s/o

CELEBRATIONS

Senior Author
William K. Durr

Senior Coordinating Author
John J. Pikulski

Coordinating Authors
Rita M. Bean
J. David Cooper
Nicholas A. Glaser
M. Jean Greenlaw
Hugh Schoephoerster

Authors
Mary Lou Alsin
Kathryn Au
Rosalinda B. Barrera
Joseph E. Brzeinski
Ruth P. Bunyan

Jacqueline C. Comas
Frank X. Estrada
Robert L. Hillerich
Timothy G. Johnson
Pamela A. Mason
Joseph S. Renzulli

HOUGHTON MIFFLIN COMPANY   BOSTON

Atlanta   Dallas   Geneva, Illinois   Palo Alto   Princeton   Toronto

Acknowledgments

For each of the selections listed below, grateful acknowledgment is made for permission to adapt and/or reprint original or copyrighted material, as follows:

"Arctic Fire," from *Frozen Fire: A Tale of Courage*, by James Houston. Copyright © 1977 by James Houston. (A Margaret K. McElderry Book) Reprinted by permission of Atheneum Publishers and McClelland and Stewart, Ltd.

"The Base Stealer," from *The Orb Weaver*, by Robert Francis. Copyright © 1948 by Robert Francis. Reprinted by permission of Wesleyan University Press.

"The Boy Who Shaped Stone," adapted from *The Toolmaker*, by Jill Paton Walsh. Copyright © 1973 by Jill Paton Walsh. Reprinted by permission of Houghton Mifflin Company and William Heinemann, Ltd.

"Change," from *River Winding*, by Charlotte Zolotow (Thomas Y. Crowell). Text copyright © 1970 by Charlotte Zolotow. Reprinted by permission of Harper & Row, Publishers, Inc. and William Heinemann, Ltd.

"Cobie's Courage," adapted from *Winter Wheat*, by Jeanne Williams. Copyright © 1975 by Jeanne Williams. Reprinted by permission of Harold Ober Associates, Inc.

"Conquering the Colorado," from *Down the Colorado with Major Powell*, by James Ramsey Ullman. Copyright © 1960 by James Ramsey Ullman. Reprinted by permission of Houghton Mifflin Company and the Harold Matson Company, Inc.

"Digging For Clues to the Past," from *Digging the Past*, by Bruce Porell. Copyright © 1979, Bruce Porell. Reprinted with the permission of Harper and Row, Publishers, Inc.

"Dog," from *Small Poems*, by Valerie Worth. Copyright © 1972 by Valerie Worth. Reprinted by permission of Farrar, Straus and Giroux, Inc.

"Dragon Doctor," from *The Flying Horses*, by Jo Manton and Robert Gittings. Copyright © 1977 by Jo Manton and Robert Gittings. Adapted and reprinted by permission of Methuen Children's Books.

"The Enchanted Steel Mills," adapted from *Portrait of Myself*, by Margaret Bourke-White. Reprinted by permission of the author and the author's agents, Scott Meredith Literary Agency, Inc., 845 Third Avenue, New York, New York 10022.

"Escape from NIMH," adapted from *Mrs. Frisby and the Rats of NIMH*, by Robert C. O'Brien. Copyright © 1971 by Robert C. O'Brien. Reprinted by permission of Atheneum Publishers and John Schaffner Associates, Inc.

"Five Under Cover," by Myrtle Nord, from *Plays, The Drama Magazine for Young People*. Copyright © 1983 by Plays, Inc. This play is for reading purposes only; for permission to perform or produce this play, write to Plays, Inc., 120 Boylston Street, Boston, MA 02116.

Continued on page 588.

Contents

3

Magazine Two

Magazine Four

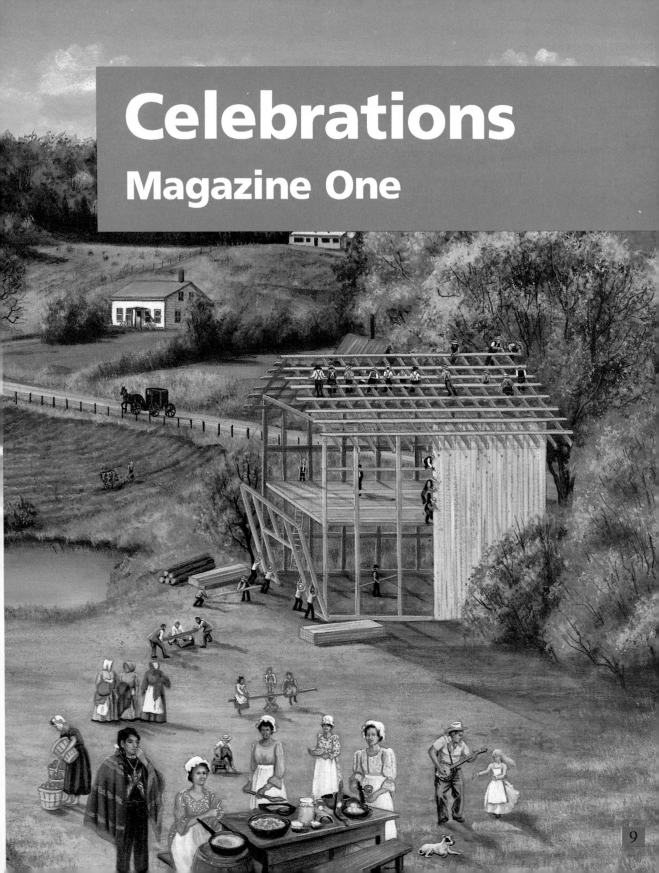

Celebrations

Magazine One

Contents

Henry Reed's Engineering Problem

by Keith Robertson

Uncle Al asked Henry to stop his lawn from flooding. The trouble sure got fixed—but was it really Henry who fixed it?

Twelve-year-old Henry Reed, who had been living in Italy with his mother and diplomat father, returned to the United States to spend the summer. He stayed with his aunt and uncle in their quiet New Jersey town. The town wasn't so quiet, however, after Henry teamed up with Midge Glass, who lived down the street, and Agony, a stray beagle he adopted. In the journal he kept, Henry recorded their summer adventures.

It rained most of the weekend, and I spent a good part of Saturday and Sunday in the house, reading. Late Sunday afternoon it began to clear, and Uncle Al and I went outside. The rain had been quite heavy, and the water had flooded down the driveway, washing half the gravel into the grass. He was completely disgusted.

"This has happened every time there's been a heavy rainstorm for the past ten years," he said. "Now, there's a research project for you or an engineering job, whatever you want to call it. Figure out some way that my driveway and maybe half the lawn doesn't get flooded every time there's a hard rain."

Although it had stopped raining, water was still flowing down the driveway. It came from a ditch beside the highway at the front of the place. When we walked up the road, we saw that there was at least two feet of water in the ditch.

"The main trouble is that culvert there," said Uncle Al. "The water from our half of the road flows down through that culvert and on down the other side of the road to the creek, but nine-tenths of the time the culvert is clogged. As a result, we have a flood."

The culvert that he was talking about is really just a big corrugated galvanized steel pipe that runs underneath the road. "The trouble is it isn't big enough," I said.

"That is a very astute observation," said Uncle Al, "and it's one that I made about nine or ten years ago. I've made it at regular intervals to the highway department ever since. When I complain, they send a man out, and he pokes a stick in there or something to get out the leaves and debris, and that's all. It works reasonably well for several rains and then clogs up again, and we have the same trouble. The last three houses on this side of the road have had their front lawns flooded at least three or four times a year for I don't know how long."

"Couldn't you put some sort of a screen over this end?" I asked.

"I tried that," Uncle Al said. "Then the stuff just clogs up and blocks the entrance to the culvert. It's a little bit easier to clean away the debris that way, but that's all."

I said that I would give the problem my attention, and I did. I thought about it several times, but I couldn't figure out an answer, except, of course, to put in a much larger culvert. I did get a long bamboo pole from the garage and poked it through the culvert. I managed to dislodge a big glob of sticks and leaves, and then the water began to go through much faster. However, there wasn't any doubt that Uncle Al was right, and it would soon clog up again the next time it rained.

On Monday, Agony disappeared someplace, and I didn't pay too much attention. Then I heard his rabbit voice, and I could tell from the tones that he was after that white rabbit again. That wouldn't have bothered me except that he was on the wrong side of the road.

The white rabbit goes back and forth across the road from Midge's house to my lot quite often. I don't worry about him, but I do about Agony. When he starts chasing that rabbit, he forgets there are such things as roads or cars. Several times he has located the rabbit on Midge's side of the street, and after chasing around over there for a while, the rabbit invariably heads for my lot. I guess all the woodchuck holes and the woods at the back make that his safest place. Two or three times they have streaked across the road, neither one paying any attention to whether there are cars coming or not.

As soon as I heard Agony barking on Midge's side of the road, I started running down the road to locate him. Suddenly Agony and the rabbit came directly toward me. About fifteen seconds later, they went flashing by, headed for the road. I shouted for Agony, but he didn't pay the slightest bit of attention.

I rushed through the shrubbery in front of the Ainsworths' house just in time to see the rabbit tear down the bank with Agony close behind him. Agony was really giving that rabbit a run for his money. He was only about three feet behind, and he was gaining. The rabbit was either tired or is getting fat. Of course he should be getting fat. He eats the best out of everybody's garden.

Instead of crossing the road, the rabbit went straight along the bottom of the ditch. When he got opposite Uncle Al's, he made a sudden and abrupt turn and disappeared in the steel culvert. Agony tried to stop, but he skidded about three feet before he could turn around. Then he poked his nose in the culvert, hesitated for a minute, and disappeared inside.

I looked up and down the road. No cars were coming, so I made a mad dash across to the other end of the culvert. I got there just too late. I was hoping that the culvert would be blocked and that the rabbit would be trapped inside, but he wasn't. I was almost there when he came scrambling out the end in front of Uncle Al's house. He was muddy and dirty and he was scared, but he got through. I made a leap for him and missed him. He hopped up the bank and disappeared in the rhododendrons in Aunt Mabel's front yard.

Midge came up beside me. "What happened?" she asked.

"Agony almost had the rabbit," I said. "He was gaining on him fast when the rabbit ducked into this culvert."

"Agony is always gaining on him," Midge said. "The trouble is he starts too far behind. Is the rabbit still in the culvert?"

"No, he managed to get through," I said. "Agony hasn't come out yet."

I leaned down to look in the culvert, but it was black inside. "Here, Agony," I called, and Agony gave a whine. I could hear him scratching but nothing else. "Come on, boy," I called. "Come on out of there."

"I'd hide, too, if I couldn't catch a big fat rabbit," Midge said.

"He's not hiding," I said. "I think he's stuck."

I went to the other end of the culvert and called, but Agony didn't come out. Now and then I'd hear him scratching and he'd whine, but we couldn't see a thing from either end. I went inside the house and got a flashlight. I could just see Agony's tail and hind end from one end of the culvert, and from the other I thought I could see the tip of his nose, but I wasn't sure. I got a long pole and put a wire on the end and managed to pull out an old rusty tin can, but that didn't accomplish anything except to let me see a little better. Agony seemed to be stuck right in the middle of the culvert, and I couldn't reach him with the pole from either end. Even if I had been able to reach him, I couldn't have done anything except poke him.

"How in the world are we going to get him out of there?" Midge asked, getting worried.

"I don't know," I said. "I'll have to figure out some way."

I sat down by the edge of the road to think about the problem. Midge believes in action. She doesn't think you can accomplish anything while you're sitting still. Maybe her brain is connected to her arms and legs and won't move unless they do. She called Agony from first one end of the culvert, then the other. Then she poked around with the stick and practically burned out the flashlight. Since she had to get down on her knees in the ditch to look in the culvert, and the bottom of the ditch was still muddy, she was certainly a sad-looking sight. She had mud all over her legs, her hands, her arms, and even her face. Finally, she stuck her head inside the culvert to get a better look and came out really streaked with mud. To make matters worse, something got in her eye.

"Don't just sit there!" she said, half crying because of the dirt in her eye.

At that moment a woman in a green station wagon came driving by. Maybe she thought Midge had had an accident or something. Anyhow, she stopped.

"Is there anything wrong?" she asked.

"Agony's inside the culvert," Midge said, wiping the tears away from her eyes. "He's stuck, and I can't get him out."

"Who's Agony?"

"A dog," Midge replied. "He went in after a rabbit, and now he can't get out. I'm afraid he'll suffocate. Or if he doesn't do that, he'll starve."

"Are you certain that he can't get out?"

"He's right in the middle," Midge replied, "and we've called him, and all he does is whine. I can't even touch him with this long pole."

The woman got out of her car to investigate or help — I don't know which. She had on a light tan silk dress, and she was dressed to go somewhere special. She took one look at the mud in the ditch and decided that she would take Midge's word for it. Just then Agony let out a howl that reverberated back and forth in the culvert, making an awful racket. Anyone who doesn't know beagles would have sworn that he was dying of pain.

"I wonder who could help," the woman said. She paused a moment, then said suddenly, "There were some men working about half a mile back on the highway."

She jumped in her car, turned it around, and disappeared down the road. I took another look in the culvert, but I couldn't see much. The flashlight gave only a weak glimmer. I went into the house to get two new batteries, and by the time I came back the woman had returned.

"Don't you worry," she told Midge. "Those men will be here in a minute. They've finished whatever they're doing and were coming this way anyhow." Midge thanked the woman, who said she had an engagement to keep and drove on.

You often see repair crews of three or four people in a truck fixing holes in blacktop roads. I thought that the woman had talked to a crew like that, but about five minutes later a whole procession came rumbling down the road.

"We have an entire construction gang coming!" I said to Midge.

In the lead was a station wagon, followed by three big trucks, one of those big air-compressor rigs, and a crawler power shovel loaded on a flatbed trailer. Way off in the distance was a huge roller chugging along slowly but steadily.

"Just pretend he's your dog," I told Midge. "Act as though you're worried sick."

"I *am* worried sick," said Midge. "Aren't you?"

"Not particularly," I said. "Not now."

The station wagon pulled into Uncle Al's driveway, and a man in a khaki shirt got out. "Where's this dog that's caught in a culvert?" he asked.

"Right in there," said Midge, doing a perfect job of looking anxious and forlorn. The man got down on his knees and looked in the end of the culvert where Midge was standing. She handed him the flashlight. "I can see his tail," he announced. He got up and came over to my end of the culvert and looked in there. "He has certainly got himself stuck in the middle, hasn't he? And *by* the middle, too, it seems."

The three trucks had stopped by this time, and the truck drivers were all gathered around. They seemed to think this was a big joke, and even Midge grinned a little. She has a peculiar sense of humor. The big air compressor and the truck hauling the power shovel pulled up beside the road and stopped. Mr. Ainsworth came out of his house and walked over to see what was going on. I could see that we were soon going to have a crowd.

The supervisor, or whoever the man was who was in charge, got up from the ditch and brushed the dirt off his knees. "I don't know how to get him out of there except with a can opener," he said.

"That culvert looks pretty rusty," said one of the truck drivers.

"Yes, it's pretty well shot," the supervisor agreed. "It's probably good for a couple of years more at the most." He looked at a short, stocky man wearing horn-rimmed glasses who had been driving the air-compressor rig. "How long do you think it will take, Jim?" he asked.

The man rubbed his chin. "We could rip up the surface in half an hour or so and have that culvert out of there by four-thirty. The new culvert is apt to be the hitch. If that arrives the first thing in the morning, we should have everything cleaned up and be away from here by eleven."

"Well, that won't be too bad. We're a little bit ahead of schedule anyhow, and I guess this classifies as a real emergency," the supervisor said. "Take these two trucks back, but the rest of you start ripping this culvert out."

In less than ten minutes, there were three men with air hammers cutting a strip from the black-top straight across the road. Another truck arrived, loaded with signs, and the foreman sent it off to put up detour signs at the two nearest corners. The power shovel was unloaded from the truck and moved over, ready for use.

"Have you got a telephone, son?" the supervisor asked. "I've got a couple of calls to make."

I took him into our house to make the phone calls, and on the way I said, "That culvert's too small anyhow. It gets blocked every time it rains and floods all the lawns on this side of the road."

"I think there has been a complaint or two about that. Well, I suppose we might just as well put in a larger one while we're at it." He looked at me and grinned. "How big a one would you suggest?"

"Big enough for me to crawl through," I replied. "Then if Agony gets stuck again, I can crawl in and get him."

"That's an idea," he said thoughtfully. "I wonder why no kids have ever been stuck in a culvert. They've been stuck everyplace else."

After they had cut through the black-top, they struck the softer dirt underneath. The power shovel was moved into position, and it began digging. By two-thirty in the afternoon they had dug a big, wide trench and were only a few inches above the culvert. They dug down on each side of it until it was lying in the open at the bottom of a wide ditch. Next they dug a hole underneath the middle of the culvert, hooked a chain on it, and hooked that on the dipper of the shovel. A couple of minutes later, the culvert was hanging in the air like a pencil tied to a string. It was almost perfectly balanced in the middle, and first one end and then the other would swing up. Agony was scared. He started howling like mad. I'll bet the late arrivals were puzzled to see that long culvert hanging in the air with those weird sounds coming out of it.

"Which end did he go in?" the supervisor asked.

I showed him, and he pushed down on that end until the culvert was tilted up in the air at about two feet above the bottom of the ditch. Then two men banged on it with crowbars. Agony howled as they banged, and a minute later he

24

came sliding out the lower end, followed by a whole mess of mud and leaves.

Everybody shouted in approval, and I jumped down in the ditch to see how Agony was. Before I reached him, he got to his feet and shook his head as though bewildered by it all. Then he scampered across through the trench that had been dug, headed toward Uncle Al's house. I thought he was scared and was getting out of there as fast as he could. Instead, when he reached the other side of the road, he began sniffing around the grass and bushes and then suddenly began baying and went flying across the front yard. All of us stood staring after him in amazement.

"You say he chased a rabbit in there?" the supervisor asked.

"Yes, the rabbit went on through."

"And out that end?"

"That's right."

The supervisor shook his head. "Now that's a real hunting dog for you," he said. "He's trapped in a culvert for three or four hours, and when he gets out what does he do? He picks up the trail and keeps right on going. Son, if you ever want to sell that dog, let me know."

The new culvert didn't arrive, and at four-thirty all the men left, leaving their equipment parked beside the road. People who normally came home by our road found it blocked with a sign saying "No through traffic." They all had to detour about two miles out of their way.

Uncle Al was lucky. He came home from the right direction and was able to get in his driveway. He parked his car and came over to where Midge and I were inspecting the road equipment.

"What's happening?"

"They're putting in a bigger culvert," I replied.

"How big?" he asked.

"Big enough for me to crawl through," I said. "At least when the man asked me what size I thought we needed, that's what I told him."

Uncle Al seemed sort of weak. He leaned against the air compressor. "How did you manage it?" he asked. "Don't tell me you blew up the old culvert?"

"No, it was all an accident," I said. "Agony was trapped in it."

Between us, Midge and I told him the story. When we had finished, he pulled five dollars from his wallet and handed it to me. "We didn't agree on any fee to solve this problem of getting a bigger culvert, but it's certainly worth at least five dollars to me. I've got to admit you gave me prompt service."

"But you don't owe us anything," I said. "It was entirely an accident. We didn't plan for Agony to get trapped."

"Maybe not," Uncle Al replied. "But you've got a way of making accidents happen. Here, take the five dollars."

"As long as the man thought he could get Agony out by digging up the culvert, I wasn't going to argue with him," I said.

Uncle Al looked at me suspiciously. "Did you have some other way of getting him out?"

"Yes. I figured that out just before they got here."

"How?" Uncle Al demanded.

"I was going to hook up the garden hose," I said. "I'd let the water run through the culvert, and it would wash the dirt out. It might have taken an hour or two, but the mud in there was still soft. Agony might have gotten a little wet, but eventually he'd have been able to go on through."

Uncle Al ran his hand down over his face and walked off, muttering to himself. I don't know what was wrong with him. Maybe he thinks that wouldn't have worked, but I'm sure it would have.

Author

Keith Robertson grew up in the Middle West. While working for a publisher, he began writing for young people. His three children and their friends provided him with ideas for his books, including the well-known Henry Reed series. The story you have just read was taken from the first of the series, *Henry Reed, Inc.*

Summary Questions

Uncle Al's problem was solved in a roundabout way. Think about how it was solved and the role Henry played in solving it.

1. What problem did Uncle Al want Henry to solve?
2. What were Henry's ideas for solving the problem? Do you think they would have worked? Why or why not?
3. A number of characters in the story contributed to the roundabout solution of Uncle Al's problem. Who were they, and what part did each play?
4. Uncle Al said that Henry seemed to have a way of making accidents happen. What do you think he meant by that? Tell the story of Henry's solution to the problem as Uncle Al might tell it.

The Reading and Writing Connection

At the end of the story, Uncle Al's problem with the over-flowing culvert was solved. However, Henry still had a problem of his own to solve. Henry's problem was how to keep Agony from chasing the rabbit and running out into the road. Imagine that you are Henry. What steps would you take to solve the problem? Write a paragraph telling what you would do. Try to use some of the following words in your writing:

debris	détour	astute	invariably

DOG

by Valerie Worth

Under a maple tree
The dog lies down,
Lolls his limp
Tongue, yawns,
Rests his long chin
Carefully between
Front paws;
Looks up, alert;
Chops, with heavy
Jaws, at a slow fly,
Blinks, rolls
On his side,
Sighs, closes
His eyes: sleeps
All afternoon
In his loose skin.

29

Unfamiliar Words

At first, one of the boys did not know the meaning of philologist. However, by reading more — on the back of his friend's T-shirt — he found a clue to the meaning. He could tell that *philologists know many words.*

Often when you read you will find words you do not know. If you read on, the words and sentences around an unknown word will help you figure out its meaning.

Look for different kinds of clues to meaning. One kind of clue to look for is an **example** of the unknown word, like the example on the back of the boy's T-shirt. Learning new words is an example of what philologists do.

Another kind of clue you may find is a **synonym** for the unknown word. A synonym is a word with a similar meaning, as in the following example:

Jesse felt *anxious* about the math test. "I am so worried," he said.

The third clue to look for is **contrast** to the unknown word. Look for words and phrases that tell how the unknown word is *different* from the other known words in the sentence. Read these sentences.

Marcie can be *eloquent* when she talks with just one friend, but when she is in a group, she fumbles for words and talks very softly.

The last part of the sentence tells us that *eloquent* means the opposite of "fumbles for words." *Eloquent* means "able to talk with grace and force."

Choose the correct meaning of each boldface word. Tell which words and phrases helped you determine the meaning.

1. Pam's **chignon** is perfect in this heat. Wearing her long hair loose became too uncomfortable.
   a. knot of hair
   b. gourmet dinner
   c. cold drink
2. The new captain was on the lookout for **marauders.** Several other ships had already lost their gold to a band of pirates.
   a. wild animals
   b. landing sites
   c. wanderers; thieves
3. I don't like to listen to Rick because he's so **grandiloquent.** I have trouble believing his exaggerated claims. He thinks he's the only man in the world who knows about space exploration.
   a. stately; noble
   b. boastful; self-important
   c. large

When you read "Maria Tallchief: Dancer with a Dream," you will find some difficult words like *hostility, snicker,* and *elated.* Remember to look at the words and sentences around the unknown words to help you figure out their meanings.

Something Extra

Become a Word Wiz! When you come across a word you don't know, write it down. Try to figure out its meaning, then check it in the dictionary. Use it in a sentence. Have a weekly contest with a friend. Have your friend give the meaning of each word on your list. Give him or her one point for each correct answer. If your friend doesn't know a meaning *and you do,* give yourself the point.

Maria Tallchief

DANCER WITH A DREAM

by Marion E. Gridley

Through trouble, sickness, and disappointment, Maria kept on dancing, hoping for her chance to be a star. She knew she could do it—but why were there so many obstacles in her way?

As a young adult, Maria Tall-chief was a famous ballet dancer—but it seemed she had already spent a lifetime working for that difficult goal. She was born Betty Marie Tall Chief in 1925 in Oklahoma. Her father was Osage and her mother Scottish-Irish and Dutch. When she was eight, the family moved to Los Angeles. There she and her younger sister, Marjorie, worked hard on their dance lessons. At seventeen, Betty Marie joined the Canadian tour of the famed Ballet Russe de Monte Carlo.[1] The next year on the tour was one of the hardest of her life — but also one of the most important.

It wasn't long before Betty Marie realized that Ballet Russe had chosen her as a wartime replacement only. She was needed for the Canadian tour, but perhaps Mr. Denham, the manager, would decide that she was not needed afterward. She would have to convince them that she had ability.

Before the company opened in Ottawa, there were hours and hours of rehearsals. Each day was a round of rehearsals and fittings. Quick meals were snatched on the run. There were only brief rest times. It was exhausting, but the excitement kept her going.

The road company was so much smaller in size than the New York Company that performers had to learn a number of parts, more than they usually would. And there was less time to learn them. Betty Marie's quick memory made it possible for her to fill in many times where the other dancers could not.

One night, just before curtain time, she was told that she would have a small part in the ballet *Gaîté Parisienne*[2]. Danilova[3] was the star.

This was a real break for Betty Marie. She had to do a series of *fouettés*[4] while on her toes. She

---

[1]**Ballet Russe de Monte Carlo**
(bă **lä′ roos′** də **mŏn′** tē **kär′** lō):
Russian Ballet of Monte Carlo.

[2]**Gaîté Parisienne**
(gət ĕ′ pə rē′ zē ĕn′)

[3]**Danilova** (dä **nē′** lō vä)

[4]**fouetté** (fwĕ **tä′**): a ballet step executed with a quick whipping movement of the raised leg, often accompanied by continuous turning.

Reprinted from Maria Tallchief: *The Story of an American Indian* by Marion Gridley. By permission of the publisher, Dillon Press, Inc., Minneapolis, MN.

always did them well, but never so well as she did them that night. The audience clapped loudly, and the principal dancers praised her. From then on, she was given other good parts that would not otherwise have been assigned to her. She never knew until almost the last moment what she would dance. Sometimes her part was changed even after she was all dressed and ready.

In Montreal the company presented a benefit performance for the war effort. The Governor General of Canada and his wife, Princess Alice, would attend. A few days beforehand, Betty Marie was told that she would have a solo role as Spring in the ballet *Snow Maiden*. This important role had first been danced by Danilova. For an unknown to follow in the steps of this great ballerina was a challenge. Never in her wildest dreams had she hoped for this.

Danilova was her idol of idols. She wanted to become just like the graceful, dynamic star whom people flocked to see. All of her heart and all of her talent went into her performance. She seemed to hear Madame Nijinska[5], her teacher, saying, "Let the music speak!" She let

herself be swept along by it, and with all of her being she reached out to her audience and carried them with her. Her dancing was pure poetry, pure rapture.

That night praise was heaped on her. Backstage callers complimented her lavishly. One of them was Princess Alice, who spoke with admiration about her lyrical dancing. "You must have worked very hard to do so well," Princess Alice said. She predicted that Betty Marie would become one of the great names in ballet. The newspaper reviews of the performance echoed the same thought the next day.

All of this was sweet to hear. Betty Marie's happiness was spoiled by only one harsh note. There was now an air of hostility towards her among the *corps*[6] dancers. They made her feel unwelcome, like an outsider.

Betty Marie knew that *corps de ballet* dancers, the dancers who performed as a group but had no solo parts, thought her standoffish. She was naturally reserved and had never had her sister Marjorie's outgoing personality. She had studied and practiced so much by herself that she was not

---

[5]**Nijinska** (nə **jĭn′** skä)

[6]**corps** (kôr)

at ease with people. Though she could respond to friendliness and wanted to be friendly, it was hard for her to make friends at once.

The new attitude on the part of the *corps* dancers was an active jealousy. They resented the fact that Betty Marie was given so many good parts. They said spitefully that this was because she was a pupil of Madame Nijinska's. There were other cutting remarks, all meant for her to hear. "Her father is a millionaire, so she can ride in Pullman cars while we have to go by coach," they said. They called her a "wooden Indian" and "Princess Iceberg."

Because Betty Marie's family had always traveled in Pullman cars, she did so as a matter of course. She had never been with a road company before and had not known it was only the principals who did so. It had not occurred to her that the other dancers would feel that she thought herself too good to ride with them.

From then on, she went by coach with the rest. But the mean remarks continued. They hurt so much that she withdrew within herself and stayed more or less alone. She was a member of

the *corps,* but not "one of the gang."

Now she worked harder than ever. She spent what time she could watching the principal women dancers practice and trying to follow their movements. This, too, aroused comment from the other dancers. "Trying to get in good," they sniffed. "She wants to be noticed."

The Canadian tour was a lonely and depressing experience. If it had not been for Helen Kramer, her only good friend among the *corps* dancers, it would have been nearly unbearable. Betty Marie suffered from the extreme cold weather and from the constant travel. The mean remarks stung like wasps and added to her tiredness and discouragement. She tried to think only of the pleasant things that took place, although the meanness rankled her. She grew pale and sad-looking. She described herself to Helen as a picked chicken. She spent much of her time resting and trying to stay well.

At last she learned to steel herself against sullen looks and cold manners. When some of the dancers complained to the dance director that she was given parts and they were not, she brushed this aside. She was more concerned about what she heard him reply. "When we get back to New York, she won't have those special parts anymore," he said. "She'll be right back in line with the rest of you." Betty Marie wondered if she would be able to get ahead in New York after all or, rather, if she could get ahead with Ballet Russe. Mr. Denham summoned Betty Marie to his office. He had been given many good reports about her. Everyone said she had a glowing future. So, he would give her a year's contract as a paid member of Ballet Russe. There would be important roles for her, but not at first. She might have to wait a long time for those. Always, she must work very hard. There would be disappointments and frustrations and constant practice for her.

"If you can't stand up to it all, then you must decide to leave now," Mr. Denham said flatly. "You have got to have what it takes to be a dancer. I think you do."

Betty Marie answered yes at once. Practice she was not afraid of; that she had always done. Hard work she was not afraid of; she had always worked hard. Disappointment she could learn to

accept. She would stay with Ballet Russe and hang on, come what might. All that mattered was that she would be dancing. The chance would come to prove herself, and she would be ready. She would not stay in the *corps* forever.

The New York season began almost at once. On opening night, Betty Marie arrived early. The great stage was ready. Soon the musicians would tune their instruments. The electricians would test the lights. The giant theater would come to life.

In the dressing room, excitement was high. Betty Marie expected to perform a high-kicking dance in *Gaîté Parisienne* with a group of *corps* dancers. It was a spirited number, and she always enjoyed it. She hurried to get ready, pulling on her long hose and slipping her costume with its flouncy skirts over her head. Make-up was put on carefully. A large flower was fastened in her sleek hair. A velvet ribbon was fastened around her throat.

The dressing room was crowded and noisy, so she waited in the wings. It was nearly time for the audience to start arriving. Suddenly, a hand was placed on her shoulder and she was given a quick shove.

"Hurry, get out of that costume," she heard the dance director say. "You are going to dance a solo. The soloist who performs the role has not arrived. She cannot be waited for."

Unfastening her costume as she went, Betty Marie ran back to the dressing room. The wardrobe mistress had her new costume ready for her. Her make-up had to be changed. In only a few moments, she was ready and about to leave for the wings. She intended to go over her steps.

Just then the soloist dashed in. There was scarcely time for her to get into the costume that Betty Marie quickly slipped off. She smiled as she gave it to the dancer, but she wanted to cry.

There was a snicker among the *corps* dancers. They were laughing at her. One girl said, "Miss High and Mighty didn't make it this time." Betty Marie remained silent. Only her great dark eyes flashed anger. She would be a good trouper and let no one see how bad she felt. She would not give them the satisfaction of letting their jabs upset her.

Quickly she became a *corps* dancer again. She danced with a smile on her face, lifting her long tapering legs in perfect *fouettés*. She knew she did them better than anyone else. It gave her a bittersweet feeling to see the envious looks of the other dancers. "They know it too," she thought. "Let them laugh at me if they want to."

As she danced off into the wings, the dance director was waiting. With him was the wardrobe mistress holding out a new costume. The director's face was scarlet. This costume was for another role. Someone had not shown up, and Betty Marie had to fill in. Her new dress was barely fastened when she was back on stage.

That night there was a party after the ballet. "You have earned the right to better roles," said Mia Slavenska, a distinguished dancer with Ballet Russe. "You will have them. But Mr. Denham wants you to have a new name — a Russian one."

Betty Marie refused. She did not want a different name. She wanted to dance as herself. But Mia said that Betty Marie was not the name for one who would be a great star.

Someone suggested the name Tallchieva. What could be more Russian than that?

To this, Betty Marie also said no. "I will not change my last name," she said. "It's a good

American name. I'm proud of it. I'm not a Russian."

No amount of argument could persuade her. Even Mr. Denham tried to win her over. "I'll change my first name," she finally gave in. "You can call me Maria. But Tall Chief must stay as it is. You can spell it as one word, if you want to." So it was decided. Maria Tallchief she would be. Maria Tallchief, the Osage dancer who would go a long way.

When she wrote home to her family, Maria said that it seemed like a miracle. But then, to dance was a miracle. She spoke no word of the mean things that had taken place. She talked only of the promise that lay ahead. When she put aside the name Betty Marie, she also put aside childish feelings. As Maria, she became a woman.

She had tried out her wings, and they had carried her on her first flight. She was eager, now, to fly to new heights.

Six months after Maria first came to New York, she had a small part in *Rodeo*. This was a new, modern ballet choreographed by Agnes de Mille. It met with tremendous success, and it was also a small success for Maria. But she was not enjoying herself. She was continu-

ally depressed, did not eat well, and grew steadily thinner. It was like a sickness, but she was not sick except in spirit.

Shortly before Maria was given the *Rodeo* part, Ballet Russe had announced that Madame Nijinska's *Chopin Concerto*[7] would be included in the list of presentations. The names of the cast were posted, but Maria's name was not among them. Maria had danced the *Concerto* in the Hollywood Bowl when she was fifteen, but she tried to tell herself she had been only an amateur then. She was still no more than a small-part dancer. She hardly expected to be included.

Yet she longed to dance the *Concerto* with all of her being. Surely she could have been given a tiny part! She wanted to dance the *Concerto* so badly that she could think of little else.

Day after day Maria watched Krassovska, one of the great stars of Ballet Russe, rehearse the same role that she had once danced. The movements had been changed somewhat. Maria studied as she watched so that they became familiar to her. She could have filled in for any of the

---

[7]**Chopin Concerto**
(shō′ păn′ kən chĕr′ tō)

soloists if an emergency arose, so well did she study all their parts.

When *Chopin Concerto* opened in the Metropolitan Opera House, Maria watched from the wings. She saw herself in every turn, in every graceful position. Her imagining was so vivid it was almost real. But it wasn't real, she was forced to admit. She was only standing on the sidelines.

The program was a great triumph. Danilova, the prima ballerina, received ovation after ovation. Krassovska, too, was applauded enthusiastically. Maria was delighted for her beloved Danilova, for her friend Krassovska, and for Madame Nijinska. But her delight was edged with despair. When was the promised time coming when she would be a great star? Where were the important roles she had been promised? She worked so hard, tried so hard, did everything that was asked of her — and stayed where she was.

In spite of her worries, Maria continued to perfect and polish her dancing. She practiced by herself for hours on end. She paid for extra lessons with her own money. She grew more wan and thin, and she was more than ever driven to succeed.

That fall, the company went on tour. Maria danced in Los Angeles for the first time since she had left home. She did not have a solo part, however; she was still one of the *corps*. It was good to see her family again. Marjorie was doing well with her dancing and was certain to find a future in ballet. Mrs. Tall Chief worried about Maria, who looked so poorly. "You should come home and rest," she urged. "You should stay in Los Angeles and dance. Maybe you should even give up ballet. It is too hard on you."

The ballet returned to New York for a Christmas Day opening. Maria worked for an hour by herself. Then, while she was exercising at the *barre,* the dance director approached her. He said that it was possible she would dance in the *Concerto* the following night. Krassovska was ill, and Maria would be allowed to dance that role. She was to begin practicing the changes.

Maria almost collapsed with joy. It was as though a magic wand had been waved and had lifted her up to the clouds. The news spread quickly through the cast, and many warm wishes were spoken for good luck. Some of the dancers who had been the most unfriendly had left the company, and there were better feelings toward Maria. It was admitted that she had been given parts because she deserved them. Maria had what the rest did not — an inner spark and more than the usual amount of skill.

Christmas night Maria was ready long before curtain time. Then came a message. Danilova wished to see her. Maria hurried to her dressing room and found Mr. Denham there, also. He looked troubled.

As Maria waited with a sinking heart, the two talked in Russian. Somehow, she knew what was being said. She clasped her hands tightly together, afraid for what she would hear.

"Danilova does not think you are ready for the *Concerto*," Mr. Denham said. "She says you have had no proper rehearsal. She says that you cannot master this difficult role in only a day's time."

Maria pleaded that she could. She knew all of the movements and the music. It was time for the Christmas performance, so there the matter was left.

The following night, Maria was at the theater early. Her friends clustered around her, eager to help with her hair, her costume, her make-up, or just to be near her in this wonderful hour. When she was ready, she stood in her usual place in the wings.

Then Mr. Denham touched her on the shoulder. She turned, her face shining with happiness. Mr. Denham could not look at her. "You will not be needed," he said shortly, and walked away.

Crushed, Maria went back to the dressing room. The *corps* dancers were shocked at her stricken face. No one said a word as she blindly took off her costume and left the room. She stumbled home to sit alone in darkness.

Nothing so terrible had ever happened to her before. "Why? Why?" she asked herself over and over. There had to be a reason. But the reason would not come. Only the hurt mounted and mounted.

For the next few days, rumors spread like wildfire. Maria was the talk of the ballet world. There were times when she wanted to run away and hide. But she had an inner toughness, an inner strength, that carried her through. She refused to be defeated by what had taken place. She stayed calm and would not discuss what had happened or what was said.

At last Danilova spoke to her. "Don't hate me," she said. "There just wasn't enough time for you to dance the *Concerto*. If you had not done well, your whole career would have been set back. Some day you will dance the *Concerto*, and you will be wonderful."

Danilova had a small part for Maria in *Le Beau Danube*[8] and urged her to take it. So Maria swallowed the lump in her throat and began rehearsing. She tried to be grateful for Danilova's attention. She would keep on doing her best.

The winter was a rugged one. One after another, the dancers became ill. Maria, too, caught a cold and was unable to shake it. She was given a solo part in *Scheherazade*[9], but her spirits remained low and her health poor. Mrs. Tall Chief again wrote for her to come home. She sensed in Maria's letters that she wasn't well. Marjorie was studying with Madame Nijinska, and Maria could study with her too.

Maria hung on doggedly. She would not let go. She went on tour with the company in April,

even though she was very ill. Her mother wrote again and said that Marjorie was dancing with the Los Angeles Light Opera Company. Maria must come home. A place would be found for her with the same company.

Again Maria refused. She had a contract with Ballet Russe and would not break it. Once she fainted at a private party. Her friends were alarmed over her health, and she begged them not to let her mother know. She continued to practice and dance, even when she should not have done so.

Then came a never-to-be-forgotten day. May 1, 1943! The day of the big chance, at last!

Krassovska injured her foot, and Maria was told that she would take her place in the matinee performance of *Concerto*. She tried to stand quietly while she was being fitted for her costume. But the words "I will show them" kept singing through her head. "I will show them. I will SHOW THEM." She wanted to leap around the room.

When the cue came, she did leap onstage and swirled into the steps as if she were another being. She was part of the music, dancing as if in a dream. She was a new and different Maria,

---

[8]**Le Beau Danube** (lĕ bō′ dän yoob′)
[9]**Scheherazade** (shə hâr′ ə zä′ də)

43

radiant, following her heart in the joy of dancing.

She finished to thunderous applause. Even Danilova stood aside as Maria took her bows. She had proven that she was a dancer — a great dancer. She was the only *corps* dancer in the company with the promise of becoming a prima ballerina. There was no higher place to go.

All of the principals were elated. They had witnessed the birth of a star. Mr. Denham, in his quiet way, complimented her too. She would dance the role until Krassovska's foot had recovered. But even when Krassovska returned, Maria continued to dance the role although it was Krassovska's name that appeared in the program. She did not mind. It was not the glory but the doing that mattered.

When Ballet Russe opened its summer season, Krassovska decided to go to Europe. Maria now had the *Concerto* role for good. So far, she had danced it only on tour. Now she would debut in the ballet in New York City. She was only eighteen years old! The world was very good.

Mr. Denham understood the happiness that shone from her eyes. He had been concerned over her sunken cheeks and her pale face, but he knew that happiness can be a great healer. Maria's health began to improve almost at once with the *Concerto* assignment.

The New York debut was outstanding. There was no question now of her stature as a dancer. Tears stood in her eyes as she saw the audience rise and heard their shouts and applause. Many bouquets of flowers were brought to the stage. One of them touched her deeply. It was a huge bouquet of roses from the *corps* dancers. For Maria, life would never again be the same.

Author

Marion E. Gridley was adopted by the Omaha and Winnebago peoples. Her interest in Native Americans led to her more than twenty books on the subject. For many years she edited the magazine *Amerindian*. Ms. Gridley died in 1974.

Summary Questions

Maria Tallchief spent many years in studying and practicing before beginning her professional career. She was a gifted dancer whose training and determination had enabled her to obtain a place in one of the most famous ballet companies in the world. However, the road to stardom was paved with difficulties for Maria Tallchief. Think about how she overcame them.

1. What were some of the obstacles Maria faced as she tried to achieve success with the Ballet Russe?
2. What did Maria do to overcome these obstacles?
3. What personal characteristics did Maria have that contributed to her eventual success?
4. The selection names several people in the world of ballet who influenced Maria's career. What part did each of the following people play in Maria's career?
   Mr. Denham
   Danilova
   Madame Nijinska
   Krassovska

5. Imagine that you are Maria and that a young person has asked you how to become a ballet star. Tell how you would answer that question.

The Reading and Writing Connection

Prepare a report on Maria Tallchief's career. You will need to include information about the ballets she performed in Ottawa, Montreal, and New York. Skim the selection and take notes on the important information. Then use your notes to help you write your report. Try to include some of the following words in your report:

> **amateur**
> **cue**
> **choreographed**
> **debut**
> **oration**

Reference Aids

You are often expected to write a research report on a subject. As you read through this lesson, imagine that your class is researching the Revolutionary War.

Knowing how to choose your sources on the subject is an important part of doing research. You should make a search plan before you begin. Think about which reference aids are best for the kinds of information you are looking for. Choose which aids you will use. Plan how you will use them. You will be more successful in getting enough information when you have formed a clear idea of how you will proceed.

In this lesson, you will review some reference aids that you may be familiar with and learn how to use some new ones. As you read, think about which reference aids are best for different purposes. After reading this lesson, you should be prepared to tell which reference aids you would use to research a subject.

Using Reference Books

The Encyclopedia: The encyclopedia can give you background information about many subjects. If you were doing a report on a broad subject, such as the Revolutionary War, you might begin with the encyclopedia. There you would find some of the important information you may need.

The Almanac: If you need quick facts and figures, you might use an almanac. Most almanacs have short articles and tables of statistics about many subjects. New editions are printed each year so that the information is kept up to date. Along with the new information, the almanac will also include facts about the past.

You can use the almanac to learn about famous people and events, weather records, distances between cities, population statistics, and many other subjects.

Most almanacs have either tables of contents or indexes. Some have both. If you want an overview of what the almanac might tell you for your report about the Revolutionary War, you can scan the table of contents. See the example below.

In the table above, you see a section called "Headline History," covering the period from 4500 B.C. to the present. To find information about the founding of the United States, you should turn to page 83 and read the following:

THE FOUNDING OF THE AMERICAN NATION

Colonization of America begins: Jamestown, Va. (**1607**); Pilgrims in Plymouth (**1620**); Massachusetts Bay Colony (**1630**); New Netherland founded by Dutch West India Company (**1623**), captured by English (**1664**). Delaware established by Swedish trading company (**1638**), absorbed later by Penn family. Proprietorships by royal grants to Lord Baltimore (Maryland, **1632**); Captain John Mason (New Hampshire, **1635**); Sir William Berkeley and Sir George Carteret (New Jersey, **1663**); friends of Charles II (the Carolinas, **1663**); William Penn (Pennsylvania, **1682**); James Oglethorpe and others (Georgia, **1732**).

Increasing conflict between colonists and Britain on western frontier because of royal edict limiting western expansion (**1763**), and regulation of colonial trade and increased taxation of colonies (Writs of Assistance allow search for illegal shipments, **1761**; Sugar Act, **1764**; Currency Act, **1764**; Stamp Act, **1765**; Quartering Act, **1765**; Duty Act, **1767**.) Boston Massacre (**1770**). Lord North attempts conciliation (**1770**). Boston Tea Party (**1773**), followed by punitive measures passed by Parliament—the "Intolerable Acts."

First Continental Congress (**1774**) sends "Declaration of Rights and Grievances" to King, urges colonies to form Continental Association. Paul Revere's Ride and Lexington and Concord battle between Massachusetts minutemen and British (**1775**).

Second Continental Congress (**1775**), while sending "olive branch" to the king, begins to raise army, appoints Washington commander-in-chief, and seeks alliance with France. Some colonial legislatures urge their delegates to vote for independence. Declaration of Independence (**July 4, 1776**).

Major Battles of the Revolutionary War: *Long Island:* Howe defeats Putnam's division of Washington's Army in Brooklyn Heights, but Americans escape across East River (**1776**). *Trenton and Princeton:* Washington defeats Hessians at Trenton, British at Princeton, winters at Morristown (**1776–77**). Howe winters in Philadelphia; Washington at Valley Forge (**1777–78**). Burgoyne surrenders British army to General Gates at *Saratoga* (**1777**).

France recognizes American independence (**1778**). The War moves south: Savannah captured by British (**1778**); Charleston occupied (**1780**); Americans fight successful guerrilla actions under Marion, Pickens, and Sumter. In the West, George Rogers Clark attacks Forts Kaskaskia and Vincennes (**1778 – 1779**), defeating British in the region. Cornwallis surrenders at *Yorktown*, Virginia (**Oct. 19, 1781**). By **1782**, Britain is eager for peace because of conflicts with European nations. *Peace of Paris* (**1783**): Britain recognizes American independence.

The overview from "Headline History" gives you a list of the important events and their dates, but little further information about them. If you need to know more about one of them, for example the Continental Congresses, use the index to find it. From the sample index, you see that information about the Continental Congresses can be found on pages 89, 546–47, and 561.

Consumers:
Credit, 43
Metric conversion tables, 350–51
Price indexes, 36, 39
Spending, 57
Continental Congresses, 89, 546 – 47, 561
Continental Divide, 472
Continental Drift, 358, 454
Continents, 454–55
Area, 457
Dimensions, 457
Elevations, 457
Explorations, discoveries, 453–54
Maps, 472–87
Populations, 112, 457
Religions, 407
See also specific continents
Controllers (of states), 646–72
Conventions, National, 586–87
Converter, Bessemer, 342
Cook Islands, 223

On page 561, you would find a short article about the early Congresses. There is also a table listing the presidents of the Continental Congresses, the dates on which they were elected, when they were born, and when they died.

Use the almanac whenever you need either a quick overview or a set of specific facts.

The Atlas: If you need information about where cities, towns, lakes, rivers, or mountains are, you use an **atlas**, a collection of maps. Suppose you have read that the Continental Congress met in Philadelphia. To see where that is, use an atlas.

Use the index to find the map. Suppose you have looked up "Philadelphia,"

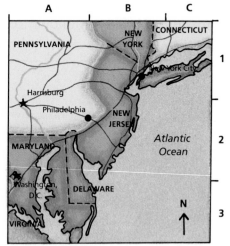

and see "53: B2." The first number tells you the page where the map is to be found. The letter and number following the page number tell you where on the map to look. Turning to page 53, you would find the map of Pennsylvania marked off in a grid, with letters across the top of the map and numbers down the side. Look at the sample map. Find the letter B at the top. Look down the side to find the number 2. You will find Philadelphia in the square that is under B and beside 2.

If you wanted to find the shortest route between Philadelphia and England, the atlas probably would not show you that. It would be better to look at a globe for that information.

Using the Library

Often you will need to go beyond the standard reference books to find the information you want. If you are going to write about a famous person in the Revolutionary War, you need to use the library to find books about that person. Using the library efficiently is an important step in doing research.

All libraries have a way of numbering books and placing them on the shelves. The system used in one library may be somewhat different from that in another, but they all work the same way.

Fiction books are usually arranged alphabetically by author.

For your report, you will probably use nonfiction books. They are given **call numbers** according to their subject matter. All the books on a subject will have similar call numbers, but each will be slightly different from the others. The call number tells you exactly where to find the book on the shelf. You might think of looking up a book's call number as something like looking up a person's address.

Some libraries have card catalogs and others have their information on computers. To find a book, you go either to the card catalog or to the computer terminal, where you read the information on a screen. Your search plan would be the same in either case.

Usually in researching a subject, you don't have a certain book or author in mind. In that case, look up your subject. Sometimes you may have to look under more than one subject. Use the cross-references to guide you to related subjects.

When you have found the call number of the book or books you want, use the numbers at the ends of the library shelves to guide you to the shelf where you will find your book.

Other Sources

Sometimes you may want more information about one part of your subject than you can find using the reference aids you have already learned about. For example, if you want to know what people thought about a past event at the time it happened, your librarian can help you find newspaper and magazine articles about it. Many libraries can use computers to get information about many subjects from many sources.

You can often get information about your subject from government agencies, from businesses, and from industries. Sometimes the most accurate and up-to-date information about a subject can come from people who are involved with it and who are willing to serve as expert consultants.

The next time you research a subject, think about how you might use some or all of these additional sources.

Choosing Reference Aids

Choose two subjects from the following list. Think of at least two reference aids that could be used to research each subject. For each, write a paragraph telling which aids you would choose and why and how you would use them.
1. Recent space shuttle flights
2. Famous sailing ships of the 1800's

3. The greatest hitter in baseball history
4. Yosemite National Park
5. Training your dog
6. The best places to fish in your state

Skill Summary

- Plan your search strategy before you start to research a subject.
- Choose the reference aids that are best suited to your subject.
- Use more than one kind of reference aid to find your information.
- Use what you have learned about the different kinds of reference aids.

TWISTER!

by George Sullivan

When a tornado cuts its path of destruction, it's time to get out of the way. But will the warning come soon enough?

The Worst Tornado

The Time: Wednesday, March 18, 1925.

The Place: Murphysboro, a small coal-mining town in southern Illinois.

The Setting: It is almost three o'clock in the afternoon. For a March day it has been unseasonably warm — hot, actually — and sticky, very sticky. There are menacing gray clouds in the sky to the west, and the rumble of thunder is beginning to be heard.

At the Joiner Elementary School, it is an hour before dismissal. Because of the growing darkness, classroom lights have been put on. Teachers glance out of the windows anxiously at what they believe to be a gathering thunderstorm.

This is no thunderstorm. A nearby cloud has become heavy and black, and from beneath it stretches a column of whirling air in the shape of a long funnel. Heavy rain and hail are falling. Brilliant flashes of lightning brighten the sky. Strong winds have begun to blow.

Now a strange, hissing sound is heard. It grows to a loud roar that sounds like a flight of passenger planes at rooftop level.

The eerie funnel-shaped cloud, whirling madly, has touched the ground at the outskirts of Murphysboro. Soon it is raging through the very heart of the city, ripping trees up by their roots, lifting people bodily, tearing off rooftops, and causing explosions.

The tornado that struck Murphysboro, Illinois, that tragic day in 1925 was the worst in history. It covered a path 220 miles long and, in some places, a mile wide.

It took 689 lives — 284 in Murphysboro. Of the 11,000 people that lived in Murphysboro, more than 8,000 were left homeless.

Could such a terrible tragedy happen today?

Tornadoes are not uncommon. In any given year, about 1,000 strike the United States. It is possible that a storm equaling the 1925 tornado in terms of size and destructive power could occur again.

However, the chances of escaping serious injury in a tornado are much better nowadays. In describing the storm that devastated Murphysboro in 1925, the *New York Times* reported: "The storm struck without warning . . ." Taken by surprise, people did not have time to

protect themselves. Today, it is not likely that a tornado could strike without warning. Weather scientists, called *meteorologists,* are better able to locate tornadoes as they are beginning to form, and so, in many cases, are able to predict their arrival.

How Tornadoes Behave

No storm is more violent than a tornado. None is so little understood. A tornado is much different from a hurricane. A hurricane is made up of spiraling rain clouds that swirl about a calm center, or eye. Its winds blow at about 100 miles an hour.

Compare this to the death-dealing winds of the tornado, which have been measured at up to 300 miles an hour.

Scientists have several theories explaining how tornadoes are formed. Whatever causes them, it is well known that the Gulf of Mexico is their breeding ground. Warm, moist air from the Gulf is carried north to the Rocky Mountains. Cold, dry air from the Rockies collides with the warm, moist air from the South. Troublesome weather is the result.

The conditions that bring about tornadoes are the same as those that cause thunderstorms.

Above: The ten-minute life history of one tornado
Below: Path and life stages of a typical tornado, lasting 26 minutes

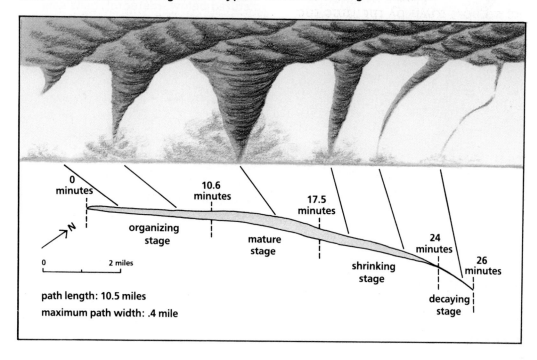

0 minutes

10.6 minutes

17.5 minutes

24 minutes

26 minutes

N

organizing stage

mature stage

shrinking stage

decaying stage

0   2 miles

path length: 10.5 miles

maximum path width: .4 mile

Indeed, tornadoes often develop along with thunderstorms. As the thunderstorm moves, tornadoes may form along its path, traveling for a few miles, then dying out.

The tornado funnel usually appears beneath the thunderstorm's dark, heavy clouds. Often it stretches down toward the ground, whirling and twisting as it moves. Sometimes the funnel never quite reaches the earth's surface. Other times it touches down briefly, then rises.

On the average, the tornado path is a quarter of a mile wide and 16 miles long. Some tornadoes have caused heavy damage for as much as 200 or 300 miles.

The forward speed of the tornado is about 40 miles an hour; however, speeds of up to 70 miles an hour have often been recorded.

Predicting Tornadoes and Warning the Public

Because of the small size and short life-span of tornadoes, it is extremely difficult for meteorologists to predict exactly where they are going to occur. What meteorologists try to do is watch for areas where tornadoes can be expected to develop.

In weather stations like the one pictured below, meteorologists keep a careful watch on developing storms.

At the National Severe Storms Forecast Center in Kansas City, Missouri, specialists are on duty around the clock. They watch for conditions that are likely to produce severe thunderstorms. Once an area has been identified as one of possible danger, a SKY-WARN system of watches and warnings goes into effect.

When the Forecast Center sends out a tornado *watch,* it is telling people in a given area that a severe storm is likely to occur.

During a watch, people can go about their business as usual, says the Center's director, but they should keep tuned in to radio or television. They should also keep a weather eye on the sky, watching the horizon for low, threatening clouds — what is called a squall line. These often produce tornadoes.

A tornado *warning* is much more serious than a tornado watch. A warning is issued by the Forecast Center when a tornado has already been sighted.

A tornado warning tells the exact location of the storm, the time it was seen, and the path it is expected to take. A person in an office building at the time should go to the designated shelter area or to an inside hallway on a low floor. To a person at home, the basement usually offers the most safety. In schools, students are often led to an inside hallway on the lowest floor. "Stay out of auditoriums, gymnasiums, and structures with wide, free-span roofs," says a bulletin from the U.S. Weather Service.

Warning Systems Save Lives

When all these safety measures are put together, the result can be a dramatic saving of lives. The tornado outbreak that struck Kansas on September 25, 1973, was extremely dangerous. It consisted of more than a dozen different twisters — the worst storm of this type in more than fifty years.

Most Kansans first learned of the tornado conditions that morning soon after they awakened. The first notice went out from the National Severe Storms Forecast Center at seven o'clock, alerting all Weather Service offices and Civil Defense units in the area.

Information continued to pour into the Forecast Center. By the middle of the afternoon, there was enough evidence to issue a tornado watch for an area south of Salina, Kansas.

Salina braced itself. Watchers never took their eyes from the twister as it bore down on the town. The Salina police chief was watching the skies southeast of the city. When debris began to fall around him, he ordered the city's sirens to sound their warning. It was 5:50 P.M.

Radio and television began to give minute-by-minute coverage of the twister's approach. Shoppers in stores heard the warning on public-address systems. Police officers in squad cars covered city streets and back roads, with loudspeakers bellowing. "Take cover to the nearest shelter! This is no drill!"

Salina, a city of 38,000, looked like a ghost town by the time the tornado arrived. The storm's greatest fury was directed toward a mobile-home park at the edge of town. The people who lived there watched the storm's approach. When it turned their way, they hurried to a thick-walled shelter that had been provided for them. As they huddled in the darkness, their trailers were destroyed and their belongings scattered over the Kansas countryside.

Next the tornado lashed out at towns to the northeast. Clay Center was a prime target, with the twister tearing through the heart of the city, destroying or damaging hundreds of buildings. Clay Center, like Salina, had plenty of advance warning, and when the tornado exploded through, people had taken shelter. Not one death was recorded in Clay Center that night.

And so it was along the path of the tornado. Hundreds of homes and other buildings were destroyed, and thousands were damaged. Three lives were lost. However, the repeated warnings had made it possible for hundreds of people to get away unharmed.

A Continuing Challenge

The tornado watch and warning system works to save lives. Scientists hope that by learning more about how storms behave, they can make it work even better. Planes and weather balloons fly into storms and record information. Radar and weather satellites track storms and report on their progress. Every year, more is known about the conditions under which tornadoes are formed. However, predicting exactly when and where the next tornado will touch down still remains a difficult task.

Author

George Sullivan taught non-fiction writing at Fordham University for many years. He says he is curious about many subjects, as young people are. His many books include *How Do They Find It?*, from which this article was taken.

Selection Wrap-up

Summary Questions

Think about the ways in which tornado warning systems can help save lives.

1. What steps are taken to warn people of an approaching tornado?
2. What kinds of places should people go to during a tornado warning? Why are these good places to go?
3. How might tornado warning systems be improved?
4. Imagine that you lived in Salina, Kansas, during the 1973 tornado. Explain what you were doing when you heard about the tornado, how you were warned of its approach, and what you did to protect yourself.

The Reading and Writing Connection

The graph below should show rotary and forward speeds of tornadoes and hurricanes. Bars have been drawn to compare rotary speeds. Copy the graph on another paper. Then use information from the article and reference aids to complete it.

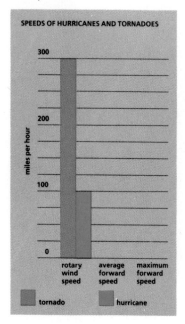

Grandpa's Miracle

by Eve Bunting

Ever since he retired, Grandpa had been hard to get along with. How could Cathy get him to be her special friend again?

Saturday, April 3

"Do you want to come to the park with me?" I asked Grandpa today. Our park is terrific; it has lots of space, and there's even a river that runs through it. That's where Grandpa taught me to skip rocks when I was little.

"I don't want to go to the park," Grandpa said, and he turned his head away.

So I went with my best friend, Laura, who lives in my building. We decided to go for a run along the river path.

As we jogged along at an easy pace, I thought about Grandpa and how he'd changed.

Laura stopped to tie her shoelace. I knew she really stopped to rest because she was huffing and puffing like a train. I decided to tell her about my problem.

"Grandpa's no fun at all these days," I told her. I wanted Laura to talk about him. I wanted her to help me understand why he was suddenly the way he was.

"Aw, he's not so bad," Laura said. What does Laura know — she's not even *related* to him.

Grandpa lives with Mom and me. He used to be my friend. Every night when he came home from work, we talked or we did something, such as building a model of the space shuttle. Grandpa helped Mom too. He did the supper dishes, and sometimes he made the best spaghetti and meatballs. His Saturday morning special breakfasts weren't so bad, either.

Since January, Grandpa doesn't go to work anymore. They told him he had to retire because he's too old. It's strange — when they told Grandpa that, he turned all moody and gloomy. I didn't tell him he was too old to do things with me, and Mom sure didn't tell him he was too old to help around the house; but all of a sudden he believes he is. All he does now is sit and sit and sit — and complain.

Wednesday, April 7

Today Judy Spencer asked Laura and me to try out for the girls' softball team. When I told Grandpa that tryouts were next week, he didn't even offer to help us practice.

"Are you sure you're good enough?" he asked.

I didn't let that get to me; I tried one more time. "Want to hit some balls to us?" I asked. "We need practice catching Texas leaguers."

"I don't play games anymore," Grandpa said. "Just leave me alone."

I'll leave him alone all right.

What has happened to him? Grandpa is the one who taught me to play all kinds of games. I still have the moonstone marble he gave me when I was eight. It's there in my secret box, all pink and blue and orange as fire.

When Mom came home from work, I helped her fix a tuna and rice casserole. When she asked me how Grandpa was, I didn't answer.

"Cathy," Mom said, "Grandpa has always been such a proud man, so independent. It's going to take him time to get accustomed to being retired. Right now he feels depressed because he thinks life is over for him."

"Well, that's stupid," I said. I felt as gloomy as Grandpa.

Saturday, April 10

Laura and I went to the park today. We took our gloves and ball so we could practice to get on the softball team. I want to make pitcher. Laura caught for me even though she wants to play first base. Instead of just crouching and catching, she kept jumping up and shouting, "Pitch it in the glove, Cathy! Get it down! Wow, is your eye ever off!"

"I just need practice," I muttered.

Laura shook her head. "You're never going to make it."

Sometimes Laura gives me an enormous pain.

We decided to visit the ducks before we left. When we were little, we used to bring bread to feed them, but we haven't done that since the third grade.

We counted eleven ducks on the river, and we were just about to go when Laura said, "Look!"

She pointed, and I saw a mother duck with her four little ducklings starting off from the river bank. They glided downstream in a row. The little ones were trying to imitate their mother, and they were adorable.

Then I saw the nest. It was by the bank close to where we were standing. I saw something else too; the mother duck had abandoned one light tan egg. It was lying there, all sparkly and shiny, and when I gently picked it up, it was as smooth as glass. It was as smooth as my moonstone, only bigger.

"She'll be back to get it," Laura said; but I knew about mallards, and I knew this family was gone for good.

"You can't keep it anyway," Laura said. "Pretty soon it's going to get smelly."

"No, it won't." I figured Laura was miffed because she hadn't found the egg first. Very carefully, I wrapped it in my flannel shirt.

We ran all the way home and found Grandpa sitting in the courtyard.

"Look!" I held the egg on my hand and imagined the baby curled inside, its head under its dark little wing. "It's a mallard's egg," I said. "The mother left it." I don't know why I said what I said next. The words just popped out. "I'm going to hatch it."

"Just how do you propose to do that?" asked Grandpa.

I hadn't thought about it yet, but quickly I said, "Well, I'll wrap it in something — maybe in a towel — and hold it all day."

"What about school?" asked Grandpa. "You going to take an egg in a towel to school?"

"I'll think of something," I said. No way was I going to let Grandpa spoil my idea.

"Here, let me see it." Grandpa took the egg and cradled it in his big hand and stared off into the distance for a long time. I tried to figure out what he was staring at, but there is just our courtyard and the fence between our building and the next one. There are trees and the TV aerials on the roofs and the ECONO GAS sign above the corner service station.

"Cathy," he said, "if this egg hatches, it will be a miracle."

I waited but he didn't say anything else. He just sat there, holding the egg.

"Are you going to just sit there, holding that egg?" I asked him.

Grandpa nodded. "Maybe. Somebody has to monitor it if the baby is to make it. Besides, who else is there who has the time and the patience and the know-how?"

64

"Nobody but you, Grandpa," I said.

Grandpa asked me to get his old woolen cap. He put the egg inside and held the cap warm in his hand. Then he started making phone calls. "Better find out for sure how to hatch a duck egg," he muttered.

I guess he found somebody who knew for sure. They talked and talked. Then Grandpa said, "That was the county agricultural agent. He gave me some suggestions. You hold the egg carefully in the cap, Cathy. I'm going to get that old aquarium from the basement."

Grandpa set up the tank with lights, a towel, and a pan of hot water.

"The water supplies humidity," Grandpa explained. He put the egg in the tank and propped a thermometer in the corner. "We can't let this water drop below 99 degrees," he said.

"Hatching a baby duck is tricky stuff," I said.

Grandpa smiled. "We can do it."

When he went to bed tonight, Grandpa put the tank on the nightstand next to his bed. He didn't seem to mind sleeping with the lights on. I guess having a baby duck is going to be worth it.

Sunday, April 11

Grandpa monitored the egg off and on all day. Once he carefully turned it.

I'm getting worried. What if that old egg is rotten? I keep hearing Grandpa say, "If this egg hatches, it will be a miracle." What if Grandpa hatches a dud? What if it *never* hatches?

Mom kids Grandpa a lot. "That little duck will be convinced you're its daddy because you'll be the first thing it sees when it breaks out of that shell. That happens with a lot of orphaned baby animals. It's called imprinting."

"Huh," Grandpa said. "I never figured on being a duck's daddy." But he didn't say it in the old, dreary way.

Grandpa crooked his finger at me. "Come here, Cathy," he said. He put the egg in my hand, all moonstone smooth, and I felt the tiniest of taps against my palm. Tap, tap, tap.

"It's in there all right," I said, "and it feels as if it's trying to get out."

"A couple more days," Grandpa said.

Tuesday, April 13

When Laura and I came home from school, we had a duckling.

It had just happened. There were little pieces of tan shell on Grandpa's pants and sticking to his sweater. The duckling was perched on Grandpa's knee, staring at him. It was a little ball of dandelion fluff with button eyes. When Grandpa put it on the floor, it walked splayfooted around his shoes.

"Oh, it's so pretty," I said.

Grandpa touched the fluffy head with the tip of his finger. "It's going to take a lot of care and attention. It's going to need feeding and . . ."

I interrupted. "I bet it would love your spaghetti and meatballs. Everybody does."

Grandpa half smiled. "For now it needs chick mash. Want to accompany me to the pet shop, girls?"

Mom duck-sat while Grandpa and Laura and I were gone. Laura and I talked a lot on the way there — and Grandpa listened. It was the first time in ages he really listened.

"Cathy's not getting the ball into the strike zone when she pitches," Laura told him.

"You have to bend your back more, Cathy," Grandpa said. "We'll work on it."

Laura nudged me and grinned. "OK," she whispered.

As soon as we got back with the duck chow, the little duck ran peep-peep-peeping straight for Grandpa.

"Duck's daddy," Mom teased, and Grandpa shook his head; but I could tell he was pleased. He got the heating pad and made a warm bed for the baby in the kitchen.

"It's going to be a while before it's self-sufficient," Grandpa said. "Till it is, we can't put it back in the river."

"How long will that be?" I asked. It's such a dear little duck that I want it to stay around. Now there's something else — I like the way Grandpa is these days. I don't want him to turn back into that old gloomy person again.

"It can't go till it's all feathered out," Grandpa said. "The downy feathers are what insulate it in the water. About a month, I'd say."

"How come you always know so much?" Laura asked.

Sometimes Laura asks good questions, especially considering that Grandpa's not even her grandpa.

"It must be a matter of longevity." There was a kind of boasting in Grandpa's voice and in the way he looked at the little duck.

Laura let the duck nip her finger. "What's its name, anyway?"

"Miracle," Grandpa said. "I told Cathy that if this egg hatched, it would be a miracle, and here it is."

Tuesday, April 27

Miracle just keeps eating and growing. For the past few weeks, Grandpa has been taking him into the courtyard of our building so that he can look for bugs in the ground.

"Miracle has to learn to forage for food," Grandpa says. "We don't want him to be dependent on humans."

Grandpa has been learning a lot about ducklings. He went to the library and got a couple of books. He read, and then he told us things he had read.

"Miracle's a male duck, so he's really a drake," he told me.

"But he's so little," I said. "Let's just call him 'duck' for now."

Grandpa talked to the pet store owner. He even made a trip to the zoo and talked to the duck-keeper. When my grandpa does something, he does it well! He wants our little duck to have the right start in life.

When he isn't hunting food, he's following Grandpa around — indoors, outdoors, through our apartment, everywhere — just like Mom said he would.

"Imprinting, remember?" I asked.

"How could I forget?" Grandpa said.

Tonight we sat in the kitchen after dinner. "Such a change," Mom smiled, cradling our duckling in her arms. I think she was talking about Miracle, but she was looking at Grandpa. He was mixing up a batch of bran muffins. We've discovered his muffins are just as delicious as his spaghetti. He put dates in them.

Saturday, June 9

Today Grandpa said it was time to set Miracle free. "He's big enough and he's strong enough and he knows enough."

I called up Laura, and we walked over to the park with Grandpa and Miracle.

When we got to the edge of the river, Grandpa set Miracle down. Right away that nosy, hungry little duck began to poke around; but when Grandpa started to edge away, Miracle started to follow him. Grandpa had to shoo Miracle back toward the river. "Go, baby," he said. "It's time to be a duck again."

"Go, Miracle!" I pointed to a bunch of ducks his size that were swimming downstream and gave him a little push.

Miracle just didn't want to go.

Then one of the ducks in the river looked right at him and called, "Quack! Quack!" That must mean something significant in duck talk because Miracle quacked back and rushed straight into the water.

We watched. The other ducks watched too; they seemed to be paddling, just waiting.

Miracle sure is a good swimmer. I could see his little orange feet churning below the greenish surface. I watched carefully because he looked just like the other ducks. I knew if I took my eyes off him, I wouldn't be able to tell which one he was. That's sad, but it's nice, too, because it means he'll fit right into a duck family.

Grandpa put his hand on my shoulder. He knew how I felt — and I knew how he felt. Grandpa and I have always known about each other, even when things weren't this good.

He smiled down at me and said, "Everything's going to be all right, Cathy." I know that he was making a promise, and I know that I don't have to worry about him anymore.

"Bye, Miracle," I said. We watched the ducks swim across the river and climb out on the bank. Then I turned to Grandpa and asked, "Want to hit a few fly balls to Laura and me? I could dash home and get my bat."

Grandpa grinned. "Sure. Dash home and get it. I can see you have plans for your old grandpa."

"Old," I said. "You're not old. You're just Grandpa!"

Author

Born in Ireland, Eve Bunting began her writing career after moving to California with her husband and three children. Among her more than one hundred books many have won awards. Her concern for wildlife is portrayed in "Grandpa's Miracle" and in her book, *One More Flight*.

Summary Questions

Think about how Grandpa's attitude changed during the course of the story.

1. How had Grandpa changed since his retirement?
2. What did Grandpa do that showed he was beginning to take an interest in things again?
3. What happened that caused Grandpa to change back to his old self?
4. At the end of the story, Grandpa told Cathy that everything was going to be all right. What do you think he meant by that? How do you think he felt about himself? Explain your answer.

The Reading and Writing Connection

Imagine that Grandpa has been asked to write a short article about Miracle for a natural history magazine. The article is to include directions for hatching a mallard egg and raising the duckling to maturity. Skim the story and make a list of the things Grandpa did. Then write the directions that Grandpa might write for hatching and raising a baby mallard. Make sure your directions have the correct steps and are in the right order. Try to include some of the following words in your writing.

mallard	downy	monitor
self-sufficient		forage

ROGER TORY PETERSON

MALLARDS

Mallards belong to the family *Anatinae*, ducks that feed on the surface of the water rather than diving. Their most common habitats are creeks, ponds, and swamps.

Females are a mixed brown, with whitish tail and white borders *on each side* of bright purplish-blue wing patches. During the summer, the males shed their bright feathers. At that time, they look much like the females. At other times of the year, males are grayish with *green head, narrow white ring around neck,* reddish breast, and white tail.

MALLARD

Water Picture

by May Swenson

In the pond in the park
all things are doubled:
Long buildings hang and
wriggle gently. Chimneys
are bent legs bouncing
on clouds below. A flag
wags like a fishhook
down there in the sky.

The arched stone bridge
is an eye, with underlid
in the water. In its lens
dip crinkled heads with hats
that don't fall off. Dogs go by,
barking on their backs.
A baby, taken to feed the
ducks, dangles upside-down,
a pink balloon for a buoy.

Treetops deploy a haze of
cherry bloom for roots,
where birds coast belly-up
in the glass bowl of a hill;
from its bottom a bunch
of peanut-munching children
is suspended by their
sneakers, waveringly.

A swan, with twin necks
forming the figure three,
steers between two dimpled
towers doubled. Fondly
hissing, she kisses herself,
and all the scene is troubled:
water-windows splinter,
tree limbs tangle, the bridge
folds like a fan.

Organizing Information

One way to organize information is to make an outline. This will help you to see how the important details are related to one another. Then, when you have to talk or write about the information, you will be able to state the points well.

In this lesson you will learn how to outline a piece of writing. You can also use what you learn to outline chapters in the books you study.

Parts of an Outline

Some of the ideas in any piece of writing are more important than others. Main topics are the most important facts given about the subject. Other facts in the piece will tell more about the main topics. In your outline, they become *subtopics*. The piece may also have additional facts about the subtopics. They become *details* in your outline. Choose main topics, subtopics, and details carefully, and place them to show how they are related to one another. This will make a clear outline that will help you to understand and remember what you read.

Finding Main Topics

Each major heading in a piece can be turned into a main topic. Use the important words in the heading to state the main topic. If a piece does not have headings, use the title to help you find main topics for your outline. After you read the title, think of questions about it that you expect the piece to answer. Then read to get answers to your questions. Your questions may begin with the words *Who, What, When, Where, Why,* or *How.*

If the piece does not answer your questions, you must think of different questions.

If you were outlining "Twister!" on pages 52–58, you could use the important words in each heading as your main topics, as follows:

Twister!
I. Worst tornado
II. Tornado behavior
III. Tornado prediction
IV. Warning systems
V. Continuing challenge

There is a Roman numeral and a period before each main topic. Only the first word begins with a capital letter.

Finding Subtopics

To choose good subtopics that tell about a main topic, first think of a question you expect the piece to answer about the main topic. Then read all or part of the piece again to get all the answers it gives.

Look at the first main topic in the outline for "Twister!" What questions would you expect the piece to answer about it? You might expect it to tell you where and when the worst tornado happened. You might also expect it to tell how much damage and what kind of damage was done. The answers to these questions become your subtopics. Below are subtopics for the first main topic in the "Twister!" outline.

Twister!
I. Worst tornado
  A. Happened in Murphysboro, Illinois, 1925
  B. Caused property damage and death
  C. Struck without warning

You can see that each subtopic is indented under its main topic and labeled with a capital letter followed by a period. The indention shows that the subtopics tell about the main topic just above them. The letters show that the subtopics tell a number of different things about the main topic.

Finding Details

How will you choose details that tell about a subtopic in an outline? First, think of a question you expect the piece to answer about the subtopic. Then read as much of the piece as you need to in order to get all the answers it gives. Look again at the subtopics for the first main topic of "Twister!" What further facts can you expect the article to give? You can expect it to answer these questions: How big was the tornado? Why was there no warning of its approach? How many people were killed? How much damage was there? After you reread the piece, you could continue the outline, as follows:

Twister!

I. Worst tornado
   A. Happened in Murphysboro, Illinois, 1925
      1. Covered 220 miles
      2. Was a mile wide at some places
   B. Caused property damage and death
      1. Killed 689 people
      2. Left 8000 homeless
   C. Struck without warning
      1. No meteorologists predicted storm
      2. No other warning system

Details are indented under the first word of the subtopic. They are labeled with an Arabic numeral and a period and begin with a capital letter.

The example shows details for each of the three subtopics. In some outlines you will not need details for each subtopic. Always read carefully to see if details are needed.

Making an Outline

Reread "Twister!" on pages 52–58. Then finish the outline for it shown on page 78. Remember to ask yourself questions that you expect the piece to answer before you list any subtopics and details. List only the subtopics and details that you feel are needed.

Skill Summary

- Outlining is one way to organize information. A good outline will help you to remember and understand what you read.
- The parts of an outline include main topics, subtopics, and details.
- Main topics are the main points that you include in an outline.
- Use subtopics to tell more about the main topics.
- Use details to give more information about the subtopics.

Understanding the Past

Learning from the past involves more than just knowing what happened last week or last year. It means studying about people in many places and times, ancient as well as modern. People have always been curious about the past. How can learning about what happened long ago contribute to life today?

The Boy Who Shaped Stone

by Jill Paton Walsh

The tribe needed the tools that only Ra could make so well; but how could Ra hunt for food and still have time for making tools?

Ra was a young man in the Stone Age in a tribe where each man made his own tools and hunted for himself.

Ra was making his summer house when he broke his axe. He was cutting long bendy branches of hazel from the coppice at the edge of the forest, and the axe wedged in the thick bole of the tree. He heaved at it to free it, and it came unstuck so suddenly that it flew out of his hand and struck a stone lying a little way behind him and broke. Ra picked up the pieces and looked at them to see if he could perhaps use them for making something else, but there were milky cracks showing in the dark flint — the pieces were useless. Ra grunted angrily and threw them away. He gathered up the sticks he had already cut and walked down the hillside, out of the hazel copse and towards the stream.

On the grassy slopes in the shelter of the wood, and just a little above the stream, his people were busy making shelters for the summer, each family building one hut. They dug away the earth of the hillside till they got down to a solid, firm floor; then they made a framework of branches and stretched over it tents made of skins. There were many skins in a tent, all carefully stitched together with overlapping edges to keep out the wind and rain. Ra had not earned one yet — his hut would be covered in bracken and brushwood. He looked enviously at the others. Nearly all the huts were almost finished, but only the great-grandmother's was completely ready, for everyone had to help with hers before starting their own. Ra's house was slowest of all because he had nobody helping him. Among the forest tribes, a boy lived with his mother's and grandmother's family, but Ra's mother had died in the snows of the winter that was just passing, and he had not yet gathered enough skins and bones and flint tools to earn himself a wife and join her family. So for the time being he was alone and had to live in a hut by himself.

He had scraped an earth floor out of the grassy slope. Now he was making a ring of pliable sticks set upright in the ground all around it. He set to work with the new bundle. First he made a hole by driving a piece of bone into the ground with a large stone for a hammer. Then he rocked the bone drill to and fro, pulled it out of the ground, and set the hazel branch in the hole, wedging it firmly with a little loose earth. Soon the ring of sticks was finished, with a gap in it for a door. Ra unwound from his waist a long strip of leather, and reaching up he bent the hazel branches down over his head one by one and tied them into a bundle with his thong.

It was getting dark now, and Ra went hastily down to the stream to find a piece of flint in the pebbles in the water to

make himself a new axe. There was no time now to gather bracken to cover the framework of his hut — that would have to wait till tomorrow. He found a big heavy stone of the right sort and then went to one of the bright fires that now blazed on the slope.

He bowed to the great-grandmother of the family, who sat between the fire and the door-hole of the hut, in the place of honor.

"Is there room beside your fire, Mother?" he asked her.

"Sit, Ra. There is room," she said. Ra sat down a little way outside the family circle and began to make his new axe, working in the firelight where it fell between the shadows of Brun and Mi, a boy and girl only a little older than Ra. First Ra broke his stone in two against the ground. Then he chose the better half and wedged it firmly against his bent knee on the ground. Then he took from his leather pouch a short piece of the leg bone of a stag, and placing one end against the axe stone, first here and then there, he struck the other end with the rejected half of the stone, making flakes of flint fly off in all directions.

Ra was good at making axes, but the light was poor, and he bent closely over his work. Even so, he could feel that someone was watching him. Ra glanced up, hoping it was Mi, and his eyes met those of Yul. Yul was a grown man, tall and strong — some said the best hunter in the tribe — and he had hunted with Ra's father long ago. Ra was in awe of him; he looked away quickly. When he had finished his axe, he stood up to go.

"May the hunt be good tomorrow to those who shared fire with me tonight," he said.

In his own unfinished house he lay down to sleep. There was nothing else to do, for the day had gone in traveling and in hut making. There had been no time to hunt, and so there was nothing to eat. Ra was used to going to bed with an

empty stomach; but all winter he had slept in a deep cave in the distant hills, and he was not used to sleeping in the open. The year had only just begun to turn warmer, and the leaves were scarcely breaking bud on the trees, when the Great-grandmother had moved them out of the caves. It was still sharply cold, and a wind swept the sloping glade. Shivering, Ra wished he had finished his house. Through the web of sticks over his head he could see the cold stars. Not only the stars disturbed him; unseen creatures moved in the forest and in the grasses all night long. The echoing tapping of dripping water in the cave had gone, and instead there were the quiet movements of living things going about their business and hunting each other in the dark. And although he slept, Ra slept so lightly all night long that he dimly knew from the sound and smell of them what creatures had come near. No wolf or wildcat came to startle him awake, but he drowsed on the chilly earth till the dawn.

When he woke, he went to the stream and drank greedily, lifting the water to his mouth in cupped hands. Cold trickles ran down his forearms. And when he returned to his hut, he had a visitor. Yul stood there.

"Is there room beside your fire, Ra?" he asked.

"There is no fire yet, but there is room," said Ra.

Yul sat down. "Show me the axe you made at our fireside last night," he said. Ra stared at Yul in surprise. Then he picked up the axe and held it out to Yul. Yul took it and turned it over and over in his hands. Then he held it with the thick end in his palm and tried it, striking it against the ground.

"This is a good axe, Ra," he said.

"It is mine," said Ra, puzzled by all this talk of his axe. "I made it."

"You were quick and deft about making it," said Yul. "I take longer. And when I have an axe to make, I gather several stones, so that I need not stop to look for another when the one I am working splits in the wrong place. You had only one stone with you."

"The stones are good to me, Yul. They almost always break as I wish them to."

"Since that is so, Ra, will you make a new spearhead for me? Hard though I try, I cannot make them balance so that the spear flies really straight. You make me a good one."

Ra was silent. This was a new thing Yul was doing; new things frightened Ra. Each man of his tribe did everything for himself. There were no rules for this sort of asking.

"I must hunt, Yul," he said at last. "I am hungry."

"Today I will bring you food. I will hunt until I have enough for two and share what I catch with you. You can sit here and make me the spear that I need. Do this for me, Ra."

"I will do it," said Ra, unhappily. Indeed one had no choice but to do what Yul wanted; he was big and strong. He could have knocked Ra down with one hand only. Ra did not dare refuse him.

So that morning Ra stood at his door, watching the men and dogs go out to hunt. The dogs ran yelping at the hunters' heels, and the men walked away into the forest, carrying spears, and bows, and bundles of arrows. The barking sounded clearly in the cold morning and echoed faintly from the bare hill above the wooded valley. The sounds came more and more distantly to Ra's ears. The quiet of the camp made him uneasy. He wanted to run after the hunt, but instead he went looking for a good piece of flint.

He returned to his hut a while later with two large lumps of flint tucked under each arm. Then he sat down and set to work. First he wedged one of his stones firmly on the ground with a little earth, to make an anvil. Then he chose the best of the stones, taking it in two hands raised above his head, and brought it hard down on the anvil stone so that it broke cleanly in two across the middle. He took the larger half and

set it down with the new broken surface upwards. And now he took his bone chisel and a spare piece of stone to bang it with. He had to get the slant of the chisel exactly right to make the flint split where he wanted it to. First he struck the stone round the rim of the new surface; at each blow a flake of stone cracked off the side, so that soon all the hard rough surface of the stone had been struck away, and he was left with a block of pure black, unweathered flint.

Now he worked more carefully still. He struck the top surface of his block near the edge, so that a long narrow flake of flint broke off the side. This flake would make a good knife; Ra put it on one side. Then he tried again and this time got a shorter, wider chip. Just what he wanted. He put the block aside and started to work on the chip. It was wafer thin at the edges and thick in the middle. Ra tapped the edges gently and broke off little pieces until he had rounded it into a leaf shape.

Then he trimmed it, holding a stick at a slant on his anvil, laying the edge of the spearhead against the stick and pressing the stick upwards under the thin edge of the stone blade until a little flake dropped off. These tiny flakes left a beautiful rippled surface on the flint, like a light wind on dark water. They also left a wavy, bitter-sharp edge. Ra was pleased. He had never made a better one.

But now that it was finished, he had time to feel hungry. He wondered about the hunt and felt uneasy. All his instincts, all the ways of his tribe, told him that when he was hungry he must hunt. He shook his head and took up the long flake of flint he had laid aside before. This had flat straight edges already, because of the way it had split from the block. Ra took careful aim and sharpened the end of it with a single blow that nicked a diagonal chip from the end. Then he took it and went up to the forest to cut more brushwood for his hut.

Ra finished his roof, tied it down securely, and gathered a pile of pebbles for a hearth. All day the women and children stared at him curiously, for it was a new thing for man or boy to stay away from the hunt. And all day Ra's ears were pricked for any sound of the men returning.

At last he heard them. Down the valley, from among the trees, came the sound of singing — a low droning song. The hunt had been good. The hungry families gathered at the hut doors to watch the hunters come. They marched out of the woods and scrambled up the slope to the camp, bringing the carcasses of deer and rabbits across their shoulders. Ra looked at them hungrily and licked his lips. He was apprehensive — what if Yul did not keep his unheard-of bargain? The night would be cold, and the cramps of hunger in his stomach would keep him awake. But Yul brought him the flank of a young doe and half a rabbit and exclaimed in delight when he saw the spearhead Ra had made for him.

"This bargain is good," he said.

Ra gathered firewood and stacked it on his hearth of stones, then went to the Great-grandmother's house to get fire. All the fires of his tribe were lit from hers, and hers had been carried on torches of pine wood all the way from the winter caves. He roasted his meat on a spit over the fire, not taking long about it, for he liked it still red and raw in the middle. He sighed with pleasure as he sunk his teeth into it, and when he had finished and sat sleepily beside his fire, the good, well-fed feeling spread through his limbs. He just sat enjoying this feeling for a long time. Then he built up his fire so that it would last the night, for it is not only humans who hunt for food, and Ra knew that he did not wake quickly when he was not hungry. Then he crept into his hut to sleep. He did not fall asleep at once. He felt odd. Never in all his life before did he remember sleeping well-fed and yet not tired from running in the hunt all day. But although the strange feeling was a new thing, he liked it.

The next morning, when Ra was collecting his arrows and tightening the thong on his bow, Brun came to him and said, "Make with me today the bargain you made with Yul yesterday. I need more arrowheads and a scraper, and my sister, Mi, wants this little bone worked into a harpoon for fishing the deep pools."

So Ra stayed at home that day, too, and worked stones beside his fire. He worried a little about his food, but not as much as he had the day before. And he discovered that making a whole lot of arrowheads all together, instead of one by one as he needed them, was in a way easier. He got defter and quicker with each one. The little sounds he made as he worked ran together into a jerky, gruff sort of song, the beat keeping time with the sharp cracking noise of the breaking flints. Ra was happy.

In the afternoon, when Ra was using his new knife to cut little notches in Mi's bone to make it into a harpoon for her, his thoughts took a new turn. The bone had to be notched to make it catch in the fishes' flesh; a smooth point just slipped out. Ra remembered how often he had lost a rabbit or a deer because the arrow with which he had hit it had dropped out of the wound as the beast ran. Why shouldn't the arrowhead be notched too? Of course, it would be very hard to make notches in stone, but the thought was good. Trembling with excitement, Ra took up one of the completed arrowheads and tried to notch the back, so that it would pierce smoothly and then lodge securely. It broke. He tried again. And again. It was hard, but before evening he had succeeded in making one tiny triangular blade with two deep notches cut in the broad end, so that it had two barbs and a little stem by which it could be tied to the shaft.

He gave it to Brun with the others in return for a hunk of wild boar, and Brun went round the whole tribe showing everyone what he had got, until Ra was surrounded by men asking him to work for them the next day and the day after that. They even promised to pay him with the skins of their catch as well as the flesh, so that he could make himself a better hut.

"This is a new thing we are doing," said Ra. "We must ask the Great-grandmother." He said this because he was becoming alarmed. Surely the Great-grandmother would keep them to the old, well-tried ways, for it was she who knew how things had always been and how they ought to be.

The Great-grandmother listened while one after another of her children told her that they wanted the tools that Ra knew best how to make.

"Tell him to work for us, and we will feed him," they said. She took the arrowheads he had made for Brun between her stick-like fingers and stroked them, learning what they were like from touch, since she had no eyes. She was very old; nobody in the tribe could remember a time when she had not

been Great-grandmother over them, and since long before Ra's birth she had been blind with age.

"What is this?" she asked when she felt the barbed arrow. Ra told her how he had thought of it and how it worked. She was silent for a time, her head tilted back on her shoulders as though she were looking at the sky, and her fingers turned the barbed arrowhead over and over. At last she said, "If Ra makes better tools, it is a good thing that he should make them for us all."

"I am afraid," said Ra. "If I do not hunt, what will happen to me when food is short? I shall starve as soon as the hunt is bad. I am afraid."

"No matter how little is brought home, you shall share what there is," said the Great-grandmother. "The tribe promises this. It shall be one of our ways."

And so Ra, who had been a hunter, became a toolmaker instead. And in Ra's tribe there were good tools for the doing of many things. The summer was good. There were many warm days, and the hunt did not fail. Ra made great axes from large stones, and the men cut down full-grown trees from the forest and built dams and fish traps across the stream; and the children's limbs rounded and plumped with the plentiful food. Several groups of strangers came trading for Ra's tools; everyone prospered and everyone was content.

Author

A native of England, Jill Paton Walsh was a teacher before turning to writing. Her interest in ancient history contributed to the setting of many of her books, including *Children of the Fox* and *Toolmaker,* from which this story was taken.

Summary Questions

Think about how the people in Ra's tribe reacted to a change in the way they lived.

1. What did people in Ra's tribe have to do for themselves?
2. What unusual bargain did Yul make with Ra? How do you think Yul felt about the bargain? How do you think Ra felt about it?
3. Why did Ra seek advice from the Great-grandmother?
4. Think about the decision the Great-grandmother made. Pretend that you are she, and explain to the tribe why you think the new division of labor will be better for the tribe.

The Reading and Writing Connection

The author of this story included information about making stone tools and weapons. Skim the story, making notes on this information. Then, arrange your notes in outline form. Try to use some of the following words in your outline.

> chisel
> anvil
> shaft
> thong
> pliable
> instincts

WHO AM I?

by Felice Holman

The trees ask me,
And the sky,
And the sea asks me
Who am I?

The grass asks me,
And the sand,
And the rocks ask me
Who am I?

The wind tells me
At nightfall,
And the rain tells me
Someone small.

Someone small
Someone small
But a piece
of
it
all.

95

Digging for Clues to the Past

by Bruce Porell

There are lots of clues to the mystery of how people lived long ago — but it takes careful work to find them.

Archaeologists study how people lived in the past. They learn from objects that people used in their daily lives. Their work is important because there are few written records of long-ago life. They help to fill holes in the puzzle of history.

Revealing Artifacts

The objects that archaeologists study are called artifacts. They are the pots we cook in and the dishes we eat from. Artifacts are the chairs and tables in your living room, the rubber ball in your bedroom, the toothbrush in the rack over your bathroom sink, and the chicken bones you threw away after supper last night. They are everywhere. They are our tools, toys, decorations, furniture, clothes, and weapons, and even the buildings we live and work in. Look around you. You are wearing artifacts, and you are surrounded by them.

Very old artifacts have often been changed by nature's forces. Some materials stand up better than others. Cloth, paper, and wood can be destroyed by water, fire, and insects. They can be impossible to recognize after only a few years. Metals such as iron, bronze, and copper can rust or corrode, if they are in damp places. Pots and stone tools are the artifacts most often found, because they last the longest. Modern plastics may last as long as pottery and stone. Some of these new materials will be around for ten thousand years before breaking down and returning to the soil.

Archaeologists at work
Opposite: Israel
Above: Mexico

Archaeologists rarely find artifacts as well preserved as the Greek coin and the Phoenician pottery shown above.

Most of the time, when things were broken or worn out, people threw them out the door or dumped them in a back-yard trash pit. New ones were made or traded for. The old ones were buried by sand or leaves, covered by growing plants, or broken down by wind and rain.

In time, they were covered by layers, or strata, of earth. As the ground level grew higher, later artifacts were piled on top of those already there. Each layer contains the artifacts from a time when a particular group of people lived there. Usually, the deeper they are found, the older they are.

However, archaeologists must study the strata very carefully. Often when new groups began to build houses, they dug into the ground and threw up dirt and artifacts that belonged in the next layer down. Archaeologists who dig these places hundreds of years later find objects from different layers mixed together. They must work carefully to figure out what all this mixing means and how it happened.

Finding a Likely Place to Dig

Archaeologists don't wait to find sites by chance. Many are in danger of being lost or destroyed by spreading cities and highways.

The archaeologist looks at maps and written records with a critical eye. Humans have basic needs that must be met. The people of long ago

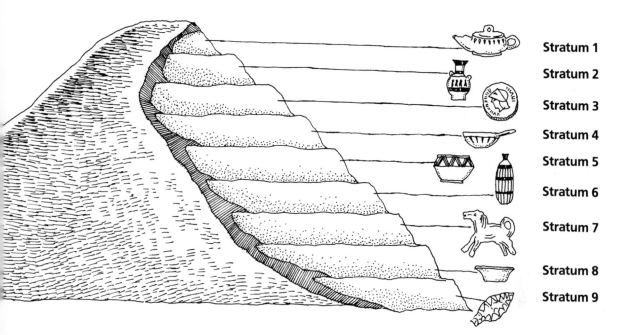

Stratum 1
Stratum 2
Stratum 3
Stratum 4
Stratum 5
Stratum 6
Stratum 7
Stratum 8
Stratum 9

had to have water and food. They had to be able to defend their homes. Thinking of their needs helps archaeologists find places where they lived. The most promising places to dig are near sources of water. People also often built homes on the tops of high hills so they would be easy to defend.

The best building sites were often used over and over again. In many places in the Near East there are places that look like great mounds of earth. These are called *tells,* places where city has been built upon city.

Preparing to Dig

First the archaeologist asks the owner's permission to look around. Then, on foot, he or she looks for any clues on the surface of the

Above: Some building sites have been used over and over. Below: A tell in England

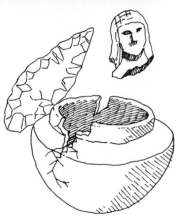

The grid of string helps the archaeologist to mark the exact location of artifacts.

ground. Sometimes it is also helpful to fly over and look down on the site. Buried walls or foundations or other features may show up from the air, even though no one could see them from the ground.

After finding a good place to dig, several things must be done before the actual excavation, or digging, begins. The area must be mapped, and a grid is laid over the map and numbered. The numbered squares make it possible to find quickly any area of the map.

Next, this pattern of squares is marked on the ground by driving stakes into the exact locations shown on the map. They are connected by a string, making a pattern of squares over the ground. When the dig begins, these squares will be used to show the positions where artifacts are found.

Excavating a Square

Let's imagine that you are an archaeologist, and that you are going to begin excavating a new square. The site has been mapped and marked with stakes. You have chosen where you want to begin. You have stretched string between the four corner stakes to outline a square.

First you search the grass in the square, looking for any artifacts that are showing on the surface. You find a broken piece of pottery, called a sherd. You put it in a plastic bag, and label it with the square location and a note that it was found in the grass. You begin to remove the turf, which is cut into squares and lifted

carefully, as you check for more finds. The sod is moved away to be replaced later.

Now you work very slowly. Each artifact must be dug up with great care so that it is not destroyed. Each one is treated as if it held a valuable clue. It must not be moved until you have recorded all the information that its location can provide.

Small tools, such as dental picks and paint brushes, are carefully used to clean off dirt. This cleaning is done without moving the artifacts.

You make notes of all of the information about your find. A photograph is taken for later study. It will also prove that the object was

The archaeologist must work slowly and carefully to avoid damaging the artifact.

101

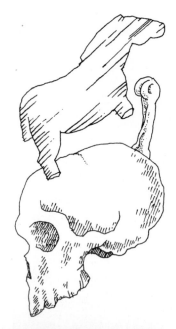

found as stated. You must note the original position and condition of the objects, as well as their relationship to each other and to the soil layers. You have only one chance to do this. Once they are moved, they are out of place forever.

All objects go to the field laboratory to be studied. There you will spend at least part of each day cleaning, cataloguing, and storing your finds. Many of them will also be measured and weighed. On some you will write their location in India ink. You will examine them all carefully before they are sent to other experts for further analysis.

Artifacts are studied by experts in many different fields of science.

Summary

Archaeologists use information gathered from the ground. They study the layers of earth and learn from the artifacts they find there. Experts from other fields of science help sort out these clues from the ground. All these bits and pieces go together to form a picture of life in the past.

Author

Bruce Porell was a science and theater arts teacher in Vermont. Archaeology was his hobby, and his interest contributed to his only book, *Digging the Past,* from which this selection was taken.

Summary Questions

Many ancient cultures left no written records about themselves and the times they lived in. In order to learn about the lives, customs, and beliefs of such people, archaeologists must rely on whatever clues they can infer from the artifacts they find. Think about the way in which artifacts contribute to archaeologists' understanding of ancient cultures.

1. Why are archaeologists interested in artifacts?
2. What difficulties do archaeologists have in trying to find artifacts?
3. Why is it so important for archaeologists to be careful about noting where artifacts are found?
4. What kinds of artifacts do you think might be most useful in helping an archaeologist understand a culture? Give reasons for your answers.
5. Imagine that it is one thousand years from now and you are an archaeologist looking for artifacts. What steps would you take to discover clues from the past? What kinds of artifacts from today's world might you find?

The Reading and Writing Connection

Still pretending that you are an archaeologist one thousand years from now, imagine that you have found an artifact from today's world. You are not sure what it is or what it was used for. Describe this artifact in a letter to another archaeologist. Tell where you found the artifact. Try to use some of the following new words from this selection in your letter:

> **excavation**
> **analysis**
> **strata**
> **cataloguing**

A Small Link with the Past

by Mary Chubb

The necklace had lain buried in the sands for several thousand years. What could it tell Mary about the person who had left it there?

Mary Chubb worked with an archaeological team in Egypt at Tell el Amarna, the home of the great Pharaoh Akhenaten and his beautiful queen, Nefertiti. See the picture on the opposite page. Mary describes one of the team's exciting discoveries.

It was one of those days. I was unscrambling the shorthand notes for the first report, which we were sending to a London paper, when a shadow fell across the doorway behind me. Young Kassar Umbarak had run up from the dig with a note. "I think we've found a necklace," said the note. "Can you come and deal with it, please?" I collected a small drawing board, pencils, brushes, tweezers, a knife, sunglasses and a hat, waved farewell to the office, and set out, grumbling mildly, into the glare. When should I get at that report again? But as soon as I was on my way, I began to think that it was rather a lark to be an odd-job person of this kind, slapping away at a typewriter one moment and digging up ancient necklaces the next.

The house with the find had been cleared, except for a heap of rubble up against one low wall. Already some rings had been found in the heap, one bearing the seal of Nefertiti; and there were glazed beads to be seen here and there on the surface. And here, said John, pointing, was obviously the main part of a necklace to which most of these fragments probably belonged. Would I cope, while he moved the team to the next house? I said I would, took one look at the problem before me, and knew for a fact that the report, far away on my desk, would *not* be ready before nightfall.

Necklaces were tricky because the threads had worn away, so that each pendant had to be lifted separately; and if a necklace had fallen in a heap before being buried, it was sometimes impossible to be sure that we reconstructed the pattern correctly. Today we were lucky. I began by blowing away the surface sand very gently from the topmost beads.

Through the thin veil of sand gleamed fragments of red and yellow and green and white. I brushed very lightly and then blew again — and there, lying on the sand, just as it had fallen more than three thousand years ago, was the main part of the necklace — a confused heap of beads at one end, to be sure, but happily a stretch of at least three inches lying quite flat, enough to show the pattern. The thread had perished, of course, but pendants and beads were lying exactly as if still threaded, in a fan shape of three rows. If I were breathlessly careful, I could save this tiny piece of knowledge.

All the pendants were fashioned like fruit and flowers. There were enchanting white daisies, blue grape-clusters, mauve-tipped lotus petals, and rust-red pomegranates. Here it was again, this delight of Akhenaten's people in the beautiful simplicity of natural design and color. I suddenly remembered, sitting back on my heels and gazing at it, a bead necklace I'd had as a little girl, which had completely fascinated me — small white daisies, yellow-hearted, linked together by fragile strings of tiny green beads. I felt sure that this necklace, too, had belonged to someone rather young, someone who had felt the same delight at wearing the pretty thing over her best white frock. I'd often wondered how the people of Amarna managed to lose so many of their possessions, as we picked up one thing after another out of the heaps of rubble — but after all, where was my daisy necklace now? Would some strange creature, three thousand years hence, digging for history beneath the grassy mounds covering London, come upon it, and finger it gently, and find it somehow pathetic?

But daydreams were a menace to neat field work. I snapped out of it and began to concentrate on the business of salvaging the necklace in good order. I made a diagram-drawing of the whole pattern on the drawing board, writing in notes about the color scheme, for some of the pendants were

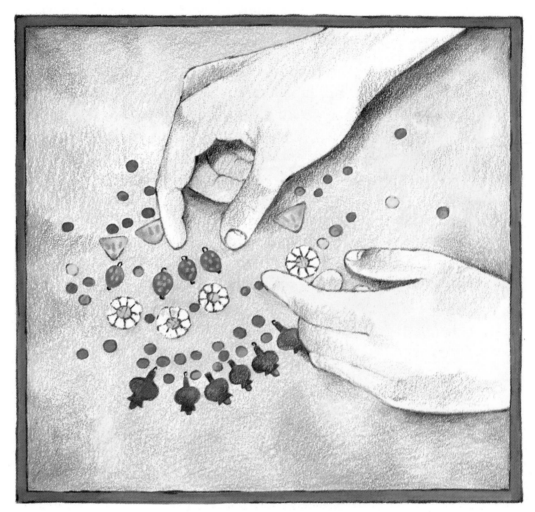

the same shape but colored differently. Then I began raising each pendant and small bead with tweezers, laying them out on the board beside the diagram in the correct order. This would save time when it came to rethreading the whole thing; but I still might need the drawing, for in the event of the necklace getting joggled out of position on its journey up to the house, or even by some misfortune spilled completely, it could still be correctly put together again by means of the diagram.

I spent the afternoon working through the heap of rubble, picking up loose pendants that belonged to the necklace. The pace had to be slow, in case of disturbing yet another stretch of beads, perhaps made up in a different way. One ruthless jab with a knife into the rubble might bring down a shower of earth, and with it a stream of beads and pendants, carrying with them the secret of their shattered pattern, lost forever.

At the end of the afternoon, Kassar and another helper carried the board up to the house without shifting a bead, and keeping perfectly calm. This was wonderful, really, as they had me nervously circling round them the whole way, rather in the manner of a cow with a new-born calf. They laid the whole thing in the antiquity room to await registration, and then trotted off to their evening meal. I had never felt grittier and sandier — or more elated.

Author

The selection you have just read came from *Nefertiti Lived Here,* Mary Chubb's first book for young people, which tells of her first experiences as a member of an archaeological team. She later joined another dig in Mesopotamia, which she described in her adult book, *City in the Sand.*

Summary Questions

Think about the aspects of Mary's job that were dull, as well as those that were exciting.

1. What did Mary have to do to reconstruct the necklace?
2. Why did the necklace seem special to Mary?
3. What personal rewards do you think Mary got from her work with the archaeological team?
4. Explain why a person would need to be enthusiastic and hardworking to be on an archaeological team. Discuss both the boring and the exciting aspects of the job.

The Reading and Writing Connection

Think of an ancient culture that interests you. Imagine that you are on an archaeological team excavating an ancient city of that culture. The beads on the necklace below include information about some tasks you might do on the dig. Use the information to help you write a paragraph about your experience. Name the culture, tell what work you do on the dig, and describe your most exciting discovery.

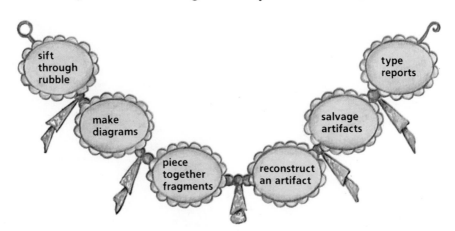

"Journey's End"

an excerpt from
Lassie Come-Home

written by Eric Knight

illustrated by Cherie Wyman

With only her animal's instincts to guide her, Lassie began her thousand-mile journey home to Joe, the boy who had never stopped hoping to see his beloved friend.

This is the heart-warming story of the bond between a boy and his dog, a bond so strong that nothing could keep Lassie from making her heroic journey. *Lassie Come-Home* is one of the most popular animal stories ever written.

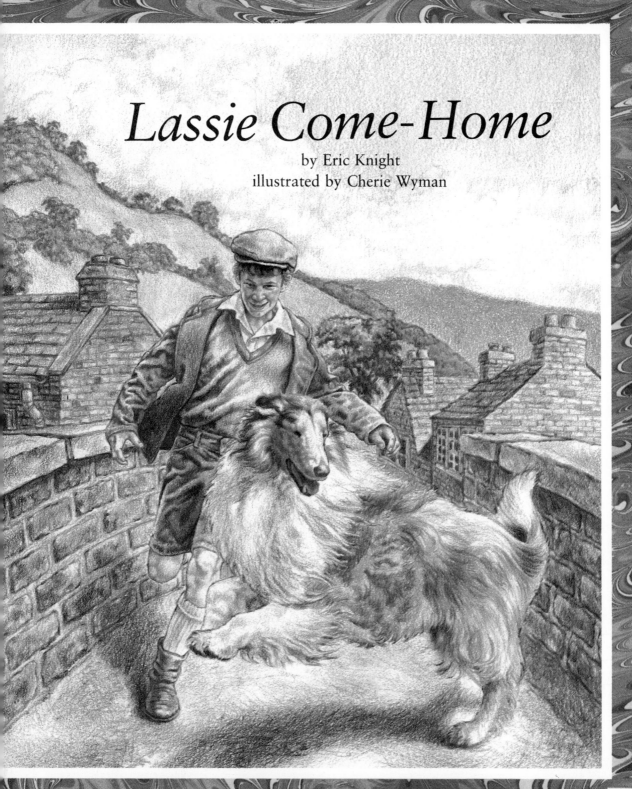

Lassie Come-Home

by Eric Knight

illustrated by Cherie Wyman

Journey's End

The Carraclough family loved their collie dog Lassie, but they had little money, and finally they had to sell her. They sold her to the Duke of Rudling, but she kept running away and coming back to the Carracloughs. Finally the duke took her away from the village that had been her home in Yorkshire, England, to his estate in the north of Scotland. Even there, Lassie escaped and headed south—longing to get home and meet young Joe Carraclough after school once again. Lassie's story is told in Eric Knight's book, Lassie Come-Home, from which this story is taken.

Slowly, steadily, Lassie came across a field.

She was not trotting now. She was going at a painful walk. Her head was low and her tail hung lifelessly. Her thin body moved from side to side as though it took the effort of her entire frame to make her legs continue to function.

But her course was straight. She was still continuing to go south.

Across the meadow she came in her tired walk. She paid no attention to the cattle that grazed on the green about her and that lifted their heads from their feeding to regard her as she passed.

The grass grew thicker and coarser as she followed the path. The track became beaten mud. Then the mud was a puddle of water, and the puddle was the edge of a river.

She stood at the trampled place. It was where the cattle came to drink and to stand for coolness in the heat of the day. Beyond her some of them stood now, knee-deep in the slow backwater. They turned and regarded her, their jaws moving unceasingly.

Lassie whimpered slightly and lifted her head as if to catch some scent from the far bank. She rocked on her feet for a moment. Then, wading forward tentatively, she went deeper and deeper. Her feet now felt no bottom. The backwater began to carry her upstream. She began swimming, her tail swirling out behind her.

This was not a turbulent river, but it was broad, and its current went firmly, carrying Lassie downstream.

Her tired legs drove with the beat and her forefeet pumped steadily. The south bank moved past her, but she seemed to be getting no nearer.

Weakness numbed her, and her beat grew slower. Her outstretched head came under the water. As if this wakened her from a sleep, she began threshing wildly. Her head went straight up, and her forefeet sent a splashing foam before her. She was a swimmer in panic.

But her head cleared again, and once more she settled down to the steady drive forward.

It was a long swim — a courageous swim. And when at last she reached the other shore, she was almost too weak to climb the bank. At the first place, her forepaws scratched and she fell back. The bank was too high. The backwater began carrying her upstream. Lassie tried again. She splashed and fell back again. Then the eddy carried her, and at last her feet touched a shelving bottom. She waded to shore.

As though the weight of the water in her coat were an extra load that was too much for her to carry, she staggered. Then dragging herself rather than walking, she crawled up the bank. And there, at last, she dropped. She could go no farther.

But she was in England! Lassie did not know that. She was only a dog going home — not a human being wise in the manner of maps. She could not know that she had made her way all down through the Highlands, the Lowlands; that the river she had crossed was the Tweed, which divides England and Scotland.

All these things she did not know. All she knew was that, as she crawled higher on the bank, a strange thing happened. Her legs would no longer respond properly, and as she was urging herself forward, the tired muscles rebelled at last. She sank, plunged a moment, and then fell on her side.

For a second, she whined. With her forepaws she clawed the earth, still dragging herself south. She was in rough grass now. She pulled herself along — a yard, another foot, another few inches. Then at last the muscles stopped their work.

Lassie lay on one side, her legs outstretched in "dead dog" position. Her eyes were glazed. The only movement was a spasmodic lifting and falling of the pinched flanks.

All that day Lassie lay there. The flies buzzed about her, but she did not lift her head to snap at them.

Evening came, and across the river was the sound of the herder and the lowing of the cows. The last notes of the birds came — the singing of a thrush through the lingering twilight.

Darkness came with its night sounds, the scream of an owl, the faraway bark of a farm dog, and the whispering in the trees.

Dawn came with new sounds — the splash of a leaping trout while the river was still veiled in mist. The sun came, and the shadows danced weakly on the grass as the overhead trees shimmered in the first breeze of the new day.

As the sun reached her, Lassie rose slowly. Her eyes were dull. Walking slowly, she set out — away from the river, going south.

Sam Carraclough had spoken the truth early that year when he told his son Joe that it was a long way from Greenall Bridge in Yorkshire to the Duke of Rudling's place in Scotland. And it is just as many miles coming the other way, a matter of four hundred miles.

But that would be for a man, traveling straight by road or by train. For an animal how far would it be — an animal that must circle obstacles, backtrack and sidetrack till it found a way?

A thousand miles it would be — a thousand miles through strange terrain it had never crossed before, with nothing but instinct to tell direction.

Yes, a thousand miles of mountain and dale, of highland and moor, plowland and path, ravine and river; a thousand miles of snow and rain and fog and sun; of wire and thistle and thorn and rock to tear the feet — who could expect a dog to win through that?

Yet, if it were almost a miracle, in his heart Joe Carraclough tried to believe in that miracle — that somehow, wonderfully, inexplicably, his dog would be there some day; there, waiting by the school gate. Each day as he came out of school, his eyes would turn to the spot where Lassie had always waited. And each day there was nothing there, and Joe Carraclough would walk home slowly, silently, stolidly, as did the people of his country.

Always, when school ended, Joe tried to prepare himself — told himself not to be disappointed, because there could be no dog there. Thus, through the long weeks, Joe began to teach himself not to believe in the impossible. He had hoped against hope so long that hope began to die.

But if hope can die in a human, it does not in an animal. As long as it lives, the hope is there and the faith is there. And so, coming across the schoolyard that day, Joe Carraclough would not believe his eyes. He shook his head and blinked. Then he rubbed his fists in his eyes, for he thought what he was seeing was a dream. There, walking the last few yards to the school gate, was his dog!

He stood, for the coming of the dog was terrible — her walk was a thing that tore at her breath. Her head and her tail were down almost to the pavement. Each footstep forward seemed a separate effort. It was a crawl rather than a walk. But the steps were made, one by one, and at last the animal dropped in her place by the gate and lay still.

Then Joe roused himself. Even if it were a dream, he must do something. In dreams one must try.

He raced across the yard and fell to his knees, and then, when his hands were touching and feeling fur, he knew it was reality. His dog had come to meet him!

But what a dog was this — no prize collie with fine tricolor coat glowing, with ears lifted gladly over the

118

proud, slim head with its perfect black mask. It was not a dog whose bright eyes were alert, and who jumped up to bark a glad welcome. This was a dog that lay, weakly trying to lift a head that would no longer lift, trying to move a tail that was torn and matted with thorns and burrs, and managing to do nothing very much except to whine in a weak, happy, crying way. For she knew that at last the terrible driving instinct was at peace. She was at the place. She had kept her lifelong rendezvous, and hands were touching her that had not touched her for so long a time.

By the Labor Exchange, Ian Cawper stood with the out-of-work miners, waiting until it was tea time so that they could all go back to their cottages.

You could have picked out Ian, for he was much the biggest man even among the many big men that York-shire grows.

Ian was a few seconds behind the others in realizing that something of urgency was happening in the village. Then he too saw it — a boy struggling, half running, along the main street, his voice lifted in excitement, a great bundle of something in his arms.

The men stirred and moved forward. Then, when the boy was nearer, they heard his cry:

"She's come back! She's come back!"

The men looked at each other and blew out their breath and then stared at the bundle the boy was carrying.

120

It was true. Sam Carraclough's collie had walked back home from Scotland.

"I must get her home, quick!" the boy was saying. He staggered on.

Ian Cawper stepped forward.

"Here," he said. "Run on ahead, tell 'em to get ready."

His great arms cradled the dog — arms that could have carried ten times the weight of this poor, thin animal.

"Oh, hurry, Ian!" the boy cried, dancing in excitement.

"I'm hurrying, lad. Go on ahead."

So Joe Carraclough raced along the street, turned up the side street, ran down the garden path, and burst into the cottage:

"Mother! Father!"

"What is it, lad?"

Joe paused. He could hardly get the words out — the excitement was choking up in his throat, hot and stifling. And then the words were said:

"Lassie! She's come home! Lassie's come home!"

He opened the door, and Ian Cawper, bowing his head to pass under the beam, carried the dog to the hearth and laid her there.

There were many things that Joe Carraclough was to remember from that evening. He was never to forget the look that passed over his father's face as he first knelt beside the dog that had been his for so many years and let his hands travel over the emaciated frame. He was to remember how his mother moved about the kitchen, silently and with a sort of terrific intensity, poking the fire quickly, stirring the condensed milk into warm water, kneeling to hold the dog's head and lift open the jowl.

Not a word did his parents speak to him. They seemed to have forgotten him altogether. Instead, they both worked over the dog with a concentration that seemed to put them in a separate world.

122

Joe watched how his father spooned in the warm liquid; he saw how it drooled out again from the unswallowing dog's jowls and dribbled down onto the rug. He saw his mother warm up a blanket and wrap it round the dog. He saw them try again and again to feed her. He saw his father rise at last.

"It's no use, lass," he said to his mother.

Between his mother and father many questions and answers passed unspoken except through their eyes.

"Pneumonia," his father said at last. "She's not strong enough now . . ."

For a while his parents stood, and then it was his mother who seemed to be somehow wonderfully alive and strong.

"I won't be beat!" she said. "I just *won't* be beat."

She pursed her lips, and as if this grimace had settled something, she went to the mantelpiece and took down a vase. She turned it over and shook it. The copper pennies came into her hand. She held them out to her husband, not explaining nor needing to explain what was needed. But he stared at the money.

"Go on," she said. "I was saving it for insurance."

"But how'll we . . ."

"Hush," the woman said.

Then her eyes flickered over her son, and Joe knew that they were aware of him again for the first time in an hour. His father looked at him, at the money in the woman's hand, and at last at the dog. Suddenly he took the money. He put on his cap and hurried out into the

night. When he came back he was carrying bundles — eggs and a small bottle of medicine — precious and costly things in that home.

Joe watched as they were beaten together, and again and again his father tried to spoon some into the dog's mouth. Then his mother blew in exasperation. Angrily she snatched the spoon. She cradled the dog's head on her lap, she lifted the jowls, and poured and stroked the throat — stroked it and stroked it, until at last the dog swallowed.

"Aaaah!"

It was his father, breathing a long, triumphant exclamation. And the firelight shone gold on his mother's hair as she crouched there, holding the dog's head — stroking its throat, soothing it with soft, loving sounds.

Joe did not clearly remember about it afterwards, only a faint sensation that he was being carried to bed at some strange hour of darkness.

And in the morning when he rose, his father sat in his chair, but his mother was still on the rug, and the fire was still burning warm. The dog, swathed in blankets, lay quiet.

"Is she — dead?" Joe asked.

His mother smiled weakly.

"Shhh," she said. "She's just sleeping. And I suppose I ought to get breakfast — but I'm played out — if I had a nice strong cup o' tea . . ."

And that morning it was his father who got the breakfast, boiling the water, brewing the tea, cutting the bread. It was his mother who sat in the rocking chair, waiting until it was ready.

That evening when Joe came home from school, Lassie still lay where he had left her when he went off to school. He wanted to sit and cradle her, but he knew that ill dogs are best left alone. All evening he sat, watching her, stretched out, with the faint breathing the only sign of life. He didn't want to go to bed.

"Now she'll be all right," his mother cried. "Go to bed — she'll be all right."

"Are you sure she'll get better, Mother?"

"You can see for yourself, can't you? She doesn't look any worse, does she?"

"But are you sure she's going to be better?"

The woman sighed.

"Of course I'm sure — now go to bed and sleep."

And Joe went to bed, confident in his parents.

That was one day. There were others to remember. There was the day when Joe returned and, as he walked to the hearth, there came from the dog lying there a movement that was meant to be a wag of the tail.

There was another day when Joe's mother sighed with pleasure, for as she prepared the bowl of milk, the dog stirred, lifted herself unsteadily, and waited. And when the bowl was set down, she put down her head and lapped, while her pinched flanks quivered.

As the weeks passed, under careful feeding and correct treatment, Lassie slowly blossomed back into the dog she had once been. The gauntness and the pinched flanks

126

disappeared, and the years of proper care that had built a strong constitution aided her now. Once more the rich coat billowed in black, sable, and white, making her a delight to the eye. The muscles of one leg had stiffened and, try as Sam Carraclough would, he could never quite cure that. But he did well with it, and massaged and rubbed the dog's muscles until her limp was so slight that only a dog expert would have noticed it. To the eye of all except the most expert of dog owners, she would have been that most beautiful thing, a perfect collie.

And each weekday, a few minutes before four o'clock, once again the shopkeepers of Greenall Bridge would look out and see that proud dog going down the street, and say, "You can set your clocks by her." And always, not long after, Joe Carraclough would come out of school and greet his dog, and they would go home together happily.

Author

Eric Knight was born in the Yorkshire countryside of *Lassie Come-Home*. He later moved to the United States, where he had a distinguished career as a writer. His works included newspaper columns, cartoons, film scripts, books, magazine articles, and short stories.

One story was based on his collie, Toots, who made a long journey home after being lost. Mr. Knight expanded the story into his only full-length children's book, *Lassie Come-Home*. The book was the basis of a feature film with many sequels and a popular television series.

Illustrator

Born in the Middle West, Cherie Wyman spent her childhood years fishing, building treehouses, playing ball, and drawing. By age twelve, she had begun to draw portraits of friends and family members. Her teachers were the great masters whom she studied from a book given to her by her grandfather. She currently lives in Minneapolis and divides her time between doing her artwork and remodeling her fifty-year-old house.

Summary Questions

Consider how the events in this story show the importance of not losing hope.

1. In the story, the author says that hope does not die in an animal. What did Lassie hope to do? What showed that she didn't lose hope?
2. What did Joe's parents do for Lassie that showed that they didn't lose hope?
3. Why do you think Joe's parents were willing to spend their savings to save Lassie?
4. How might Lassie have become a symbol of hope and courage to the people in Joe's village?

The Reading and Writing Connection

Lassie Come-Home, the story of a faithful and courageous dog, became the basis of a movie. A later television series based on the Lassie character told of the dog's adventures in the United States. Use what you know about Lassie to write an idea for a television script that describes an adventure Lassie might have had, either in England or in the United States, after recovering from her journey. Try to use some of the following words in your script:

stolidly	terrain	triumphant	turbulent

Synonyms

Look at the drawings of the dog and the cat above. If you needed to describe them to someone who had not seen them, you could say that in each drawing, both the dog and the cat were moving. However, that would not give anyone a very clear idea of what the drawings are really like. You would need to use more exact words that tell something about how the animals moved.

There are many synonyms for *moved* in the English language. Some of them give an idea of how fast someone or something moved.

Such words as *sprinted, scampered, shot,* and *darted* are used to describe fast motion. Slow motion is described by such words as *plodded, trudged, shuffled,* or *dawdled.*

Other synonyms can give an idea of the direction in which someone or something moved. These include such words as *circled, backtracked, climbed,* and *descended.*

Some words for motion tell you about the amount of effort used in moving. Such words as *threshed, struggled,* or *dragged* suggest that the person or animal had some trouble in moving. Others, such as *flitted* or *sauntered,* suggest easy moving.

Many animals have characteristic ways of moving. Ducks *waddle;* rabbits *bound.* Read each sentence below and think about how the animal or animals moved. Then select a word from the box that you could use instead of the word *moved* in each sentence. Be prepared to discuss your choices.

shuffled	**plodded**
darted	**scampered**
scurried	**shot**
crept	**sprinted**
lumbered	**dawdled**

1. The two horses moved through the fields.
2. Bears moved along the forest trails.
3. The hummingbird moved from one flower to another.
4. A deer moved into the bush.
5. Squirrels moved high in the trees.
6. A beetle moved along the vine.
7. Two fat geese moved along the river bank.
8. Quail moved toward the woods from the garden.
9. The shark moved through the water.
10. The old elephant moved through the trees.

Something Extra

Make a list of other synonyms for *move.* For each synonym, list an animal or animals that might move in that way.

Magazine Wrap-up

Literary Skill: Narrative and Expository Writing

You have learned that narrative writing tells a story or describes one or more events. Narrative writing can be either fiction or nonfiction.

Expository writing explains something factual. It does not tell a story or describe events. Expository writing is nonfiction.

Look at the Magazine One table of contents on pages 10–11, and find the titles of all the selections that are *not* poems. They include expository writing as well as fiction and nonfiction narrative. One selection includes both narrative and expository writing.

On a sheet of paper, list the following headings: Narrative Fiction, Narrative Nonfiction, Expository Writing, Narrative and Expository Writing. Under each heading write the titles that belong there.

Vocabulary: Finding Base Words

The teacher said there were too many **erasures** on my paper.

The word *erasures* may be new to you. However, if you look closely at its parts, you will see that it has an ending added to the base word *erase*, which is probably familiar to you. Recognizing base words can help you understand the meaning of many new words.

Read each of the following sentences, paying special attention to the boldface words. Each has a base word that you probably know. Write the base word. Then write in your own words what the sentence means.

1. Lack of sleep can be **injurious** to your health.
2. The Romans used a different **notation** system for writing numbers.
3. The smoke from our grill **activated** the fire alarm.
4. The clumsy dishwasher had to pay a **breakage** fee.
5. We put up a **partition** between the two rooms.

Language: Conversation

Imagine that your family could invite one of the characters listed on page 133 to have dinner in your home. Choose the character you would like to invite. Think of the kinds of topics you might discuss with that person during dinner. Be prepared to report on your proposed conversation topics to your class.

- Henry Reed
- Maria Tallchief
- Cathy
- Ra
- Mary Chubb
- Joe Carraclough

Books to Enjoy

Ida Early Comes Over the Mountain
by Robert Burch
   Ida Early's storytelling and her unconventional ways as a housekeeper perplex and charm four motherless children.

Have You Seen Hyacinth Macaw?
by Patricia Reilly Giff
   With her police friend Garcia, would-be detective Abby helps to solve the mystery about Hyacinth.

Going on a Dig
by Velma Ford Morrison
   This historical overview of archaeology in the United States emphasizes Amerindian cultures.

Help! There's a Cat Washing in Here!
by Alison Smith
   Henry takes over the housework so his mother can take a new job.

Celebrations
Magazine Two

Contents

THANK YOU, JACKIE ROBINSON

by Barbara Cohen

Sam wanted the Dodgers to sign a baseball for his
sick friend—but that wouldn't be easy.

This story takes place in the late 1940's. Sam loves baseball, especially the Brooklyn Dodgers. Sam's special friend is Davy, a sixty-year-old man who shares Sam's love for baseball and takes him to his first major-league game. When Davy goes into the hospital, Sam buys a baseball and sets off for the ballpark to get it autographed as a get-well present for Davy.

All the baseball players named in the story were real people. Jackie Robinson was the first black player in major-league baseball and played for the Brooklyn Dodgers from 1947 until he retired in 1956. In 1962, Robinson became the first black player to be named to the Baseball Hall of Fame.

I had gone into the kitchen real early in the morning, before anyone else was up, and made myself a couple of egg-salad sandwiches. I had them and my money and the baseball, which was still in its little cardboard box. I walked the mile and a half to the bus station because there'd be no place to leave my bike if I rode there. I took the bus into New York City, and I took a subway to Ebbets Field. I didn't have to ask anyone anything — except the bus driver for a ticket to New York City and the man in the subway booth for change for a quarter. There was one thing I'd learned, and that was if you know how to read you can do anything. Right in the middle of the subway station was a big map of the subway system, and Ebbets Field was marked right on it in large black letters. I didn't even have to change trains.

You could see flags flying above the ballpark when you climbed up out of the subway station. You had to walk three blocks, and there you were. Inside, it was as it always had been, as bright and green as ever, remote from the sooty streets that surrounded it, remote from all the world. In the excitement of being there, I almost forgot about Davy for a moment. I almost forgot why I had come. Then when the

Cubs' pitcher began to warm up, I turned to Davy to ask him if he thought the Dodgers' manager was going to give Jackie Robinson's sore heel a rest that day; but Davy wasn't there, and I remembered.

I thought maybe I'd better start trying right away. My chances were probably better during batting practice than they would be later. I took my ball out of its box and stashed the box underneath my bleacher seat. Then I walked around to the first-base side and climbed all the way down to the box seats right behind the dugout. I leaned over the rail. Billy Cox was trotting back to the dugout from home plate, where Carl Erskine had been throwing to him.

I swallowed my heart, which seemed to be beating in my throat, and called out, "Billy, hey Billy," waving my ball as hard and high as I could. But I was scared, and my voice wasn't very loud. I don't think Billy Cox heard me because he disappeared into the dugout.

Marv Rackley came out of the dugout, and then Carl Furillo. I called to them, too, but they didn't seem to hear me either.

This method was getting me nowhere. I had to try something else before the game began, or I'd really lose my chance. I looked around to see if there were any ushers nearby, but none was in sight. It was kind of early, and the place hadn't really started to fill up yet. I guess the ushers were loafing around the refreshment stands.

I climbed up on the railing and then hoisted myself onto the roof of the dugout. That was something you could not do at many places besides Ebbets Field. That was one of the few advantages of such a small ballpark. Of course, you know, you couldn't go see Ebbets Field now if you wanted to. They tore it down and put an apartment building there.

I could have stood up and walked across the dugout roof to the edge, but I figured if I did that an usher surely would see me. I sneaked across the roof on my belly until I came to the edge, and then I leaned over.

It was really very nice in the dugout. I had always kind of pictured it as being literally dug out of the dirt, like a trench in a war, but it had regular walls and a floor and benches and a water cooler. The only trouble was there were just a couple of guys in there — Eddie Miksis and Billy Cox, whom I'd seen out on the field a few minutes before. I was disappointed. I had certainly hoped for Campy's signature, and Gil Hodges's, and Pee Wee Reese's, and of course Jackie Robinson's, but I figured Davy would be thrilled with Miksis's and Billy Cox's, since their names on a ball would be more than he'd ever expected. Anyway, I figured that a few more guys might come meandering in before I was through.

No matter how hard I swallowed, my heart was still stuck in my throat. "Eddie," I called. "Eddie, Billy." Hardly any sound came out of my mouth at all.

Then all of a sudden I heard a voice calling real loud. Whoever it was didn't have any trouble getting the sound out of *his* mouth. "Hey you, kid, get down off that roof," the voice said. "What do you think you're doing?" I sat up and turned around. An angry usher was standing at the foot of the aisle, right by the railing, screaming at me. "Get yourself off that roof," he shouted. "Right now, or I'll throw you out of the ballpark."

I scrambled down as fast as I could. Boy, was I a mess. My chino pants and my striped jersey were absolutely covered with dust and grime from that roof. I guess my face and arms weren't any too clean either. I looked like a bum.

"I'm going to throw you out anyway," the usher said, "because you don't have a ticket."

I got real mad when I heard him say that, especially since I certainly did have a ticket.

"You can't throw me out," I shouted back at him. "I've got as much right to be here as you have." I had suddenly found my voice. I was scared of the ballplayers, but this usher didn't frighten me one bit. I pulled my ticket stub out of my pocket. "See?" I said, thrusting it into his face, "I certainly do have a ticket."

He made as if to take it out of my hand. I guess he wanted to look at it closely to make sure it was a stub from that day and not an old one I might have been carrying around in my pocket for emergencies, but I pulled my hand back.

"Oh, no, you don't," I said. "You can't take this ticket away from me. You won't give it back to me, and then you'll throw me out because I don't have a ticket!"

"You crazy, kid?" he asked, shaking his head. "This is what I get for working in Ebbets Field. A bunch of crazy people.

Next year I'm applying for a job at the Polo Grounds."

"Go ahead," I said, "you traitor. Who needs you?" I turned away from him and leaned over the rail.

"I better not see you on that roof again," the usher said. "I'll have my eye out for you — and so will all the other ushers."

"Don't worry," I said.

Then I felt his hand on my shoulder. "As a matter of fact, kid," he said, "I think I'll escort you to your seat where you belong — up in the bleachers where you can't make any trouble!"

Well, right then and there, the whole enterprise would have gone up in smoke if Jackie Robinson himself had not come trotting out onto the field from the dugout that very second. "Hey, Jackie," I called, "hey, Jackie," in a voice as loud as a thunderbolt. I mean there were two airplanes flying overhead right that minute, and Jackie Robinson heard me anyway.

He glanced over in the direction he could tell my voice was coming from, and I began to wave frantically, still calling "Jackie, hey, Jackie."

He lifted up his hand, gave one wide wave, and smiled. "Hey, kid," he called and continued on his way to the batting cage. In another instant he'd have been too busy with batting practice to pay any attention to me.

"Sign my ball," I screamed. "Sign my ball."

He seemed to hesitate briefly. I took this as a good omen. "You gotta," I went on frantically. "Please, please, you gotta."

"He doesn't gotta do anything," the usher said. "That's Jackie Robinson, and everyone knows that he doesn't gotta."

I went right on screaming.

"Come on, kid," the usher said, "we're getting out of here." He was a big hulking usher who must have weighed about eight hundred pounds, and he began pulling on me. Even though I gripped the cement with my sneakers and held onto

the rail with my hand, he managed to pull me loose — but he couldn't shut me up.

"Please, Jackie, please," I went right on screaming.

It worked, or something worked. If not my screaming, then maybe the sight of that monster usher trying to pull me up the aisle and scrungy old me pulling against him for dear life.

"Let the kid go," Jackie Robinson said when he got to the railing. "All he wants is an autograph."

"He's a fresh kid," the usher said, but he let me go.

"Kids are supposed to be fresh," Jackie Robinson said.

I thrust my ball into Jackie Robinson's face. "Gee thanks, Mr. Robinson," I said. "Sign it, please."

"You got a pen?" he asked.

"A pen?" I could have kicked myself. "A pen?" I'd forgotten a pen! I turned to the usher. "You got a pen?"

"If I had," the usher said triumphantly, "I certainly wouldn't lend it to you!"

"Oh, come on," Jackie Robinson said, "don't be so vindictive. What harm did the kid do, after all?"

"Well, as it happens, I don't have one," the usher replied smugly.

"Wait here," I said. "Wait right here, Mr. Robinson. I'll go find one."

Jackie Robinson laughed. "Sorry, kid, but I've got work to do. Another time maybe."

"Please, Mr. Robinson," I said. "It's for my friend — my friend, Davy."

"Well, let Davy come and get his own autographs," he said. "Why should you do his dirty work for him?"

"He can't come," I said. The words came rushing out of me, tumbling one on top of the other. I had to tell Jackie Robinson all about it, before he went away. "Davy can't come because he's sick. He had a heart attack."

"A heart attack?" Jackie Robinson asked. "A kid had a heart attack?"

"He's not a kid," I explained. "He's sixty years old. He's my best friend. He's always loved the Dodgers, but lately he's loved them more than ever."

I guess Jackie Robinson could tell how serious I was about what I was saying. "How did this Davy get to be your best friend?" he asked.

So I told him. I told him everything, or as near to everything as I could tell in five minutes. I told him how Davy worked for my mother and how I had no father, so it was Davy who took me to my first ball game. I told him how we had always talked about catching a ball that was hit into the stands and getting it autographed.

Jackie listened silently, nodding every once in a while. When I was done at last, he said, "Well, now, kid, I'll tell you what. You keep this ball you brought with you. Keep it to play with, and borrow a pen from someone. Come back to the dugout the minute, the very second, the game is over, and I'll get you a real ball, one we played with; and I'll get all the guys to autograph it for you."

"Make sure it's one you hit," I said.

What nerve. I should have fainted dead away just because Jackie Robinson had deigned to speak to me, but here he was, making me an offer beyond my wildest dreams, and for me it wasn't enough. I had to have more. However, he didn't seem to care.

"Okay," he said. "If I hit one." He had been in a little slump lately.

"You will," I said. "You will."

And he did. He broke the ball game wide open in the sixth inning when he hit a double to left field, scoring Marv Rackley and Duke Snider. He scored himself when the Cubs pitcher, Warren Hacker, tried to pick him off second base. Hacker overthrew, and Jackie, with that incredible speed he had, ran all the way home. On top of that, Jackie worked two double plays with Preacher Roe and Gil Hodges.

The other Dodgers had a good day too. On consecutive pitches, Carl Furillo and Billy Cox both hit home runs, shattering the 1930 Brooklyn home-run record of 122 for a season. The Dodgers scored six runs, and they scored them all in the sixth inning. They beat the Cubs, 6–1. They were hot, really hot, that day and that year.

I really didn't watch the game as closely as I had all the others I'd been to see. I couldn't. My mind was on too many other things — on Jackie Robinson, on what was going to happen after the game was over, on that monster usher who, I feared, would yet find some way of spoiling things for me, but above all on Davy and the fact that he was missing all of the excitement.

Then I had to worry about getting hold of a pen. You could buy little pencils at the ballpark for keeping box scores, but not pens. It was the first — and last — time in my life I walked into a ballpark without something to write with. And I didn't see how I could borrow one from someone, since in all that mess of humanity I'd never find the person after the game to return it — unless I took the person's name and address and mailed it back later.

It didn't look to me like the guys in the bleachers where I was sitting had pens with them anyway. Most of them had on tee shirts, and tee shirts don't have pockets in them for pens. I decided to walk over to the seats along the first-base line to see if any of those fans looked more like pen owners. I had to go in that direction anyway to make sure I was at the dugout the second the ball game ended. I took my ball with me.

On my way over, I ran into this guy hawking cold drinks, and I decided to buy one in order to wash down the two egg-salad sandwiches I had eaten during the third inning.

This guy had a pen in his pocket. As a matter of fact, he had two of them. "Look," I said to him, as I paid him for my drink, "could I borrow one of those pens?"

"Sure," he said, handing it to me after he had put my money into his change machine. He stood there, waiting, like he expected me to hand it back to him after I was done with it.

"Look," I said again, "maybe I could sort of buy it from you."

"Buy it from me? You mean the pen?"

"Yeah."

"What do you want my pen for?"

"I need it because Jackie Robinson promised me that after

the game he and all the other guys would autograph a ball for me." Getting involved in all these explanations was really a pain in the neck.

"You don't say," the hawker remarked. I could tell he didn't believe me.

"It's true," I said. "Anyway, will you sell me your pen?"

"Sure. For a dollar."

I didn't have a dollar. Not anymore. I'd have to try something else. I started to walk away.

"Oh, don't be silly, kid," he called to me. "Here, take the pen. Keep it." It was a nice pen. It was shaped like a bat, and on it was written "Ebbets Field, Home of the Brooklyn Dodgers."

"Hey, mister, thanks," I said. "That's real nice of you." It seemed to me I ought to do something for him, so I added, "I think I'd like another drink." He sold me another, and between sipping first from one and then from the other and trying to watch the game, I made very slow progress down to the dugout. I got there just before the game ended, in the top of the ninth. The Dodgers didn't have to come up to bat at all in that final inning, and I was only afraid that they'd all have disappeared into the clubhouse by the time I got there. I should have come down at the end of the eighth, but Jackie Robinson had said the end of the game. Although my nerve had grown by about seven thousand per cent that day, I still didn't have enough to interrupt Jackie Robinson during a game.

I stood at the railing near the dugout, waiting, and sure enough, Jackie Robinson appeared around the corner of the building only a minute or two after Preacher Roe pitched that final out. All around me, people were getting up to leave the ballpark, but a lot of them stopped when they saw Jackie Robinson come to the rail to talk to me. Roy Campanella, Pee Wee Reese, and Gil Hodges were with him.

"Hi, kid," Jackie Robinson said. He was carrying a ball. It was covered with signatures. "Pee Wee here had a pen."

"A good thing, too," Pee Wee said, "because most of the other guys left the field already."

"These guys wanted to meet Davy's friend," Jackie Robinson said.

By that time, Preacher Roe had joined us at the railing. Jackie handed him the ball. "Hey, Preacher," he said, "got enough strength left in that arm to sign this ball for Davy's friend here?"

"Got a pen?" Preacher Roe asked.

I handed him the pen the hawker had given me. I was glad I hadn't gone through all the trouble of getting it for nothing.

"Not much room left on this ball," Roe said. He squirmed his signature into a little empty space beneath Duke Snider's, and then he handed me both the pen and the ball. Everybody was waving programs and pens in the faces of the ballplayers who stood by the railing, but before they signed any of them, they all shook my hand. So did Jackie Robinson. I stood there clutching Davy's ball and watching while those guys signed the programs of the other fans. Finally, though, they'd had enough. They smiled and waved their hands and walked away, five big men in white uniforms, etched sharply against the bright green grass. Jackie Robinson was the last one into the dugout, and before he disappeared around the corner, he turned and waved to me.

I waved back. "Thank you, Jackie Robinson," I called. "Thanks for everything." He nodded and smiled. I guess he heard me. I'm glad I remembered my manners before it was too late.

When everyone was gone, I looked down at the ball in my hands. Right between the rows of red seaming, Jackie Robinson had written, above his own signature, "For Davy. Get well soon." Then all the others had put their names around that.

I took the ball I had bought out of the box and put it in my pocket. I put the ball Jackie Robinson had given me in the box. Then I went home.

Author

Barbara Cohen always wanted to be a writer and began writing in the fifth grade. She writes from her own experience. *Thank You, Jackie Robinson,* from which this story was taken, and another of her books, *Gooseberries to Oranges,* were named American Library Association Notable Books.

Summary Questions

Think about the lengths to which Sam went to help his friend Davy feel better.

1. Why did Sam want the Dodgers to sign his baseball?
2. How do you know that Davy's friendship was important to Sam?
3. Why do you think Jackie Robinson offered to get Sam a "real ball," signed by all the players, instead of just signing the ball for Sam?
4. Pretend that you are Davy. Tell what happened at the hospital when Sam brought you the ball. Describe how you felt when he told you how he got it.

The Reading and Writing Connection

Suppose you are a newspaper reporter who hears about Sam and the baseball. You think this story would be a good human-interest article for your paper. You want to get as broad a viewpoint as possible, so you interview each of the following people: Sam, Jackie Robinson, the usher, and Davy. Think about what each of these people could have told you about the event. Then write your article, using some of the following words you have learned in this selection.

enterprise	autographed	dugout	hawking

The Base Stealer

by Robert Francis

Poised between going on and back, pulled
Both ways taut like a tightrope-walker,
Fingertips pointing the opposites,
Now bouncing tiptoe like a dropped ball
Or a kid skipping rope, come on, come on,

        Running a scattering of steps sidewise,
        How he teeters, skitters, tingles, teases,
        Taunts them, hovers like an ecstatic bird,
        He's only flirting, crowd him, crowd him,
        Delicate, delicate, delicate, delicate — now!

The Newspaper

You have learned how to use many different resources for information in a library, but you have one resource for up-to-date information that can be available in your own home every day. From it you can learn about important events in other parts of the world; what the weather is likely to be tomorrow; what shows will be on your television tonight; what items are for sale in stores near you; how your favorite sports team is doing; and even if there are any part-time jobs that you might be interested in. Your local newspaper tells you this and more.

There are differences among newspapers, but most are alike in many ways. If you know the things they have in common, you can use any newspaper quickly and easily.

Sections in a Newspaper

Most newspapers have major sections that appear in about the same order each day.

News: The first part of a newspaper has news stories. The most important news is likely to be on the front page. You can first check the front-page headlines to find news stories that interest you. The size of the headline generally shows how important the editors of the paper thought the news story was. The largest headlines are used for the most important stories.

Here is an example of a headline and other information that might come before a news story.

MAN BITES DOG
by Bill Brown
WASHINGTON (AP)

Beneath the headline is the name of the person who wrote the news story. This is called a by-line and appears in some, but not all, news stories.

Next comes the dateline, which shows the origin of the story. Since this imaginary story took place in Washington, the dateline shows the name of that city. Some datelines are followed by letters such as (AP) or (UPI). These letters stand for the news service, such as Associated Press or United Press International, that wrote the story. A news service produces and sells stories to many different newspapers.

A well-written news story has the most important information in the first paragraph. That paragraph should tell who or what the story is about as well as when and where it took place. When you read the first paragraph of a news story, try to find answers to the questions *Who? What? When?* and *Where?* Then you can decide whether or not you want to read the entire story.

Sports: Most papers have a section called SPORTS. You will find information about both amateur and professional sports. There are reports about sports events near you and in other parts of the country. This section may also have stories about athletes as well as columns that give the opinions of sports writers. When your own school's teams play, you are likely to find reports about the games in your newspaper.

Editorials: Most papers also have an EDITORIALS section. Here you may read about some of the same events and issues that are covered in the news section, but they are presented in a different way. News stories are supposed to give just the facts. Editorials give the opinions of the writers. People often write letters to the editor, and the letters may be printed in the editorials section.

Entertainment: If you want to know about movies, plays, or concerts that are near you, look in the section with a title such as ENTERTAINMENT. There you may find reviews that can help you decide if you want to go to a certain show. Titles and starting times of the movies playing near you are also given.

Living: Many papers have a section about home and family living, with a title such as LIVING or HOME LIFE. It usually has recipes, health advice, and stories about community events.

Classified: Most papers have a CLASSIFIED or WANT ADS section, with ads for many kinds of products and services. Job openings may be listed under *Employment, Job Opportunities,* or *Help Wanted*. Under *Automobiles* or *Cars for Sale* you will find ads by car dealers and private owners. Ads for houses and apartments will be found under *Real Estate, Houses for Sale,* or *For Rent*. Ads for new and used items, such as furniture or bicycles, may be grouped under a heading such as *For Sale*.

Special Features in a Newspaper

Besides the major sections, a newspaper also has regular features. Most newspapers use part of an inside page for reporting the weather in different parts of the country. A brief weather forecast may also be on the front page.

A television schedule lists the programs to be shown and tells where and when they can be seen. A schedule for radio programs may be on the same page.

Cartoon strips are on the comic pages. You may also find a crossword puzzle and other word games in the newspaper.

Most newspapers have special columns that appear every day or once a week. The authors' by-lines appear on these columns. Some may be written by members of the paper's own editorial staff. Other *syndicated* columns may appear in newspapers all over the country. The columns deal with many subjects. Some answer questions from readers. Others give the authors' opinions on a wide range of topics. Some are written to entertain or amuse.

Display advertisements will be found throughout the newspaper. They can help you if you want to buy something or want a service performed.

A Newspaper Index

You can find a major section or a special feature quickly by using the index on the first or second page of most newspapers. The major sections and some special features are listed in alphabetical order. Numbers and sometimes letters show the pages on which they will be found. The sample index below may look like the one in your local paper.

Today's Index

Ask Amanda	3c
Business	12-14a
Classified	6-12d
Comics	7-8b
Crossword	6b
Death Notices	6c
Editorials	10-11a
Entertainment	1-5b
Living	1-5c
Sports	1-5d
TV-Radio	6b
Weather	15a

In some papers the pages are numbered in order, as they are in a book. Pages in other newspapers are shown by both numbers and letters, as in the sample index. The first section is labeled **a**, the second **b**, and so on. Pages are then numbered in order within each section. The first page of Section b would be numbered **b1** or **1b** and the second page as **b2** or **2b**.

If you are looking for something that is not listed, you can still use the index to help you find the section where it is likely to be. Suppose you wanted to find out when and where a flower show was being held. By thinking about the kinds of subjects covered in each section, you would know this announcement would probably be found in the living section and would look for it on pages **1-5c.**

Newspapers as Reference Sources

Old newspapers are sources of information about past events. Most public libraries have them available for you. However, they are not printed on paper as you are used to seeing them. Paper takes up a great deal of space and does not last well. Libraries keep their back copies of newspapers on *microfilm*, on which the pages have been photographed greatly reduced in size. Libraries can store thousands of microfilmed newspapers in the same space that it would take to store just one copy of the original paper. To read a microfilmed newspaper, you use a machine that projects an image on a screen.

To gather information from old newspapers you will usually have to know the date or the approximate date that the newspaper you want appeared. If you wanted to know what the weather was like and what other important things happened on the day you were born, you could ask to read the microfilm for the newspapers that were published on that date.

A few of the larger newspapers and the news services have computerized indexes that would be available to you in some libraries. You use this index in the same way as a book index. You have to decide on the main topics and subtopics you want to look up, and the index tells you where the information you want can be found.

Many newspapers also keep indexes of their old editions. This information is usually kept only for people who work for the newspaper. However, you may be able to ask your newspaper to help you find what you want. If you give them the topic, they can tell you the dates on which articles on that subject appeared in their newspaper. You can then ask your librarian for microfilms of the papers published on those dates.

The next time that you do a research project on something that happened in the past, use this valuable source of information to help you write your report.

Using the Newspaper

Use the sample index on page 159 to decide where you would look in the newspaper to answer these questions.

1. Did the high-school team win the game last night?
2. Are there any used tents for sale?
3. What are some opinions about the recent election?
4. What programs are on television at 8:00 P.M.?
5. Is it likely to rain in the local area tomorrow?
6. How much are the tickets for the circus that is in town?
7. What is the answer to the word game in yesterday's paper?
8. What did readers think about a recent article in the paper?
9. What advice is given in the health column?
10. What did the reviewer think of a movie that just opened?

Skill Summary

- Most newspapers have News, Sports, Editorials, Living or Home Life, and Classified or Want Ads as major sections.
- Newspapers have regular features that may include radio and television listings, columns, and advertisements.
- The index in a newspaper shows the major sections.
- Back issues of newspapers can be found on microfilm in most public libraries, and are a source of information about people and events of the past.

THE
Gorillagram

by E.M. Hunnicutt

Jan and Barbara were making lots of money in the drama business — until they met up with a very unfriendly critic. Would he spoil their act?

Jan Peabody said to me, "Barbara, you and I are going on the River Club canoe trip."

"Where's the money coming from?" I asked.

"Think positive," she said, "and don't bog down in such technicalities."

I have a lot of confidence in Jan. Take last summer. Mr. Timmerman, who'd always let us play softball on the lot next to his house, moved away. When this new lady moved in, she said we were too noisy and the balls were coming too close to her hollyhock bed. She told us to clear out.

Jan remembered that each week the local radio station gives a good citizen award. The station tells about the person on the air and mails a free pair of movie tickets. Jan wrote the station a letter saying this lady was preserving the town's history by growing hollyhocks, a flower popular with the first settlers. An announcer read Jan's letter on the radio, and the lady was so pleased she invited us back.

"Where'd you find out about hollyhocks?" I asked Jan.

"In the library," she said, "under *H*."

"Mr. Timmerman planted those flowers."

"A technicality, Barbara," she said. "Nobody can say the lady isn't doing her best to preserve them." We shifted the bases a little to protect the flower bed, and those hollyhocks grew to be six feet tall.

For Halloween, back when we were in fourth grade, Jan decided we should fix up her garage as a haunted house and take people through for a quarter each. We were the first in town to do it, and we made enough money to buy tickets to all the hockey games that winter.

So when I said to Jan, "Between us, we have fourteen cents for gear and supplies," I was prepared for anything. Our folks had already said it was up to us to earn the money.

We were in Jan's basement. I was sitting beside a plastic cup that was four feet high, and Jan was holding the headpiece of one of two gorilla suits on her lap, stroking the fur thoughtfully. Jan's dad is a photographer for an advertising agency, and the house is always full of these weird props.

"I'm thinking positive, Jan," I said. "So what's next?"

She put on the headdress and began pounding her chest and jumping up and down.

"It's too early for Halloween," I said. "Take off the mask."

Jan said, "You are surrounded, hairless ape!" Except through the gorilla mask, it sounded like, "You have found Harold's grapes!"

I was getting bored with the cup. I circled Jan and went over to a cardboard telephone that was taller than I was. It looked like an ordinary phone except for a sign in the middle of the dial advertising this dry-cleaning place that picks up and delivers.

Jan took off the gorilla headpiece and handed it to me. Then she picked up the telephone receiver and pretended to be the smallest person in the world calling the "Guinness Book of World Records."

I put on the headdress. "Jan, what can we do?"

"And happy birthday to you, too!" she said.

"I didn't say happy birthday."

"It sounded like it," Jan said. "Remember singing telegrams?" She sang a full chorus of "Happy Birthday to You" into the cardboard telephone.

I'm used to Jan. From the outside, all her antics just look like horsing around, but that's how she creates. She takes a little of this and a little of that, whatever happens to be around, and puts it together in her own way. By the time she hung up the phone, she had it.

"Barbara," she said. "We're going to sell Gorillagrams."

"What's a Gorillagram?"

Jan put on the bottom of one gorilla suit and started swinging her arms and showing her teeth like a monkey.

"Someone has a birthday; people call us. We put on the suits, go knock on the door, and sing 'Happy Birthday.' Except we also ham it up, put on a little act, give people their money's worth. We can do graduations, anniversaries, whatever the ladies and gentlemen want!"

On "ladies and gentlemen," she took a bow and did a little dance step. "Barbara, there's nothing people like better than a good laugh."

"Maybe so, but I'm no actor."

"Look," she said, "do you want to go on the canoe trip?"

"Sure," I said.

"Then start pounding your chest and scratching your fleas."

The first step was to talk to Jan's dad.

"So you want to rent the suits?" Mr. Peabody asked.

"Strictly on a business basis," Jan told him.

"Strictly business," Mr. Peabody said, but he was grinning. I guess anyone who works with cups four feet high has to have a sense of humor. "Okay, the money for the first three Gorillagrams comes back to me for suit rental," he said.

"After that, everything you make is yours, free and clear." Then he bought the first two Gorillagrams himself and wanted to know how soon we could deliver them.

First, we had to fix the headpieces of the suits so people could understand what we said. We put wads of newspaper in the top, and that brought the mouth openings up into good position. Then we practiced singing "Happy Birthday."

"Jan, I don't sing so good," I said.

"You're a gorilla, Barbara. Nobody expects a gorilla to sound like a rock star." Then she taught me the words to "Anniversary Waltz," and we practiced dancing, which was really pretty dumb.

"Which is exactly what we want," Jan said. "The dumber the better." Jan's mother sewed a little pink skirt for one of the suits, and we named ourselves "Gonzo" and "Gloria."

Mr. Peabody sent the first Gorillagram to his mother, Jan's grandmother. It wasn't any special occasion. Just a "Have a Nice Day" greeting. He gave us plenty of material to use. She had won a dance contest when she was eighteen, dancing the Charleston. She'd been a teacher in a one-room school. She had eloped to Baltimore with Jan's grandfather. We worked it all into the act, sang a couple of songs, and did a dance Jan said was pretty close to the Charleston.

Jan's grandmother is past eighty. She laughed until tears ran down her cheeks, and I have a feeling she may still be laughing.

The second Gorillagram went to a friend of Jan's dad, a man who ran a real-estate office downtown. "I can't walk into a business office in this get-up," I told Jan.

"Sure you can," she said. "Nobody will know who you are. Besides, the whole Gorillagram doesn't take more than ten minutes. That's not much of an interruption."

"What if someone calls the police?"

"They won't call the police," Jan said. "The dogcatcher, maybe."

This man had just finished some big job, so the message was "Congratulations." But Jan's dad had us work in a lot of other stuff. His friend had been a big football star back in high school, and he spent every other weekend working on his boat because it broke down a lot. We put it all in, passed a football around the office, and sang a couple of choruses of "Row, Row, Row Your Boat." Then we wound up with a dance Jan invented called the Grumba, a cross between "gorilla" and "rumba." The Grumba worked out so well we made it a regular part of the act.

We were a big hit in the real-estate office and got two more jobs on the spot. Word about us soon got around. We went to two nursing homes and four birthday parties for small children. Then there was a silver wedding anniversary party and several more "Have a Nice Day" jobs, just for people who wanted to play a joke on a friend.

We couldn't believe how well things were going. We'd kept our price low to encourage business. Even so, the money was rolling in.

By the end of June our goal was in sight, and we had two weeks left to sign up for the canoe trip. Then disaster struck.

It was Saturday afternoon, and we were on our way to a birthday party. Usually our mothers took turns driving us to jobs, but this one was only four blocks away — three if we cut across behind the school. We had decided to suit up at home and walk over. We were halfway across the school yard, and I was daydreaming. I could see my canoe cutting silently through beautiful clear blue water.

Then Jan stopped suddenly. "Barbara," she whispered, "how fast do you think two gorillas can run?"

Then I saw it. About fifty yards away was this big gray dog, ears laid back, teeth bared, an evil-sounding snarl churning out of his throat. He was poised like a steel spring, set to go for us.

"Jan," I whispered, "I've seen that dog around. I think he's a stray. He's never been mean."

"He thinks we're real animals," Jan said softly. "He's scared, scared bad, and he's big enough to do real damage."

"If we could get out of these suits," I said, "let him see we're really people . . ."

"Maybe," Jan said, "if we just had enough time. But if we're tangled up in the suits, and he decides to come after us, we're trapped. We won't be able to move at all."

"And any move we make now could spook him into a charge," I said.

We were in the wide-open space between the basketball court and the swings.

"Barbara," Jan whispered, "what this school needs is a *jungle gym*."

Any other time, it would have been funny.

The whole thing couldn't have lasted more than half a minute, but it seemed to go on forever, with the dog snarling and the two of us frozen like statues. Then he charged.

The school building was the closest solid object, and we made for it, hobbling along in the suits as best we could. Then the only direction to go was up. There was a rainspout fastened to the corner of the building. I lunged for it, hoping the screws in the brackets were twisted in tightly. They were,

169

and somehow I made it to the roof. The dog caught Jan in the seat of the pants and ripped the back out of the suit, but Jan made it all the way up.

We got out of the suits and leaned over the edge of the roof to talk to the dog. "Easy, boy," I said. "Easy now."

He had taken up sentry duty beside the rainspout, and there was no calming him down. He hadn't liked two wild animals running around loose, and he didn't like two people sitting on top of the schoolhouse any better. Suits or no suits, it didn't look right to him. He just stood there snarling.

"We'll sneak across the roof," Jan said, "and climb down the other side."

But you can't sneak past a dog's ears. He knew what we were up to before we'd taken two steps. When we got across the roof, he was down below, waiting for us.

"Jan, I don't believe this," I said.

"Believe it, Barbara," she said. "Believe it."

I cupped my hands and yelled. "Help!" Someone was sure to come along soon.

Jan recovered her good nature and started inventing imaginary newspaper stories. "'Today a courageous dog, acting alone, saved our city from two vicious gorillas.'"

"Help!" I yelled again. There was nobody in sight.

"'When asked by reporters to comment on his heroic deed, the dog made no reply. He just wagged his tail modestly.'"

"Jan, I never realized how deserted it is around a schoolhouse when school's out."

She ignored me. "'Shortly after the gorillas escaped from the zoo, Herbert, an ordinary-looking dog with nerves of steel, picked up their scent.'"

"Herbert?"

"The name fits him, don't you think?"

"Okay. Herbert. Jan, how much is that ripped-up suit going to cost us?"

171

"I'd better not tell you," she said. "You're too depressed already."

"Help!" I hollered.

"They'll miss us soon," Jan said. "Someone will come looking for us."

"No, they won't," I said. "When we don't show up, your folks will think you're at my house, and my folks will think I'm at your house. The people at the birthday party didn't know we were coming. It was going to be a surprise. And the dog is a stray. Nobody will miss him."

That's exactly what happened. Nobody guessed we were missing. When night came, it turned chilly. We got back into the suits to keep warm.

Herbert never left his post. "'The determination and dedication of this lone dog amazed everyone,'" Jan said through chattering teeth.

"You're always full of bright ideas," I said. "Now's the time to come up with one." But for once, it wasn't Jan's imagination that pulled us through. It was the moon. The moon came out full, and Herbert started to howl. Once he started, he never stopped.

"'Herbert the singing dog,'" Jan said, "'kept his captives entertained with several bass-baritone selections.'"

After half an hour of howling, some family down the street called the police about the noise. In the dark, the officers couldn't see our suits, which was just as well. By the time they found a ladder and got us down, we'd had time to explain everything.

As soon as we were back on the ground, Herbert turned friendly. He seemed to think he was a hero. He licked everybody's hand and nearly wagged his tail off.

The newspaper made a big thing of it. We had to go back in daylight the next day and re-enact all of it for the photographers. Everyone felt sorry for us, and somebody wrote to the radio station recommending us for the good citizen award. The letter said the Gorillagrams had brought joy to hundreds. The station agreed and sent us two pairs of movie tickets.

"I don't think it was actually 'hundreds,'" I said to Jan.

"A technicality, Barbara," she said.

We were sitting in Jan's basement, between the giant cup and the oversized telephone. In one way, we had a lot to feel good about, being honored by practically the whole town. On the other hand, the cost of a new gorilla suit was going to wipe out our chances to go on the canoe trip.

Jan was still composing newspaper stories. "'Our heroes have glory, honor, and movie passes . . . but no money.'"

"If Herbert had an owner, we could make him pay for the suit," I said.

"'Herbert the dog told reporters that he is, unfortunately, penniless.'"

Then the phone rang, the real phone upstairs, and we could hear Jan's dad answering it. A few minutes later he poked his head in the doorway, and there was a big smile on his face.

"You know that rainspout you girls climbed on? A man from the company that manufactures them just called. He read the story in the newspaper and saw the rainspout in the photographs. The company wants to use your picture in one of its ads, and you'll be paid for it."

Jan jumped up and started pounding her chest. "'This rainspout of ours is strong enough to support King Kong! Holds up under extreme conditions! Keeps schoolhouses hazard-free and saves innocent young lives!'"

Mr. Peabody grinned and shook his head. "You're overacting, as usual, but that's the general idea."

"It *was* the rainspout that saved us," I said. "No question about that."

What the manufacturer paid us for using our picture covered the cost of the gorilla suit and gave us a little cash to spare.

After we got that settled, we went over to the pound, where the police had taken Herbert, and Jan adopted him. We took him back to Jan's and showed him the gorilla suits up close and in good light.

"These are not real animals," Jan told him, and she produced a dish of chopped liver to clear away any doubts Herbert might have.

The dog caught on right away. He's smart. Jan says that when we get back from the canoe trip, she's going to teach Herbert the Grumba and take him along on Gorillagrams. A dancing dog sounds a little far-fetched, but with Jan you never know.

Author

Ellen Hunnicutt is a resident of upper New York State. As a music teacher, she has written articles for professional journals. Her experiences as a mother and her sense of humor have contributed to her stories and articles for young people.

Summary Questions

Jan and Barbara knew what would make people laugh. As you read the story, think about the parts that made you laugh.

1. What was the most distinctive element of Jan's personality? What happened in the story that demonstrated this?
2. How did Jan and Barbara turn a sense of humor into money for the canoe trip?
3. What was funny about the girls' adventure with Herbert?
4. Near the beginning of the story, Jan says that there's nothing people like better than a good laugh. What happened in the story that gave you a good laugh?

The Reading and Writing Connection

Many people in town got to know about Jan and Barbara's enterprise after their story was featured in the newspaper. Their names and pictures also appeared in a display advertisement for the rainspout company.

Think about how Jan and Barbara might make use of the newspaper as their business continues to grow. For example, if they needed a third person for their act, they could place an ad under "Help Wanted" in the Classified section. Think of ways the other sections of the newspaper could help them. Then write a letter telling them how to make use of the newspaper for those purposes. Try to use the following words in your letter.

| antics   dedication   technicalities |

Roots

Many English words are made up of parts that have been borrowed from other languages. These borrowed word parts are called *roots*. Knowing the meaning of just a few roots can help you understand many different words.

The roots below were borrowed from Greek. Think about the meaning of each root as you read the English word that comes from it.

graph Something that writes, or is written. (geo*graph*y)
gram Something written, drawn, or recorded. (mono*gram*)
phon A sound or voice. (sym*phon*y)
scope To see. (tele*scope*)
tele Far; distant. (*tele*vision)
photo Light. (*photo*graph)
auto Self. (*auto*matic)
micro Small. (*micro*scope)

Use what you have learned about roots to help you explain the meaning of each of these words:

telegram
microphone
autograph

Now use words made with the Greek roots to complete these sentences.

1. People all over the country watched the _____ program about the space shuttle.
2. After the concert, many fans lined up to get the singer's _____.
3. The scientist examined the new bacteria under a _____.
4. The astronomers used a new kind of camera to _____ the rings of Saturn.

A scientist using a microscope.

Another language from which we have borrowed many roots is Latin. Read the following Latin roots with their meanings:

aqua Water.
aud Hear.
dict Say.
man Hand.
min Small.
script Write.

Use the Latin roots to answer these questions.

5. What is a *manuscript*?
6. Would you use a *microscope* or a *telescope* to look at a *miniature*?
7. What does an *aqualung* help people do?
8. What does a *dictator* do?

Something Extra

Use Greek and Latin roots to help you become an inventor. For example, you might invent an *autoscope*, a pair of magic glasses to help you see yourself as others see you. What might a *photophone* be? See how many other inventions you can think up using Greek and Latin roots.

MR. ALVA WILL PRESENT
THE WINNER OF THE CONTEST

THE MURAL

by Emilia Durán

Mercedes knew how she wanted the mural to look, but Inez had other ideas. How could they paint it together?

The class party was almost over when Mercedes saw Mr. Alva standing in the door. He was holding a large portfolio. Here it was, the moment she had been waiting for all those weeks, ever since she had entered the art contest. The winner would paint a mural on the side of Mr. Alva's store, overlooking the little park. The mural would symbolize the neighborhood's Chicano heritage, and all the students in the school had been invited to submit ideas for its design. Mr. Alva had brought the winning picture to show the class.

Mercedes held her breath. "Please," she thought, "please let it be mine — I've never wanted anything so much!" She could hardly sit quietly through Mr. Alva's long introduction, but finally she heard him say, ". . . in fact, it was impossible for us to choose between two such excellent entries. The contest is a tie between two members of this class — Mercedes and Inez Gálvez. We want them to paint the mural together."

Mr. Alva took two pictures from his portfolio and held them side by side. Mercedes's painting represented the history of Mexico. It showed a pyramid, a large calendar stone, Spanish *conquistadores*[1] on their horses, and a Mexican figure in the center to represent the blending of the Aztec, Mayan, and Spanish cultures. The sky flamed with the colors of a brilliant sunrise.

"Oh, no," Mercedes thought. "Not a tie. That's almost worse than not winning at all!" She looked at Inez's picture and wondered, "What did they see in *that?*" Inez had painted the city of the future, with many buildings and machines. In the sky there were rockets and moving sidewalks. A large banner was decorated with symbols of Chicano achievements. It was exciting, with a lot of action, but Mercedes couldn't see that it had much to do with the purpose of the contest. "I *hate* it!" she thought.

---

[1] conquistadores (kōn kēs'tä **dōr'**äs) Conquerors.

Then the other thoughts crowded in, the ones Mercedes had been trying not to have. "Why do I have to share everything with Inez, just because we are cousins and were born on the same day? They try to treat us the same, but it never comes out the same. The same clothes look better on Inez; when I make 95 on a test, she makes 98. Why does she always seem to get the bigger half of everything?"

Mercedes hated being jealous of Inez. What would her family think of her if they knew, she wondered. Her parents; her big brother, Daniel; Abuelita[2]; Tío[3] Ernesto; and Tía[4] Diana — all seemed to think she and Inez were twins, or something. What if they knew she didn't want to be a twin? They would be ashamed of her for being so selfish, especially Abuelita, who had brought them all up always to respect one another.

Mercedes managed to smile through the rest of the party, the congratulations of her teachers and friends, and their farewells for the summer, but she was thinking, "What a way to start a vacation — having to act all enthusiastic about painting my half of a mural with rockets zooming all over the other half. What kind of mural is that? It will look stupid!"

She hoped to slip away without having to talk to Mr. Alva or Inez, but they stopped her at the door. "Mr. Alva wants us to go with him to the paint store and pick out the colors and the brushes we want to use," Inez told her. "We must call Abuelita and tell her we will be late. She is expecting us to help with the plans for Daniel's homecoming party."

When they had delivered their supplies to Mr. Alva's store, he suggested, "Let's have a look at the wall you're going to paint. I've put a barricade of sawhorses around it so the children won't get underfoot while you paint. When you come tomorrow, we will stretch a plank between two ladders, and

---

[2] **Abuelita** (ä′bōō ä lē′tə)   [3] **Tío** (tē′ō)   [4] **Tía** (te′ä)

you can stand on the plank to reach the top of the wall. You must tell me if there's anything else you need."

As they walked around to the side of the building, Mercedes remembered how excited she had been the year before, when Mr. Alva had bought the store and the vacant lot beside it, and had donated the lot to the community for a playground. Until then, the lot had been an eyesore, full of weeds and rusty tin cans.

What a difference now! It had been a lot of work, but everybody on the block had pitched in last summer to clean up and plant things — grass and flowers and a hedge to keep children from chasing balls into the street. By the end of the summer, the neighbors had begun bringing picnic suppers and spending long evenings eating, playing games with the children, singing songs, and telling stories. It was wonderful.

There was still work to be done. Several of the neighbors had volunteered to build benches and equipment for the little children to play on. Best of all, the mural would give the neighbors something nicer than a blank concrete wall to look at. Or at least half the wall would be nice to look at. Mercedes wasn't so sure about the other half.

All the way home, Mercedes wondered how she would get through the family dinner that night, with everybody congratulating her on winning the contest. As things turned out, it wasn't so bad after all because everyone was full of plans for Daniel's return from college the next evening. Mercedes was grateful for the opportunity to slip away quietly and go to bed early.

After tossing and turning for most of the night, Mercedes overslept the next morning. When she finally arrived at Mr. Alva's store, Inez was already up on the plank — looking great in an old pair of coveralls and whistling a little tune. How could she be so cheerful, so early?

Mercedes climbed onto her end of the plank and began quickly to fill in the blue part of her sky. She could hardly wait to get the background filled in so she could start on the sunrise. Now that they had started painting, Mercedes realized that some parts of the mural were going to be tricky. With a picture of the past on one side and the future on the other, what were they going to paint in the middle? Something about the present, obviously, but what?

When she stepped down to change brushes, she sneaked a quick glance to see what Inez was doing over on her side of the picture. She could hardly believe what she saw — Inez busily

painting a big yellow sun peeking out from behind a sky-
scraper. "Why are you putting that sun there?" Mercedes
asked.

"Oh, I just thought of it," Inez replied airily. "The picture
seemed to need something else up in this corner."

"What this picture *needs* is my sunrise," thought Mercedes.
"Inez knew that was an important part of my painting, and
now she has put the sun on her side instead. We can't have two
suns, one on each side of the picture. It just wouldn't make
sense. Now that she has taken the sun away from my half, what
am I going to paint over here? How thoughtless can she be?"

Furious, Mercedes climbed back onto the plank and began slapping blue paint on the wall.

"Hey, look out!" shouted Inez. "You're splashing paint all over. It's all running down in streaks." She stepped down to get a better look at what Mercedes was doing. "Besides," she continued, "that shade of blue you are using is too dark. Your sky should match my sky."

For a moment Mercedes stood absolutely still. Then, very slowly and without speaking she stepped down, picked up the broadest paintbrush, dipped it into the black paint, climbed back up, painstakingly painted a broad black stripe down the middle of the wall, and stepped back down on the ground.

"What are you doing?" Inez demanded. "What's the matter with you today, anyway? What is this all about?"

Controlling her anger, Mercedes looked directly at Inez for the first time and spoke slowly and quietly. "This is not one picture any longer. It is two. That is your side. This is my side. What happens over here is none of your business. Now, if you will excuse me, I think I won't paint any more today."

All the way home, Mercedes was torn between anger at Inez and dismay at her own behavior. Never in all her life had she behaved so rudely toward her cousin — or anyone else, for that matter. What would Abuelita think of her, if she knew?

Mercedes had hoped to sneak into her room unnoticed, but as soon as she opened the door, she heard her grandmother moving about in the kitchen. Abuelita must be starting to prepare the *empanadas*,[5] Daniel's favorites, for tonight's celebration dinner. Later, the whole family would pitch in to help, since it took many hands to prepare the large number of *empanadas* needed for all the aunts and uncles and cousins who would be coming to dinner.

---

[5] **empanadas** (ĕm'pä nä'dəz)

Abuelita must have heard the door open because she called to Mercedes to come and help her. As Mercedes sidled into the kitchen, Abuelita gave her a sharp look and handed her a mixing bowl and a spoon.

Working silently alongside Abuelita, Mercedes realized how much she wanted her grandmother's help in straightening out her feelings, but how could she ask for it when she felt so ashamed? Why didn't Abuelita say something — anything? Were they going to go on like this all afternoon?

Finally, Abuelita put down her mixing bowl and asked, "Why are you looking so angry? What has happened?"

"It's Inez," Mercedes burst out. "She is ruining the mural. Furthermore, she is trying to tell me how to paint my half." Little by little, the whole story of the argument came out, and the more Mercedes talked, the angrier she felt. Then she concluded, ". . . and I'm going to let her paint it all by herself. Let her ruin things without any help from me. I quit."

Abuelita spoke sternly. "Mercedes, you surprise me. In this house, we do not speak ill of our family. We also honor our commitments. There will be no more criticism of Inez, and no more talk of quitting. Now, what is behind this? What is this ruining you say Inez is doing?"

"The mural is supposed to show something about Chicano life. When I made my picture, I was remembering the time when I was just a little girl and you took Daniel and me to Mexico City to that museum. I saw where part of our culture came from. Later when we climbed the old Aztec pyramids, I felt a sense of drama.

"I wanted to put the drama and importance of our history into my picture, but Inez wants to show a lot of tall buildings and rockets. She calls it the city of the future. I hate it, and it doesn't have anything to do with us!"

Abuelita was silent for a long time. Finally, she spoke, "Mercedes, it is true that the past is important, but so are the

present and the future. You and Daniel have done things I never dreamed of. Now Daniel is in college, and one day you will be. Daniel plans to be an architect, and the buildings he designs will probably look more like Inez's city than your pyramid. Those tall buildings do have something to do with us. Do you see?"

Mercedes nodded silently, and Abuelita continued. "Do you remember the murals that we saw in Mexico City? Most of them were not one scene, or two scenes, but many small scenes incorporating many different things. If great artists have room for such variety in their paintings, surely you and Inez can find room for all your ideas in one mural. You will have to work it out together.

"However, I find it hard to believe that all this anger comes about because of what is to be painted on a wall. It seems to me that there is something more involved here — something that you perhaps have not wanted to tell me. Is it not true?"

Hardly daring to look at Abuelita, Mercedes managed to mumble, "Having to share everything with Inez gets to be a real pain sometimes."

Abuelita spoke thoughtfully. "The family has always kept you together, as if you were sisters. Both of you have only brothers, and it is a fine thing to have a sister. When you were small, the two of you wanted to do everything together.

"Now you are growing older, and I remember how it was with my sisters. We had always done things together, but as I grew older, I did not always want to be with them. Sometimes, I wanted to do things alone. I still loved them just as much as ever, but I also needed some time to learn to be by myself. Perhaps it is the same with you two. It may be that Inez, also, feels that there can be too much of a good thing.

"I will speak to the family tonight after dinner. They will understand. In the meantime, you and Inez must settle your differences concerning the mural. Have you sat down and talked together about what you should paint, or has each of you tried to go her own way? In this family, we talk to one another."

"In this family. . . ." thought Mercedes. "I've been so busy being angry with Inez that I haven't even thought about how wonderful it is going to be when we are all together tonight. Of course they will understand. They always do."

Mercedes hugged her grandmother and said, "Abuelita, I have to go now. It is high time I did talk with Inez about the mural. Besides, I think I am getting an idea about how to do it, and I want to share it with her. I can't tell you because it's a surprise."

On the way to Mr. Alva's store, Mercedes thought about the middle of the mural — the part that would have to show something important about the present. The most important thing that she could think of was the family. Inez would think so too — the family as the link between the past and the future. They could paint pictures of their family and their neighbors and their families in the center. Of course — that was what the park and the mural were all about.

Mercedes began to hum a little tune, the same tune Inez had been whistling that morning. Maybe working together on this mural wasn't such a bad idea, after all.

Author

Emilia Durán has enjoyed an extensive career working with young people of various ages. Her experiences as a teacher and mother have contributed to her writing for children.

Summary Questions

Think about how Mercedes's and Inez's feelings about their heritage helped them to finally work together, despite their differences.

1. What kinds of things did Inez want to put in the mural? What kinds of things did Mercedes want?
2. What view of Chicano heritage did each girl's ideas reflect?
3. What important idea about Chicano heritage would Mercedes and Inez probably agree on?
4. Imagine that Mercedes and Inez decided to tell Daniel about the mural during his homecoming party. What might each girl say?

The Reading and Writing Connection

Mercedes and Inez resolved their problem by painting a mural that reflected the feelings that both girls had about their background and heritage. Think about what kind of mural you might paint to show what you know or what you like about your heritage or your neighborhood. Make a list, or make sketches, of some of the objects in the mural. Then write a proposal to the mayor that explains exactly what your mural would look like and in what way it would benefit the community. Try to use some of the following words in your proposal.

> **heritage**
> **mural**
> **symbolize**

Home from School

by Jean Little

**Sal had longed to be back home again with her family
— but now that she was here, would she get the
support she needed?**

While Sal Copeland had been away at school, her family had moved into a new home. Now she was taking her first close look at the room she was to share with her younger sister Meg.

With unabashed delight, Sal sat and stared around her new room. The drapes were yellow. So were the tiny flowers in the wreaths on the wallpaper, and so was the sheepskin rug between the beds. There was a huge bookcase, the top shelves filled with her favorite books, the bottom shelves full of her old favorites, which now belonged to Meg. There was the tall mirror which had always stood in her parents' room in the old house. Sal had never paid much attention to it before, but now she liked it at once.

"Do you like it, Sarah Jane?" Mother asked, gently.

"It's a beautiful room," she cried. "It's . . . it's beautiful!"

"It's *my* beautiful room too," Meg put in, sounding not quite sure.

"Of course it's yours too, funny face," said Mother. "Let's get ready for breakfast, shall we?"

As Mother began to help Sal into her braces, Meg put down the sock she had just picked up.

"Why do you have to wear that?" she asked.

Sal had known the question was coming. She waited for Mother to explain, but Mother was fitting the braces into the high shoes Sally wore, and she paid no attention to Meg.

"Well . . . it's . . . I have to wear them so I can walk," Sal mumbled at last.

"Why?" Meg countered.

Sal hesitated.

"Why?" Meg repeated, a little louder, as though she imagined Sal had not heard the first time.

"Because," Sal snapped.

She knew that would not satisfy Meg, and she looked at

her mother again, but Mother was still busy doing up buckles. Sal thought hard. Until today, somebody else had always explained for her.

"Because I have cerebral palsy. It makes you so you can't walk and maybe your hands don't work just right. It makes you kind of stiff."

Then, remembering Bonnie and Alice, Jane Ann, and Hilary, she stopped. All of them had cerebral palsy — and yet every single one of them showed it in a different way. Bonnie only limped a bit with her left leg. Alice couldn't walk but sat in a wheelchair all the time. Hilary walked without much trouble, but she could not use a fork or a pencil. Then there was Louise, who could walk and use her hands fairly well, but had a terrible time talking. They all had cerebral palsy; and yet it suddenly seemed to her that there were dozens of different handicaps among them. She stared helplessly at Meg's waiting face.

Mother caught her expression of dismay and laughed.

"Cerebral palsy is pretty complicated to explain, isn't it, Sally? Let's wait till next weekend. You have an appointment then with Dr. Eastman in Toronto, and we'll take Meg along. I could explain, but he told Mindy about it when we first found out you had it, and he did such a good job I'd like to see him do it again. Also, right this minute, everybody else in this house is just about ready for breakfast!"

She got up and fetched some clothing from Sal's dresser and the closet.

"Try these on for size, honey." She laid them within Sal's reach and smiled down on her. "You'll find the clothes are brand new — to match your new room."

Then, without another word, she walked out.

Sal lay very still and stared after her. In one frightened instant, the safe, warm feeling that had been growing inside her since Mother first hugged her the night before vanished.

Why, she couldn't dress herself! There were always slippery little blouse buttons impossible to do up and zippers with metal tabs so small your fingers couldn't keep hold of them! Didn't Mother know that? At school, there was always somebody there to help with the hard parts no matter what Miss Jonas said.

Sal lay very still. She lay and watched the door through which Mother had disappeared. Inside, she could hear a voice shouting: She didn't even ask! She just left me! She's not ever going to stay! She doesn't care! She just left! She just left me alone!

"Aren't you going to get dressed now, Sally?"

Sal looked away from the door. She had forgotten Meg. How small and sure of herself she looked, sitting cross-legged on the floor, tugging on her sock. Sal almost smiled. Then she knew Meg was no help. She was too small. She couldn't take the place of a whole schoolful of girls with cerebral palsy. She couldn't drive away the fear that now surrounded Sally.

With a jerk, Sal rolled away from her little sister to face the wall, her braces clanking together. A giant sob ached in her throat. As her first tears wet the pillow under her cheek, she took back the wish she had been making so faithfully for such a long time, the wish "come true" just last night. In spite of the feeling she had had when Mother hugged her in the car, in spite of the beautiful room, in spite of all the years of waiting and wanting to go home to stay, Sally wanted to go back, back to where she was known and safe and never left alone for a minute. She wanted to go back to school!

"Don't cry!" Meg begged, her voice shrill with alarm. "I'll get Mother. Don't cry, Sally!"

Sal wept on, and Meg scurried off to get help. She always ran to Mother with her own tears. By some special magic, Mother knew every time whether to cure them with a bandage or a kiss. Sal, crying into her pillow, was counting on Mother in much the same way.

"Thank you, honey. Now go on down to the kitchen and help Mindy with breakfast."

Sal stiffened. There she was now. There. That was Meg leaving. Now Mother would come in and take her in her arms, and everything would be all right again.

Footsteps crossed the room. There was a creaking sound over by Meg's bed. Then a door closed and silence fell. Nothing moved. Nobody spoke. Nothing at all happened.

Sal was stunned. Surely Mother had come in! Yes, of course she had! She had heard her talking to Meg. She had even heard her walking across the room. So why didn't she do something . . . or say something?

The answer came to her suddenly. Mother probably thought she was asleep. She must be being extra quiet so as not to waken her. Sal sniffed again, but this time the sniff was very small and uncertain.

At once, the silence swallowed it.

Sal waited. There was nothing else she could think of to do. A minute passed. It seemed an hour. She began to feel sure someone was watching her. Another minute passed, and another. She stuck it out for one more long, long minute. Then, with a gasp, she turned over.

Mother was sitting on Meg's bed.

"That's better," she said quietly, as Sal stared at her. "I'm not in the habit of talking to people's backs. Now suppose you tell me what your trouble is."

Sal was so taken aback she couldn't think of a word to say.

"Don't you know I can't do it all by myself?" she finally burst out, new tears streaming down her face.

"Do *what* all by yourself?" Mother asked evenly.

"All those buttons, that's what!" Sal shouted, glaring.

"Sally, I have a story to tell you," Mother said.

She tucked her feet up under her as though she had all the time in the world. A little of the fear went out of Sally.

"One summer there was a four-year-old girl who had an older sister and a brother just turned two. Her parents packed up their three children and some clothes and rented a cottage by Lake Huron for one week. The moment they arrived, they all got into their bathing suits, even the baby, and went down to the lake to swim."

Sal said nothing. Her eyes were dark and startled.

"The baby ran right into the water as though it were his bath at home. It was very shallow, so his mother wasn't worried. She just stayed close to him and watched. When the

waves hit him, he tried to catch them in his fists, and he laughed as though it were a game. The older girl went in more slowly, but before long, she was in up to her neck. Only the little four-year-old girl did not join in and have fun with the others. She began to scream as soon as she saw the water. She buried her head in her father's shoulder. No matter what anyone said, she wouldn't let even her toes be put into the lake."

Mother paused, but Sal was silent.

"The little girl's family stayed at the lake for a week. Every day the whole family went in swimming — all but the little girl, whose name was Sarah. Sarah wouldn't have anything to do with that water.

"On the next-to-the-last day her father grew tired of coaxing. He knew that, by then, Sarah had herself so scared she'd never go in unless someone went with her, so he picked her up and carried her in."

Sal's tears had dried on her cheeks. She remembered that day. It was so long ago it seemed almost a dream, but she could still feel the way she had clutched at Dad and shrieked as he had walked to the lake.

"Her father tried to be gentle" — Mother remembered too — "but Sarah cried and fought, so at last he just put her down. It was so shallow it wasn't dangerous, and Sarah had to stay there whether she wanted to or not. Maybe you remember what happened, Sally, when that little girl stopped crying long enough to notice what the water was really like."

Sal nodded slowly. It didn't seem like a dream any longer. The lake had been calm that day. Greenish ripples had broken softly against her. Her brother Kent had crowed with excitement and galloped around her, churning up a frothy sparkle. Nearby, Mother had been holding Mindy on her stomach, making her "swim" on top of the bright water. Suddenly giving in completely, she, Sal, had called to Dad, "I want to swim too. Make me swim like Mindy, Daddy."

"Five long days at the beach — wasted!" remarked Mother, as though Sally had spoken her memories aloud. "Five days wasted because Sarah didn't wait to find out whether there was anything to cry about before she started crying. . . . Of course, she was only four. You can forgive a little girl like that for not taking time to think."

Sal blushed, a slow, deep, burning blush right up to her ears. She looked at the rug.

"Have you really looked at the clothes I put out for you?"

Unable to speak, Sal only shook her head. Mother rose and reached for the clothes. One piece at a time, she spread them out across Sal's knees.

"Now show me those buttons you're so worried about!"

With her head bent and her heart thumping uncomfortably, Sal inspected the clothing. The expression on her face grew more and more sheepish as she looked.

There were no buttons. Not a single button anywhere! In fact, the clothes on her lap were the simplest clothes to put on that Sal had ever seen. No zipper! No tricky fastening at all! No hooks and eyes! All the things that made dressing difficult were missing — and yet the clothes themselves looked lovely.

"I — I'm sorry. They're wonderful clothes," Sal gulped.

Mother dropped down on the bed beside her and circled Sal lightly with her arms.

"Sally, Sally, don't be so afraid," she said softly. "You're scared to death that I'm going to walk out and leave you with nobody to look after you. Don't you know that I would never do that if I didn't know, for sure, that you didn't need me?"

Astonishment held back Sal's tears. How could Mother see inside a person's thoughts like that?

"Now guess who suggested those new clothes for you."

"You must have," Sal faltered.

"Wrong. Miss Jonas did."

"Miss Jonas!"

"Miss Jonas. When you left Allendale, she wrote us a long letter about you. She told us that if we all, including you, started working on it right away, there will come a day when you will be an independent adult — a person who decides things for herself and does things for herself and for others. It would mean having your own job, your own friends, your own money, your freedom."

To Sal it sounded frightening and far-off, but fun too. Her own friends! She had wanted a special friend badly for a long time now.

"To be independent someday means beginning practicing independence *today,* and the first step is dressing yourself.

Now get busy, Sal. When you're dressed, you can look at yourself in this mirror." Mother put Sal's crutches within reach and left.

For one long moment, Sal sat and stared down at the clothes beside her. Then she began to move. Just the same, it took a long time. Wriggling into and tugging at each garment in turn soon had her puffing and red in the face. Her fingers, always a little awkward, seemed to stiffen on purpose to make things harder. She put her arm through the hole in her blouse that was meant for her head, and it took ages to pull it free again. The skirt twisted itself around her legs, and however hard she yanked at it, it refused to straighten out. More than once she came close to giving up, but something kept her going doggedly until she was done.

She looked down at herself and drew a sharp little breath of excitement. She had managed it! She was dressed. She wriggled forward until her feet were firmly on the floor and reached for her crutches. Leaning down, she got her braces locked and then put her weight solidly on the handgrips. After trying a couple of times, she was up. Holding her breath, she turned and started for the mirror.

Without warning, the door swung wide and the other Copelands crowded in. Forever afterwards, Sal was to wonder whether they had been watching her through the keyhole.

"Is that Sally?" Meg asked, her eyes round.

Kent gave a whistle, and Mindy breathed "Gee!"

"Hush," Mother said. "Let her see for herself."

Shyly, shakily, Sally approached the glass. As she caught sight of herself, she stopped in her tracks. Even though she had known she would be different, she was totally unprepared for this girl in the mirror.

Sal was not used to seeing herself in a looking glass. At school she had practiced walking in front of one, but the therapist had always been telling her to watch her knees or

keep her elbows in. Over the years, Sally had grown to look at herself a piece at a time. She had come to have a vague picture of herself, a girl all elbows and knees and crutches, with a face and clothes too ordinary to notice much.

This was a new Sally.

She was dressed in bright, soft colors. Her hair was smooth and shining with no part at all. It was short with bangs straight across the front, and it curved in just a little on the ends. From all her hard work and excitement, her cheeks glowed like roses. In spite of herself, her mouth tipped up in a delighted smile, and her blue eyes shone bluer than ever with wonder.

Sal glanced away from the glass at her family. At the admiration on their faces, her cheeks grew rosier.

"I look like somebody else," she half-whispered at last. "Not me."

"Somebody beautiful," smiled Dad, and he bowed to her with a flourish.

Author

Jean Little was born in Taiwan and grew up in Guelph, Ontario. Blind at birth, she later gained some sight in one eye and graduated from the University of Toronto. *Mine for Keeps,* from which this story was taken, was her award-winning first book.

Summary Questions

Think about the important lesson Sal learned on her first morning home.

1. What kind of support was Sal expecting from her mother? How did Sal feel when her expectations were not met?
2. Why do you think Sal's mother reminded her of what happened at the lake when Sal was four?
3. Why did Sal's mother refuse to treat Sal the way she had been treated at school?
4. Contrast Sal at the beginning of the story with Sal at the end. Explain how you think Sal's experiences on her first morning in her new home will affect the way she meets new challenges.

The Reading and Writing Connection

Soon, Sal will be entering public school and making new friends. Think of the kinds of school activities that sixth graders enjoy participating in. Then think of some of the new skills Sal will need in order to participate with her friends. Make a list of five things that Sal will want to do as she becomes more independent. Then choose one of the items on your list and write a paragraph about it. In your paragraph, explain what it is that Sal will want to do, what skills she will have to learn, and how she can overcome the difficulties that might arise. Try to use some of the following words in your paragraph: *unabashed, doggedly, faltered, handicaps.*

Change

by Charlotte Zolotow

The summer
still hangs
heavy and sweet
with sunlight
as it did last year.

The autumn
still comes
showering gold and crimson
as it did last year.

The winter
still stings
clean and cold and white
as it did last year.

The spring
still comes
like a whisper in the dark night.

It is only I
who have changed.

Taking Tests

Many people get nervous when they take a test. Being a little nervous is natural. However, the best way to keep from being *too* nervous is to be prepared and to know as much as possible about test-taking. This lesson will tell you how to prepare for a test and give you strategies to use when taking tests.

Getting Prepared

The only way to be prepared for a test is to study for it. Try to find a special time and place to study every day. You will study best when there is nothing to distract your attention.

Make sure that you have everything you need before you begin to study. Use the SQRRR method to review your textbook. Review all the notes in your class notebook. Also read over all of your old test papers. You can always learn from any mistakes you made before.

Finally, get a good night's sleep and eat a good breakfast. You will perform better on a test if you are rested and alert.

True-False Test Items

Three of the most common types of test items are true-false, multiple choice, and matching. They test your ability to recall information.

True-false test items require you to decide if a statement is true or not. Be sure you know whether your teacher wants you to write *true* and *false* or *yes* and *no* or whether you are to circle *t* and *f* or *y* and *n*. Then read each item carefully. Look at the following example:

_____All states have two U.S. senators and four members of the U.S. House of Representatives.

After reading carefully, look back at the important words: *all, two,* and *four.* If any part of a statement is false, the entire statement is false. Because all states have two senators but not all have four representatives, this statement is false.

In some true-false items, one word can make the statement true or false. Pay special attention to words like *no, not, never, all,* and *always.* They mean that there are no exceptions. Suppose you had this item on a test: "All trees lose their leaves in the fall." Because you know that there are trees that do not lose their leaves, you would answer *false.*

Multiple-Choice Test Items

Multiple-choice items require you to select the answer from several choices. Sometimes the choices will include "all of the above," "none of the above," or "*a* and *c.*" Usually you will be asked to write only the letter of the correct answer. Look at the following example:

_____What is the capital of Wisconsin?
(a) St. Paul
(b) Madison
(c) Lake Charles
(d) none of the above

Read the question and all of the answer choices. If you still do not know the answer, see if you can figure it out. If you know that St. Paul is in Minnesota and that Lake

Charles is in Louisiana, you have eliminated two choices. Perhaps now you might remember that Madison is the capital. You might not always remember the answer to every question. If this happens, eliminate those answers you know are wrong. From the ones left, choose the answer that makes the most sense to you. Try not to leave any questions unanswered.

Sometimes you will take tests that have paragraphs followed by multiple-choice items. You may find it helpful to read quickly the questions and possible answers before you read the paragraph. Use a flexible reading rate so that you will not waste time. Finally, take into account any knowledge you may already have about the subject of the reading passage before you answer the questions.

Matching Test Questions

In matching test items you must match the items in one column with the items in another column. Sometimes the two lists will contain the same number of items. Sometimes there will be items in one column that you do not use or items that you will use more than once. Look carefully at the following example:

Match the following states with their state flowers.

1.	Indiana	a.	peony
2.	Vermont	b.	iris
3.	Kansas	c.	clover
4.	Virginia	d.	sunflower
5.	Tennessee	e.	dogwood

To complete this example, you should read the first item in the left-hand column. Then start at the top of the right-hand column and read to the end. Even if you find an answer you think is right, you should read to the end to see that there is not a better choice. Then continue filling in all the answers that you are sure of. This will give you fewer choices for the remaining items. The fewer the choices, the better the chance you have of being correct.

Again, try to answer every question. First answer all of the questions that you know. Then go back and answer the others, selecting the answers that seem best. Finally, check to see that all your answers are easily read. For example, do not make *e*'s that look like *c*'s.

Short-Answer Test Items

Many tests also contain short-answer items. They also test your ability to recall information. In some short-answer items, called *fill-in-the-blank*, you must write in a missing word or words. Look at the following example:

_____ _____, a tree-planting holiday, began in the state of _____ on April 10, 1872.

Even if you think you know the answer, read the entire item. Sometimes the context and the order of the words can provide you with clues to the answer. In the example the context tells you that the name of a two-word holiday that is celebrated by planting trees should be written in the first two blanks. The name of a one-word state belongs in the third blank.

In answering other short-answer items, you may have to write a few words or even a complete sentence. Look at the following example:

Who discovered penicillin and when did he discover it?

Before answering, read the question carefully. What should you notice before you write your answer? First, you should have seen that your answer will have two parts: a name and a date. Second, you should have seen that the person to be named is a man.

Your answer to the example item could be written in two ways. You might write

Sir Alexander Fleming; 1928

Or you might write

Sir Alexander Fleming discovered penicillin in 1928.

Before answering short-answer items, check with your teacher for the correct form.

When you take a test, remember to use your time wisely. Do not linger over items you are unsure of, but try to go back to them before the time is up. Always check your paper before you hand it in. Careless mistakes can cost you valuable points. Finally, save your test papers. Correct any answers you missed and use your papers when studying for future tests.

Answering Test Items

Decide whether each of the following statements is true or false.

1. Use the SQRRR method to help you study for a test.
2. If part of a true-false statement is true, answer it *true.*
3. The most common objective tests are true-false, multiple choice, and matching.
4. Never make wild guesses on a test.
5. In short-answer questions, you always write a complete sentence.
6. Always check your paper before you hand it in.
7. When you get your paper back, look at the score and then throw the paper away.

Skill Summary

- Start studying as soon as you know a test is planned. Choose a quiet place and make sure you have all equipment you need.
- The most common test questions are true-false, multiple choice, and matching.
- Answer short-answer questions with either words or sentences, as your teacher instructs you.
- In all test questions, look for important words that tell you what to do and may be clues to the answer.
- Answer all questions. If you are not sure of an answer, eliminate those choices you know are wrong. From the remaining choices, select the one that seems best.
- Always check your paper before handing it in. Save test papers to study from later.

Social Studies

Social studies books describe how groups of people live. They may tell what happened in the past, what is going on now, or what might happen in the future. You can get more out of reading social studies if you understand and use good reading and study habits.

Using SQRRR

When you read social studies, *survey* the headings to see what is in the lesson and how it is organized. Turn each heading into a *question*. That will help you predict what the author will tell you. After you *read* carefully, use the *recite* and *review* steps to help you remember what you read.

Social Studies Writing

You will understand your social studies books better if you understand what is special about social studies writing. You can think of a social studies writer as one kind of reporter. Like the newspaper reporter, the social studies writer must answer these questions: *Who? What? When? Where?*

Why? How? (Reporters call these *the five W's and the H.*) When you read social studies textbooks, try to see how the author is answering the questions. The *who* and *what* may seem easy, but to understand them fully you have to be able to understand the answers to the other questions as well.

The *when* and *where* often mean learning about times and places that are new to you. As you read, think about how these times and places are alike and different from those you already know about.

Study carefully any **maps** in the book. You may also use an atlas or a globe to get a clear idea of where the important places are. **Time lines** can help you relate what the author is telling you to other things that were happening at that time, as well as what happened before and after. Most social studies books use **pictures** and **diagrams** to show you what people, places, and objects looked like. Studying them, with their titles, captions, and labels, can help you understand what you read.

The *how* also means connecting

what is new to you with what you already know. In many ways, people are more alike than they are different. All have to meet basic human needs. The ways people meet these needs may differ from one group to another. As you read, think about what is like your own experience and what is different. Make a list or chart of likenesses and differences. Use the pictures and other graphic aids to help you understand.

The *why* is sometimes the most interesting question and the most difficult to answer. Events may have more than one cause. Social scientists themselves do not always agree on exactly what caused certain events.

As you read, pay attention to words like *because* and *therefore* that signal cause-effect relationships. Ask yourself *how* the cause could bring about the effect.

Studying Vocabulary

Like most subjects, social studies has its own vocabulary which you must learn in order to understand what you read. Sometimes the words themselves are new and unfamiliar; names of people, places, and objects may come from languages other than English. At other times, short and familiar words that seem easy to read may stand for very complex ideas — such as *freedom, democracy,* and *justice.*

As you read, notice the new words in the lesson. List the important people and places. Learn to pronounce their names, using the pronunciation key in the glossary or in a dictionary.

After reading, go back to the words that stand for major ideas and concepts. Ask yourself how the lesson contributed to your understanding of these ideas.

Summary

Good reading and study habits are important in understanding social studies. You have to know when and where things happened. You have to think about how what you read is similar to and different from what you have experienced. You must understand cause and effect relationships. You have to learn the names of people, places, and concepts.

Preview

The next selection, "Taming the West," resembles a chapter that you might read in a social studies textbook. As you read it, use the reading strategies that you have just learned.

Taming the West

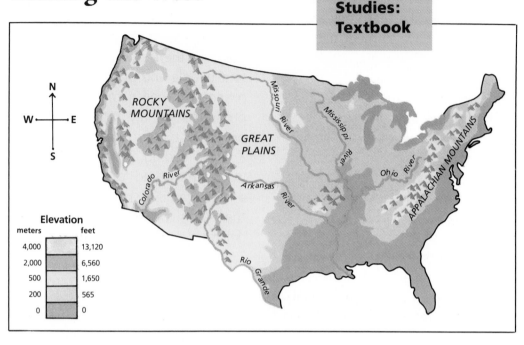

The United States of America

The Last West

When people from Europe first migrated to North America, they established colonies in the East, along the Atlantic Coast. To the west lay the frontier, the edge of the unsettled territory. This unexplored area was vast, but the early colonists paid little attention to it. Their ties were still with Europe.

In the mid-1700's, the frontier began to shift westwards. First, settlers pushed into the Appalachian Mountains. By the early 1800's, pioneers were staking out claims as far west as the Missouri River. When gold was discovered in California in 1848, thousands of people rushed to the Pacific Coast. Many followed the overland trails that had been blazed by early explorers. To get to the West Coast, they had to cross an "ocean of grass" — and most of them were glad to get across it.

If you look at the map on page 213, you will see that for a long time a vast area — from the Missouri River to the Rocky Mountains — was largely unsettled.

The last frontier was not the Pacific Coast. It was the central plains of North America.

The Great American Desert

The plains were unlike anything Americans had seen before. This was not an environment that made new settlement easy. Winter winds tore across the flat grasslands, bringing icy cold and raging blizzards.

In the summer, the winds were very hot. The few rivers became shallow and muddy. The winds brought lightning, hail, and violent tornadoes that twisted across the open land.

Although the plains were covered with grass, few trees grew there. Without trees, there was no wood to build houses or fences, and no fuel to cook or keep warm with. No shade shielded the plains from the summer sun. No barrier broke the force of the constant winds. People called the treeless plains the Great American Desert.

Wagon Trains

How, you may wonder, was this region ever settled? For one thing, the trip to the Pacific Coast was long and hard. Wagons broke down; horses and oxen died. People got sick or ran out of food. Some could simply go no farther and decided to stop where they were. They settled on the plains.

Former Civil War soldiers and freed slaves came too, looking for a new life. Immigrants from Europe came to find land that would be their own. These first settlers took up all the acreage near the few rivers and streams where cottonwood trees grew. For the thousands who came after 1870, there were only the arid plains left. At least by then there was a railroad, and that made the trip easier.

Expansion of Settled Area by:

1790
1850
1890
largely unsettled by 1890

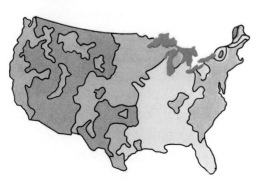

U.S. Settlement: 1790-1890

A Transcontinental Railroad

By the 1860's there were railroad lines throughout most of the eastern part of the United States and in California. After the Civil War, the government chartered two companies to construct a railroad that reached all the way across the country. With the transcontinental railroad, a journey that had once taken months could now be made in weeks.

Millions of Acres

Together, the two railroad companies had laid almost 1,800 miles of track. For each mile of track, the government had given the railroad companies ten square miles of land to sell. The companies advertised all over the East for settlers. They sent agents to Europe to spread news of cheap land for sale in America. Many thousands came. The rush to settle the plains had begun.

In 1862, Congress passed the Homestead Act. Under this law, any person could have 160 acres of land free if he or she built a house on the land and lived there for five years. This brought thousands of people from the East and from Europe. As these people soon found out, life on the vast and windswept plains was far from easy.

The daring men and women who settled the plains had to find new ways to:
— build houses
— find water
— farm the land
— protect their crops
— plow the soil
New inventions helped the pioneers solve some of their problems. The pioneers had to find the solutions to other problems for themselves.

Sodbusters

The grass that covered the dry plains had long, strong roots that reached deep into the earth. (This top layer of soil and grass is called *sod*.) When the farmers started to prepare the soil for planting, they found that they could not cut through the tangled mass of grass, roots, and soil. Their iron plowshares either stuck or broke.

Back East, one person and a horse could plow a field. On the plains, teams of six horses found it hard to pull a plow through the tough sod. Only when the

A sodbuster family

homesteaders could afford to buy the newly invented steel plow could they turn the soil easily.

As homesteaders wrestled with the tough sod, however, they soon realized that it would make good building material. There was a seemingly endless supply of sod. It could be plowed up in long strips, and then cut into "bricks."

Sod Houses

Many of the first homesteaders lived in dugouts — caves dug into the side of a bank. These often had a dirt floor, three dirt walls (a canvas wagon made a fourth), and a roof of earth. A dugout was a dark and dusty place.

Once they learned to prepare sod bricks, some homesteaders built houses of sod.

Sod houses had their drawbacks. Snakes, mice, and insects were often part of the household. Dirt filtered down from the roof and walls. However, there were also advantages. The thick walls were fireproof and kept the family cool in summer and warm in winter.

Water and Windmills

In the East water was plentiful, but for the plains settlers getting water was a major problem. Homesteaders without access to wells had to load their wagons with barrels and drive to the nearest river or stream to fill them. This could mean a trip of many miles and many hours by wagon. The water they brought back would have to suffice for drinking, cooking, bathing, and washing clothes until another trip could be made.

Under these conditions, people were naturally eager to have wells on their own land. Digging wells was no easy task for the homesteaders, however. They

A prairie windmill

might have to go down three hundred feet to reach water. Even after drilling rigs were invented, most wells were dug by hand — shovelful by shovelful. It was a back-breaking, dangerous task.

Even with a well, bringing up the water was a slow and tedious job. It had to be done one bucketful at a time. The homesteaders solved this problem with the help of the wind and technology. The wind was something they always had with them, a ready source of free energy. They learned to build windmills to harness this energy — and soon there were windmills everywhere.

Fences

Another problem facing homesteaders was protection of their crops. Stray cattle and wild animals often trampled the wheat growing in the field. They ate or crushed everything in the vegetable garden. There was no wood or stone available, which people used in the East for building enclosures. There was wire, but no one had yet designed a wire fence that could keep cattle out. Then in 1873 Joseph Glidden solved the problem with the invention of barbed wire. Glidden had been thinking about the thorned shrub. He took two long strands of wire and twisted them together. Between these strands, he twisted short pieces of wire with sharp ends, which stuck out like the thorns on the shrub.

The points, or barbs, discouraged cattle or other animals from pushing against the wire and breaking the fence. Glidden's barbed wire was a real boon to the plains farmers, enabling them to keep stray animals out of their fields. At first, the barbed-wire fences caused serious trouble between the farmers and the ranchers, who wanted their animals to be able to graze freely on the open range. However, as more and more settlers came to farm the land and fence the prairies, the vast open range gradually disappeared.

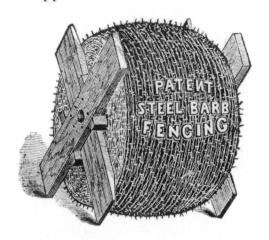

A roll of barbed-wire fencing

Prairie farmers

New Ways of Farming

Eventually, the settlers found new and better ways to farm the plains. They planted a hardy kind of wheat that did not need much water. They learned how to preserve moisture in the soil by "dry farming."

Dry farming meant plowing very deeply, and keeping the planted earth broken up so that it did not become hard. The farmers kept a layer of dust over their fields and let some fields lie fallow every other year, giving a two-year supply of moisture for the next crop.

Fortunately for the plains settlers, many new farm implements were being invented. Mechanical reapers, threshers, and binders made the farmers' work easier, and allowed them to plant larger areas.

The End of the Great American Desert

In many ways, life on the plains was more primitive than life in the East. In fact, most settlers lived the way Easterners had lived more than a hundred years earlier.

Each family had to provide for most of its own needs. Parents were often the doctors, nurses, and teachers of the family. Candles, soap, and clothing were made at home. The family worked together to build houses and barns, grow food for the table, and raise the crops that were sold for money.

Together, the family shared many experiences — some of them difficult. They lived through droughts that withered their crops. They watched helplessly as hordes of grasshoppers ate every green thing growing. Their endurance was tested, but the settlers who survived those trying early years transformed the "Great American Desert" into the "Breadbasket of the World." They were the true tamers of the West.

Summary Questions

1. Why did the great plains remain empty of settlers for such a long time?

2. What factors contributed to settlement of the plains after 1860?

3. What were the major problems that the homesteaders faced in settling the prairie?

4. What technological advances made plains life easier, and how did they help?

5. The author described the sodbusters as "the true tamers of the West." What does that mean?

Oral History

Historians learn about life in the past from many kinds of sources. Most often, they use books, newspapers, letters, and journals written at an earlier time. Another important way of learning about the past is through **oral history—** interviewing people about their experiences of past events.

While you may not be able to talk with someone who lived during the time the prairie was settled, you can be an oral historian. Think of someone you know who has lived in a time or place that was very different from your own. Interview the person about what life was like at that time and in that place, and how it is different from the life he or she has now. Be prepared to report on your interview to your class.

Cobie's Courage

by Jeanne Williams

Somewhere out on the darkening prairie, Cobie's little sister was lost in the snow. Cobie was determined to find her — but how?

To Cobie Lander and most of her family, the freedom to follow their Mennonite religion made life on the harsh prairie near Harmony, Kansas, worthwhile. Because they had little money, the Landers traded work for help and supplies. Cobie worked one day a week for Elder Wiese, whose wife was not well. The Landers found pleasure in their close family life and in new friendships. Stede Martin, who spoke German, the Mennonites' language, and Bedad, who had lived for years on the prairie, had settled nearby and helped with the farming. Prairie life was difficult and unpredictable, though, and danger could appear often.

Farm winters were usually spent doing outside chores as quickly as possible and catching up on things there was no time for in the busy crop period from spring to late fall. Father mended harnesses, made rough furniture from timber he felled by the creek, and when snow was off the ground, cut prairie grass from Elder Wiese's land and hauled it home where it was used for both fodder and fuel.

Mutti, as the girls called their mother, sewed and mended and knitted while Cobie and Rebecca did most of the household work. Each Friday, except in severe storms, Cobie crossed the footlog to the Wieses' comfortable snug home and swept and scrubbed, dusted and ironed, churned butter, and helped once a month with the washing.

She came to understand that Mrs. Wiese was very lonesome, for the older woman talked continuously when her husband was not around. She always gave Cobie a fine lunch and usually managed to send some treat to vary the Lander table, though she tried to do this when Elder Wiese wasn't watching.

Bedad often came by. He always played buffalo with little Gaby, who regarded him as her special property, and when it was not too cold, he took her for rides on his mule,

Belshazzer, who accepted this with resigned floppings of his long ears. Bedad had learned a surprising amount of German, and now that Rachel and the twins were familiar with some English from school and were using it with the family, the Landers could communicate with Bedad. He and Mutti often sat for long periods, Mutti sewing, Bedad playing with Gaby, each trying out the words they knew of the other's language.

Stede and Bedad claimed they deserved no baking, washing, or mending in winter, when Father needed no help with chores. He pointed out to them that he would need a lot of their time from spring onward and that it was only right that the services they got in return should go on throughout the year.

So each Saturday Stede and Bedad came for dinner, always bringing some gift of food, as well as their washing and mending, which would be done during the week so that they could take it home the next Saturday. Each Saturday they carried five loaves of crusty, fresh-baked bread back to their tepee.

"Don't you get cold in a tent?" asked Rachel during one freezing spell.

"It's warmer than the schoolhouse." Stede, who was the teacher, laughed. "Anyhow, we're not inside much except to sleep, and then we bundle up in warm buffalo robes. You ought to see Bedad all wrapped in his old bearskin! You'd think for sure he was a grizzly!"

"I skinned that hide off a bear that stood taller'n you, back when you were a baby," Bedad growled at his friend, who translated the remark for the Landers.

"Yes, and it looks like it," Stede added. "Full of moth holes!" He turned back to Rachel. "When the weather gets nicer, all you girls must come visit us and see what a good home a tent can be!"

One cold Friday morning, Rachel went to school alone because the twins had feverish colds. Father was spending the day helping a neighbor make furniture, so he was able to drive Cobie to the Wieses' on his way. It was one of those long, gray, bleak days that seemed to stretch on and on, especially since Mrs. Wiese was in bed with an ague that periodically troubled her.

Cobie put out the four o'clock meal of bread, butter, zwieback, and tea for Elder Wiese and his son, Heinrich, and carried Mrs. Wiese's to her on a tray. As soon as she had cleared away the dishes and set the table for supper, she gave the borscht a final stir and started home through powdery, dry snow halfway up to her knees.

It was slow moving, and she was exhausted as well as cold when she trudged up to the sod house to find Mutti watching anxiously from the window.

"You haven't seen little Rachel?"

Cobie stopped taking off her sheepskin coat. "Isn't she home yet?"

Mutti shook her head. "I thought perhaps she had waited to walk with you."

It was now a little after four; darkness would fall by six. It had been snowing about the time school let out. Rachel might have lost her way — but the snow had stopped. She should have come home by this hour even if she had been mixed up for a time by the storm.

"Father's not home yet?"

Mutti shook her head. Cobie pulled the sheepskin back on and wrapped the scarf more securely about her ears and face, which still felt half-frozen.

"Oh, Cobie!" cried Liese, snuffling with her cold and with alarm. "Don't you get lost too!"

"Of course I won't," said Cobie, more bravely than she felt.

"Child — " began Mutti, and then pressed her hands tight together. Tears showed in her eyes. "Be careful!"

"I'll just go toward school and shout now and then," said Cobie. "I can follow my tracks back. But if I can't find her, I'll go ask Mr. Martin and Bedad to help."

"Can you find their place?"

"Mr. Martin says he can walk right out of the school door and keep going straight east to the tepee," Liese put in. "He's promised to take the whole school there someday when the weather turns fine."

"As if it could ever do that!" sniffed Rebecca. "Don't go, Cobie! Rachel's probably throwing snowballs or idling with the other children. I need help to do the milking and other chores, with the twins sick and Father not back."

"If you'll look for Rachel, I'll do the chores," said Cobie. "But one of us has to go — now!"

"Always pretending to be a hero!" Rebecca scolded.

Cobie shrugged and started out. Rebecca caught her in a tight hug. "I'm sorry, Cobie! Forgive me! Of course, someone

must go and I — I'm afraid! I'm afraid to go look for my little sister!"

"There's plenty to do here," Cobie said. She could find only pity in her heart for Rebecca, so beautiful, so unfitted to this raw land. "I don't mind going, truly! I'll be back soon, Mutti, don't worry!"

She plunged into a cold that stung her face, hands, and feet, which had not had a chance to warm thoroughly. How she hoped Father would drive into sight! Sol, the ox that was singly pulling the wagon that day, would scarcely show against the snow, but the green wagon would stand out plainly.

It did not come into view, though, and Cobie soon had to turn in the opposite direction to reach the school, abandoning the hope of meeting her father. Every hundred yards or so she called Rachel's name and got a sinking feeling when there was no answer. At least it wasn't snowing, and there was no wind to blow over her tracks.

The other schoolchildren lived on the opposite side of the schoolhouse, on farms scattered for several miles. Their families would help search if necessary, yet Cobie's first impulse had been to ask Stede and Bedad.

"Rachel!" shouted Cobie so loudly that her throat hurt.

How could the child just vanish! There were no thick woods hereabouts, no gorges or ravines. A person could get lost in a blinding storm, but Rachel knew the country well enough so that she should quickly right herself when she could see.

There were coyotes and wolves, but they didn't attack people unless they were hydrophobic, and, of course, in that condition skunks and even squirrels bit. That seemed unlikely.

But hadn't Bedad warned them about old abandoned wells? He had said discouraged homesteaders often left without bothering to board over such holes, and there were a few abandoned claims near the school. On the way to church, Cobie had glimpsed several caved-in dugouts some distance from the road.

If Rachel had strayed in the snow, and *if* there was an open well, she could have fallen into it. Cobie's spine felt colder than her feet as she pictured Rachel lying in a hole, perhaps drowned, perhaps with a broken leg.

Across the white prairie, Cobie saw one of the ruined dugouts. She hurried toward it, shouting, and halted some distance from the house. Floundering around in the failing light, she herself could pitch into a well.

But what if Rachel was unconscious or — dead? Cobie shuddered and pushed on toward the place where she remembered seeing the other dugout. If she didn't find her sister there, she'd go east of the school and get Stede and Bedad to help her before it was completely dark! Surely, surely, Father would come soon!

Panting and sobbing through the drifts that came above her knees in places, Cobie felt entirely alone and helpless.

"Rachel!" she cried. Her breath turned to frosty smoke. What if her sister was trapped out in such weather? "Rachel!"

Cobie tripped hard over the skeleton of a cow. Kicking free of the ribs that settled again under the snow, she pushed on. A battered cattle shelter loomed ahead, snow-covered thatch slanting to the ground and roof pole jutting into the air. Beyond it was the doorless ruin of the other dugout.

Cobie stopped, caught her breath, and cupped her hands. "Rachel! Rachel!"

Her voice died slowly, seeming to mock her. It was no use. She must get help. It was almost dark, and somewhere on this prairie Rachel might be lying hurt or dead.

For a moment she thought the faint sound was an echo of her own cry. Then it came again, dim, moaning.

"Rachel!" Cobie shouted, running forward. "Where are you?"

"Down here! Be careful — you'll fall too!"

Cobie moved gingerly toward the voice. "Are you all right?"

"I — I think so. I hurt my knee, but I can stand on it. But Cobie! Help me get out! I'm so cold! I've been so scared!"

Cobie edged near the mouth of the well. Her sister's pale face showed in the darkness fifteen feet below.

"I don't have a rope," Cobie said. "My scarf's not long enough. Rachel, I'll have to go for help!"

"Don't leave me!" Rachel wailed. "I — I can't stay here anymore! Please, Cobie, get me out!"

"I want to, dearest! Can you climb part way? Is there anything down there to help?"

"I tried to get out. There's a wide casing around the bottom almost as tall as I am, and I got on it and worked up a little way, but I fell back down."

"How wide is the well?"

Rachel snuffled, estimated, and said after a moment, "When I stretch out my arms, I can touch both sides."

"Could you find Mr. Martin's from here? It's beginning to get dark."

Rachel began to weep. "Of — of course I could find him if I weren't down here! He's just east of the school. Don't make fun, Cobie! Please get me out!"

"Listen!" Cobie spoke so sharply that Rachel gulped down her sobs. "One of us has to bring help, but if you're afraid to stay here, maybe I can get down and then boost you up on my shoulders. But you've got to make it, Rachel, or we'll both be stuck down there!"

"I — I'll make it if you hold me! Please, Cobie, please don't go off and leave me!"

Cobie hurried over to the falling-down cattle shelter and dragged the roof pole free. It was still sound; it would hold her. She laid it across the well, gripped it, and lowered herself, stretching out her legs to feel the sides.

Releasing the pole, she slid till her feet lodged on opposite sides of the casing. "Up with you!" she commanded, leaning to give Rachel a hand. "Get on top of the casing the way you did before. Then I'll bend as much as I can to let you climb up on my shoulders. From there you can reach the pole and scramble out."

"But you'll have to stay in this nasty, dark hole!"

"One of us must! So hurry!"

Stubble and earth showered down as Rachel's toes dug into the unlined sides of the pit. Cobie pushed with all her might at her sister's shoes. Gasping, Rachel dragged herself out. A final rain of snow and rubble came down. Cobie shook it out of her face and slid to the bottom. There was no use trying to hold that strained position while Rachel fetched Stede and Bedad.

"I'll run all the way!" Rachel shouted from above.

"Just don't get lost!"

It was too dark to see much of her prison. Rachel had trampled down the snow. There was no water in the well. Perhaps its going dry had been one of the reasons the homesteader had left.

The hours poor Rachel had been trapped here must have seemed an eternity. Even knowing that help would come shortly didn't make it pleasant. Cobie sat down, huddling her arms and face against her knees for warmth.

Rachel was found. She wasn't hurt. But, oh, supposing she had broken her neck in the fall! Or that Bedad's warning hadn't echoed in Cobie's brain and Rachel had frozen to death before she was found!

It seemed that help would never come. By the time voices roused her, Cobie had almost dozed off in exhaustion. She sprang up eagerly.

"Here we are!" Rachel shouted.

"We'll have you up in a jiffy!" came Stede's reassuring voice. "Slip this loop under your shoulders, hold on to the rope, and we'll haul you out!"

In seconds she stood in the snow, hugged tight in Rachel's arms. Bedad gave her a rough dusting off. "I'll board this well up tomorrow — should have done it long ago!"

"For tonight let's get you girls home to your folks," said Stede, coiling up the rope and tying it to his saddle horn.

He got in the saddle and helped Cobie up behind him on Raven, his horse. Bedad and Rachel occupied Belshazzer, who snorted at the burden and shambled through the snow as if utterly disgusted.

It was now dark, but the snow shone underfoot, and they could see dark shapes at a distance. Halfway home Stede said, "There's someone coming!"

"Cobie!" came the faint sound. "Is that you?"

"Yes!" cried Stede. "She found Rachel!"

In minutes Rachel tumbled off Belshazzer to embrace her father, and shortly after that they were all in the sod house warming themselves and eating supper.

Author

Jeanne Williams, who grew up in the Midwest, became interested in the history of the frontier while at college. In her books, she drew upon her study of history and her grandparents' tales of their homesteading days. *Winter Wheat,* from which "Cobie's Courage" was taken, was a Notable Children's Trade Book in the Field of Social Studies.

Summary Questions

Think about what it took for Cobie to rescue Rachel.

1. How did Cobie's family show courage in their daily life in Kansas?
2. How did Cobie show courage during her search for Rachel?
3. What other qualities did Cobie have that helped her in her search for Rachel?
4. Pretend that you are Cobie. Tell your father what happened after you learned that Rachel was missing. Explain how you kept your courage up, and tell who you counted on for help.

The Reading and Writing Connection

Although Cobie was very courageous in her search for Rachel, she was not fearless. She shuddered at the thought that Rachel could be hurt, and she sobbed as she searched. Yet she was able to reassure Rachel and climb into a dark well to rescue her.

Write a paragraph telling how you would define courage. Give examples of courageous people or actions that you have read about or heard about. Try to use some of the following words in your paragraph.

> **reassuring**
> **shuddered**
> **loomed**
> **gingerly**

"Escape from NIMH"

an excerpt from
*Mrs. Frisby and
the Rats of NIMH*

written by Robert C. O'Brien

illustrated by Jan Pyk

They were just ordinary rats
from the city, caught by scientists for use in a very unusual
experiment. The experiment was
successful — more successful
than the scientists could have
predicted — and it would change
the lives of these once-ordinary
rats forever. Theirs is an exciting
story, an adventure with an
unexpected twist that has made it
a popular classic with young
readers everywhere.

*Mrs. Frisby and the Rats of
NIMH* was awarded the John
Newbery Medal in 1972.

Mrs. Frisby and the Rats of NIMH

by Robert C. O'Brien

illustrated by Jan Pyk

Escape from NIMH

One evening a young rat, Nicodemus, and his friend, Jenner, were feasting with dozens of other rats in the market square at the edge of the city. As they began to eat, Nicodemus noticed a white truck parked nearby. Printed on both its sides were the letters NIMH. Suddenly, several people jumped out of the truck, surrounded the rats, caught them in nets, and dumped them into a wire cage at the back of the truck. The doors shut, and they drove away.

After several hours, the truck came to a stop beside a large building. The rats were taken into a large, white room with a lot of bottles, boxes, and mysterious-looking equipment. One whole end of the room was filled with small cages. A man whom the others called "Dr. Schultz" locked each rat into a cage and left. Nicodemus and his companions wondered where they had been brought, and for what purpose.

234

That cage was my home for a long time. It was not uncomfortable. Yet just the fact that it was a cage made it horrible. I, who had always run where I wanted, could go three hops forward, three hops back again, and that was all. But worse was the dreadful feeling — I know we all had it — that we were completely at the mercy of someone we knew not at all, for some purpose we could not guess. What were their plans for us?

As it turned out, the uncertainty itself was the worst suffering we had to undergo. But of course we didn't know that when we arrived, and I doubt that any of us got much sleep that first night. I know I didn't. So, in a way, it was a relief when early the next morning the lights snapped on and Dr. Schultz entered with a young man and a young woman dressed in laboratory coats. He was talking to them as they entered the room.

". . . three groups. Twenty for training on injection series A, twenty on series B. That will leave twenty-three for the control group. They get no injections at all — except, to keep the test exactly even, we will prick them with a plain needle. Let's call the groups A, B, and C for control; tag them and number them A–1 through A–20, B–1 through B–20, and so on. Number the cages the same way, and keep each rat in the same cage throughout. Diet will be the same for all."

"When do we start the injections?" the woman asked.

"As soon as we're through with the tagging. We'll do that now. George, you number the tags and the cages. Julie, you tie them on. I'll hold."

One by one we were taken from our cages and held gently but firmly by Dr. Schultz while Julie fastened around each of our necks a narrow ribbon of yellow plastic bearing a number. I learned eventually that mine was number A–10.

A little later in the morning they came around again, this time pushing a table on wheels. It was loaded with a bottle of some clear liquid, a long rack of sharp needles, and a plunger. Once more I was lifted from the cage. I felt a sharp pain in my hip; then it was over. We all got used to that, for from then on, we got injections at least twice a week. What they were injecting and why, I did not know. Yet for twenty of us those injections were to change our whole lives.

During the days that followed, our lives fell into a pattern, and the reason for our captivity gradually became clear. Dr. Schultz was a neurologist — that is, an expert on brains, nerves, intelligence, and how people learn things. He hoped, by experimenting on us, to find out whether certain injections could help us to learn more and faster. The two younger people working with him, George and Julie, were graduate students in biology.

"Watch always," he told them, "for signs of improvement, faster learning, quicker reaction in group A as compared to group B, and both as compared to the control group."

My own training began on the day after the first injections. It was George who did it; I suppose Julie and Dr. Schultz were doing the same test on other rats. He took my cage from the shelf and carried it to another room. He placed the cage in a slot against a wall, slid open the end, opened a matching door in the wall — and I was free.

Or so I thought. The small doorway in the wall led into a short corridor, which opened, or seemed to, directly onto a green lawn. Were they letting me go?

I made a dash toward the open end of the corridor — and then jumped back. I could not go on. There was something dreadfully wrong with the floor. When I touched my feet to it, a terrible, prickling feeling came over my skin; my muscles cramped, my eyes blurred, and I got instantly dizzy. I never got used to that feeling, but I did experience it many times and eventually learned what it was: electric shock.

Yet, I was in a frenzy to reach that open lawn, to run for the bushes, to get away from the cage. I tried again — and jumped back again. No use. Then I saw, leading off to the left, another corridor. It seemed to stop about five feet away in a blank wall. Yet there was light there; it must turn a corner. I ran down it, cautiously, not trusting the floor. At the end it turned right — and there was the lawn again, another opening. I got closer that time; then, just as I thought I was going to make it — another shock. This was repeated over and over; yet each time I seemed to get a little closer to freedom.

But when finally I reached it and the grass was only a step away, a wire wall snapped down in front of me, another behind me; the ceiling opened above me; and a gloved hand reached in and picked me up.

A voice said, "Four minutes, thirty-seven seconds." It was George. I had, after all my running through the corridors, emerged into a trap only a few feet from where I had started, and through a concealed opening up above, George had been watching everything I did.

I had been in what is called a maze, a device to test intelligence and memory. I was put in it many times again. You might ask: Why would I bother to run through it at all if I knew it was only a trick? The answer is: I couldn't help it. When you've lived in a cage, you can't bear *not* to run, even if what you're running toward is an illusion.

There were more injections and other kinds of tests, and some of these were more important than the maze, because the maze was designed only to find out how quickly we could learn, while some of the others actually taught us things — or at least led up to actual teaching.

One was what Dr. Schultz called "shape recognition." We would be put into a small room with three doors leading out — one round, one square, and one triangular. These doors were on hinges that were easy to push open, and each door led into another room with three more doors like the first one. But the trick was this: If you went through the wrong door, the room you entered had an electric floor, and you got a shock. So you had to learn: In

the first room, you used the round door; second room, triangular door; and so on.

All of these activities helped to pass the time, and the weeks went by quickly, but they did not lessen our longing to get away. I wished I could see my mother and father and run with my brother to the marketplace. I know all the others felt the same way; yet it seemed a hopeless thing. Still, there was one rat who decided to try it anyway.

He was a young rat, probably the youngest of all that had been caught, and by chance, he was in the cage next to mine; I might mention that like Jenner and me, he was in the group Dr. Schultz called A. His name was Justin.

It was late one night that I heard him calling to me, speaking softly, around the wooden partition between our cages.

"Nicodemus?"

"Yes?" I went over to the corner.

"How long have we been here?"

"I don't know. Several months — I think, but I have no way to keep track."

"I know. I don't either. Do you suppose it's winter outside now?"

"Probably. Or late fall."

"It will be cold."

"But not in here."

"No. But I'm going to try to get out."

"Get out? But how? Your cage is shut."

"Tomorrow we get injections, so they'll open it. When they do, I'm going to run."

"Run where?"

"I don't know. At least I'll get a look around. There might be some way out. What can I lose?"

"You might get hurt."

"I don't think so. Anyway *they* won't hurt me."

By *they* he meant Dr. Schultz and the other two. He added confidently, "All those shots, all the time they've spent — we're too valuable to them now. They'll be careful."

That idea had not occurred to me before, but when I thought about it, I decided he was right. Dr. Schultz, Julie, and George could not afford to let any harm come

240

to us. On the other hand, neither could they afford to allow any of us to escape.

Justin made his attempt the next morning. And it did cause a certain amount of excitement but not at all what we expected. It was Julie who opened Justin's cage with a hypodermic in her hand. Justin was out with a mighty leap, hit the floor with a thump, shook himself, and ran, disappearing from my view, heading toward the other end of the room.

Julie seemed not at all alarmed. She calmly placed the needle on a shelf, then walked to the door of the laboratory and pushed a button on the wall. A red light came on over the door. She picked up a notebook and pencil from a desk near the door and followed Justin out of my sight.

A few minutes later Dr. Schultz and George entered. They opened the door cautiously and closed it behind them. "The outer door is shut too," said Dr. Schultz. "Where is it?"

"Down here," said Julie, "inspecting the air ducts."

"Really? Which one is it?"

"It's one of the A group, just as you expected. Number nine. I'm keeping notes on it."

Obviously the red light was some kind of a warning signal, both outside the door and in — "laboratory animal at large." And not only had Dr. Schultz known one of us was out, but he had expected it to happen.

241

". . . a few days sooner than I thought," he was saying, "but so much the better. Do you realize what this . . ."

"Look," said Julie. "He's doing the whole baseboard — but he's studying the windows too. See how he steps back to look up?"

"Of course," replied Dr. Schultz. "And at the same time he's watching us too. Can't you see?"

"He's pretty cool about it," said George.

"Can you imagine one of the lab rats doing that? Or even one of the controls? We've got to try to grasp what we have on our hands. The A group is now three hundred per cent ahead of the control group in learning, and getting smarter all the time. B group is only twenty per cent ahead. We have a real breakthrough. I think we should go ahead now and do the next injection series."

"Look," said Julie, "A–9 has made a discovery. He's found the mice."

George said, "See how he's studying them? Should I get the net and put him back?"

"I doubt that you'll need it," Dr. Schultz said, "now that he's learned he can't get out."

But they were underestimating Justin. He had learned no such thing.

Of course, Justin did not escape that day, nor even that year. When Julie put on a glove and went to pick him up, he submitted meekly enough, and in a short time he was back in his cage.

Yet he had learned some things. He had, as Julie noticed, looked at the air ducts, and he had studied the windows. Mainly he had learned that he could, occasionally at least, jump from his cage and wander around without incurring any anger or injury. All of this, eventually, was important. For it was Justin, along with Jenner, who figured out how to get away. I had a part in it too. But all that came later.

During the months that followed, two things were happening: First, we were learning more than any rats ever had before and were becoming more intelligent than any rats had ever been. The second thing could be considered, from some points of view, even more important — and certainly more astonishing — than the first. As far as Dr. Schultz could detect, in the A group the aging process seemed to stop almost completely. No one could see any signs that we were growing older at all. Apparently (though we seldom saw them) the same thing was happening with the G group, the mice who were getting the same injections we were.

Dr. Schultz was greatly excited about this. "The short life span has always been a prime limiting factor in education," he told George and Julie. "If we can double it, and speed up the learning process at the same time, the possibilities are just enormous."

The one important phase of training began one day after weeks of really hard work at the "shape recognition" that I mentioned before. But this was different. For the first time they used sounds along with the shapes and pictures, real pictures we could recognize. For example, one of the first and simplest of these exercises was a

picture, a clear photograph, of a rat. I suppose they felt sure we would know what that was. This picture was shown on a screen, with a light behind it. Then, after I had looked at the picture and recognized it, a shape flashed on the screen under it — a sort of half circle and two straight lines, not like anything I had seen before. Then the voice began: "Are . . . Are . . . Are."

It was Julie's voice, speaking very clearly, but it had a tinny sound; it was a record. After repeating "are" a dozen times or so, that particular shape disappeared and another one came on the screen, still under the picture of the rat. It was a triangle, with legs on it. And Julie's voice began again: "Ay . . . Ay . . . Ay."

When that shape disappeared, a third one came on the screen. This one was a cross. Julie's voice said: "Tea . . . Tea . . . Tea."

Then all three shapes appeared at once, and the record said: "Are . . . Ay . . . Tea . . . Rat."

You will already have recognized what was going on: They were teaching us to read. The symbols under the picture were the letters R—A—T. But the idea did not become clear to me, nor to any of us, for quite a long time. Because, of course, we didn't know what reading *was*.

It was Jenner who finally figured it out. By this time we had developed a sort of system of communication, a simple enough thing, just passing spoken messages from one cage to the next. Justin, who was still next to me, called to me one day, "Message for Nicodemus from Jenner. He says it is important."

"All right," I said, "what's the message?"

"Look at the shapes on the wall next to the door. He says to look carefully."

My cage, like Jenner's and those of the rest of A group, was close enough to the door so I could see what he meant: Near the doorway, there was a large, square piece of white cardboard fastened to the wall — a sign. It was covered with an assortment of black markings to which I had never paid any attention. Now, for the first time, I looked at them carefully, and I soon grasped what Jenner had discovered.

The black marks up there on the top line were instantly familiar: R—A—T—S; as soon as I saw them, I thought of
the picture that went with them; and as soon as I did that,
I was, for the first time, reading. Because, of course, that's
what reading is: using symbols to suggest a picture or an
idea. From that time on, it gradually became clear to me
what all these lessons were for, and once I understood the
idea, I was eager to learn more. The whole concept of
reading was, to me at least, fascinating. I remember how
proud I was when, some months later, I was able to read
and understand that whole sign. I read it hundreds of
times, and I'll never forget it: RATS MAY NOT BE RE-
MOVED FROM THE LABORATORY WITHOUT WRITTEN
PERMISSION. At the bottom, in smaller letters, we could
read the word: NIMH.

Apparently Dr. Schultz, who was running the lessons,
did not realize how well they were succeeding. We leaped
way ahead of him. I remember well, during one of the
lessons, looking at a picture of a tree. Under it the letters
flashed on: T—R—E—E. But in the photograph, though the
tree was in the foreground, there was a building in the
background, and a sign near it. I scarcely glanced at
T—R—E—E but concentrated instead on reading the sign.
It said: NIMH. PRIVATE PARKING BY PERMIT ONLY.
RESERVED FOR DOCTORS AND STAFF. NO VISITORS
PARKING.

I'm sure Dr. Schultz had plans for testing our reading
ability, but apparently he did not think we were ready for
it yet. I think maybe he was even a little afraid to try it;

because if he did it too soon, or if for any other reason it did not work, his experiment would be a failure. Dr. Schultz wanted to be very sure, and his caution was his undoing.

Justin announced one evening around the partition, "I'm going to get out of my cage tonight and wander around a bit."

"How can you? It's locked."

"Yes. But did you notice, along the bottom edge, there's a printed strip?"

I had not noticed it. I should perhaps explain that when Dr. Schultz and the others opened our cages, we could never quite see how they did it.

"What does it say?"

"I've been trying to read it the last three times they brought me back from training. It's very small print. But I think I've finally made it out. It says: To release door, pull knob forward and slide right."

"Knob?"

"Under the floor, about an inch back, there's a metal thing just in front of the shelf. I think that's the knob, and I think I can reach it through the wire. Anyway, I'm going to try."

"Now?"

"Not until they close up."

About half an hour after Dr. Schultz, George, and Julie left that night, Justin said, "I'm going to try now." I

247

heard a scuffling noise, a click and scrape of metal, and in a matter of seconds I saw his door swing open. It was as simple as that — when you could read.

"Wait," I said.

"What's the matter?"

"If you jump down, you won't be able to get back in. Then they'll know."

"I thought of that. I'm not going to jump down. I'm going to climb up the outside of the cage. It's easy. I've climbed up the inside a thousand times. Above these cages there's another shelf, and it's empty. I'm going to walk along there and see what I can see. I think there's a way to climb to the floor and up again."

"Why don't I go with you?" My door would open the same way as his.

"Better not this time, don't you think? If something goes wrong and I can't get back, they'll say it's just A–9. But if two of us are found outside, they'll take it seriously. They might put new locks on the cages."

He was right, and you can see that already we both had the same idea in mind: that this might be the first step toward escape for all of us.

And so it was. By teaching us how to read, they had taught us how to get away.

Justin climbed easily up the open door of his cage and vanished over the top with a flick of his tail. He came back an hour later, greatly excited and full of information. Yet, it was typical of Justin that even excited as he was, he stayed calm; he thought clearly. He climbed down the

front of my cage rather than his own and spoke softly. "Nicodemus? Come on out. I'll show you how." He directed me as I reached through the wire bars of the door and felt beneath it. I found the small metal knob, slid it forward and sideward, and felt the door swing loose against my shoulder. I followed him up the side of the cage to the shelf above. There we stopped. It was the first time I had met Justin face to face.

Justin said, "Nicodemus, I've found the way out."

"You have! How?"

"At each end of the room there's an opening in the baseboard at the bottom of the wall. Air blows in through one of them and out the other. Each one has a metal grid covering it, and on the grid there's a sign that says: LIFT TO ADJUST AIR FLOW. I lifted one of them. Behind it, there is a thing like a metal window; when you slide it wide open, more air blows in. But the main thing is that it's easily big enough for us to walk through and get out of here."

"But what's on the other side? Where does it lead?"

"On the other side there's a duct, a thing like a square metal pipe built right into the wall. I walked along it, not very far, but I can figure out where it must go. There's bound to be a duct like it leading to every room in the building, and they must all branch off one main central pipe — and that one has to lead, somewhere, to the outside. Because that's where our air comes from. That's why they never open the windows. I don't think those windows *can* open."

He was right, of course. The building had central air conditioning; what we had to do was find the main air shaft and explore it. There would have to be an intake at one end and an outlet at the other. But that was easier said than done, and before it was done, there were questions to be answered. What about the rest of the rats? There were twenty of us in the laboratory, and we had to let the others know.

So, one by one, we woke them and showed them how to open their cages. We all knew each other in a way, from the passing of messages over the preceding months; yet except for Jenner and me, none of us had ever really met. We were strangers — though, as you can imagine, it did not take long for us to develop a feeling of comradeship, for we twenty were alone in a strange world. The group looked to me as leader, probably because it was Justin and I who first set them free, and because Justin was obviously younger than I.

We did not attempt to leave that night, but went together and looked at the metal grid Justin had discovered, and made plans for exploring the air ducts. Jenner was astute at that sort of thing; he could clearly foresee problems.

"With a vent like this leading to every room," he said, "it will be easy to get lost. When we explore, we're going to need some way of finding our way back here."

"Why should we come back?" someone asked.

"Because it may take more than one night to find the way out. If it does, whoever is doing the exploring must be back in the cage by morning. Otherwise Dr. Schultz will find out."

Jenner was right. It took us about a week. What we did, after some more discussion, was to find some equipment: first a large spool of thread in one of the cabinets where some of us had seen Julie place it one day; second, a screwdriver that was kept on a shelf near the electric equipment — because, as Jenner pointed out, there would probably be a grill over the end of the airshaft to keep out debris, and we might have to pry it loose. What we really needed was a light, for at night the ducts were completely dark. But there was none to be had, not even a box of matches. The thread and the screwdriver we hid in the duct, a few feet from the entrance. We could only hope that they would not be missed, or that if they were, we wouldn't be suspected.

Justin and two others were chosen as the exploration party. They had a terrible time at first: Here was a maze to end all mazes; and in the dark they quickly lost their sense

of direction. Still they kept at it, exploring the shafts, night after night. They would tie the end of their thread to the grid in our laboratory and unroll it from the spool as they went.

Time and time again they reached the end of the thread and had to come back.

"It isn't long enough," Justin complained. "Every time I come to the end, I think, 'If I could just go ten feet farther . . .'"

And finally, that's what he did. On the seventh night, just as the thread ran out, he and the other two reached a shaft that was wider than any they had found before, 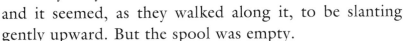 and it seemed, as they walked along it, to be slanting gently upward. But the spool was empty.

"You wait here," Justin said to the others. "I'm going just a little way farther. Hang on to the spool, and if I call, call back."

Justin had a hunch. The air coming through the shaft had a fresher smell where they were, and it seemed to be blowing harder than in the other shafts. Up ahead, he thought he could hear the whir of a machine running quietly, and there was a faint vibration in the metal under his feet. He went on. The shaft turned upward at a sharp angle, and then, straight ahead, he saw it: a patch of lighter-colored darkness than the pitch black around him, and in the middle of it, three stars twinkling. It was the open sky. Across the opening there was, as Jenner had predicted, a coarse grill.

He ran toward it for a few seconds longer and then stopped. The sound of the machine had grown suddenly louder, changing from a whir to a roar. It had obviously shifted speed; an automatic switch somewhere in the building turned it from low to high, and the air blowing past Justin came on so hard it made him gasp. He braced his feet against the metal and held on. In a minute, just as it had begun roaring, the machine returned to a whisper. He looked around and realized it was lucky he had stopped; by the dim light from the sky he could see that he had reached a point where perhaps two dozen air shafts came together like branches into the trunk of a tree. If he had gone a few steps farther, he would never have been able to distinguish which shaft was his. He turned in his tracks, and in a few minutes he rejoined his friends.

We had a meeting that night, and Justin told all of us what he had found. He had left the thread, anchored by the screwdriver, to guide us out. Some were for leaving immediately, but it was late, and Jenner and I argued against it. We did not know how long it would take us to break through the grill at the end. If it should take more than an hour or two, daylight would be upon us. We would then be unable to risk returning to the laboratory and would have to spend the day in the shaft — or try to get away by broad daylight. Dr. Schultz might even figure out how we had gone and trap us in the air shaft.

Finally, reluctantly, everyone agreed to spend one more day in the laboratory and leave early the next night. But it was a hard decision, with freedom so near.

Then, just as we were ending our meeting, a new complication arose. We had been standing in a rough circle on the floor of the laboratory, just outside the two

254

screen doors that enclosed the mice cages. Now, from inside the cabinet, came a voice: "Nicodemus." It was a clear but plaintive call, the voice of a mouse. We had almost forgotten the mice were there, and I was startled to hear that one of them knew my name. We all grew quiet.

"Who's calling me?" I asked.

"My name is Jonathan," said the voice. "We have been listening to your talk about going out. We would like to go too, but we cannot open our cages."

As you can imagine, this caused a certain consternation, coming at the last minute. None of us knew much about the mice, except what we had heard Dr. Schultz dictate into his tape recorder. From that, we had learned only that they had been getting the same injections we were getting and that the treatment had worked about as well on them as on us. They were a sort of side experiment, without a control group.

Justin was studying the cabinet intently.

"Why not?" he said. "If we can get the doors open."

Someone muttered, "They will slow us down."

"No," said the mouse Jonathan. "We will not. Only open our cages when you go, and we will make our own way. We won't even stay with you, if you prefer."

"How many are you?" I asked.

"Only eight. And the cabinet doors are easy to open. There's just a simple hook, halfway up."

"The cages open the same way as yours," said another mouse, "but we can't reach far enough to unlatch them."

"All right," I said. "Tomorrow night we'll open your cages, and you can follow the thread with us to get out. After that, you're on your own."

"Agreed," said Jonathan, "and thank you."

The next day was terrible. I kept expecting to hear Dr. Schultz say, "Who took my screwdriver?" And then to hear Julie add, "My thread is missing too." That could have happened and set them to thinking — but it didn't; and that night, an hour after Julie, George, and Dr. Schultz left the laboratory, we were out of our cages and gathered, the whole group of us, before the mouse cabinet. Justin opened its doors, unlatched their cages, and the mice came out. They looked very small and frightened, but one strode bravely forward.

"Nicodemus?" he said to me. "I'm Jonathan. Thanks for taking us out with you."

"We're not out yet," I said, "but you're welcome."

We had no time for chatting. The light coming in the windows was turning gray; in less than an hour it would be dark, and we would need light to figure out how to open the grill that was at the end of the shaft.

We went to the opening in the baseboard.

"Justin," I said, "take the lead. Roll up the thread as you go. I will bring up the rear. No noise. There's sure to be somebody awake somewhere in the building. We don't want them to hear us." I did not want to leave the thread where it might be found: The more I thought about it, the more I felt sure Dr. Schultz would try to track us down, for quite a number of reasons.

256

Justin lifted the grid, pushed open the sliding panel, and one by one the others went through. Then I went in myself, closing the grid behind me and pushing the panel half shut again, its normal position.

With Justin leading the way, we moved through the dark passage quickly and easily. In only fifteen or twenty minutes we had reached the end of the thread; then, as Justin had told us it would, the shaft widened; we could hear the whir of the machine ahead, and almost immediately we saw a square of gray daylight. We had reached the end of the shaft, and there a terrible thing happened.

We were approaching the lighted square of the opening when the roar began. The blast of air came like a sudden whistling gale; it took my breath and flattened my ears against my head, and I closed my eyes instinctively. I was still in the rear, and when I opened my eyes again, I saw one of the mice sliding past me, clawing uselessly with his small nails at the smooth metal beneath him. Another followed him, and still another, as one by one they were blown backward into the dark maze of tunnels we had just left. I braced myself in the corner of the shaft and grabbed at one as he slid by. It was a white mouse. I caught him by one leg, pulled him around behind me, and held on. Another blew face-on into the rat ahead of me and stopped there; it was Jonathan, who had been near the lead. But the rest were lost, six in all.

In another minute the roar stopped, the rush of air slowed from a gale to a breeze, and we were able to go forward again.

I said to the white mouse, "You'd better hold on to me. That might happen again."

He looked at me in dismay. "But what about the others? I've got to go back and look for them."

Jonathan quickly joined him. "I'll go with you."

"No," I said. "That would be useless and foolish. You have no idea which shaft they were blown into, nor even if they all went the same way. And if you should find them, how would you find your way out again? And suppose the wind comes again? Then there would be eight lost instead of six."

The wind did come again, half a dozen times more, while we worked with the screwdriver to pry open the grill. Each time we had to stop work and hang on. The two mice clung to the grill itself; some of us braced ourselves behind them, in case they should slip. And Justin, taking the thread with him as a guideline, went back to search for the other six — but it was futile. To this day we don't know what became of those six mice. They may have found their way out eventually. The opening was there in the grill for them, just in case.

The grill. It was heavy metal, with holes about the size of an acorn, and it was set in a steel frame. We pried and hammered at it with the screwdriver, but we could not move it. It was fastened on the outside; we couldn't see how. Finally the white mouse had an idea.

"Push the screwdriver through the grill near the bottom," he said, "and pry up." We did, and the metal bent a fraction of an inch. We did it again, prying down, then left, then right. The hole in the grill was slightly bigger, and the white mouse said, "I think that's enough." He climbed to the small opening, and by squirming and twisting, he got through. Jonathan followed him; they both fell out of sight, but in a minute Jonathan's head came back in view on the outside.

"It's a sliding bolt," he said. "We're working on it." Inside we could hear the faint rasping as the two mice tugged on the bolt handle, working it back. Then the crack at the base of the grill widened; we pushed it open, and we were standing on the roof of NIMH, free.

Author

Robert C. O'Brien was the pen name of Robert L. Conly, a writer and editor for newspapers and magazines. His several books for young people include *The Silver Crown* and *Mrs. Frisby and the Rats of NIMH*, winner of the Newbery Medal and other awards.

Illustrator

Jan Pyk, a talented Swedish artist, grew up in Stockholm, where he studied art. In 1963, he moved to New York. He has illustrated a number of children's books that have been widely enjoyed. Jan Pyk likes traveling and sailing and is currently building his own sailboat on Long Island.

Selection Wrap-up

Summary Questions

Think about how the experiments on the rats at NIMH had unexpected results.

1. How did the injections change Nicodemus and the other rats in the A group?
2. How did learning to read help the rats?
3. In what ways did learning to run through the maze prove helpful to the rats when they made their escape?
4. The rats in the A group learned a number of skills. Which do you think was the most important? Explain your answer.

The Reading and Writing Connection

The map below shows some of the skills the rats in the A group learned during their captivity.

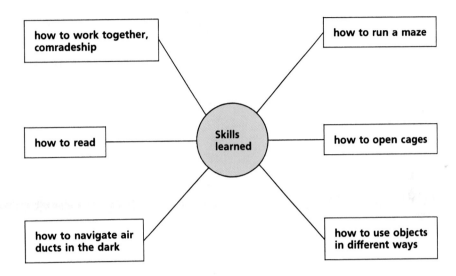

Copy the map on a large sheet of paper. Then expand it by adding other skills you think the rats may need to relearn in order to survive in the outside world once again. Select one or more of the skills on the expanded map and write a brief story telling how the rats used the skill or skills in an adventure outside NIMH. Try to use some of the following words in your story.

> consternation
> futile
> reluctantly
> underestimating

Acronyms

Imagine that after the rats escaped from NIMH, some of them decided to share their knowledge with other rats. They might have formed their own organization, **R**ats for **E**ducation **a**nd **D**evelopment — or **READ**.

In naming their organization READ, the rats used an acronym, a word made from the first letters or syllables of a string of words. A part of each important word is used to make the new word. An acronym often becomes accepted as a word in its own right; we may use it without even knowing that it is an acronym.

Organizations are often known by acronyms. For example: A government agency concerned with **H**ousing and **U**rban **D**evelopment is referred to as **HUD**. The **A**merican **S**ociety of **C**omposers, **A**uthors, and **P**ublishers is called **ASCAP**.

Technology has added a number of acronyms to the English language. **RADAR** stands for **Ra**dio **D**etecting **a**nd **R**anging. RADAR is so common in the language that it has become a word in its own right.

Another such acronym is **SCUBA**, which stands for **S**elf-**C**ontained **U**nderwater **B**reathing **A**pparatus. You have probably heard of SCUBA divers, who carry their supply of oxygen in tanks carried on their backs. In the case of SCUBA and RADAR, you can see how the acronym is a quick and easy substitute for a long and complicated name.

Look at the acronyms and strings of words below. Match each acronym with the words it stands for. Sometimes not all the words are included in the acronym.

NASA   National Institute of Mental Health

MODEM   Women's Army Corps

NIMH   Zone Improvement Plan

LASER   Modulator/Demodulator

WAC   Light Amplification by Simulated Emission of Radiation

ZIP   National Aeronautics and Space Administration

The Town Mouse and The Country Mouse

by Aesop

A Country Mouse was very happy that his city cousin, the Town Mouse, had accepted his invitation to dinner. He gave his city cousin all the best food he had, such as dried beans, peas, and crusts of bread. The Town Mouse tried not to show how he disliked the food and picked a little here and tasted a little there to be polite. After dinner, however, he said, "How can you stand such food all the time? Still, I suppose here in the country you don't know any better. Why don't you go home with me? When you have once tasted the delicious things I eat, you will never want to come back here."

The Country Mouse not only forgave the Town Mouse for not liking his dinner but even consented to go that very evening to the city with his cousin. They arrived late at night, and the Town Mouse, as host, took his Country Cousin to a room where there had been a big dinner. "You are tired," he said. "Rest here, and I'll bring you some real food." He brought the Country Mouse such things as nuts, dates, and fruit.

The Country Mouse thought it was all so good he would like to stay there; but before he had a chance to say so, he heard a terrible roar, and looking up, he saw a huge creature dash into the room. Frightened out of his wits, the Country Mouse ran all around the room, trying to find a hiding place. At last he found a place of safety. While he stood there trembling, he made up his mind to go home as soon as he could get safely away; for, to himself, he said, "I'd rather have common food in safety than dates and nuts in the midst of danger."

Magazine Wrap-up

Literary Skill: Setting

The setting of a story is the time and place in which the events happen. In some stories, the setting is very important. For example, "The Boy Who Shaped Stone" could not be set in modern times. "A Small Link with the Past" could only have happened at an archaeological dig. In other stories, such as "Grandpa's Miracle," the time and place are less important to what happens.

Read the titles of the stories for Magazine Two listed on pages 136–137, and think about their settings. Select one story in which

the setting is very important and one in which it is less important. Be prepared to discuss your choices with your classmates.

Vocabulary: Roots and Prefixes

Study the meanings of these prefixes and roots.

Prefixes

pro-	Forward; ahead.
e-	Out; away from.
in-	In; into.
sub-	Below; under.

Roots

ject	Throw.
spect	Look.

Read each numbered sentence below. In each, there is a blank. Combine a prefix and a root from the list to make a new word to complete the sentence. The meaning should be the same as the phrase in parentheses below the sentence.

1. The umpire _____ the unruly player from the game.
   (threw out)
2. The health officers were _____ the kitchen.
   (looking into)
3. The king made a speech to his new _____.
   (people he had conquered)

4. The veterinarian gave the sick dog several _____.
   (doses of medicine shot under the skin)
5. Planning for our trip was a pleasant _____.
   (look ahead)

Writing: Play Form

Select one incident from one of the stories at the top of the second column. Write it out in play form. Be sure to indicate which character is to speak, and how the lines are to be spoken. You may add lines to the story dialogue if you wish. Be sure to include stage directions to describe how the characters move and act. Rehearse and act out your play with your classmates.

- "Thank You, Jackie Robinson"
- "The Gorillagram"
- "Cobie's Courage"

Books to Enjoy

The Stolen Lake by Joan Aiken
In this exciting fantasy, enterprising Dido Twite recovers a stolen lake for a 1300-year-old queen.

Hazel Rye by Vera and Bill Cleaver
The Poole family, who move into a small house by Hazel's orange grove, help her to have a new outlook on life.

Baseball Fever
by Johanna Hurwitz
Winning a computerized chess game helps Ezra convince his scholarly father of the value of his son's baseball knowledge.

Roll of Thunder, Hear My Cry
by Mildred D. Taylor
This Newbery Award-winning story tells of the struggle of Cassie's family to keep their land during the Depression years in Mississippi.

Celebrations

Magazine Three

Contents

Arctic Fire

by James Houston

Stranded on a drifting piece of ice, Matthew and Kayak never expected to see home again. . . .

Matthew Morgan and his father were newcomers to the Canadian Arctic. Matthew was attending school in Frobisher Bay while his father, a geologist, was prospecting.

Mr. Morgan and his helicopter pilot, Charlie, set out in a storm — and failed to return. When bad weather continued to prevent an air search for the missing men, Matthew and his friend Kayak went off secretly by snowmobile to look for them.

After abandoning their snowmobile when it ran out of gas about 120 kilometers from Frobisher, the two boys continued on foot across the frozen tundra. After several days, their food supply was exhausted, and they had no hope of obtaining more. They realized that their only chance for survival was to give up their search and try to return to Frobisher.

The next day a cold, sharp wind blew against their backs and seemed to drive them forward. Matthew was so hungry he felt light enough to take off and sail across the snow. They entered the mountains just before darkness came, and they hurried through a long valley.

"Just a little farther," Kayak called to him. "I want to build our igloo right up there."

When they reached the height of land, darkness had come.

Kayak ran to Matthew and gripped him by the arm and shook him. "We did it! We did it!" he whispered.

Matthew could not tell if Kayak was laughing or crying.

"See over there. Across the bay. See the glow of lights? That's Frobisher. That's where we came from!"

Far away on the horizon, Matthew could see a faint yellow glow in the sky, as though some strange moon was about to rise.

"I wonder if my dad is over there," said Matthew. "Let's keep on going!"

Matthew took a step forward, but his legs bent like spongy rubber that might let him down at any moment.

"No, no," said Kayak, "that glow must be forty-eight kilometers away." He drew the long snow knife from his pack. "We'll build an igloo here and sleep. We'll feel stronger in the morning."

They left at dawn and traveled down the long slope toward the bay. When they reached the ice, Matthew felt lightheaded.

Kayak squatted in the snow, and taking the broken half of the bow that he had saved, he lashed the snow knife to its grip.

"Why are you doing that?" asked Matthew.

"See that black fog rising way out there?" said Kayak. "The ice has changed. It's broken open. When we get out there, I'm going to have to feel beneath the snow for open water. I don't trust moving ice. You walk only in my footsteps," he added as he carefully probed the ice before him. "Hurry," he said. "See that crack up ahead. It may be opening. It may be getting wider."

They ran toward the blue-green line that zigzagged like a frozen streak of lightning across their path. To the south Matthew could see a great green shining lake where the seawater had flooded over the ice.

"Too wide for us to cross," exclaimed Kayak.

He hurried north along the edge of the crack. Matthew dreaded the look of the dark water that stood gaping before them, sometimes a meter, sometimes a meter and a half, wide.

"We'll never get across," said Matthew, and he felt like falling down and weeping.

"Come on," said Kayak. "We have to keep on moving!"

The crack stretched like a long ragged tear in a piece of white paper for as far as Matthew could see.

"Look over there." Kayak pointed. "There is our only chance."

Matthew saw his friend run forward and reach out for a

four-foot chunk of ice that had cracked away from the main
ice. Kayak caught it with his snow knife and slowly drew it to
him.

"I'll go first," he said, putting one foot on the ice pan.

Matthew saw it shudder and sink a little.

"It should hold me," Kayak said.

As though he were treading on eggs, he carefully eased one
knee and then the other onto the trembling pan of ice.

"Now push the ice," he said to Matthew. "Not so hard
you'll tip me in, but hard enough to float me over to the other
side."

Matthew lay on his stomach and with both hands gave the
ice a steady push. Kayak was on his hands and knees. A light

breeze whipped across the ice and caught him like a sail, so the ice pan turned half around. Matthew closed his eyes.

"Thanks a lot," he heard Kayak shout, and when Matthew opened his eyes, he saw Kayak scrambling onto the ice on the other side of the widening crack.

Kayak then began to chip two holes in the ice pan about four inches apart. He worked downward in a V-shape until the two holes touched. Then he forced a piece of tent line through the ice and tied it tight.

"Get ready," he called to Matthew, and pushing the ice with his foot, he sent it drifting back across the crack. "You're heavier than I am and that ice is very tippy even though it's thick," shouted Kayak. "You be mighty careful how you climb onto it."

With the deadly cold water all around him, Matthew felt like an elephant balancing on a cold round ball. Slowly, cautiously, Kayak drew Matthew toward him across the widening gap between the heavy shore ice of the bay and the great central body of ice, until Matthew, too, could crawl onto the strong ice.

If the two boys could have seen where they were going from an airplane, they would not have been in such a hurry to cross that deadly gap, for the ice in the center of Frobisher Bay was broken into a dangerous jigsaw puzzle of slowly moving pans of ice, rising and falling as much as three meters on the huge tides pulled by the terrifying forces of the moon.

"I think we're going to be all right now," Kayak called to Matthew. "The wind should make it easier to get onto the shore ice across the bay near Frobisher."

He was wrong. Dead wrong. For the next six hours they hurried across the vast broken ice fields, driving the knife in before taking every step, testing. Kayak warned Matthew a dozen times to step only in the footprints that he himself had made.

In the late afternoon they watched with terror as the huge tide flooded the ice, creating deadly lakes just south of them. With each step Matthew imagined he could feel the broken ice beneath them moving south toward the Hudson Strait, where they would be swept to certain death in the North Atlantic Ocean.

As darkness came again, Kayak squatted on the ice and placed his head in his hands. He was trembling, and Matthew could not tell whether it was from cold or hunger or fear.

"It's no use going any farther," said Kayak. "I can feel it; we are being swept away. The tide is carrying us too far south. We will never reach the other side."

"What do you mean?" said Matthew, horrified.

"See that hill?" asked Kayak, pointing. "It was far to the south of us this morning when we crossed the tide crack. Now it is so far to the north I can scarcely see it. We have moved twenty-four kilometers south already. By morning we will have drifted forty-eight, almost sixty-four, kilometers away. We are lost, I tell you. Lost forever. Look. Look how the ice has split." Kayak showed him. "We were once on pans a kilometer square in size. Look how all of them have broken. You could not walk fifteen paces now without falling into water. I am sorry, Matthew, we are truly finished."

A cruel blast of wind swept out of the north, driving chilling swirls of ice fog around them.

"We must build an igloo," said Matthew, unlashing Kayak's knife from the broken bow.

"It is too difficult out here," Kayak mumbled. "The snow is wet with salt water."

"Still, we must try our best," said Matthew, and he paced out the small circle as he had seen Kayak do and began to cut the thin, damp blocks. Big wet flakes of snow came driving on the wind.

"Come and help me," Matthew called to Kayak.

"Don't move," answered Kayak in a whisper. There was terror in his voice.

Cautiously Matthew turned and saw a white head with black beady eyes move snakelike through the icy water. When it reached the small ice pan on which they stood, the huge polar bear heaved its bulk out of the water and shook itself like an immense dog. It looked yellow against the stark white snow.

Matthew saw the great bear swing its head back and forth, sniffing the air suspiciously. Its huge blue-black mouth hung open, showing its terrible teeth. With a rumbling growl, the giant bear lowered its head and came shambling toward them.

Matthew and Kayak lay as still as death on the ice, their heads turned so that they could watch the bear. Matthew clutched the snow knife like a dagger and trembled inside as he felt the wet salt water seep up from the snow and soak his clothing.

The bear did not even pause to look at them as it stalked past. They saw it crouch down flat against the snow.

Matthew looked ahead and saw a seal's dark head, alert and motionless in the water. The bear was watching it intently.

Seeing nothing move to frighten it, the seal relaxed and let its back float to the surface as it drew a large breath of air into its lungs and dove beneath the ice in search of food.

The bear snaked forward cautiously until it reached the very edge of the ice where it had seen the seal. It reached out its paw and scratched against the ice.

The seal must have heard the sound beneath the water, and being curious, it once more raised its head above the surface. Seeing nothing but a yellowish heap of snow, it swam along the edge of the ice.

Suddenly, with lightning swiftness, the bear's right paw shot out and struck the seal's head a killing blow. The left paw lunged forward and hooked the seal inward with its great

curved claws. Using its sharp teeth, the bear easily hauled the huge seal up onto the ice pan.

Matthew watched as the bear started to devour its prey. "Be still," Kayak hissed through his teeth, now chattering from cold and fear.

At last Matthew saw that the big bear was finished eating. They watched it as it licked its lips and, like a huge cat, carefully wiped the seal fat from its mouth. It turned and shambled toward them, paused and sniffed the air. With its belly rumbling, it padded once more to the edge of the ice and slipped silently into the freezing water. Kayak sat up carefully as the bear swam south. It climbed up on another pan and ambled off, disappearing into the whirling snow.

Kayak rolled stiffly onto his hands and knees. Then crouching like an animal, he still watched the place where they had last seen the bear.

"I'm soaking wet." He trembled. "Get up," he called quietly to Matthew. "We're in trouble now, worse than we've ever been before."

The north wind seemed to press its freezing hand against Matthew's soaking clothes. It glazed them with a thin white sheath of ice as stiff as armor.

"Being wet will kill us sure," said Matthew, shivering like a dog. "What will we do?"

"I don't know. We'll have to think of something," said Kayak, and he went forward and felt inside the seal.

In the half darkness Matthew saw him cut the big artery and then pull the seal's heart out and set it on the ice.

"Quick; we've got to build a shelter. Work hard and it will warm you up a little. Move your arms and legs," Kayak said, "so your clothing won't freeze stiff."

On one end of their pan, sheets of ice the size of tabletops lay scattered like playing cards, forced there by the pressures of the rising tides. Kayak stood three upright, leaning them against one another. Then together they hauled two more into place to form a rough circle.

"Now gather snow," said Kayak. "We'll chink up the holes and cracks between the ice to make it strong. If the house should blow down with the wind tonight, we could never build a new one in the dark."

When their crude shelter was finished, it looked like nothing but another miserable pile of ice.

Kayak hurried away and returned with the frozen heart and the torn remains of the seal. He dragged them inside the little ice cave.

"It's just as cold in here," said Matthew. "We've only built a grave for ourselves."

"Unless we make a fire."

Kayak took the last matches carefully from his pocket and felt them. "They are soaking wet," he groaned, "and their heads have come off. Useless," he said, and flung them on the snow.

"Then we can't make a fire," cried Matthew through his chattering teeth. "We've got no lamp, no matches, and everything is soaking wet."

He saw Kayak take the snow knife and hack white chunks of seal fat from the inside of the carcass and set the frozen heart up in the snow like a small melon with its top cut open.

"Give me your little knife," he said, and with it he trimmed a narrow piece off the back tail of his shirt in a place where it was still dry.

"I hope I didn't lose it," Kayak said, searching his pockets with his freezing hands. "I've found it. My little piece of flint." He handed it to Matthew. "Hold it carefully. Don't drop it. It's worth more to us than gold."

Matthew had to help Kayak cut open the freezing front of his parka so that he could reach into his inside breast pocket to get his little carving file and a wad of fine steel wool.

"They're soaking wet," said Kayak. "Feel in your hip pockets. They're still dry. Can you find any pieces of lint or string?"

"Only this bit of string," said Matthew. "Nearly nothing."

"It may be enough. Roll it into a loose ball," Kayak said. "Now, Matthew, you do everything exactly the way I tell you. If you get your hands a little burned, don't mind it, understand me?"

Matthew wanted to laugh at him or cry. "How are you going to burn my hands? They're almost frozen."

He watched as Kayak struck the flint along the steel teeth of the little file. On the third try, sparks flew into the wet steel wool, and Matthew gasped in surprise as he saw the fine steel wire spark and begin to flare red and burn. The fire fizzled out.

"Now," said Kayak. "If I can light it again, you put the dry string in the spark with your finger. Do it right! My hands are freezing."

He struck the file again a dozen times before the steel wool sputtered into running sparks. Matthew held the wad of string against the tiny flame.

"Hold it there. Don't let it go out."

Kayak took the shirttail wick that he had made, rubbed it with seal fat, and held it in the tiny glow.

"Don't breathe on it just yet," he said, and waited.

Matthew felt a blister raising on his finger.

"Don't move the wick," Kayak ordered.

Slowly the seal fat sizzled; then a real flame burst into life. Kayak blew gently on it and then carefully stuffed one end of the wick into the well of glistening seal fat that he had stuffed into the open cavity of the frozen seal heart. The white, candlelike flame expanded as the seal fat softened and soaked upward into the homemade wick. Working as painstakingly as a surgeon, Kayak spread the cloth wick with his knife until the flame widened. He let out his breath in satisfaction when he

saw that at least three inches were burning hotly. The ice shelter reflected the joyful light. Matthew held his hands out, spreading his stiffened fingers in the life-giving warmth.

"I would never have believed," Matthew said quietly, "that you could make a lamp stove out of a frozen seal's heart and make wet steel wool burn."

With Matthew's knife Kayak cut strips of rich red seal meat from the carcass where the bear had scarcely touched it. Together they warmed the strips over the little lamp and ate them. Matthew thought he had never tasted anything so good.

"Now come on," Kayak demanded. "We go out of here and run around this little house as many times as you have fingers on your hands and as I have toes."

When they came inside once more, Matthew felt warm all over, as though the seal meat in his stomach were fuel on fire within him. His face and hands seemed to burn in the strong warmth and flickering light of Kayak's clever lamp.

Kayak unrolled the sleeping bags, which were only a little damp.

"Tonight we sleep resting on our knees and elbows," he said. "The snow's too wet for us to lie down."

Kayak pulled off his parka and beat it with the piece of broken bow until the sheath of ice fell away; then he put his parka on backwards.

"Why are you doing that?" asked Matthew.

"Because I'm going to pull up my hood and breathe into it. That way I catch all my body heat. You do the same. It's a trick I heard about from my mother's relatives. It might help to save our lives."

In the first light of morning, Matthew heard the ice grinding and had the uneasy sense that their whole house was slowly turning. Kayak pushed out the piece of ice that he had used to block the entrance.

"Look up there!" he yelled at Matthew.

Matthew, still crouching stiffly, looked up and in the sky saw a long, thin, white contrail.

"It's the big plane," said Kayak, "going into Frobisher Bay or maybe over to Greenland. No use waving your arms," he said in a discouraged voice. "It can never see you. It must be two miles high."

Matthew whirled around, dived back through the entrance, reached into his pack, and leaped outside holding the snowmobile's mirror.

"Give me the knife, the knife!" he shouted.

With its point he scratched a small cross in the coating on the back of the glass. Then, standing in the rays of the morning sun, he placed the mirror against his eye and looked through the cross for the plane. Through the tiny opening, he could see it moving through the cold blue sky like a slow silver bullet. He tipped the glass back and forth, back and forth, back and forth. He continued to watch the airplane through the hole until it was out of sight.

"What's that? Some kind of magic you are doing?" Kayak asked him.

"No," answered Matthew. "It was nothing, I guess. My dad told me that sometimes a pilot can see a mirror flashing from a very long way off."

"Well, it didn't make them turn around," said Kayak. "They're all just sitting up there warm and dry and comfortable, drinking coffee in the sky."

"I guess you're right," said Matthew, and he dropped the mirror in the snow.

"The ice, it's breaking in half," cried Kayak. "Quick!"

He grabbed Matthew by the arm and forced him to jump across the gap. As they watched, half of their shelter broke apart and slipped into the water.

"The sleeping bags and pack are gone," cried Matthew, and he lunged forward to grab the heart lamp and the seal remains.

Just before evening they took the few pieces of flat ice that had not slipped into the water and once more tried to build a shelter, though it was scarcely big enough to house a wolf. When they had finished stopping up the holes with soggy snow, Kayak stepped up, pulled off his wet mitt, and solemnly shook hands with Matthew.

"I wish we had known each other for a longer time," he said, "but I . . . I'm going to say good-by to you now, Matthew."

"Oh, don't say that." Matthew spoke in a choked voice.

"Why not?" said Kayak. "What is going to be — will be."

He started to pull the last remains of the seal into the crude little house and then suddenly changed his mind and began to circle round the house, pressing down hard, leaving a dark red trail of seal blood in the snow.

"Now you're trying magic, aren't you?" Matthew cried. "What good will that do?"

Kayak didn't answer him. The only sound was the moaning of the ice in the gathering gloom. Together they crawled inside and huddled side by side and ate some seal meat.

They slept, crouching like animals in the lamp's faint glow, until the first light of morning filtered through their icy shelter.

"What's that noise?" gasped Kayak. He cocked his head and listened.

"I don't hear anything," said Matthew. "Wait! Wait! Yes, I do. I do!"

They kicked away the thin ice door and scrambled out the narrow entrance.

Thug-thug-thug-thug-thug.

They heard a helicopter's engine driving the whirling blades through the glittering ice fog overhead.

"Look at us, we're here! Right here!" screamed Kayak.

"Come back! Don't go away!" they yelled together, waving their arms.

284

"It's going! It's going. It can't see us in the fog," said Kayak. "And we were in the house."

Thug-thug-thug-thug-thug.

"It's turning! It's coming back!" Matthew shouted and danced upon their pan of ice that was now shaped like a broken marble tombstone.

Then suddenly the helicopter loomed through the fog, hovered like a giant bird, and then swept toward them. Like a pair of partly frozen scarecrows, they danced a jig together.

"It's Charlie's helicopter!" Kayak yelled. "It's the *Waltzing Matilda.*"

285

They could see Charlie in the gleaming bubble, waving at them wildly. One door of the helicopter slid open, and Charlie flipped out a short rope ladder with metal rungs. Kayak staggered across the ice pan and grabbed it.

"I'm too weak to climb," he screamed at Matthew.

"I'll help you," Matthew shouted, and with his last remaining strength, he heaved Kayak onto the dangerously swaying ladder.

"Get in!" Charlie shouted over the roar of the engine.

Kayak grabbed Matthew by the hood of his parka and helped pull him up the ladder. Matthew slumped down behind them. There was little room inside.

"You two all right? Feet not frozen? No bones broken?" Charlie shouted.

They shook their heads.

He reached across Matthew, slid the door closed, and then gunned the engine. *Waltzing Matilda* whirled up above their little ice shelter. Kayak looked down for the last time at what had almost been their grave.

Charlie pointed down and said, "Whoever made that red circle around that ice shack of yours certainly saved your lives. I would never have found you without that red bull's eye. Where did you get the paint?"

"It's not paint," said Matthew. "He thought of the idea." Matthew nodded toward Kayak. "He saved us."

"It worked like magic," Charlie shouted. "And where did you get the mirror? The one you flashed at the airplane that was coming into Frobisher. If the flight crew hadn't seen that mirror shining, we'd never have found you. The aircraft and the rescue teams were looking for you inland. That mirror saved your lives!"

"Matthew thought of that," said Kayak.

"There's lots of people who are going to be mighty glad to

see you two. I imagine you could use a good hot meal. Here," he said and handed each of them a chocolate bar.

Kayak's hands were so weak and trembling from the climb up the ladder that he had to tear the wrapper with his teeth.

"Is my dad okay?" asked Matthew.

But Charlie had his earphones on and was speaking excitedly into his microphone and did not hear the question.

Matthew felt lightheaded as they began to rise through the dangerous ice fog. Beneath them spread the deadly puzzle of broken ice widening into dark open water to the south. He had never felt so glad to be away from any place in all his life. In the cabin's warmth his head nodded forward, and he fell into an exhausted sleep.

Twenty minutes later Matthew awoke as the helicopter landed in a whirling haze of snow crystals. Charlie turned off the engine, and the big blades stopped and hung silent in the harsh Arctic light of morning. Matthew, tears running down his cheeks, saw his father amid the stream of people running out of the hangar toward them.

Author

James Houston lived among the Inuit people on West Baffin Island for twelve years, and introduced Inuit art to the rest of the world. Recipient of many awards, he has written for adults and children. The story you have just read was taken from *Frozen Fire,* whose characters appear again in *Black Diamonds* and *Ice Sword.*

Summary Questions

Think about how Matthew and Kayak used objects in un-conventional ways in order to survive.

1. Where were Matthew and Kayak traveling? Why were they worried about their survival?
2. What did Matthew and Kayak build with blocks of ice?
3. What three uses did they find for the dead seal?
4. How did they use the mirror? Why was this object the right one to use in this situation?
5. "Necessity is the mother of invention" is an old saying. Explain what you think it means and how it can be applied to the boys' actions in the story.

The Reading and Writing Connection

It takes resourcefulness to make new uses out of everyday objects, as Matthew and Kayak did when they made a wick out of the tail of a shirt. Think about a time when the saying "Necessity is the mother of invention" could have been applied to you. Write several paragraphs about it. Explain what problem you faced and what resourceful means you used to solve it. Try to include some of the following words in your writing.

> **gloom**
> **devour**
> **treading**
> **bulk**

Arctic Words

Wherever you live, you use special words and phrases that describe what that place is like. Below are some words for land and water features that are found in parts of the Arctic.

bay   A body of water partly surrounded by land but having a wide outlet to the sea.

fjord[1]   A long, narrow inlet from the sea between steep cliffs or slopes.

glacier   A large mass of slowly moving ice, formed from snow packed together by the weight of snow above it.

ice cap   A mass of ice and snow that covers an area throughout the year.

sound   A long body of water, wider than a strait or channel, connecting larger bodies of water.

tide crack   A crack caused by the tide separating the shore ice from the sea ice.

tundra   A cold, treeless area of arctic regions, having only low-growing mosses, lichens, and stunted shrubs as plant life.

---

[1]**fjord** (fyôrd)

Which of the Arctic words that you have just read describe land areas? Which refer to the sea?

Which of the words and phrases describe features that may also be found in other parts of the world?

Read each of the following sentences. Choose the arctic word or phrase from the preceding list that best completes each sentence. Be prepared to discuss your answers.

1. Reindeer and caribou graze on the _____.
2. Icebergs are formed when huge chunks of ice break off from the moving _____ as it meets the sea.
3. A _____ in the ice separated the travelers from the safety of the shore.
4. The small ship made its way carefully between the steep walls of the _____.
5. The _____ covering most of Greenland is two miles thick in some places.
6. The boys paddled their canoe through the _____ that connected the two bays.

FOG

by Carl Sandburg

The fog comes
on little cat feet.

It sits looking
over harbor and city
on silent haunches
and then moves on.

On Little Cat Feet

by Lee Kingman

Fishing for lobsters was hard, dirty work, and Uncle
Merlin gave one order after another. Would Jo be
able to work with him all summer?

The day began gray-colored and raw-cold, not promising for Jo's first day on her summer job — which was to be her great-uncle's seeing-eye girl.

"What duds you got on?" was Uncle Merlin's greeting.

"Dad's old shirt and my old pants."

The old man pinched the cloth with fingers so thickened and scarred it was surprising that he could feel anything with them. "Yacht club stuff. You'll freeze. Bring a sweater. There's oilskins and rubber aprons on board."

Jo led the way from the cottage to the cove below. Uncle Merlin stepped carefully, his knee-high rubber boots thunking and swishing with each step. "The dinghy — that little boat — is tied to the third ladder on the pier. Now, Jo, let's get things straight. You're the crew, the lookout. I'll depend on you to spot buoys and on-coming boats and to gaff things. I'm the captain. I give orders. You act. Quick. That saves time and accidents. You have everything to learn about boats, and we have a lot to learn about each other. I'll try to be patient. You try to learn fast. Deal?"

"What kind of a deal was that?" Jo wondered. He expected her to be a speed-learner while he just offered to be patient? She tried to see the warm, fun-loving uncle her father remembered, but his impatient gruffness put her off. She wasn't exactly afraid of him, yet she worried about how demanding he would be and how much his "failed" eyes could take in. She wondered how much of the unexpected ache in her stomach came from anxiety about being seasick or frightened out on the water and how much from her increasing uneasiness about putting her trust in a brusque, half-blind old man. *Whatever* had made her think that she, a fourteen-year-old girl who grew up in Ohio and had never seen the ocean before, could help a seventy-year-old man with his lobstering anyway? Uncle Merlin's offer to share the profits — that was the *big* whatever, one that could help out her family as well as her great uncle. Her notions that the sea was calm and wonderful to be on and that lobstering could be fun were suspect now that she had seen the ocean and the boat.

When his uncle had phoned to tell Dad about his problem — that he needed help on the *Trudy* — and to ask if Jo's older brother Roger could spend the summer helping him, Dad remembered how much he'd liked lobstering. He'd helped Uncle Merlin summers while he went to college. He said Roger would have a great time. "And Uncle Merlin says his legs and his back are still fine. He just needs young eyes. If Roger will provide the sight, he'll give us half his summer's profits. What do you say, Rog? You know how much a good hunk of money coming in would help us all." Roger agreed to go, but two days before he was to leave, he broke his leg. Dad, who was already counting on Roger's earnings, was terribly upset.

"Let me go!" Jo pleaded. She'd been listening to Dad reminisce about summers at the cove. He remembered dazzling days of sunshine and sparkling ocean and his turning a tan so deep it took all winter to fade away. "If all Uncle Merlin needs is my eyes, I can help him."

Dad had made a summer by the sea — and a terrific tan — sound so glamorous that Jo longed to be there. On the phone he had persuaded Uncle Merlin that his great-niece, Joanne, was strong and capable and resourceful.

That did it. Uncle Merlin said, "Come." He gave instructions for her to take the bus to Boston, the train to Cape Ann, and a taxi from the station to his house by the cove.

Then yesterday, in the late afternoon, seen from Uncle Merlin's porch, the ocean confronted her as a vast, wet, unfriendly space, and the great waves pounding with unceasing blows on the rocks made her shiver at their sound and force. But her father expected Jo to be a help — not to run home in fear — and she was the one who had insisted on

coming. So here she was about to embark in a twenty-two-foot boat onto that huge ocean.

"Take a look over the seawall," ordered Uncle Merlin. "What's the water like?"

"What's it *like*?" She didn't dare answer "Wet."

"Choppy? White-caps? Long swells? Never mind. I can feel where the wind's coming from and hear how light the surf sounds. So there shouldn't be any white curls on the waves out in the bay. Right? Good day for you to start."

His hand found the top of the ladder. He climbed down, caught the dinghy below with his boot-toe, and then stepped confidently in. "Let that bait bucket down on that rope," he called. "Scared of heights?"

Jo didn't want to admit she was. Leaning over to play the bucket down the fifteen-foot drop made her dizzy. Then, white-knuckled, she eased onto the ladder, clutched its slippery rungs, and slowly descended. "Step in easy, untie the dinghy, sit down, and we're off," the captain ordered.

"I can see shapes and tell light from dark," Uncle Merlin said as he deftly paddled with a broken oar between a white speedboat and a dark-hulled lobster boat. From habit he knew where to put his hand under the bow of the *Trudy* to unhook a mooring line; where to snub the dinghy against the stern so the girl could climb on board; and where to hook the dinghy to the mooring and release the *Trudy* from it. On board, too, his movements were measured by sureness of habit — showing her where to check the gas gauge so they wouldn't run out of fuel, checking the position of the outboard motor, adjusting the choke, turning on the motor, and catching its "Sputt-sputt-tut-tut-tut-tutter" in a "Whoooooom-whooom-whooom" as the boat began to move.

"All right, Jo Eyes. What's ahead? Call it like the clock. Boat at three o'clock or speedboat coming up fast at ten o'clock. It's not nautical but it's quick. And yell *cut engine* if I should stop in a hurry."

Once she'd directed Uncle Merlin beyond the granite breakwater and into the bay, Jo looked around the untidy boat. The filthy empty buckets were almost as pungent as the full bucket of fish heads. There were sponges and rags, a pump, and a hose she kicked out of the way so Uncle Merlin wouldn't trip. She made herself pick up a dead fish and throw it over before he slipped on it.

"Housekeeping?" he asked. "Smells bother you? This may not be the right job for you."

There was a challenge in his voice. He'd gotten her into this, yet he almost seemed to be goading her about it. Jo was annoyed. He complained about his failing eyes. Did he want her to fail too? Perhaps it was hard for him to depend on a great-niece. She took a deep breath, expecting a lungful of the fresh Ipswich Bay air her father had recalled — "That wonderful sea air!" Instead she choked on fumes from the motor.

Uncle Merlin cut the engine and let the *Trudy* drift while he sent Jo crawling out over the deck to the bow to display the wooden marker, painted white with a blue cross, that floated above each pot. "That identifies me with my pots to the Fish and Game guys," he explained. He showed her the lobster gauge — a metal device that measured the lobster from the back of the eye to the end of the shell of its body. A lobster that didn't measure up was called a short. Those big enough were called keepers. "There's a big fine for taking shorts," he said. "Big enough to wipe out your half of the profits if you take shorts. So watch it, Jo."

Jo hoped all she had to do was watch it — not actually pick up a lobster to measure it. "How many lobsters do you get each time you haul the pots?"

"Out of eighty pots, maybe a hundred lobsters or more. But if I get thirty keepers out of that, I'll be lucky."

Eighty pots! A hundred lobsters! Jo's hopes for only two or three hours a day on the water sank. The best she could hope for, if the sun ever came out, was that great tan and a good profit.

The *Trudy* drifted among the thousands of buoys that bobbed on the surface, scattered as randomly and colorfully as confetti. "Some fellows run three or four hundred pots. I used to," he said. "I'll go easy on you today. We'll just check my 'east forty.'"

Jo spotted one of his buoys. "At two o'clock!"

Uncle Merlin swung the boat to the right, cut the engine, and handed her the gaff. It had a metal hook on a long wood handle. "Catch the buoy, and I'll haul her in." She swiped and missed. He put the boat in reverse. They tried again. This time she caught the buoy, and he took hold of the rope, pulling it over a pulley that hung from an iron pipe. He hauled on the

rope until the trap burst through the surface; then he yanked the trap on board. "What have we got?"

"Just some yucky-looking fish in a red net bag."

"That's the bait. Lobsters love it." He threw the trap over.

The next trap held a lobster and a flounder that he told her to keep for bait. He couldn't see well enough to untangle the lobster from its grip on the bait bag. "Grab it behind the claws," he told Jo, "and pull."

The creature waved one of its ugly claws and flared its tail. "I've got to do this," Jo told herself. "I hate it, but I've got to." She clutched the mottled-green carapace and found it smooth and firm, not scaly nor slimy. It didn't feel so dreadful, but the claws were weapons until Uncle Merlin showed her how to slip elastic bands over them with lobster pliers.

"Your first catch, young lady." He gave her a jolting slap on the back. "You can eat it for supper if you like."

With loathing she threw the creature into the bucket. "Never!"

Uncle Merlin laughed. "Too bad. They say crustaceans are gourmet food — except restaurants wreck 'em with crumbs and herbs and stuff. When you get sick of hot dogs and cold cuts, I'll boil you a lobster. You eat it hot out of the shell, and you'll change your mind."

They hauled thirty pots that day. Jo missed spotting ten. The next day the sun came out, and at last she was warm while they pulled the "west forty." The third day Uncle Merlin predicted she could find all his pots. He said he wouldn't mind being out all day to haul them. She did find them all! All morning the sun sparkled on the ocean, making the facets of the surface dazzle so the buoys were hard to distinguish. Her face was dry and red. Her hands were wet and red. Her eyes ached, and her back ached. Then the wind changed, and insistent waves bounded against the boat, bouncing it, so she often missed gaffing the buoys. She realized the sunlight was dimming and pulled on a sweatshirt. She forgot to keep an eye on the traffic. It was her great-uncle's keen hearing that made him yell, "What o'clock?"

Jo looked up to see a large speedboat headed for them, driven full out. "Three o'clock!" Uncle Merlin spun the wheel hard away. The speedboat swooshed past. Its driver, laughing with friends, was not paying attention to where he was going.

The *Trudy* was hit and tossed violently by the series of battering waves thrown up by the speeding boat. Jo lost her balance and fell, hitting her face against the edge of the iron pulley. Blood gushed from her nose. The gaff was loosened from her grip with the force of an arrow. The hook just missed Uncle Merlin as it flew overboard.

"Reckless driver!" he yelled. "I hope your propeller gets fouled, but not in my lines."

"The gaff! I've lost it."

"It'll float. How about you? I heard a whack."

"I don't know." She gasped as his roughened hands explored her face, feeling her temples, tracing the bones in her cheeks and her nose.

"Nothing broken," he announced. "Wet a sponge in that cold salt water, and hold it on your nose."

"What about the gaff?"

"I'll buy another. You know, people think lobstermen are rich, but they don't know about our lost gaffs, lost pots, lost lines, and gas costing like gold. How many keepers we got today?"

"Eighteen. Forty-four throw-backs." She snuffled into the sponge. Its stench was so dreadful it kept her from feeling faint when she saw how much blood still oozed from her nose.

"Same thing happened to your pa," Uncle Merlin said, trying to comfort her. "Only he got two black eyes."

Jo sponged at her tears. Everything hurt so — but she had one satisfaction. Uncle Merlin couldn't see that she was crying. Why that was important to her she didn't know. Yet it was! What was she doing here — feeling sore and bruised and exhausted — helping an old man, who shouldn't even be out in a boat, earn a living? Helping him help her family, she reminded herself — but that wasn't enough. She wasn't helping him that much. Lost gaffs. Lost time. She knew he was barely making back his gas money because it took her so long to find and gaff his pots. Almost anyone else, one of those kids that hung around the cove, could be more help to him. She should tell Uncle Merlin that this just wasn't working out for either of them.

Uncle Merlin had let the *Trudy* drift while Jo kept wringing a sponge out in the cold water. "Stay still. We'll go in." He turned the key, but the motor didn't catch. He gave the gas line a squeeze and adjusted the choke. It still didn't catch. "Running so slow all the time fouls the plugs," he muttered. "If I could just see to clear those plaguy things."

He couldn't, though. And Jo, who did know a wrench from a hammer but had never been confronted by the puzzling insides of an outboard motor, suspected she would only make things worse if she tried to help. Besides, she was feeling woozy. Suddenly she had to stretch out flat. She closed her eyes and concentrated on not throwing up.

She listened to the old man feeling about in the tool box, blaming the motor, the wrong wrench, his lack of adequate sight, and the uncaring driver whose speeding boat had caused their problems. The one person he didn't blame was Jo, who, as lookout, should have warned him to take the *Trudy* out of the way in time.

The boat steadied down to a shallow rocking motion. She was drained of energy. She fell asleep.

When she woke, it was to find Uncle Merlin sitting beside her. On his tired face was a look of great concern. Her nose had stopped bleeding, and she struggled to sit up. It was then that she saw that not only was the motor not fixed, but the *Trudy* was encased by a gray mist. At first she blinked, wondering if her eyes, like Uncle Merlin's, had failed.

"We're in a fog!" Uncle Merlin told her. "It came in just like Sandburg wrote — on little cat feet. Not a sound. I knew it must be fog when the whites turned gray and the darks turned gray and it all turned damp. Here — put that oilskin on. I just laid it over you. Stay as warm as you can. We're out here drifting because, old fool that I am, I didn't look to see that the rope at the other end of the anchor was securely tied before I threw it over. It wasn't."

How naturally he said he hadn't *looked to see,* as if he still expected to see everything if only he paid attention. That made Jo feel even worse. "I'm sorry I fell asleep. What can we do now?"

"Wait for the fog to lift and signal for help. I was toying with buying one of those CBs for emergencies, but I didn't. Too late to mourn that now — but you can blast that horn now and then. Maybe someone will hear it." He handed her the horn, which looked like a metal funnel stuck into a rubber bulb. When she squeezed it, it made a mooing "Oooooh-aaaah" sound.

"Where are we? Off the cove?"

Uncle Merlin sat listening, and Jo became aware of the sounds that seemed to sandpaper away at the silence, rasping the edge of it: the slip, slip, slap of small waves on the hull; the swash, crash, swash of waves farther away reaching the shore; the scrabbling of lobsters in the buckets; Uncle Merlin's sudden sigh; a metallic CLANG-click, CLANG-click that kept up insistently.

"Hear that bell buoy?" Uncle Merlin asked. "That's off Halibut Point. Now if we pick up another bell that sounds sort of clangety-cluck, we'll be drifting around the Cape; and when we hear the foghorn on Thatcher's Island, we'll know where we are."

"Headed out to sea?"

"I didn't say that, did I?"

"No. Not quite."

"You just lie down, Jo. I'll tell you a story about your pa when he spent his first summer lobstering with me."

One story led to another and another. The fog turned even more opaque as day turned to night. Jo's head ached; her nose throbbed. The damp wooden deck tortured her bones. Even droplets of moisture seemed to have a burdensome weight. The bell buoys gave stereophonic clangs as the *Trudy* drifted between them. Uncle Merlin fell asleep mid-tale and woke to carry on with it. How uncomfortable he must be, Jo realized — yet he kept on telling her stories, talking, talking, keeping her from panic as she heard the vibrating blast of the foghorn change from its remote moan to frightening immediacy and then dwindle into desolate mourning, farther and farther away. At last they both slept from exhaustion.

When Jo woke next, she found the fog had lifted. The sun wasn't up, but there was a luminous brilliance to the sky and an intensity of light at the eastern horizon. She pulled herself up and looked around. Behind the *Trudy* was the shoreline. She could see houses — far away and miniaturized — but there would be people in them, perhaps even looking out to sea with binoculars. There would be people setting out in big

boats and little boats to fish. The day would come alive, and she and Uncle Merlin would be rescued. She knew it; and until that happened Jo knew she was safe on the *Trudy* — that smelly but sturdy boat — and with Great-Uncle Merlin, who was just waking up.

She grabbed his hand to help him, and suddenly he seemed as new to her as the morning. He wasn't a stupid old man who should give up his lobstering and his way of life. He was brave to keep on, using every sense he had to the utmost. He had spent the night telling her about his world — a world her father had loved too — and he was offering her a chance to make it a new world of her own. That world could at times be uncomfortable, hard, dirty, frustrating, and exasperating — but it could also provide wonders: like the great red sun flaring up from the pearl-pink water; like the swift curve of a tern gracing the flowing sky; like Uncle Merlin's smile as he felt the warmth on his face.

"Hungry?" he asked.

"I could even eat a lobster."

Author

Lee Kingman, a longtime resident of Cape Ann, Massachusetts, has written many books for children and young adults. A number of them portray her experiences on the Cape and her interest in its Scandinavian heritage. Ms. Kingman has also been an editor and reviewer. She shares with her family an interest in graphic arts and design.

Summary Questions

Think about how Jo's feelings about her summer on the coast changed during the course of the story.

1. How did Jo feel about Uncle Merlin at the beginning of the story?
2. How did Jo feel about Uncle Merlin by the end of the story?
3. What experiences and events in the story made Jo change her mind about her uncle?
4. Tell what you think will happen during the rest of Jo's summer with Uncle Merlin. Be sure to explain why you think the summer will or will not be a success.

The Reading and Writing Connection

In this story, Jo learned to appreciate and enjoy a new environment—one that was very different from any she had experienced before. Think about what Jo saw, felt, smelled, and heard during her time on the water with her uncle. Then think of an experience you have had at a river, lake, or ocean beach. Write a poem expressing the sights, sounds, and feelings you experienced there. Try to include some of the following words in your poem.

> **remin___**
> **confro___ed**
> **opaque**
> **resourceful**

Propaganda Techniques

Some things you read or hear are meant to persuade you to be for or against something or someone. Things written or said to persuade you are called propaganda. The writer hopes the reader will favor certain things, people, or ideas. To make wise decisions, you must be able to tell when someone is using propaganda techniques to influence you.

Bandwagon

One kind of propaganda is called bandwagon. The name comes from political campaigns of long ago. A parade for a person running for office was often led by a band that rode on a large wagon pulled by horses. As the wagon went slowly by, people would climb on the bandwagon if they were for the person. They hoped that others would climb on, too, to show their support. Getting on the bandwagon came to mean doing what other people were doing.

Someone who uses this technique hopes to get you to do something by telling you that many other people are doing it. Study the following example to see how the writer has used the bandwagon technique:

Thousands are switching to Squeaky-Clean.

Do they know something that you don't?

The writer hopes that you will buy the soap because you are told that others are buying it. However, unlike times when people could be seen getting on the bandwagon, you cannot be sure that others are doing what the writer says. Although the statement is given as fact, it may not be true. Even if it is true, this soap may still not be the right soap for you.

Testimonial

Another propaganda technique is called testimonial. Here, the writer uses the words of a famous person to persuade you. Along with the words, you will usually see a picture of the person. Read the following ad:

Gloria Sweet, famous actress and model, says, "When I run, I always wear No-Slide shoes. They run away from the rest."

The shoes may be good, but your decision to buy them should be based on what you know about them, not what Gloria Sweet says. Being a famous actress and model does not make her an expert on running shoes. Remember also that people who give testimonials to sell something are almost always paid to do so.

Transfer

Transfer is another propaganda technique. Sometimes the faces but not the names of famous people may be used. No direct quotation from the person will be used. Most transfer ads use professional models. These beautiful people look as if they are having a wonderful time. The writer hopes that you admire these people and will transfer your feelings to the advertised product. Look at the following example:

When winning is important, go with the winner:

the Windup Watch

Again, you should not be guided by the picture of someone you admire, famous or not. You need more information before deciding to buy a watch.

Repetition

Another widely used propaganda technique is repetition. Read the following ad:

The name of the person running for office is repeated four times. The writer hopes that repeating the name will cause you to remember it and to vote for the senator. However, the ad gives no information that would help you to make a wise decision when you vote. You should know how the senator plans to meet these goals before deciding to vote.

Emotional Words

Sometimes writers try to lead you to act or think in a certain way by using emotional words to make you feel strongly about something or someone. Can you pick out the emotional words in the following ad for a sports car?

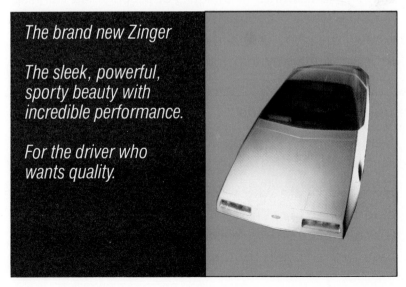

The writer hopes, of course, that these words will persuade the reader to buy a Zinger without further thought. The wise reader wants much more information than the ad gives.

Being Aware of Propaganda

From the previous examples, you have learned that advertising often contains propaganda. Do not think, however, that all advertising uses propaganda to deceive or mislead you. Many ads provide a useful service by bringing to your attention needed goods or services. Ads are also used to tell you about helpful organizations and worthy causes. Other ads might ask you to help prevent forest fires or air pollution.

Propaganda techniques can also be found in newspaper and magazine articles written by persons who want to persuade you to support particular ideas. For example, you might read a newspaper article about plans to tear down a building and make a parking lot. If the article contains only favorable statements, you might decide that it was written to persuade rather than to inform.

Learning to recognize techniques of propaganda will help you to think wisely for yourself. When you know that propaganda is being used, you can then decide whether you want to think or act in the way that you are being encouraged to.

Recognizing Propaganda

Read each of the examples below and decide which technique is used.

1. More people are watching WBX News Tonight than ever before. Tune in.
2. For the most restful, relaxing, soothing sleep that you have ever enjoyed, try the marvelous Miller Mattress.

3. Rough Cut lawn mowers are the very best. Rough Cut starts easily. Rough Cut runs smoothly. Rough Cut lasts and lasts. Rough Cut — you owe it to your lawn.
4. A picture of a famous basketball player throwing a piece of paper into a trash can has this caption: "This city belongs to all of us. Pitch in. Keep it clean."
5. A happy young couple is pictured beside their new camper, with this caption: "Haven't you waited long enough? Be good to yourself."

Skill Summary

- Propaganda is ideas or information meant to persuade people to think or act in certain ways.
- Five common kinds of propaganda are bandwagon, testimonial, transfer, repetition, and emotional words.
- Propaganda is often used to persuade you to buy something, but it may be used for many different purposes.
- When you recognize propaganda, you can decide more wisely how you yourself want to think and act.

From Idea to Air:
Making a
Television Documentary

by Salem Mekuria
as told to Elizabeth Owen

A television show that will take an hour to watch takes months to make. What happens during those months?

Salem Mekuria is associate producer of a documentary program produced by a public broadcasting television network. In this interview she describes how a show is put together from the initial idea to the finished program.

Question: How do you decide on a topic for a show?

I think what usually happens is that an idea strikes the producer — either something in the news or something from books or magazines. Or there may be a topic the producer has been dying to produce. If not, we spend a lot of time browsing through many, many periodicals and books. We consult with the executive producer about some priority topics for the series. We talk to people about what is currently of interest to them.

Most often, we compile a list of possible topics and do some preliminary research on each one. Questions we ask at this point include: Is this something we are really interested in doing? If we aren't, we won't be able to make it interesting to the audience. *Can* we do it? Is it something people want to know about? Is it current? Will it still be interesting a year from now? Is there enough to say about it to hold people's attention for a whole hour?

One of the main questions to ask is whether there will be anything interesting to look at on the screen. Many beautiful topics cannot be done well on television because they are too abstract. All you can do with them on the air is talk about them. There would be nothing to look at. You can't just show people sitting and talking into the camera for a whole hour — what we call "talking heads" — so a major question is what can be pictured.

Other things also have to be considered. Who are the people who know about the subject, and can they talk to us? Many defense topics are top secret. Other subjects may be too sensitive or too personal. So we keep eliminating until we have selected a topic that will work. Once we have decided on the topic, we are ready to start producing the show.

Question: How long does the production take?

The average is about six months. A show we started working on in June might be scheduled to air the following January.

Question: What happens during those six months of production?

There are several stages, each with its own set of tasks. The first stage is in some ways the most critical of all.

Research: This stage takes about eight weeks. During this time, we do intensive research on the subject and decide how it will be presented. If we don't do everything right in the research period, it doesn't come out right in the show. We have the motto that if anything at all can go wrong in the filming, it will. It is

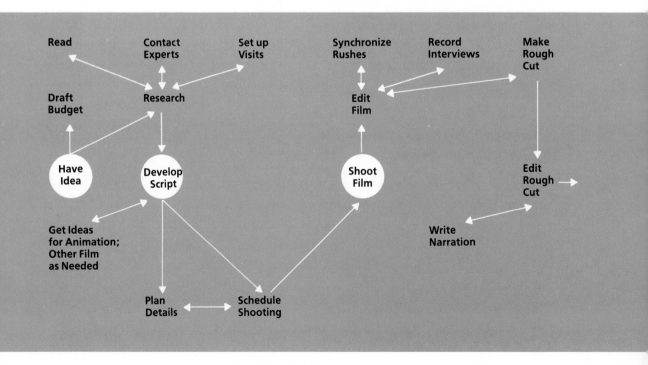

our job in the research period to see that nothing *can* go wrong.

First, we gather as much information about the subject as we possibly can. We read books, periodicals, newspapers, records of congressional hearings, research reports, and any other sources we can find in print. We inundate ourselves with information and live with the subject full-time. The purpose is to identify the major issues and questions surrounding the topic. Then we talk to the people who wrote the books and articles and did the research — the experts in the field. They help us to understand the critical issues. They recommend other things to read and people to talk with.

During this time, we are figuring out how we will deal with the subject — what we will include in our story and how we will tell it. This becomes the treatment of the show — what the program will look like. All the background research must be done carefully because once we have a treatment and start filming, we are locked in to our choices of people, issues, and places.

Steps in documentary production

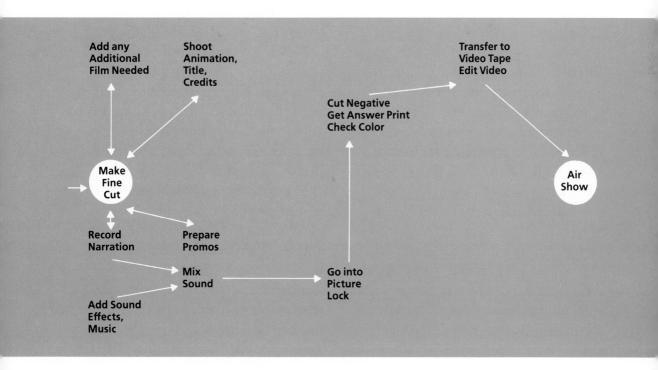

One of the decisions we have to make is whether to use video tape or film. Each has its own advantages and drawbacks. With video, you can look at the tape as soon as you have finished recording it. You get instant feedback. If you have missed something or something isn't right, you have a chance to do it over right then. Because film has to be developed, you don't see the results until later, and by that time it may be too late. Also, since our final product is transferred to video before putting it on the air, when we use video we know that what we see is what we will get. With film you have to have more faith.

However, the video equipment we must use for our show is very heavy and bulky. I remember one show when we lugged twenty-five pieces of luggage all across the country for eighteen days. Video is also difficult to use in some locations, such as in a small boat.

Another drawback to video is that there are so many sizes of tape. Film is more standard. This is important because many of our shows are bought for viewing in other countries. Since 16-mm film is the same the world over, it is more exportable.

During the first eight weeks, we are also thinking about a budget for the show. Once we have a treatment, we know where we will be going, whom we will interview, and how many feet of film we will use. We know how much the show will cost. When the budget for the show has been approved, we are locked in to all those decisions that we made in the first eight weeks. That's why we have to do our research so thoroughly and carefully. If we miss something important then, it may mean going over budget to go back and pick it up later.

Getting Ready to Film: This step is much more complicated than people may realize, and involves many, many hours on the telephone — making appointments, making reservations, making schedules. All the people and all the necessary equipment must be brought together in the right place at the right time.

Every last detail must be planned ahead of time and checked and rechecked. For example, if we need to rent cars, we have to be sure to get station wagons because the equipment won't fit into compact cars. We have to be sure that when we get where we are going, there will be

Filming underwater

dollies available for moving the equipment around. You cannot get to a location just a few minutes before you are due to start filming and find that you don't have something you need. You can't get behind schedule. You know that if one thing goes wrong, a lot of other things will go wrong that day.

For example, suppose you have just arrived in a city and have to film two people at opposite ends of town. You have an hour to get from one appointment to the next, and it takes an hour to set up, and the second person you are filming has to leave at three o'clock. If something doesn't go right in the first filming, and you don't get to the next one until one-thirty, you've lost half an hour of precious set-up time. That's why all those seemingly minor, minute things must have been taken care of before you leave home.

Filming the Show: I'm going to describe what happens when we use film. Some of the technical details would be different with video, but the major steps we go through would be similar.

If our film location is nearby, we usually take our own film crew. If we are filming in a distant city, we may hire a local film crew. The film crew consists of three people: the camera person, who does the actual filming; the assistant camera person, who assists with the lighting and changes the film; and the sound person.

As part of the research, we have identified the people we want to interview on camera. Usually we have the interview in the person's home or office. We don't like to show the person just sitting there trying not to look uncomfortable during the introduction, so we set up a little scene with the person walking into the office, or something. This gives the narrator a chance to explain who the person is. That's one way our show is somewhat different from other shows that use interviews on camera. In our show, you do not see or hear the person who asks the questions. Instead, we use an off-camera narrator whose voice is added later.

We usually just like the interview to flow naturally, without too many interruptions. After the person has finished talking, we sometimes do retakes of some

Shooting an interview

parts of the interview. Since we do not use an on-camera interviewer, we do not have to retake the person asking the question as well as the person answering the question. That saves time and film. At the end of the interview, we film what are called *cutaways* and *wallpaper*. These are general fillers.

When people talk, on or off film, they pause occasionally to collect their thoughts, or they may put in short phrases such as "Hmmm" and "You know." This is not usually noticeable in every-day conversation, but it does slow down the pace on television. We know that we are going to have to cut these pieces out of the final film. We need to be able to show something else where these cuts have occurred. We can't just let the screen go black, not for even 1/60 of a second, or cause what is known as a *jump cut*. It would be very jarring to the eye. What we do in this case is show something else on the screen while the person continues to talk under it. In that way, we can take out the pauses and false starts from the speech without interrupting the picture. We also know that it is not very interesting visually just to watch those talking heads for a whole hour. There has to be something else to look at from time to time. We also use the fillers as transitions from one thought or person to another. These fillers are better if they are somehow related to the issue being discussed.

For these reasons, while we are filming we take a lot of extra shots that we can use later to fill in the gaps. We cannot get back to the editing room and say, "Now, how do I get from this place to that place? I need an extra five seconds of film that I don't have." Those five seconds could be very important, so before we stop filming we make

sure that we have them. We cannot go back several months later and get them.

We use some of these extra shots to give the viewer a sense of what the person does. For example, a scientist might be filmed working in the lab.

When we leave the film location, we will have taken about ten to fifteen times as much film as we will actually use. This gives us room in which to pick out the very best shots to put on the air. It also ensures that we will have those crucial five-second pieces when we need them.

At the end of every day of filming, we send that day's film to our laboratory to be developed, and they make them into prints called *rushes*. The rushes are sent back to the studio, where an assistant editor synchronizes the sound with the picture and has it ready for us to edit when we return from location.

Preliminary Editing: When we get back to the studio, we look at the rushes for a few days to see whether we got what we set out to get. After about four weeks of playing around with different ways of putting the rushes together, we make what

Editing the picture

we call a *rough cut* of the show. The rough cut is about twenty to thirty minutes longer than the show will be. We show the rough cut to the executive producer, who makes suggestions about what to keep, what to drop, and what to add. Any reorganizing of our original script is done at this time.

We also plan for any other kinds of film footage we may need to add. For example, if we were doing a show with something in it about circulation of the blood, we would need to show how that works. We would have a short animated film made to illustrate that part of the show.

Adding the Sound: While this is going on, work is being done on the sound that will go along with the picture. Any music that will be heard is recorded on tape, along with any sound-effects that are needed. For example, if the picture shows cars passing by, the sounds of passing cars would be recorded on the sound-effects track.

Choosing the correct sound can be very important. In one

show we needed to have the sounds that are made by a certain kind of seal. We had recordings of sounds made by different seals, and to us they all sounded the same — we thought they sounded like sheep or goats. We spent a lot of time on the telephone with seal experts, having them listen to a seal and then tell us what kind of seal makes that sound. If we had used the wrong one on the show, someone somewhere would say, "But that animal doesn't sound like that!" This is the kind of checking and rechecking we must do. We have to make sure that every detail is exactly right.

By now, we will have written a script for the narrator. We hire a professional narrator who comes to the studio, usually for one day, to record the narration on tape. This may be done either while the narrator watches the picture, or by timing the narration exactly so that it matches the picture.

At this stage, all the sound is recorded on 16-track tape. Later all the tracks will be merged together into one or two tracks, just as you will hear it on the air.

After these steps are completed, perhaps in two weeks, we make what is called a *fine cut*. If

it is approved, we go into what we call *picture lock* — locking the picture and the sound together. Up until now, all our work on the film has been on copies. The original negative is still at the film lab. Now directions are sent to the film lab, and the original negative is cut exactly to our specification.

When the lab has cut the negative, they make one print and send it to us. This is the *answer print*. Its purpose is to enable us to be sure that all the color in the final film looks the way it should. We project the answer print on a large screen and examine it very carefully. A person with a trained eye might see that in one shot someone on the screen looked a little too pink. The answer print would be sent back to the film lab with directions to correct the color.

The *sound mixing* can be done either before or after the negative is cut. The sound mixer adjusts the sound. For example, you may not have noticed that every room has its own sounds — what are called *room tones*. Most shows have scenes in more than one room, each of which has different room tones. It is the sound mixer's job to make sure that the room tones match when the show is released. This can be done by taking out one set of room tones and adding another.

All the sounds must be at the correct level. If there are sound effects in the background, they must not be loud enough to interfere with what someone is saying. The sound cannot be too loud one minute and too soft the next. The sound mixer adjusts the levels.

The sound mixing takes about two days. All the sounds from the sixteen tracks are synchronized with the talking heads track, and mixed down to one or two channels, just the way you will hear it when the program goes on the air. You may never have realized that the sound you hear came from sixteen different sources. Now everything is transferred to one-inch video tape, and the show is almost finished. We put the title at the beginning and the credits at the end. The program is complete, but there is still work to be done before it goes on the air.

Adjusting the sound

Post Production: At this time, our post-production department goes to work on the *promos*. These are the announcements you see on television: "Watch for such and such." We choose the most exciting, appealing shots from the show and write copy to go with them.

Then we take the program and the promos to the final step. We put the title and the series opening at the beginning, the names and titles (IDs) of the talking heads in the body, and the production credits at the end.

We also send printed transcripts of our shows to people who write to ask for them. The transcripts have to be printed before the show is aired so that they can be mailed out as soon as the requests start to come in.

Then we write the letters. We must thank all the people who helped us with the show. We notify them when and where the show will appear. All this needs to be done as promptly as possible. It is an important part of our job in producing the show.

By the time the show gets on the air, it has been six months in preparation. Many people, with many different kinds of skills, have been involved.

Question: How did Salem Mekuria get involved?

My background is basically journalism, political science, and educational media. I had started out to be in education, but became interested in media. I had a little experience in commercial television as a volunteer and an intern and did some free-lance work.

I originally came here as a secretary. I had a master's degree in educational media, and I knew that what I really wanted was to be in production, but the secretary's job was the one that was open. It was a way of getting into educational television. I later became a production assistant and then associate producer. It's a competitive field, and a person would not expect to come in and be hired as an associate producer immediately.

On a show like this, you need the ability to read and absorb a great deal of information quickly, to find out what is important in a field, and to know what questions to ask and of whom.

One of the wonderful things about this job is that it is so stimulating. Every topic we do is something new, so it's like a whole world opening up every time we do another show. It's fascinating.

I had always wanted to be involved in media, but hadn't found the way I wanted to do it in commercial television. Here I am doing exactly what I wanted to do. I love it.

Author

Elizabeth Owen has always been interested in reading and writing children's books. She taught elementary school for a number of years, and has taught college undergraduate and graduate courses in reading and children's literature.

Summary Questions

Consider all the steps involved in the complex process of producing a television documentary. Think about what is most important about each step, and why.

1. What crucial steps must a documentary filmmaker take before filming can begin?
2. Why does the author describe the research stage as "in some ways the most critical of all"?
3. What are some of the complications involved in setting up the filming schedule?
4. What important steps must be taken after the filming is completed?
5. Which of the steps do you think would be the most interesting? Why?
6. What are some of the things that must be kept in mind when adding the sound? Which of these do you think would be the most noticeable if it were neglected? Why do you think this?
7. Pretend that a friend of yours says, "I'd like to make a documentary film. It seems so easy —much easier than writing a research paper or a book report." Explain how you would answer your friend. Give examples to support your answer.

The Reading and Writing Connection

Imagine that you have just finished producing a television documentary. Now you need to write promos to advertise it. Tell what the subject of your documentary is. Then use three of the propaganda techniques you have learned about to write three ads for your program. Try to use one or more of the following words in your promos.

competitive
crucial
inundate

Extending Frontiers

People have always longed to push back frontiers, to go beyond the known. In the past, explorers charted unknown territories of the earth. Today, new frontiers of knowledge, ideas, and experiences continue to challenge and inspire those who dare to test them.

Conquering the
COLORADO

by James Ramsey Ullman

Each day the Grand Canyon had seemed more threatening, and now some of the explorers talked of turning back. Their lives might depend on Major Powell's decision — but how could he decide, not knowing what lay ahead?

In the summer of 1869, John Wesley Powell set out with eight companions and several boats on one of the greatest adventures of all time. Powell and his men planned to travel hundreds of miles through unknown parts of the western United States.

Powell was a naturalist, explorer, and former army officer who yearned to learn everything he could about this wild country. Although his right arm had been amputated above the elbow as a result of a war injury, he never turned away from danger. With him were his younger brother, Walter; Bill Dunn, Jack Sumner, and Billy Hawkins, war veterans and pioneers; George Bradley, a tough ex-officer from New England; Oramel and Seneca Howland, brothers from Colorado; and Andy Hall, a young wanderer.

In August, after an exhausting journey through Wyoming and Utah on the Green River, the men entered the Colorado River. Finally, after traveling through many canyons, the group reached the mightiest canyon of them all — the Grand Canyon.

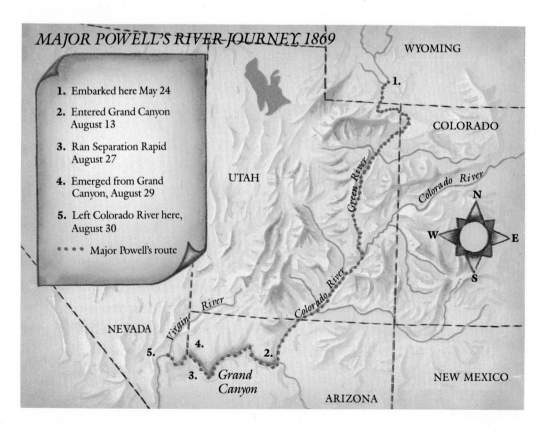

MAJOR POWELL'S RIVER JOURNEY, 1869

1. Embarked here May 24

2. Entered Grand Canyon August 13

3. Ran Separation Rapid August 27

4. Emerged from Grand Canyon, August 29

5. Left Colorado River here, August 30

•••• Major Powell's route

WYOMING

COLORADO

UTAH

Green River

Colorado River

NEVADA

Virgin River

Colorado River

Grand Canyon

NEW MEXICO

ARIZONA

N
W   E
S

For anyone else, those next days would have been a wild adventure. For Powell and Company they were almost routine. They lined, portaged, ran rapids, leaped falls. The *Emma Dean* was swamped and plunged down a hundred yards of cataract, with her crew clinging to the gunwales. At midday the sun poured down as if it would fry them alive. Then the rain would return in torrents and cloudbursts, and at night, in their rocky bivouacs, they sat hunched in misery. "The little canvas we have," Powell wrote, "is rotten and useless; the rubber pouches have all been lost; more than half the party is without hats, not one of us has an entire suit of clothes, and we have not a blanket apiece. . . . We sit up all night on the rocks, shivering, and are more exhausted by the night's discomfort than by the day's toil."

They guarded their precious flour supply as if it had been sacks of gold, keeping it always in watertight compartments and dividing it equally among the three boats — so that if one of the boats cracked up (which seemed sure to happen at any moment) only a third of it would be lost. They were down to nine days' rations, then eight, then

The Start from Green River

seven. With a week in the canyon behind them, they had traveled well over the one hundred thirty miles of its straight-line length; and with each bend of the river, their eyes strained ahead for a glimpse of the Grand Wash Cliffs, which would mean the end of the canyon, but still no Grand Wash appeared. Mile after mile, day after day, the vast gorge of the Colorado twisted on through the earth, as if its waters would pound and roar for all eternity.

On August 20, their eighth day in the Grand Canyon, the river relented, becoming briefly broader and smoother. Then it pinched in again and raced forward, but without any falls or cascades, and they made ten miles in less than an hour. On the twenty-first, to their joy, they came out of the black granite walls into softer red limestone and thought for a time that their troubles were over, but the next day the granite rose up again as menacing as ever. Soon they were again lining and portaging past raging rapids.

They were still a mile deep in the earth, at the bottom of a canyon-within-canyons. From a vantage point to which Powell climbed on the inner walls, the steep eroded wilderness stretched on as far as the eye could see. It was back to the boats again and again; back to the rapids and chutes and falls and waves and whirlpools. From here on, at least, they were only part of the time in granite, and the rest in softer rock; and the little fleet moved on with new life and hope, on what Powell now called their "race for dinner."

On August 23 they made twenty-two miles; the next day, twenty; the next, a fabulous thirty-five — past a long-dead volcano and great floods of cooled lava — and Powell wrote in his diary a heartfelt "Hurrah!" Then came another stroke of good luck, when on the 26th,

with their flour almost gone, they saw a sight they could scarcely believe. Thus far along the Grand Canyon, they had seen a few ancient ruins, but no sign that any living Indians ever came down to the river from the canyon rims. Now, suddenly, on the bank, they found a garden planted with corn and squash. The corn proved too young to eat, but the squash was ripe, and there being no one about, they helped themselves.

They dined ravenously that day on a feast of roast squash, the first fresh vegetable food they had had since seven weeks before. With hunger gone, and another thirty-five miles behind them before the day was over, they were suddenly a cheerful and optimistic crowd of scarecrows.

"A few days like this," Powell wrote in his journal, "and we are out of prison."

Or so they hoped.

The great prison of the Grand Canyon was not to let them out that easily; on the very next morning the dreaded black granite once again loomed before them. They heard a roaring, saw rapids ahead, and when they reached the head of the rapids, it was to face a sight that made

Climbing the Grand Canyon

their hearts sink — the worst stretch of wild water, according to Powell, that they had met on the whole thousand-mile course of their journey.

To run it, he thought somberly, would be sure destruction. This was not all of the problem; there was no shoreline for portaging and no visible route along the cliffs above from which they could line the boats down. Desperately, they searched. They climbed high on the walls, but on one side there was no route at all; and on the other there were so many crags and pinnacles that they could not even glimpse the river below, let alone find a vantage point for lowering the boats.

Trying for a better view, Powell climbed far out on a crag and, with only his one arm to hold on with, found himself presently "rimmed" — unable to move either forward or back. Although several of the men were nearby, they were unable to reach a position directly above him, from which to let them — or anything — down. While his companions maneuvered about, Powell clung motionless to the wall, four hundred vertical feet above the river, supported only by one foot on a narrow ledgelet and his one hand wedged into a tiny crevice.

After several futile tries, the others managed to reach him a rope, from off to one side, but he was unable to let go long enough to grasp it. Then some of the men hurried down to the boats and came back with oars. While Powell, now all but exhausted, hung straining to the rock, they succeeded in pushing one oar into a crevice beyond him, so that it held him in against the wall; then they jammed a second oar against the rock, near his feet, enabling him to step on it and move slowly off the crag.

So the rescue was completed. Another emergency had been faced and resolved, but the *big* emergency still remained: the question of how to go on, or even if they *could* go on, or whether they would have to abandon the boats and try to climb up out of the canyon. Shaken though he was by his experience on the cliff, Powell went on clambering and searching. Even after all the others had gone down in the gathering darkness, he roamed the steep canyon walls, looking for some feasible way to line the boats down the rapids.

He found none. Directly below the camp was a twenty-foot fall, flanked by a strip of shore, and over this they could conceivably lower the boats. Beyond it, lining was out of the question. They would have to run the rapid, and he himself had already given the opinion that "to run it would be sure destruction."

And yet . . .

Yet, as he studied the rapid, as he strained to absorb its every feature with eyes and mind and imagination, he was no longer so sure. He began to change his opinion — perhaps because he so desperately wanted to change it. There might, just possibly, be a way, he decided. There must be a way. *They must find a way.* By the time he reached camp he had made his decision.

"We will run the rapid in the morning," he told the men.

The men looked at him and said nothing.

They had been together now for more than three months. They had had their arguments and dissensions; indeed, few days passed on the whole trip during which someone had not grumbled about something, but no one had even come close to quitting. Through all their adventures, all their dangers and hardships and conflicts of opinion and personality, the will to stick together to the end had been the greatest of their strengths.

Now at last, however, that will was crumbling. In the darkness, Oramel Howland rose and, going to Powell, said he wished to speak to him; and the two went off a little way from the others. The senior Howland was the oldest member of the party. He was loyal, dependable, good-natured, and had never been one of the grumblers. Now, he told his leader, the time had come when he must speak out. It was madness, he said, to go on. The rapid ahead was impassable, and the only sane course was to leave the boats and climb up out of the canyon. If Powell insisted on still following the river, three of them, at least, would not go with him. He had been talking it over with his brother, Seneca, and Bill Dunn, and together they had made their decision.

Howland lay down again and slept, but there was no sleep for Powell for the rest of that night. In the darkness he paced slowly up and down the shore. He checked and rechecked the tiny food supply. Over and over he struggled with the problem of

what to do — of what was *right* to do. There were moments when he was almost persuaded to agree with Howland. Almost, yet not quite. In his journal, now, he set down his final decision, writing: "But for years I have been contemplating this trip. To leave the exploration unfinished, to say that there is a part of the canyon which I cannot explore, having already almost accomplished it, is more than I am willing to acknowledge, and I determine to go on."

At dawn they all breakfasted in silence. Then, when they had finished, Powell asked the two Howlands and Dunn if they would not change their minds. Oramel Howland and Dunn shook their heads; their decision was final. Seneca Howland wavered. On his own, he would probably have chosen to stay with Powell, but in the end he decided to go with his older brother; and so the matter was settled.

There are those who, in later years, have called the three men deserters. But Powell did not feel that. It was in sorrow that he accepted their decision, but not in anger or bitterness; for they had been good and faithful companions through the long trip,

Noonday Rest in Marble Canyon

and he realized that they could well be right in their choice and he himself wrong. He offered them two rifles and a shotgun, which they accepted, and their fair share of the remaining food, which they did not (saying that they could shoot enough game to keep them fed). Billy Hawkins, the cook, without saying anything, left them a pan of freshly baked biscuits.

With only six men going on, three boats were too much to handle, and Powell sadly decided to abandon his pilot boat, the *Emma Dean*. The other two, the *Maid of the Canyon* and the *Kitty Clyde's Sister*, were emptied of all cargo not absolutely needed, so as to make them as light as possible. Then, with the two Howlands and Dunn helping, they were carefully lined down over the fall at the head of the rapid.

From here on, the six who were continuing would have to ride the boats, and the rapid, and the time for parting was at hand. The records of the expedition had been kept in duplicate, and each group took a copy, against the possibility that one or the other would not get out alive. Powell wrote a letter to his wife and entrusted it to Oramel Howland; and Sumner gave Howland

his watch, asking that it be sent to his sister if he was not heard of again. "Each party," wrote Powell, "thinks the other is taking the dangerous course," and each tried for the last time, unsuccessfully, to persuade the other to change its mind.

It was no use: The decisions had been made. Hands were shaken. A few tears appeared on hard, leathery, bearded faces. Then the expedition split up, at what ever since has been known as Separation Rapid.

The Howlands and Dunn planned to climb up out of the canyon by way of a side gorge that entered the Grand at this point. First they climbed to a crag, high above the river, to watch the others take off. Meanwhile, down on the river, Powell, with his *Emma Dean* gone, boarded the *Maid of the Canyon*, along with two companions; and the other three took their places in the *Kitty Clyde's Sister*. For a last long moment the leader studied the sweep of white water and black rock that lay before them. Then he gave the signal, and they pushed off into the wild torrent.

The day before, on his explorations, he had convinced himself that he had found a possible route, and now it was up to him to prove it. Taking the lead, the *Maid of the Canyon* scudded along the right wall of the canyon, grazing a huge rock on the way. Then a fall appeared ahead, as big as the one down which they had just lined, but here there could be no lining, no landing. The only hope was that they could reach a sort of chute that grooved the center of the fall between the huge boulders on either side; and rowing like madmen, they swung toward midstream. The boat rocked and pitched, so that half the time their oars were flailing the air and the other half were buried handle-deep in water. But they reached the groove. They shot into it and then over the fall. The prow of the boat dug deep into the river, and the men were up to their shoulders in boiling foam.

Yet the boat did not sink. They were not thrown out. Bouncing and thudding down another rapid, they saw ahead a great rock extending halfway across the stream, against which the water piled in a roar of white fury. Again they heaved at their oars, struggling to avoid it — and again they succeeded. For though a mighty wave lifted them, carrying them high up toward the rock, they did not smash against it or go over its top, but angled off to one side; and the next instant, suddenly, blessedly, they were in a quiet pool below the cataract. In a few moments the *Kitty Clyde's Sister* had joined them safely. The whole wild run had taken each boat no more than a minute.

Beyond the rapid there were again shores, and they landed and bailed out. Although, when they looked back, they could see no sign of the three who had left them, they fired off their guns to announce that they were safe, with the hope that the others would board the *Emma Dean* and join them, but there were no answering shots; no glimpse of the Howlands and Dunn. So, presently, they were on their way again, to whatever the river — and fate — held in store.

What they held, first, was more rapids roaring on and on between black granite cliffs. For a while, though, they were no worse than many they had run before, and they almost dared hope their troubles were over. The Grand Canyon, however, was not through with them yet; for early in the afternoon, some six miles below Separation

Running a Rapid

Rapid, they came to a place as wild and fearsome as any they had ever seen. Directly before them was still another fall; beyond it more falls, more rapids, a vast cataract, with the water everywhere "lashed into mad white foam." Even more than Separation, it looked impossible to navigate. Again Powell clambered about on the shoreless cliffs, looking for a way to let the boats down on lines. This time the cliffs were easier. He did not get "rimmed." He found what he thought might be a way, but when he returned to the river, it was to face a crisis that threw all his plans to the wind.

For some reason, the others had already let the *Kitty Clyde's Sister,* with George Bradley in it, down toward the rim of the fall. The current was so swift that they could not pull it back — indeed, could barely hold it where it was — and the line was too short to be taken up on the cliff and maneuvered along it, as Powell had planned. Securing the rope around a rock, some of the men scurried for a second rope to tie onto it. Meanwhile the boat was swinging back and forth across the torrent like a crazy pendulum, now hanging on the very lip of the fall, now crashing into the rock wall at water's edge.

Bradley was doing his best to hold it off, to keep it steady and gain control, but it was a losing fight. With each new swing, it seemed, the boat would either smash to bits on the rock or break loose and plunge over the fall. From the shore, Powell saw Bradley glance off the riverbank. He saw him look at the frayed, straining line. Then the cool and courageous man

Head of the Grand Canyon

made his decision and took out his knife to cut the line.

Before he could move, however, the river took the decision from him. Unable to bear the strain any longer, the whole sternpost of the *Kitty Clyde's Sister,* to which the line was attached, broke off with a mighty jerk; and in the same instant the boat was loose in the current. Bradley lunged for the steering oar. By a miracle of strength and skill, he managed to turn the boat so that it was no longer broadside to the river, but pointed downstream. Then he went over the fall. He disappeared — reappeared. Incredible as it seemed, he was still alive, still in the boat, still fighting with all his might against the furious tide. As he plunged on down the cataract, half under water, half out of it, the others, watching with straining eyes and pounding hearts, saw him snatch off his hat and wave it in triumph.

It was a gesture never to be forgotten: one of the great moments in the history of adventure. Powell was still not sure that Bradley was safe, and now he, too, sprang into action. Shouting to his brother and Sumner to make their way down along the cliffs, he leaped into the *Maid of the Canyon* with Hawkins and Hall, pushed off, and in a moment was following Bradley's wild course down the river. It was the one wholly reckless thing he had done on the entire trip — and a true measure of the desperation that he felt, with both victory and defeat so close. He might well have been killed, and Hawkins and Hall along with him, but like Bradley before them, they had skill, courage, and luck. And in a few minutes they were past the fall, past the raging rapid, past great waves that rolled them over and over — and in quiet water, in a gentle eddy, where Bradley, himself alive and unharmed, briskly fished them up out of the river.

That was the last great roar of the Colorado. When they camped for the night a few miles farther on, the water was smooth, the cliffs no longer of granite. At noon the next day — August 29 — they sighted the long-sought sweep of the Grand Wash Cliffs and left the Grand Canyon behind them.

There were no more big canyons ahead; that Powell knew. From here on the river flowed through known country to the sea. "Now the danger is over," he wrote. "Now the toil has ceased." That night he added: "The quiet of the camp is sweet. Our joy is almost ecstasy."

"All that we regret," wrote George Bradley in his journal, "is that the three boys who took to the mountains are not here to share our triumph." Weeks later, word came that the three men were dead — their bodies had been found on the high plateau above the river.

John Wesley Powell mourned the passing of his companions. However, their deaths did not quell his enthusiasm for adventure. In the years that followed, he became one of the leaders in the exploration and development of the West.

341

The Gate of Lodore

Author

World traveler and mountaineer James Ramsey Ullman had a distinguished career as a writer. Five of his books were made into motion pictures. His *Banner in the Sky* was a Newbery Honor Book and received the Lewis Carroll Shelf Award. Before becoming a writer, Mr. Ullman was a producer in the theater.

Selection Wrap-up

Summary Questions

The survival of Powell and his party depended upon their being able to think quickly and clearly. Each member of the party had to be able to make critical decisions at almost every turn of the river. Think about the critical decision each explorer had to make at Separation Rapid.

1. Why did Major Powell decide to take the risk of running Separation Rapid?
2. What assumption were the Howlands and Bill Dunn making when they decided to abandon the river?
3. Why do you think Major Powell didn't insist that the Howlands and Dunn stay with the rest of the group?
4. Pretend you are one of the men on the journey. You have to decide whether to leave with the Howlands and Bill Dunn or to go on with Powell and the others. You have no way of knowing what will happen to each group. Which group would you join? Why?

The Reading and Writing Connection

Imagine that you are Powell, just returned from the Grand Canyon expedition, and that you are preparing a speech to a group of young people whom you hope to persuade to join a future expedition. For this talk, you decide to focus on the most exciting part of your recent adventure, from the time you entered the Grand Canyon on August 13 until you sighted the Grand Wash Cliffs on August 29.

Begin by making a time line that shows the major events of that period. Refer to the time line as you write a brief speech that might inspire others to join your next expedition. Try to use some of the following words in your speech.

maneuvered
optimistic
bivouacs
vantage point

Borrowed Words

Just as you might borrow something from a friend, we often borrow words we need from other languages. Such borrowing is very common in English. By learning where the words came from, you can often learn a lot about the history of English-speaking people.

The largest-scale borrowing of words in English probably started in 1066. In that year, William the Conqueror invaded England and became its king. William and his followers brought their native French language to England with them. Eventually, both the rulers and the people spoke one language, English, but with many words borrowed from French. Below are a few of them.

bivouac A temporary outdoor camp. In French, a *bivouac* meant a "night watch during military campaigns."

rapids A swiftly running part of a river, often with rocks. In French, *rapide* means "quick."

portage To carry boats and supplies overland from a river or lake. In French, *porter* means "to carry."

journal A daily record of events. In French, **jour** means "day."

Other words were introduced into English by the Spanish who explored the southwestern parts of the United States. They include:

canyon A narrow valley with high, steep sides. In Spanish, *cañon* means "tube or funnel."

mesa A small, high plateau with a flat top and steep sides. The Spanish inherited their word *mesa* from the Latin *mensa*, meaning "table."

In addition to bringing words with them, the explorers sometimes took home with them words borrowed from the Native Americans. For example, Columbus discovered that the Carib people paddled *canoes* — small, narrow boats that are pointed at both ends.

The name for squash came from the Narragansett word *askutasquash*, meaning "the green things that may be eaten raw."

Use the borrowed words discussed here to complete the following paragraph:

The river explorers faced many dangers. They spent most of their days between steep _____ walls. At night they set up a _____ on a narrow strip of sand. In the morning, they launched their _____ and ran the _____. When the river became too dangerous, they had to _____. Once, they climbed the walls and saw a tall _____ standing in the distance. On another day, they found a few ripe _____ for their dinner. All these events were written down in the leader's _____.

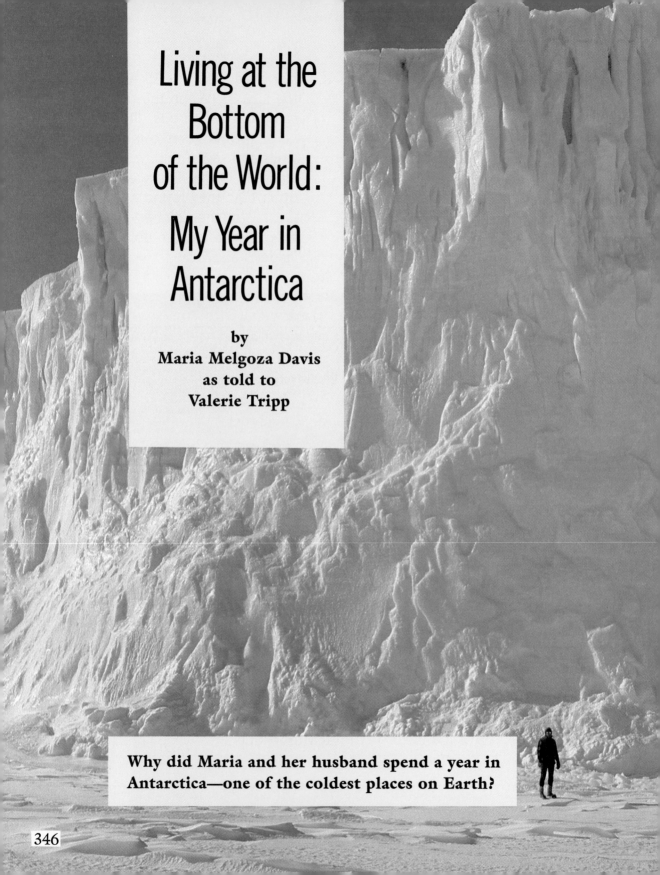

Living at the Bottom of the World:
My Year in Antarctica

by
Maria Melgoza Davis
as told to
Valerie Tripp

Why did Maria and her husband spend a year in Antarctica—one of the coldest places on Earth?

Imagine a world white with snow all year, where it can be so quiet you can hear your heart beat and so cold that metal will freeze to your skin. That's where Maria Melgoza Davis and her husband, Randy, lived for a year — one of the wildest, windiest, coldest, snowiest places on Earth — Antarctica.

In Antarctica the seasons are reversed, with summer in January and winter in June. There are no cities, super highways, shopping centers, schools, or office buildings. It seems an unlikely place for Maria Melgoza Davis, who grew up in bustling towns in Mexico and Southern California. Why was she there?

Maria and Randy went to Antarctica to study the behavior of the Weddell seals. It is believed that these unique seals were named for James Weddell, the British navigator who explored Antarctica in the 1800's. Weddell seals are the only seals known to survive under shorefast ice, ice that is attached to land. Maria and Randy wanted to find out how the seals keep warm and what they eat during the long cold season. This kind of information may someday help humans survive in cold places.

What was it like for Maria to live at the bottom of the world? This is her story of her year in Antarctica.

January

I'll never forget landing at McMurdo Station, the largest United States base in Antarctica. It was January, the Antarctic summer, a

bright blue day. I had never seen snow on the ground before. It was lovely, bright, and white. I couldn't wait to get outside and touch it, but when the door of the plane opened, the air was so cold it felt like a solid wall. I wondered how I would make it to the airport building without freezing.

If the cold was a small shock, the landscape was a big surprise. Antarctica is spectacular! Most people think it is a desolate place, just barren stretches of white snow, but that's wrong. It is one of the most beautiful places on Earth. There are dark purple and black mountains looming on the horizon and brown beaches at the shore. When the sun comes out, it bathes the snow in a golden glow. As it reflects off the ice crystals, it makes rainbows in the sky.

By the end of January, Randy and I were settled in our camp, about twelve miles south of McMurdo, at the foot of White Island. Our camp wasn't actually *on* White Island but rather on the permanent ice shelf that surrounds it. This shelf is so thick and hard that airplanes can land on it. Yet it floats on the water; it is not solid land.

We had two small rectangular huts, one for living and one for working. They were connected by a passageway that served as a wind shelter and storage area. We also had a Quonset hut for our electric generator and our vehicles. We had snowmobiles for short trips. For longer trips we had a heavy, orange land vehicle, with treads like a tank.

What a great day it was when we first saw the seals! They are graceful creatures, with sleek, torpedo-shaped bodies. Adults can be seven feet long and weigh a thousand pounds. They have huge dark eyes and short soft fur that is brown or black with white spots. They have small flippers on their sides and a big hind flipper. When their jaws are closed, the seals look as if they are smiling. When they yawn, their jaws open wide to show a big pink mouth.

We counted twenty-five seals on White Island and made a chart for each seal, noting its size, color, sex, and approximate age and weight. This was summer, and we observed that the seals seemed to take it easy. They lay around on the ice as if they were working on a suntan. They dozed, then dove into the water to catch a fish, and then dozed some more.

I could tell by the bones and shell fragments I sometimes found that the seals ate fish and krill. Krill are tiny shrimplike creatures that are food for whales, penguins, fish, and squid. The fact that the Weddell seals stayed strong and healthy eating krill was important. As people take up more of the earth's space, and less land is available for farming, people may have to turn to other food sources — such as krill from the ocean.

The seals had no fear of us, so we could get close enough to attach time-depth recorders to their hind flippers. The recorders registered how frequently the seals dove, how long they stayed underwater, and how deep they dove.

The seals' more frequent dives lasted for ten or twenty minutes and were about four hundred feet deep. However, we were surprised to learn that the seals were capable of holding their breath for an hour and of diving to a depth of almost two thousand feet. The deepest dive ever made by a human wearing scuba equipment is only 437 feet. To avoid lung damage, the seals expel air gradually as they dive.

February

Once the last supply plane left in February, I knew I was committed to spending the winter in Antarctica. This is called wintering over. Planes can't fly safely in the extreme cold of an Antarctic winter.

Ships can't make their way through the ice-clogged water. Except during extreme emergencies, no one comes in or goes out for at least four months.

March

In March, as autumn began, the surface of the sea froze. The air temperature dropped lower every day. The sun set — and would not rise again until September.

To our surprise, the seals disappeared. We knew they could not live in the severe winter weather, but we didn't expect them to vanish into thin air.

We soon learned that they had vanished into the water under the ice. We couldn't see them but we knew they were there because we could hear them. On land, seals bleat and baa like sheep. Underwater, they sing. We stood on the ice and heard the seals peep, chirp, gurgle, and whistle, and knew they were under our feet.

For several weeks we recorded the noises the seals made underwater. We lowered a special underwater microphone, called a hydrophone, into the water and connected the hydrophone to equipment in our hut. Randy and I took turns listening to the seals, and we made tape recordings of their mysterious vocalizations. We think the seals use their chirps, buzzes, and whistles to communicate with each other. Perhaps the sounds are warnings of danger or invitations to share a good fishing spot or a breathing hole.

To avoid the cold, the seals spend the entire winter in water. The water is warmer than the air even though it is under a thick crust of ice. There the seals are protected from the wind and are close to their food source. Their blubber, a thick layer of fat, insulates them against the cold water.

Since seals are mammals, they have to breathe air. How do they get air through the ice? The answer was another surprise. In one place on the Island, the ocean tide had made a crack in the thick ice. Here, where the ice was only a few inches thick, the clever Weddell seals chewed breathing holes. They held onto the ice

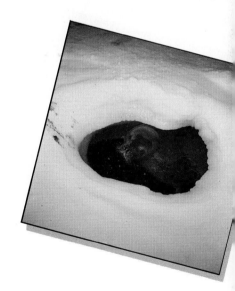

with their lower teeth and sawed back and forth until they broke through to fresh air. If the breathing hole froze over, we would observe a seal chew through the new ice to open it again. Sometimes a few seals would share a breathing hole. Weddell seals are the only seals who chew breathing holes in the ice this way.

We discovered the breathing holes when we walked along the ice next to the crack and heard the seals puffing out air like a bellows. We watched the breathing holes for hours and learned that the seals usually stayed under for fifteen or twenty minutes and then came up for a breather. When they wanted to sleep, they propped themselves upright, nose in the breathing hole, body under the ice, and slept.

April

We observed the seals every day during April except when the weather was very stormy and we were hut-bound. Then we listened to our tapes of music, read, played games, or rode our exercise bike. There was also work to do, keeping our logs of weather and activities up to date.

People had warned me about the isolation and cold of the long, dark winter. Some find it terrifying, but I didn't. On calm nights, the brilliant full moon was like a nighttime sun. It seemed huge and close, and three-dimensional. The stars were big and dazzling. Auroras — streamers of light — would dance across the sky like silver dust. I never tired of the winter

sky. I always thought, "This is the closest I will ever come to being on another planet."

May

In May, Randy and I moved our camp after it had been buried in snow. Before we had put all the finishing touches on these new quarters, we were hit by a terrible storm. We were sleeping when the storm hit. The shrieking wind woke me. It was completely dark inside the hut. Suddenly, crash! — a shock of frigid air swirling with snow blasted into the hut. I jumped out of my bunk and saw that the wind had ripped the east door off its hinges and blown it into the hut. The torrent through the gaping hole was battering the west wall. The escape hatch in the roof burst open. The chain holding it shut had snapped.

Randy and I struggled to prop the door back in its frame. I held it in place while Randy tried to tie the west door open to relieve the wind's pressure on the wall. With a wham, the west door slammed shut. The knob was frozen, and Randy was outside. Somehow, he managed to pull the door open and get inside. Meanwhile, I leaned against the east door with all my might, but it was like trying to keep a lid on a geyser. Randy came to help me. Together, we nailed a board across the door. Then we tied the escape hatch shut with a rope. When we finished, I realized I was standing waist-deep in snow. The hut was blown, battered, and full of snow, but we were safe.

Every four weeks Randy and I would go to McMurdo. I had a darkroom there because one of my jobs was to develop all our film. During our year in Antarctica I developed over 3,400 pictures, mostly of seals. On these trips we could see movies and go to the library for new books. We also got enough food, fuel, and supplies to last a month. One great treat was freshly baked bread made right at McMurdo.

June 21, the first day of winter, is called the winter solstice. We had a big party in McMurdo to celebrate. Now the sun would get closer to the horizon and the days get longer. The sky is very dramatic as winter ends. Where the sun comes up, the sky appears as red as fire, while on the other horizon, it is black.

July

Earlier we had drilled a hole in the ice. Every day we lowered traps through the hole to catch fish so that we could tell what was there for the seals to eat. We caught sea spiders, isopods, krill, and ice fish.

We also lowered instruments to measure the water currents and temperature.

Sometimes Randy dove into the water through the hole. He wore thick underwear, a dry suit, and two pairs of gloves to protect himself from the cold. With spotlights, he used his underwater camera to take pictures of the under surface of the ice and the seals. The spotlights helped us photograph the seals as they swam through the dark water under the ice — though how the seals navigate in the dark is still a mystery. The hydrophone recordings helped us keep track of our wet friends during those three months, when their only window to the outside world was their breathing hole at the tidal crack.

August–September

One day we drove to the north side of White Island in our land vehicle. It was a gray day. Everything was the same dull color — a condition called whiteout. It was hard to tell the difference between the snow on the ground and the sky. Randy seemed to be walking in mid-air when he got out of the land vehicle to look for seals. When we were driving home I was suddenly jerked hard against the back of the seat. I looked behind me and saw a huge hole. The back part of the vehicle had fallen into a crack called a crevasse. Randy gunned the motor, and we pulled out just in time to avoid getting trapped under the ice.

Later, we went back to the crevasse because we thought the seals might be using it. They weren't. The crevasse was eighty feet deep, and beautiful. Inside, it was like an ice palace: a deep, shining blue cave full of huge, sculptured chunks of ice.

October–November

In spring, October and November, the seals came back to the top of the ice. It was a happy occasion, made happier by the births of baby seal pups soon after.

The seal pups were born right on the ice. A newborn seal's fur, called lanugo, is wet and soon freezes into a stiff coat of ice. The pup begins to shiver, which warms it up and makes its furry coat fluff out and dry off.

When a seal pup is only a few days old, its mother starts to teach it to swim. The baby seal starts out making short, five-minute dives. Gradually, the pup dives deeper and longer. After six weeks, the baby is expected to find its own food and make its own air holes. The seal pup is not a helpless baby for long.

December

It was a sad day in December when Randy and I left Antarctica. As I took a last look around, it seemed to me that the snow glittered and sparkled even more than usual, and the sky was a more brilliant blue. It was as if Antarctica had polished itself up to look its very best on my last day.

Our trip was a scientific success. We had lived with the Weddell seals for a year. We learned how they survived the winter, what they ate, and how they behaved in all four seasons.

I learned a lot about myself too. I had tested my endurance to the limit and found I was capable of doing more than just surviving. Like the seal, I had adapted to Antarctica's demanding climate. I could do my share of hard work and stay cheerful in dark isolation.

The adventure of living with the seals and the beauty of Antarctica far outweighed every inconvenience, hardship, and danger of the year. I will always think of my year at the bottom of the world as the most exciting and the best year of my life.

Author

Valerie Tripp, a professional writer for over ten years, especially likes writing for young people. She has visited every state except Alaska. She likes traveling the back roads through small towns. This way she gets to meet and talk with people who often become her friends and sometimes become characters in her books.

Summary Questions

Think about the rewards and difficulties of spending a year in Antarctica.

1. Before her arrival, what had Maria imagined Antarctica would be like? In what ways was she surprised?
2. What kinds of accommodations were available for housing and for transportation?
3. What were some exciting facts about Weddell seals that Maria and her husband learned during their year in Antarctica?
4. Why was wintering over in Antarctica difficult?
5. Why, do you think, did Maria and her husband choose to face those difficulties?
6. There were many hardships involved in studying the Weddell seals. Would you be willing to spend a year in Antarctica to study seals? Explain your answer.

The Reading and Writing Connection

Pretend that you are Maria and that you are trying to convince a friend to accompany you on another educational trip to Antarctica. Your friend does not want to leave the busy city for the isolation of Antarctica. Write a letter in which you use the best arguments you can think of to convince your friend to join you. Try to include some of the following words in your letter.

isolation
insulated
barren

The Way Things Are

by Myra Cohn Livingston

It's today,
This road,
This knowing the road is there.
A few brambles,
A few tangles,
A few scratches,
A rough stone against your toe,
But still, you've got to go
And take it.
Fast, sometimes,
Or slow,
But go —

        everywhere.
        anywhere
        You need
        to go.

The Dragon Doctor

by Jo Manton

Dr. Ma knew how to cure sick horses and sheep and cows — but how would he handle a sick dragon?

Long, long ago, in the days of the Yellow Emperor, lived a farmer called Huang. His home was in a remote place, where three or four farmhouses clustered around a horse pond. The men of the hamlet plowed, the boys minded the geese and ducks, the women and girls tended the gardens. Each farm had its horse in the stable, sheep or cow in the paddock, hens in the roost, doves on the roof ridge, pigs snug in the sty, and cat stretched out in the sun. Far off you could see hazy smoke rise from the roofs. Nearer at hand you might hear a dog bark somewhere in the lanes, a cock crow at the top of the mulberry tree, or the girls chat as they milked the cows. Anyone who was not happy in that place would never be happy at all.

All these country neighbors honored Huang, for he was a wonderful doctor of sick animals. When the sheep coughed, or the cow would not calve, or the piglets failed to thrive, they would run to fetch him. Then Huang would look at the sick beast intently, speak to it quietly, and handle it gently with steady brown hands. He seemed to see through the illness to the nature of the creature itself, and the animals he treated with herbs or surgery were always healed. No wonder the farmers called him Dr. Horse — in Chinese, Dr. Ma.

Ma was standing at the door one day, looking around his walled courtyard with its stables and barns, when a sudden shadow blotted out the sun. Slowly a flying dragon circled above the farm and glided down to land in front of him. Naturally Ma knew all about dragons in theory, for the dragon was chief of the three hundred and sixty scaly reptiles. He knew that four Dragon Kings rule the four seas, that the Celestial Dragon rules the sky, that the Earth Dragon marks out lakes and rivers, and that the Hidden Treasure Dragon guards the gold and silver deep in the earth. Dragons, he knew, were certainly magical. One foolish man invented a recipe for cooking dragon meat, but he never could catch one, so his skill was all wasted. The great Confucius himself said, "Birds fly, fishes swim, and beasts run; you may snare those that run, hook those that swim, and shoot those that fly. But when it comes to a dragon — a dragon can ride on the wind, and I can't imagine how to catch one." Like everyone else, Ma also knew that a friendly dragon brings good luck. That is why people so often have them painted on dishes or screens. Yet, strangely enough, he had never seen one.

Now the dragon shuffled toward him on golden claws. Red, green, and azure rippled through its golden scales from head to snaky tail, the patterns changing with every breath. Yet the gorgeous dragon's head and tail hung limp, its ears drooped, and from its open jaws a trail of spittle fell to the stones. Its topaz eyes gazed at him piteously.

"Why," thought Ma in instant recognition, "this dragon is ill and wants me to cure it!" Seeing only a suffering beast, he lost all sense of the fabulous monster. He examined it with a strong, gentle touch; searching the scaly temples, he felt the racing pulse of pain. The trouble was not hard to find — a red and angry boil on the jaw.

"Easy, old fellow," said Ma, as though to a horse; and the dragon, hearing that quiet voice, stood trustingly under his hands. Ma fetched his case of acupuncture needles. Deftly, still talking calmly to the patient, he slid the fine gold and

silver needles into the skin. After five minutes he slipped them out, so gently that the dragon seemed to feel nothing.

Ma knew all the three hundred and sixty-five points of the body at which a doctor may practice this craft. "Unhealthy fluids will drain away," he explained reassuringly, "the swelling will go down, the healthy balance of the body will be restored, and the pain will go away." Topaz eyes gazed at him, as though the dragon understood.

The dragon rested that night in the barn. Ma, in his workroom, pounded licorice root to make soothing medicine, which the dragon appeared to enjoy, for it finished every drop and licked its chops. Next day, Ma was pleased to see the boil draining and the dragon resting comfortably, coiled in the straw. By the third morning it was cured and flew away, rainbow scales glittering along the white fingers of the clouds, until it dwindled into the distance. Next day, it came back, with a pair of red jade slippers in its claws. Ma was deeply touched. "Bless you, I want no reward," he said. "Jade slippers are not for the likes of me, nor are any of your magic tricks, like floating through the air or passing through solid rock. If you feel well, that's all the thanks I need."

The dragon, like many human patients, was now deeply attached to its doctor. It went to live in the depths of the village pond, and every time it felt out of sorts, it appeared in Huang's courtyard, like a persistent invalid at morning sick call. Ma knew what it wanted and kept a jar always filled with the dragon's favorite dark, syrupy licorice medicine.

Of course, this strange friendship could not long remain unknown. A dragon is only a dragon, you might think, but foolish people can make it a god. Soon news spread through the land that a Holy Dragon lived in the village horse pond. Happiness or grief, rain or drought — before long, people were saying that it was all the dragon's doing. Crowds came on foot, nobles on horseback, and ladies in carrying chairs. They built a stone shrine beside the pool. They poured offerings over the water mint and burned sacrifices of young pig on the rocks; the foxes that came at night grew fat with finishing it all up. All day the crowds chanted prayers, waved silk umbrellas, threw paper money into the water, or banged gongs and drums. Sightseers from town trampled the barley fields, picked the flowers, and frightened the hens until they stopped laying. No longer did the villagers stoop to see how their grain was growing, look up into their mulberry boughs, or enjoy a friendly chat with the neighbors about the weather or crops. They were all too busy selling rice cakes and tea to the tourists. Ma escaped to gather herbs in the calm shadows of the summer woods. Even there, loud picnic parties drove him away. "It's as bad as a barbarian invasion," he thought gloomily.

What did the dragon think of this incessant hubbub? Though worshippers implored it loudly, it refused to come

out from its lair at the bottom of the pond. Finally, one morning before sunrise, Ma found it waiting at its old place in the yard. Bowing its head and spreading its great bat wings, the dragon invited him to mount. No sooner had Ma swung a leg over the scaly golden back than the dragon soared into the clouds. They winged through the sky, red mists of morning wrapping them around like a cloak under the high canopy of space. The doors of the Jade Emperor's heavenly palace swung

open, and Ma wandered freely through the halls of the stars. Servants washed him in showers of rainbow spray, dressed him in silk robes, and girded him with a belt of jewels, while the dragon went off to the stables of the sky. Then they led Ma to the banquet hall, to eat the Food of Long Life. Now his fame and glory would last forever.

Like most people, Ma had expected one short life. "The world is an inn," he had said to himself, "and we are passing travelers." He was prepared to grow old, to find his hair and beard every day a little whiter, to lean each day a little more heavily on his thornwood stick, to honor the memory of friends gone before, and in his turn to meet the Common Change of death. "By then," he had said, "the world and I will have had our fill of one another."

Yet now that the dragon had carried him to the kingdom of the sky, Ma found everything quite unexpectedly usual. For there, every department of the Chinese Empire on earth has an everlasting counterpart. The Celestial Emperor has his court, his eighteen provinces with their governors, his judges, treasurers, and mandarins, each with a host of attendant clerks, doorkeepers, and police. Naturally there is a celestial Ministry

of Health, and the Minister soon sent for Ma.

"Welcome to our Ministry," he said with a polished official smile. "I now appoint you to my staff, with the title of Infallible Dr. Ma. Your duties will be to make a study of all the medicinal plants on earth for the Office of Remedies. When you have finished it, kindly present your report to your senior officers, the Superintendent of the Celestial Pharmacy and the Eternal Apothecary." Before Ma had time to open his mouth, a black-robed clerk bowed him out the door.

So, as Infallible Dr. Ma, he worked many centuries collecting healing plants on earth and planting a medicinal garden in the sky. There he grew, in neat flower beds, eight hundred and ninety-eight vegetable drugs: peppermint and rhubarb for the stomach, wintergreen for sprains, witch hazel for bruises, lime blossom for headache, vervain to calm the thoughts, balsam for wounds, and soybeans for strength. For centuries to come, everyone in China swore by Dr. Ma's infallible remedies. When this garden was finished, Ma received another appointment — to be patron and protector of all the veterinary surgeons on earth. What an important job for a country horse doctor!

Indeed, Ma might have felt overwhelmed but for one faithful friend. Every so often the golden dragon would appear outside the Celestial Pharmacy and wait patiently, with drooping ears and appealing gaze. Ma did his best not to show how pleased he was to see it.

"There is nothing wrong with you," he said in a firm voice. Yet the dragon continued to look up in its peculiar way. It knew that if it waited long enough, its favorite Dr. Ma would pour it a dose of Heavenly Licorice Medicine.

Author

British author Jo Manton has written several distinguished books for adults and children. She often collaborates with her husband, poet and biographer Robert Gittings. "The Dragon Doctor" is from her book *The Flying Horses: Tales from China.*

Summary Questions

According to Chinese folklore, friendly dragons bring good luck. Consider which characters in this story benefited from such luck.

1. What kinds of good luck did the dragon bring to Dr. Ma?
2. Did Dr. Ma bring good luck to the dragon? Explain your answer.
3. Do you think the dragon brought good luck to the village? Why or why not?
4. Give evidence to support this statement: both Dr. Ma and the dragon considered themselves lucky to have a unique friendship.

The Reading and Writing Connection

How might this folktale be different if its setting were a small town in the United States? How would it be different if set in the present? In pioneer days? Think of a setting and write a story about a fanciful creature who brings good luck to someone who lives in such a setting. You may want to write the story so that it teaches a lesson about something. As you write, try to include some of the following words:

incessant	**infallible**	**jade**	**patron**

Understanding Stories

In earlier lessons, you have learned that an author giving information about a subject uses expository writing. You have learned to pay attention to how the ideas are organized when you read science, social studies, and other expository writing.

An author telling a story uses narrative writing. The ideas in a story are developed through the author's use of **setting, characters, plot,** and **theme.** These are sometimes called **story elements.**

In this lesson, you will learn more about how authors use setting, characters, plot, and theme to develop stories. Knowing this can help you understand and enjoy stories and appreciate the styles of different authors. Thinking about how to use these elements can also help you write better stories of your own.

The lesson will use "On Little Cat Feet" to show how one author has used setting, characters, plot, and theme in telling a story.

Setting

The setting is the time and place in which the story happens. It provides the background for the events. When you read, thinking about the setting helps you understand when and where the story events happen. This is important for understanding how and why things happen as they do.

Some stories could happen in almost any time and place. In other stories the setting is very important. The story could not have happened the way it did in any other time and place. This is true of "On Little Cat Feet." The story is set on the New England coast, where catching lobsters is a way of life for many people. It is a modern story. The people use power boats. It is summer — the time when Jo is not in school. The whole story tells about Jo's problems in getting used to her new job in this setting. Understanding the setting is an important step in understanding what happens in the story.

Characters

The characters are the people or animals that appear in the story.

A story may have major characters, who carry most of the action, and minor characters, who also appear but who are less important.

The major characters in "On Little Cat Feet" are Jo and Uncle Merlin. They carry the action. Jo's father and her brother Roger are minor characters. The author has used them to show how Jo came to work with Uncle Merlin. They do not take part in the major action of the story.

Another minor character is the driver of the speedboat that almost rams the *Trudy*. This person moves the action forward by starting a chain of disasters.

Usually an author wants us to know what the major characters are like, as well as what they do. Sometimes the author does this by speaking more or less directly to the reader. At other times the author lets you infer what the characters are like by watching them and listening to them.

Read the part of the story where Jo and Uncle Merlin are starting out in the *Trudy* for the first time, from paragraph 2 on page 295 through paragraph 2 on page 296. Notice how much you learn about Uncle Merlin from the few things he says to Jo. He is very direct, and a man of few words. He knows a great deal about the ocean. Instead of just telling you these things about Uncle Merlin, the author has let you infer them from what he says — and what he does not say.

Plot

The plot is the series of events in the story. It has a **beginning, middle, climax,** and **conclusion.**

The beginning introduces the characters and the setting. The middle describes the conflict or problem. The climax is the high point or turning point of the action, and the conclusion clears up the problem.

To see how the author has constructed the plot of "On Little Cat Feet," read the first eleven paragraphs of the story. They make up the beginning of the plot. You learn who the characters are and something about what they are like. You learn where they are and why they are there. You know what the problem is going to be.

Notice how much the author has managed to tell you in a short space. Notice also that she has done this through telling you what the characters said and thought, not through explaining directly.

The middle of the story starts with paragraph 1 on page 297 and continues through paragraph 3 on page 299. In this part you learn more about the problems that Jo has in learning to help Uncle Merlin with his work. By the third day, she is getting better at finding the lobster pots, but she is finding the work hard and disagreeable. She is struggling to keep herself from giving up and going home.

The buildup to the climax of the story begins with paragraph 4 on page 299, when the *Trudy* is almost hit by the speedboat, and continues to paragraph 1 on page 302, when Jo wakes up to see that the fog has lifted and that they have not drifted out to sea after all.

Notice that there are really three minor climaxes in this part of the story: what happens with the speedboat; failing to start the engine; and the closing in of the fog. Each of these events puts Jo and Uncle Merlin in greater danger than they were before. Each time Jo blames herself for what has happened.

The turning point of the story comes when Jo realizes that Uncle Merlin is well able to cope with their emergency. He knows exactly where they are and how much danger they are in. He keeps Jo's fears from running away with her by telling her stories. By example, he shows her how to get through a crisis.

The author concludes the story quickly by letting us know that Jo and Uncle Merlin will be rescued. We also know that facing real danger has taught Jo several things. She has learned that Uncle Merlin is a brave and dependable person who understands her. She is willing to try to share his appreciation for life at sea. You know that Jo will find things to enjoy about her summer, after all.

Theme

The theme is the main idea that runs through the story. The author may state the theme directly or may let the reader infer it. Some common themes include

Person against person: One character opposes another. This may take the form of good against evil.

Person against self: A character tries to better his or her own self.

Person against environment: A character tries to master something in the environment.

These are not the only themes used by authors. Others might be cooperation and consideration for others.

Sometimes a story may have more than one theme. The major theme of "On Little Cat Feet" is Jo's struggle to master her own fear and longing to run away — person versus self. Another important theme, however, is Jo's learning to master a new and sometimes dangerous environment. In this story, the two themes are tightly woven together.

Mapping Stories

One way to get a visual picture of how an author has put together the elements of a story is to make a story map. This is a drawing that shows the setting, theme, characters, and plot. Look at the story map of "On Little Cat Feet" on the opposite page.

A person making a story map will begin by drawing four boxes on a large sheet of paper. These will be labeled "Setting," "Characters," "Plot," and "Theme." Below these, other boxes will be drawn to show the major details of the story. Lines are drawn to connect the detail boxes with the story elements to which they belong.

For example, notice that under "Characters" are two boxes labeled "Major" and "Minor." Each is connected by a line to the "Characters" box. Under "Major" you find Jo and Uncle Merlin. Under "Minor" you find Dad, Roger, and the speedboat driver.

Following the connecting lines helps you see what goes with what. Using different shapes of boxes for different levels of detail can make the story map easier to understand.

Understanding Setting, Characters, Plot, and Theme

Reread the story "The Boy Who Shaped Stone." As you read, make notes about the setting; the major and minor characters; the events that signal the beginning, middle, climax, and conclusion of the plot; and the theme.

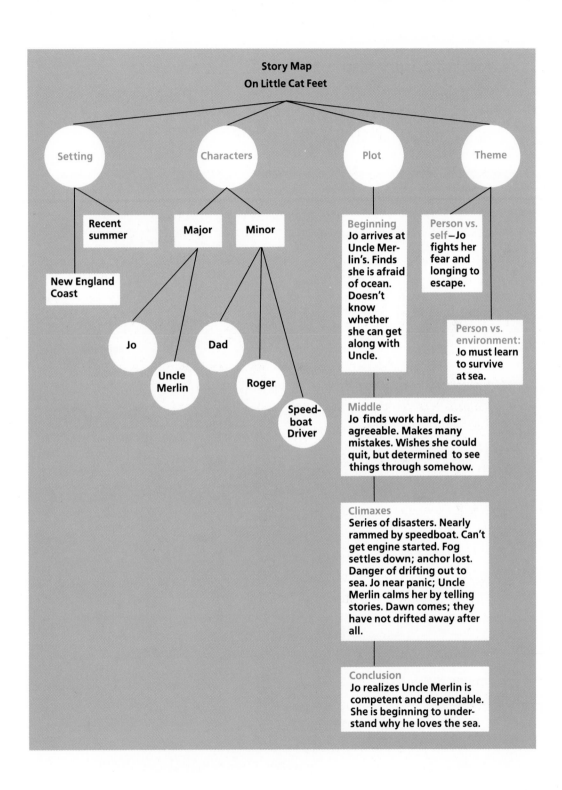

Story Map
On Little Cat Feet

Setting

Characters

Plot

Theme

Recent summer

New England Coast

Major

Minor

Jo

Uncle Merlin

Dad

Roger

Speed-boat Driver

Beginning
Jo arrives at Uncle Merlin's. Finds she is afraid of ocean. Doesn't know whether she can get along with Uncle.

Middle
Jo finds work hard, disagreeable. Makes many mistakes. Wishes she could quit, but determined to see things through somehow.

Climaxes
Series of disasters. Nearly rammed by speedboat. Can't get engine started. Fog settles down; anchor lost. Danger of drifting out to sea. Jo near panic; Uncle Merlin calms her by telling stories. Dawn comes; they have not drifted away after all.

Conclusion
Jo realizes Uncle Merlin is competent and dependable. She is beginning to understand why he loves the sea.

Person vs. self—Jo fights her fear and longing to escape.

Person vs. environment: Jo must learn to survive at sea.

Making a Story Map

Below is a format for a story map of "The Boy Who Shaped Stone." Copy it on a piece of paper. Using your notes, fill in your story map.

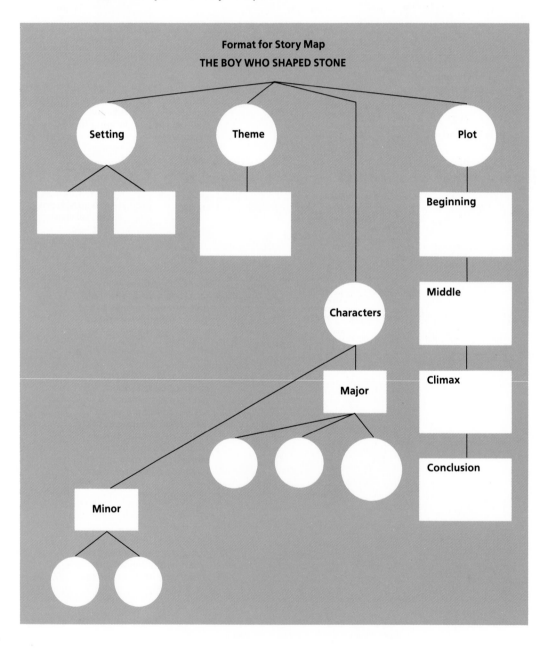

Format for Story Map
THE BOY WHO SHAPED STONE

Setting   Theme   Plot

Beginning

Middle

Characters

Major   Climax

Conclusion

Minor

Skill Summary

When you read narrative writing, notice how the author has used various elements to tell the story. A story map can be made to show a picture of these elements. The elements of a good story include

- Setting — the time and place.
- Characters — the people or animals in the story. Major characters carry most of the action. Minor characters support the major characters and action.
- Plot — the series of events that the author uses in the story. The plot has a beginning, a middle, a climax, and a conclusion.
- Theme — the main idea around which the story is developed.

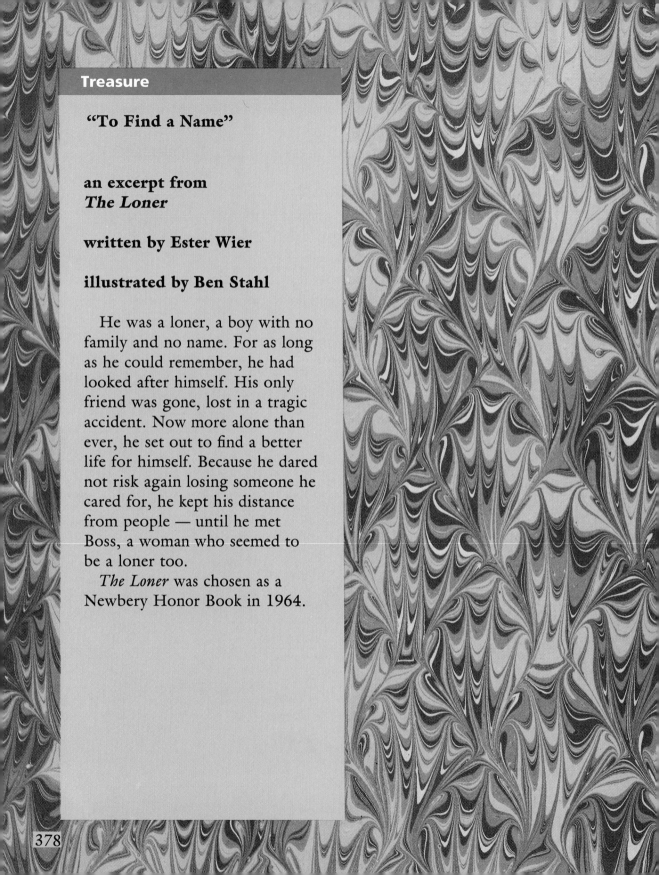

"To Find a Name"

an excerpt from
The Loner

written by Ester Wier

illustrated by Ben Stahl

He was a loner, a boy with no family and no name. For as long as he could remember, he had looked after himself. His only friend was gone, lost in a tragic accident. Now more alone than ever, he set out to find a better life for himself. Because he dared not risk again losing someone he cared for, he kept his distance from people — until he met Boss, a woman who seemed to be a loner too.

The Loner was chosen as a Newbery Honor Book in 1964.

THE
LONER

by Ester Wier

illustrated by Ben Stahl

To Find a Name

For as long as he could remember, the boy had lived among the crop pickers, moving from camp to camp with the harvest. No one could remember whether he had ever had a family. He did not even have a name — he was just "Boy."

His friend, Raidy, had promised to think of a name for him, but she had been killed in an accident. Overcome with grief, the boy left the pickers' camp and set out on his own to find a better life in California. The winter was already beginning, and he'd better get there as fast as he could.

The boy stood in the middle of the road, gazing up at the wedge of wild geese high in the sky above him. Their noisy honking broke the immense quiet that lay like a blanket, spread from the mountains beyond to the endless plains far below. He turned slowly, watching the birds disappear to the south, thinking how Raidy would have liked seeing them. She would have made up something about them, like saying they were an Indian arrowhead flung across the sky by some unseen arm behind the mountains.

He shook his head dully, pushing Raidy out of his mind, and looked down at his feet. There was little left of the sneakers now, only the ragged canvas around his ankles, the raveled strings which held them on, and what had not been gouged from the soles on the long walk from the highway many miles behind him now.

A late afternoon wind was rising, biting into his legs through the threadbare dungarees and into his body under the worn flannel shirt. The crack in his lower lip opened again and his tongue, touching it, tasted blood. He put a chapped hand against his lip and pressed hard. Every inch of his body ached, ached with weariness and hunger and the terrible emptiness of losing Raidy.

Beyond him the road climbed another hill, and upon the crest, spruce trees bent in the wind, and shadows spread like dark water seeping from the mountainside. The ruffled edges of the clouds had turned gold, and for a moment it seemed that the whole world had become golden, the dried slopes about him reflecting the coming sunset. He was used to being out of doors at all hours, but he had never seen anything like this, and he stood, swaying wearily, caught by its splendor. In the distance off to his right, a herd of deer, driven from the higher ridges by the first signs of winter, moved slowly across the bronze grass. Except for birds, they were the first signs of life he had seen in days of struggling through this country, and suddenly the enormity of the space around him and the loneliness of its silence became more than he could stand, and he found himself running toward the animals, leaving the road and scrambling over sun-scorched pasture land in a fury of haste.

"Wait!" he called, fighting through bushes and over hillocks. "Wait!" he shouted foolishly with all his strength, his voice carrying through the thin air. The deer poised for a moment and then faded into the landscape. He watched them go, still calling frantically and running toward them. They were alive, and at this moment he needed to be near something living, something besides endless stretches of hills and plains.

When he realized they were gone, his breath began to come in long shaking sobs. The reserve strength he had called on in trying to reach them left him, and he fell headlong on the earth beside a cluster of pale-gold serviceberry bushes. The impact knocked the air out of him, and he lay without moving, his tear-streaked face pressed into the rough dry grass.

Finally the boy tried to raise his body, his shaggy brown hair falling over his eyes. He couldn't go any farther. He was through, finished, beaten. How long had it been since he left the potato fields and started off on his own across this unfamiliar country? Which way was he headed now? How many meals had he made on berries and the raw potatoes he carried in his pockets? He didn't know. He didn't care. Nothing mattered now.

He burrowed deeper into the earth, rolling his body into a ball against the bushes, the weariness spreading through him like a soothing syrup. He cried himself out and slowly his hands relaxed and his eyes closed. Like a small animal seeking the warmth of the earth, he pressed his face against the grass and slept.

The woman waiting on the rise of the hill stood six-foot-two in her boots. They were sturdy leather boots, laced to the knee. Above them she wore wool trousers and a heavy, wool-lined jacket. On her head was a man's old felt hat, pulled down to cover her ears and the gray hair cut short all over her head. She stood with the grace of an athlete, relaxed yet disciplined. She lifted a hand and called, "Come!" and the dog, Jupiter, below the hill beside some serviceberry bushes, raised his head and looked at her. He came from a line of the finest sheep dogs of northern Scotland, and it showed in his deep chest, his remarkable height, his proud balance of body.

He looked at the woman and took a few steps toward her, then flung his head high and growled low in his throat. He retraced his steps to the bushes and looked at her again. Barking for a sheep dog was always the last resort in an emergency and one sure to excite the sheep, so he held his voice deep in his throat, and the sound carried no farther than to the woman on the hill.

"What is it, Jup?" she asked, watching him. "If I walk down there and find it's only a rabbit, I'll skin you alive."

He led her back to the bushes where the boy lay. How had the boy been led here, a stone's throw from the only human being within miles?

"Well," she said at last, "if it were a sheep and as scrawny as this, I'd say it was hardly worth the finding. How do you suppose he got here, Jup? Where does he belong? Hardly enough clothes or flesh on him to cover his bones. You found a real stray this time."

384

The wind from the mountains carried the icy threat of snows soon to come. The sunset was over and night blue had spread across the sky. The first stars appeared and the chill turned to raw cold.

"Back to the sheep, Jup," the woman said. "I'll handle this." The collie hesitated for a moment in leave-taking, then sped off toward the bed-ground, the white tip of his tail moving through the fast-falling darkness.

The woman bent over the sleeping boy. Traces of tears were on his face, streaks through the dust and dirt. His thin body was curled against the cold, and the straight brown hair hung ragged against his neck. "What a miserable little critter," she said softly. "I wouldn't let a sheep get into such a wretched condition." She studied for a while how to move him and decided against awakening him. Carefully she placed an arm underneath and slowly raised him so that he lay against her, reminding her of stray lambs she had so often carried back to the fold. He stirred, a long convulsive shudder running through his body, then lay quietly in her arms.

She carried him up the hill and across the hundred yards to the sheep wagon. Jup was waiting for her, his head turned toward her, yet his senses alert for any movement among the sheep on the bed-ground. They lay, over nine hundred of them, close together on a slanting rise beside the wagon. Around the bed-ground, several feet apart, stood the flags to scare off marauding animals.

The other dog, Juno, sniffed daintily, her nose pointed up at the boy. Her rough white coat moved in the wind, and her dark mahogany-colored ears stood three-quarters erect, with the ends tipping forward.

"It's all right," the woman assured her. "Now you two get back to your posts and keep a sharp lookout for coyotes. If they get a sheep tonight, I'll skin you both alive." Jup whined softly and moved toward the sheep, Juno following a parallel course on the opposite side of the flock.

Smoke curled from the stovepipe atop the sheep wagon, drifting south with the wind. The woman mounted the steps to the door, pulling it open carefully so as not to disturb the boy. Once in, she shut it behind her and looked about. The benches on either side of the long narrow room were hard and bare, so she carried the boy to the end where the bed was built crosswise into the wagon. She pushed aside the soogan, the heavy square comforter, and laid him on top of the blankets. The room was warm, and the boy sighed as he turned over and adjusted himself to the softness.

The woman took off her heavy coat and old felt hat and went to the kerosene stove, which stood to the right of the door. Taking a kettle, she poured water into it from a bucket, salted it, and set it on the flame. She seemed to fill the end of the wagon, her head clearing the ceiling by only a few inches. While the water came to a boil, she raised a trap door in the long bench on the left and pulled out two wool sacks stuffed with straw, two blankets, and another soogan. She made up a bed quickly on the bench, then returned to the stove and poured cornmeal into the

boiling water. When the mush was ready, she put it into a bowl and punctured a can of milk. She left the bowl on the stove to keep warm and went back to the bed where the boy lay.

"Come," she said, rousing him. The boy's eyes flew open, and he lay staring up at her. Confusion was on his face and a wary look about his eyes. "Here's some food," she said. "You look as if you could stand it." She went back to the stove and picked up the bowl.

The boy sat up and backed into a corner of the bed. He looked around the strange room and then up at the woman again. "Who're you?" he asked.

The woman handed him the bowl and poured milk on the mush. "Eat," she said. "I'll talk while you fill your stomach." She wanted to wash his hands and face before he ate, but she knew at the moment his need was more for nourishment than for cleanliness.

"Eat!" she said again. The boy stared at her, then picking up the spoon, he began to eat, placing the hot mush in his mouth and swallowing hungrily.

"Take it slow," she said. "There's more if you want it." She sat on the bench and leaned forward. "My dog found you a while ago, and I carried you here and put you to bed. I figured you must be hungry, so I fixed you something to eat. And I wanted you to know where you were so that when you woke up in the morning, you wouldn't be scared to find yourself here."

The boy listened as he ate. "Who're you?" he asked again.

"You can call me Boss, I guess. It's been years since anyone called me anything else. I've got a flock of sheep outside and this is my wagon, and it's resting on the winter range.

"Now, suppose you tell me what to call you," she said.

The boy looked at her silently for a long time. Distrust and caution played over his face, and Boss had the notion that if he could squirm out of the corner and past her, he would make a dash for the door.

"This isn't a home for children?" he asked.

Boss laughed. "It's a home for me; that's what it is. Now, what's your name?"

The boy's eyes narrowed. "Boy," he said. "That's what folks call me, unless they're mad at me."

The woman knew she had been right about his being a stray. He was underfed, uncared for, and didn't even have a name. Right now he looked like a hunted animal, a lonely animal fighting for its life in a world where nobody cared about it. It made her mad all over.

"All right," she said, "I'll call you Boy for now." She knew there was no use asking him questions. Let him settle down and relax first. There would be time enough to find out where he belonged and decide what to do with him later.

She took the bowl back to the stove and filled a pan with water from the kettle. In a corner of the dish cupboard beside the stove she found a towel. She got some soap and carried it all back to him.

"Wet a corner of the towel and wash your face. Then scrub your hands," she said. "And use the soap! I'll find something for you to sleep in."

The boy looked at the water and soap. "Is it Saturday?" he asked. In the crop-pickers' camps no one ever bathed except on Saturday evening.

"No, it isn't Saturday, but I want you clean because I'm letting you sleep in the bed tonight. I won't have it messed up with a lot of dirt. Now, get to washing!"

She turned her back on him, then lifted the bed she had made to get to the trap door of the bench again. When she found the garment she wanted, she came back to him and dropped it on the bed. "Wipe your hands and get into this shirt."

"It's big," he said. "Is it yours?"

She shook her head. "Belonged to old Bezeleel, who used to live here. I found it when I moved in. It's clean."

"Where are you sleeping?" he asked.

She pointed to the wool sacks on the bench. "I'll sleep here tonight, soon as I get my boots off."

"You going to wash too?"

"I've already washed. I do that as soon as I come in from the range and get the sheep settled. And I keep my boots handy. Good herders sleep with one ear on the sheep and the other on the dogs, and never know from one minute to the next when they'll have to get out there and scare off a coyote or two."

"That why Beze—the other sheepherder—isn't here any more? 'Cause he was a sound sleeper?"

Boss laughed. He was quick all right . . . "No, that's not why." She stood up and straightened her bed.

"You'd be a good crop picker," the boy said, studying her. "You could lift a sack of potatoes easy, or even a full hamper of beans."

The woman knew he had paid her a compliment. So that's where he had come from, she thought. Probably from the potato fields in Idaho. Why is he here, and who does he belong to?

She raised the blankets on his bed and told him to crawl under. "It's going to be cold when I turn off the stove, so dig down deep and keep the potatoes warm." She picked up a sack of potatoes and put them under the covers beside him. "When you sleep in this bed, that chore goes with it."

He looked at her as though she were crazy. "Sleep with potatoes? Why?"

"So they won't freeze. Now, no more questions. I'll leave the stove on in the morning when I start out, and the window over your bed cracked just enough to give you some air. I'll leave biscuits on the stove and a pot of beans, and the rest of the canned milk. Sleep all you can, and I'll see you when I get home at sundown. Don't go outside in those thin clothes."

"Where you going?"

"Out with the sheep. They're ready to leave the bed-ground at sunup, and they'll graze a few miles from here tomorrow. Now, no more questions. Go to sleep."

She turned off the lamp and lay down on the straw-filled wool sacks, drawing the blankets and soogan over her. She listened for the dogs but heard nothing. Not a sound came from the sheep. The wind was dying down, and she thought gratefully that perhaps tonight she would be able to sleep straight through. Jup or Juno would warn her if the coyotes came near, or if the sheep became restless and decided to look for higher ground, or if the lead sheep felt she hadn't had enough grass and set off to find more, with the rest of the flock following her.

She would think what to do with the boy tomorrow while she was out on the range. Right now she was tired, and sunup was too few hours away.

When the boy awoke in the morning, he was startled by his surroundings. Slowly it came back to him. He lay snug and warm under the blankets, examining the room. Boss had left her bed on the long bench neat, the blankets pulled smooth and the soogan folded lengthwise. The hinged window above his bed was held open a crack by a short stick, and he pulled himself up to look out.

He found the beans and a pan of biscuits warm on the stove. Opening a biscuit, he heaped beans into it and ate, standing beside the stove, the long flannel nightshirt dropping in folds upon the floor.

Satisfied, he returned to the bed and slipped under the blankets. It was time to think about where he was and what he should do next. Boss hadn't asked him where he had come from. She wasn't nosy like some of the people who had given him rides along the highway.

He had to be getting on to California before the winter set in. Somehow he must have got turned in the wrong direction, so he would have to go back and find the highway again. He looked around the sheep wagon. It was all right here, nice and warm, and there was plenty of food to eat. Boss was all right too. She had given him her bed and this nightshirt, and she had even covered him up. No one had ever bothered so much about him before, no one but Raidy. He lay back and closed his eyes, suddenly tired again.

When he awakened, a man was standing in the doorway looking at him. The man was young, with dark weather-beaten skin and very light-blue eyes. His clothes were rough and well-worn. He held a bag of flour and tins of food under his arm. Closing the door behind him, he came to the short bench and laid the articles on it.

"Where's Boss?" he asked, and the boy immediately knew he was a Texan. He had the same way of saying words, drawling them slow and easy, like the overseers in the bean fields.

He sat up. "Out with the sheep," he said, feeling comfortable with this man right away.

"When I saw smoke from the chimney, I wondered if she was sick." The man removed his greasy hat and extended a hand. "I'm Tex," he said, "camp tender."

His words meant nothing to the boy, but they shook hands. "I've got kerosene and wood and more groceries in the truck outside. Some mail here." He removed it from his pocket.

"My job is to come up here every week to see how Boss is makin' out and to bring provisions. Now, there's snow blowin' up in the northwest, so I'm bringin' supplies in early. Tell Boss we're in for some Montana weather, first of the season."

The boy asked, "Is that where I am?"

"Sure. Where did you think you were?"

"I didn't know, but it didn't seem like what I'd heard about California. Wasn't warm enough. Any crops to pick around here?"

"Yes, you're in Montana. But there's no crops to be picked here now. Did you run away?"

The boy considered the question. "No. I just left."

"What about your folks? They'll be worried."

Amazement showed in the boy's eyes. "Worried about me? Nobody's going to be worried about me. I never had any folks."

"Who takes care of you?"

"Takes care of me? I take care of myself, always have."

Tex chuckled. "You sound like a real loner for sure. You might say I used to be a loner too. One of those who didn't believe anyone cared about them or wanted to help. I figured it was up to me to take care of myself, and I didn't need help from anyone."

394

The boy nodded. This man understood.

"Let me tell you, boy, that's a poor way of livin'. A mighty selfish one too. Somebody will care if you just give 'em a chance."

The boy thought of Raidy.

"There's always people who need you as much as you need them. Don't you forget that. All you got to do is find 'em. When you do, you find you're happier carin' about someone else than just about yourself all the time. You thinkin' about stayin' around here? This is mighty pretty country. It's sheep country."

The boy thought it over. "I was planning to get on to California, but I might stay a little while — if she'll let me."

"You stay here with Boss for a while if she'll let you, hear? But don't tell her I said so. Ever since Ben was killed, she doesn't take kindly to people figurin' out what she should do."

"Who's Ben?"

Tex didn't answer for a few minutes. He teetered back on the bench, and his eyes looked far off. He seemed to be making up his mind. Finally he decided, and he leaned forward.

"I'm goin' to tell you about Boss so you'll understand her a little better. She won't tell you; that is for sure. She doesn't talk much and never about herself. Maybe later on she'll get around to explaining to you about Ben, but I think you should know now. Don't you tell her that I've been talkin' about her. Ben was her son. He was killed by a grizzly, a bear, two winters back when he was out huntin'. Boss spent a whole year lookin' for that bear and never did find it. There was never anyone in the world like Ben to her. She should try to hire a herder, but she won't listen. These ewes in her flock are the best on the ranch, the real money-makers, so it's a special job and Boss decided to do it herself."

He slapped his leg and stood up. "I've talked enough for one day. Got to go now. I'll bring the food and kerosene in and lay the wood under the wagon." He moved toward the door.

"You still a loner?" the boy asked.

A grin spread over Tex's face. "I been gettin' over it lately; that's how come I gave you all that good advice. You better get over it too." He winked. "You put up with Boss as long as she'll have you. When she does talk, you'll hear a lot about Ben and about the bear and about sheep, but I reckon you can stand that. Seems to me you two belong together."

When Tex finished his chores, the boy watched him walk down the hill and get into the provision truck. He watched until the truck disappeared down the road between the cottonwoods and the quaking aspens and willows.

The boy thought about Ben and Boss, the bear, and Tex for a long time. Tex had advised him to stay here if he could. It made sense. Maybe Tex was right. If Boss would have him, he'd like to stay here for a while, maybe until next spring.

He began to study how to make Boss want him to stay. He remembered how she'd made him wash last night. That must mean that she liked for people to be clean. All right, if he had to be clean to stay, then he'd get used to it. Finding the pan he had washed in before, he poured water into it from the bucket. The water was warm from standing near the stove, so he used it as it was. He stripped off the nightshirt and dropped the soap into the pan. Then, with the end of the towel, he washed himself thoroughly, better than he ever had in his life.

He ate another biscuit with beans and climbed back into bed. His body cried out for sleep and rest, and he curled up under the blankets, grasping the bag of potatoes close to him, although the wagon was warm now. There was no way of knowing what time it was, and even if he had known, it wouldn't have mattered. Boss would be home at sundown. Until then he would sleep.

The boy awoke to sounds outside the wagon. He pulled himself up to the window and looked out. The sheep were slowly coming toward the bed-ground, grazing as they moved forward. Boss wasn't in sight, but he saw a dog working one side of the band. It ran up and down on the outer edge of the flock, guiding, directing the sheep toward the bed-ground. He saw it go after one sheep that had strayed a little way off from the others. Taking it gently by the ear, the big black-and-white dog

led it back to the others, left it there, and went on with its work.

He heard a low-pitched whistle and then saw another dog, smaller, and all white except for dark-brown ears, appear from the other side, working the sheep to the right so that they headed toward the bed-ground.

Boss opened the door a few minutes later, pulling her hat off and running her hands through her short hair as she entered the wagon. "Been all right today?" she asked. Her gaze was so sharp that he felt she knew at once he had bathed, but she didn't say anything about it. He nodded, surprised again at her size.

She saw the new supplies and the mail. "Tex been here?"

The boy nodded again. "He said to tell you weather was coming so he brought things out today."

"I'm going out and feed the dogs and count the sheep," she said. "Then I'll come in and clean up and get us some supper."

The boy looked at her, round-eyed. "You know enough numbers to count all of them?" he asked. To him the sheep were endless, covering the ground all around the wagon.

She laughed and drew him to the window. "Look out there. You'll see some black sheep among the rest. They're the ones I count. There's one of them for every hundred white and we call them markers. If all nine are there, it's safe to figure we haven't lost any."

She left the wagon with the bowls of dog food, and the boy stayed at the window and looked out. He counted the number of black sheep he saw. There were only six, but he couldn't see all the flock. He couldn't see Boss or the dogs either, but he guessed she was feeding them right outside the wagon.

After a while Boss came back into the wagon. "No wind tonight," she said, "though it may blow up later if weather's coming. That's the biggest worry I have, along with coyotes."

"Wind doesn't blow them away, does it?" the boy asked.

Boss looked at him quickly to see if he was joking.

"No, though it does seem to blow their wits away. A sheep doesn't like to feel its wool ruffled, so it's just as apt to get up and walk into the wind. If one goes, they all go."

The boy thought about that. "Guess they're pretty dumb, huh?"

Boss whirled on him. "Dumb? They're not dumb. They're just about the most helpless creatures alive. They've lost all their instinct to take care of themselves because they haven't had to. But it isn't their fault. It's ours. We've bred all the wild animal's independence and cunning out of them for our own gain, to have their meat and their wool with the least possible bother from them. Don't ever use that word about them again in my hearing. I won't have it!"

She stood there, red-faced with anger, and the boy swallowed hard. He wasn't off to a very good start at making her like him and want him to stay. It was a new game to him, and he realized he wasn't very good at it. But if he wanted to stay enough, he could learn how to think of what she'd like before he did or said anything.

Slowly her face relaxed. "I know people call them stupid. They say they're the only animals alive that are born determined to get themselves killed one way or another as soon as possible. But I happen to love those sheep, every one of them, and Ben did too. He spent his time caring for them from the time he was just a child. He kept them from straying off and getting lost, kept them out of the coyotes' way, kept them from eating the locoweed that drives them crazy. I know they seem to be bent on doing things that will destroy them, but that's the reason I'm here. To keep them safe and together."

Evening had come, and the sheep had settled down. The wagon was warm and comfortable, and the deep weariness of his body was almost gone. He thought about what Boss had said. It surprised him to hear her talk like that about sheep. People he'd known spent their time taking care of themselves. Boss took care of sheep.

She pulled the table up and propped it with the folding leg. They ate stewed tomatoes and scrambled eggs and some of the biscuits left over from morning. She poured a cup of half canned milk and half water for the boy.

After she cleared away the dishes, Boss brought her boots and a jar of grease to the table. She worked the grease into the leather with her fingers and wiped it off with a cloth. Her large hands were rough, but the nails were evenly trimmed and clean. "Ben cleaned his boots every night of his life," she said. "I never had to tell him to do it."

The boy was glad he had bathed. It had been the right thing to do, something Ben would have done without being told.

When she finished, she put the boots on the floor and went to the long bench. Inside it she found a book and brought it back to the table.

"I've been thinking all day about a name," she said. "Seems to me you ought to pick one out for yourself. There's a lot of fine names in the Bible here.

"I decided the best way was to let you hold the Bible and turn to wherever you want — then to put your finger on the page and see what it says."

He took the book and held it between his hands. The cover was of smooth leather, and there were gold letters across the front of it. He hesitated, thinking of Raidy. He wished she could be here now to see him get a name, his own name.

Opening the book, he pressed the pages flat on his knees. Then he placed his finger on a place and held it there. Boss covered his finger with her large one and took the book. For a minute she didn't say anything.

The boy couldn't stand the waiting. "What does it say?" he asked.

Her voice was very low. "You put your finger on these words, 'Send me David thy son, which is with the sheep!'"

"That mean my name is David?"

She shut the book slowly. "It's a fine name. . . ."

He was curious. "Who was he?"

"A shepherd," Boss said. "A very brave and loyal shepherd. When he was only a boy in charge of his father's flock, he risked his life to protect his sheep. That's what shepherds are for, to look out for their sheep even if it means risking their own lives. You could be very proud of a name like that, but you'd also have a lot to live up to."

She rose and put the book away. "Get into bed. This one." She was pointing to the one on the bench. "You'll use it after this — David."

He lay in bed thinking about his name, trying it over and over until it began to sound familiar on his tongue. He heard the dogs barking in the night, and then was aware that Boss was leaving the wagon. He got up and watched out the window while she built a fire, and saw by its light the sheep huddled close together. Far off he heard a weird high-pitched howl. The dogs stood alert at the edge of the flock, and Boss walked around the bed-ground, a flaming stick in her hand.

Lying down again, the boy curled up under the soogan and thought sleepily that it was strange how he had picked out a shepherd's name. Now he was going to be a shepherd too.

In the months that followed, David did learn to live up to his new name. It was not easy, for there were dangers and hardships to be faced. David didn't give up, though, and the new friends he made helped him through the bad times.

405

Author

As wife of a naval officer, Ester Wier has lived in many parts of the world. While her children were in high school, she published magazine stories, articles, poems, and adult books. *The Loner,* her first book for young people, was a Newbery Honor Book and was made into a TV movie. Mrs. Wier says, "My fervent wish is that when children read a book of mine, they find something besides a story to hold their interest, hopefully the opening of a new world of some kind."

Illustrator

Ben Stahl has lived and traveled in many parts of the United States and has spent three years teaching art in Amsterdam. At the present time, he lives in Norwalk, Connecticut. He has no formal art training and claims that he has learned what he knows about illustration by looking over other artists' shoulders. He has received many awards, including one from the National Science Teachers' Association for an "outstanding science book for children" in 1976.

Summary Questions

Think about how being together will change the lives of Boss and David.

1. Why was David so lonely at the beginning of the story?
2. Do you think Boss was lonely before she met David? Why or why not?
3. How did talking with Tex change David's decision to go alone to California? Why was David willing to listen to Tex?
4. David and Boss were both used to being alone. How do you think being together will enrich their lives? What difficulties might they have?

The Reading and Writing Connection

The word map below shows some words that could be used to describe David when he first came to Boss's sheep wagon. Think about why David felt or looked each way.

Imagine that a year has passed since the end of this story. Write a description of David that tells what he was like when he arrived and how he has changed since he met Boss. Be sure to include several of the descriptive words from the map.

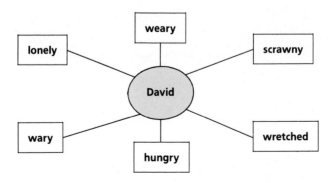

Magazine Wrap-up

- Matthew in "Arctic Fire"
- Jo in "On Little Cat Feet"
- Major Powell in "Conquering the Colorado"
- Maria Melgoza Davis in "Living at the Bottom of the World"
- David in "To Find a Name"

Imagine that you are each of these characters. For each, finish this sentence: "The most important thing I learned from this experience was _____."

Literary Skill: Theme

In several stories in Magazine Three, the characters were involved in a struggle to survive in a new and difficult environment.

Think about each of the following characters and how he or she changed as a result of the events in the story.

Vocabulary: Meaning from Context

Often you can use the context to get the meaning of a word that is new to you. When you come to an unfamiliar word, pay close attention to the other words around it. You may find an explanation or a synonym in the sentence. You may be able to figure out the word by contrasting it with another word. Sometimes the general sense of the sentence will give you a clue to the new word's meaning.

Read each of the following sentences. The boldface word may be new to you, but the context of each sentence gives clues to its meaning. Write what you think each one means. Be prepared to discuss the clues that helped you arrive at your answer.

1. The kitten tried to **extricate** it-self from the tangled yarn.
2. On the hundredth anniversary of our town's founding, we held a **centennial** celebration.
3. Do you want your new scarf to be all one color, or do you pre-fer the **variegated** ones?
4. The fact that no one voted against the measure showed the **unanimity** of our opinion.
5. The trick in learning to ride a bicycle is learning to keep your **equilibrium.**

Comprehension Skill: Evaluating Opinion

When you need an expert opin-ion, you ask someone with knowl-edge and experience in the field. Read the Magazine Three table of contents on pages 268–269. Think about the real people and the major and minor fictional charac-ters you read about in those selec-tions. Most of them had special knowledge and experience.

Imagine that you wanted a quali-fied opinion on each of the follow-ing subjects. Tell which person or character you would ask about that subject, and why.

1. The best way to train a new puppy
2. Future directions for media
3. The best places to go for rock climbing
4. Advantages and disadvantages of outboard motors
5. The best kind of garden to plant in wet places

Books to Enjoy

I, Rebekah, Take You, the Lawrences
by Julia First

A spunky twelve-year-old shares the warmth and luxury of her adoptive home with her orphanage friends.

A Morgan for Melinda
by Doris Gates

Melinda's friendship with an eld-erly woman writer helps the girl overcome her fear of horses and learn about herself.

The Land I Lost: Adventures of a Boy in Vietnam
by Huynh Quang Nhuong

Dramatic, true adventures cap-ture the flavor of Vietnamese vil-lage life before the war.

Courage at Indian Deep
by Jane Resh Thomas

Cass and his dog are the only ones who can help the survivors of a sinking ship during a blizzard on Lake Superior.

Celebrations
Magazine Four

Contents

James Forten Goes to Sea

by Brenda A. Johnston

When he signed up to be a sailor, James was dreaming
of sea battles and adventure. Dreams sometimes have a
way of taking unexpected turns.

In 1781, the city of Philadelphia was a center of activity for the American Revolution. Coming and going from the harbor were many ships whose mission was to capture British ships. James Forten was one of many young Americans who wanted to seek adventure at sea.

James was a fifteen-year-old who lived with his mother and sister in a community of free blacks. James's father, a sailmaker, had drowned when James was ten. Educated in a school for blacks, James helped to support his family by doing jobs for the sailmaker who had once employed Mr. Forten.

There was excitement along the harbor, and James joined the crowds watching the *Royal Lewis,* Philadelphia's own privateer, bringing its captured British vessel into port. Since Philadelphia was the capital of the new nation, James witnessed many auctions of captured British cargo at the wharves and marveled at the proceeds that the captain and the crew shared as a reward. The privateers were not part of the navy, but American ships whose mission was to stop the British merchant ships. Their reward was patriotic glory, the wealthy cargo from the captured ships, and a small monthly allotment as well.

James wanted to join the privateer crew more than anything else in the world, but he had already learned that it was useless to plead with his mother. As he walked home from the docks, he passed the London Coffee House, where he met his friends Larry and Fred standing outside.

"Guess what?" They greeted him in excitement.

"What?" asked James coolly, careful not to betray his curiosity.

"Guess who got signed up for the *Royal Lewis*'s next trip?"

James was interested. "Not you, I know," he said, hoping with all his heart that they were not going before he could.

"Daniel Brewton," they answered him. Daniel was one of their white friends.

"I'm going to sign up too," said James decisively.

"You're too young," said Fred.

"Daniel and I are the same age almost," said James.

"Your mother'll kill you," declared Larry. "Besides, we already tried."

James left them standing there while he approached a man sitting at a table taking down names. He stood before the man and cleared his throat.

The man looked at him inquiringly. James was already nearly six feet tall and walked with a slow, self-confident gait. He had acquired the habit of gazing unfalteringly into a person's eyes while talking, taking care that none of his own feelings were ever reflected in his dark eyes. He now fixed his gaze on the man and waited.

The man finally said, "You're on. What's your name?"

"James Forten," he answered quickly, already wondering what he was going to tell his mother.

The man's voice broke through his thoughts. "We sail in three days, James. See you then."

He walked back to his friends and said, "Well, boys, the *Royal Lewis* and I sail in three days."

They were astonished. "How?" they asked. "What did you say?"

James laughed at their dismay and patted their heads.

"I think," he said, "that you two are just a little too short." He started for home.

In spite of his apprehension about telling his mother the bad news, James was humming with joy when he reached home. His spirits were so high that even his mother and his sister, Abigail, caught his mood. James put off telling his mother until he had read to her from the Bible that evening, but as he closed the book, he looked at her and started.

"Mother, may I join the crew of the *Royal Lewis*?"

She didn't answer but just returned his direct look. For a panicky moment, he wondered if someone had already told her what he had done. She acted as if she knew.

"They are taking twenty black sailors with them, Mother," he finally said.

She still would not answer. James wildly thought that either she was a mind reader or she had talked to Larry's mother.

"I'm one of the twenty," he said at last, shamefacedly.

His mother folded her arms and shook her head but did not say anything. It was the only time James had ever defied her. Now he felt sorry.

"Is it all right?" he asked, his voice pleading.

"You did what you wanted to do already, didn't you?" She sounded tired.

"Oh, I'll never get a job in the sail loft so long as the war lasts," said James. "Business keeps getting slower and slower. This way I'll get a chance to do lots of things. Travel. Defend my country." His eyes sparkled in excitement, and he suddenly laughed aloud.

"Oh, Mother," he exclaimed, "I've always wanted to ride in a ship and see the sails from the other side."

"But, James," she said, her voice almost breaking, "it's so dangerous."

"Not for our ship," said James, "the *Royal Lewis,* commanded by Captain Decatur — King of the Sea."

"Promise me," his mother said, finally relenting, "that you will read your Bible every night. You'll never know how much your father wanted you to be able to read."

"I promise," said James. "Only, Mother, no one can forget how to read. It's like forgetting how to walk."

Three days later James went down to the docks, taking only the clothes he wore on his back, his mother's Bible, and a bag of marbles. His mother had stayed home and had waved good-by to James from the door as if he were leaving, as always, only for the day.

Powder boy on the *Royal Lewis* was the lowest and dirtiest of jobs, and James soon realized that it consisted of more than just preparing for battle. He was often called to serve meals, act as cabin boy, and do whatever else no one in particular was assigned to do.

He was eager for his first battle, and it seemed forever until the day that the cry came from the ship's lookout that the British ship *Activist* had been spotted. The quiet *Royal Lewis* became a whirl of activity as the regular privateers, in a disciplined manner, began running to their respective posts and shouting out orders. James's head was spinning. He had forgotten all he had learned. He didn't know where to start.

"James Forten," a voice called out impatiently, sounding as if it had called him many times before. "Over here!"

James ran over to the gun crew and stood in position near the powder and balls and waited, hoping that no one would notice his trembling. The *Royal Lewis* came remarkably close to the other ship, it seemed, before the voice of the British captain broke the silence.

"This is His Majesty's ship *Activist*," he called. "What ship is that?"

Captain Decatur's answer was to signal his men to attack. Almost immediately there was a deafening roar, followed by a flash of fire from the cannon, and the deck shook under James's feet. The smell of smoke filled the air and blinded him, making him cough and sneeze. By blind instinct, he began passing the powder and cannonballs to the loader, who forced them down the muzzle with a ramrod.

Now that the battle was really on, James could see the extreme danger of his job as powder boy. When the ammunition was low, James had to run below deck to the magazine for more powder and cannonballs. He would then have to run back to his post, shielding the explosive powder from the flying sparks, which could ignite an explosion fatal to him. All around him the sparks flew, forcing him to keep moving. The battle seemed to last an eternity, and both ships appeared to be utterly destroyed.

The two ships were so close now that the crew from the *Royal Lewis* began jumping over to the deck of the *Activist* to continue the battle in man-to-man combat. James, however, stayed at his post, passing ammunition until his arms felt like rubber. The battle finally took an upward swing when the *Activist* began burning in several places and the captain was seriously wounded. Soon the British flag was lowered in surrender, and the long battle had ended at last.

One day, about three months after that first battle, as the *Royal Lewis* approached a British warship called the *Amphyon,* the lookout suddenly spotted two more British vessels in the distance. Realizing the impossibility of fighting three ships at one time, the *Royal Lewis* decided to make a run for it, but the British took up the chase. Before long, they were close enough to begin firing. At the first shot, Captain Decatur immediately gave orders to strike colors. The American flag fluttered down in surrender.

It was then that James went into a complete panic. He wanted to run and scream. He knew that black sailors were never kept for prisoner exchanges but were sold into slavery in the West Indies as part of the cargo. Running below to his bunk, he had just enough time to snatch up his blanket, Bible, and marbles before he was ordered on deck by one of the British officers. The crew of the *Royal Lewis* was divided into

three groups and sent to the three British ships. James was with the group taken by the *Amphyon*. As the prisoners filed past the captain, James was stopped, and the captain asked sharply, "What's in that bag, boy?"

"What bag?" said James in confusion, looking down. His marbles in a small cloth sack dangled from his wrist.

"How old are you?" demanded the captain.

"Fifteen," answered James.

"What's in that bag?" the captain demanded again.

"Marbles," James answered, feeling very embarrassed and childish. He didn't know what had made him bring them.

"What's your name?" asked the captain.

James figured this was the end for him. The captain probably already had a prospective buyer in mind. He stood tall and answered without faltering. "My name is James Forten."

The captain smiled and waved him on. A few hours later, while James sat with the other prisoners, a British youth with rosy cheeks, straight brown hair, and a pouting mouth approached him.

"Are you James Forten, the powder boy from the *Royal Lewis*?" he asked.

James nodded.

"I am Willie Beasley, the son of Sir John, the captain of the *Amphyon*," he said with a heavy British accent. "My father tells me that you brought a bag of marbles on board. I'm a champion. Would you like to play a game?"

James took out his marbles with great pride now and followed Willie on deck. They placed the marbles on the floor between them. It was the first of many games, and in spite of themselves, the boys became fast friends, so James was in no way treated as a prisoner. At first he thought the other prisoners would be angry, but they didn't seem to notice. Sir John was glad that Willie had met someone his own age to entertain him, since the trip had turned out to be a long and boring one for the boy.

During one of their long days together, Willie asked James to go back to England with him. James instantly flared.

"I'll never be a traitor!" he snapped.

"What difference does it make, since you're nothing but a slave in your own country anyway?" asked Willie.

"I am not a slave!" said James angrily. "I was born free."

"Well, you're just a black prisoner now," retorted Willie, "and you have only two choices. You will either be sold as a slave, or you can come to England with me as a friend." He suddenly dropped his belligerent attitude. "Oh, come on, James," he begged. "England abolished slavery. You'll get an education and live in a beautiful home. Father likes you. He thinks you have a fine mind."

James didn't answer. He was tempted, but somehow it didn't seem right. When Sir John sent for him the next day, James stood before him and refused his offer to go to England.

"You must be a fool!" exclaimed Sir John in perplexed anger.

"I am an American prisoner," said James. "I cannot be a traitor to my country."

Willie broke in. "America is not your country, James. All you are there is a slave."

"I am not a slave," answered James, quietly this time.

"Well, what kind of future will you have?" asked Willie. "I could understand your loyalty if you were white."

This time James didn't answer.

Sir John sighed. He had spoiled Willie by trying to give him everything he wanted. Now he hated to see him disappointed. In an effort to change James's mind, he said, "You know you'll have to be sold."

James didn't know what to say. He opened his mouth to speak but changed his mind and said nothing.

"Well?" asked Willie.

"I cannot be a traitor," James answered. Lifting his dark, pain-filled eyes and looking directly at Willie, he almost whispered, "I never want to be a slave." He turned and quickly left.

The next day before the prisoner exchange, Willie Beasley approached James.

"You will be transferred to the *Jersey* with the other prisoners," he said. As soon as he started talking, his eyes filled with tears. "It is nothing but a floating death trap. No one gets off alive." He handed James a white envelope. "This is from Father to the captain of the *Jersey*. It will help you. Good-by, James." He turned and hurried away. Looking down at the white envelope, James realized that Willie was one of the best friends he would ever have. Somehow he knew that they would never meet again.

When James boarded the *Jersey*, he handed the white envelope to the officer in charge, who barely glanced at it and waved him on without comment. He was sent below to the main prisoner quarters, where his nostrils were immediately assailed by a loathsome odor. All around the dark hole he could hear the ravings and groanings of the sick and dying.

James knew that he was probably the only black on board. His mind went back to his school lessons on how the slaves were captured and brought to America in the pits of ships. He now knew just how they must have felt. He knew why they were so submissive and broken when they were finally sold. James thought of his great-grandfather, who had survived the slave ship, and of his grandfather, who had bought his freedom. From the number of African slaves in America, James realized that quite a few of them must have survived, and in a sudden surge of pride, he reminded himself that he was of the same race. He would make it too.

When the prisoners were brought on deck the next day, James recognized Daniel Brewton, his white neighbor from Philadelphia, who looked gravely ill. They were glad to see each other, and because of their past association they quickly became friends. This relationship was hard on James because Daniel was so sickly that James ended up doing chores and hustling food for both of them. Nevertheless, James was still able to volunteer for extra jobs, and he picked the ones that kept him on deck and out of the stinking hole as much as possible. He loaded supplies and scrubbed the deck. Not only did James survive, but he also grew tough.

He never knew if it was the letter Sir John had written that prompted another prisoner to seek him out one morning while he was doing his chores. The man told James that he, an officer, was being exchanged for a British prisoner and that he was taking a trunk with him that would hold one person. Joy flooded James's heart to think that he might finally escape, but instinct warned him not to tell Daniel. Somehow he felt like a traitor leaving him behind to die. He rudely avoided Daniel for the remainder of the day. That night when Daniel sought him out in the dark pit where they usually talked about Philadelphia and old times, James pretended he was sleepy.

"Leave me alone, Daniel!" he snapped.

"What's wrong?" asked Daniel.

"Nothing," James snapped again. "I'm just sick and tired of waiting to get off this boat."

"I don't think I'm ever going to get off," said Daniel. "I don't think I'm ever going to see Philadelphia or my home again." His voice cracked, and James knew that he was crying.

Long after Daniel had fallen asleep, James still lay awake, hating himself for what he knew he had to do. The next morning Daniel did not even want to go up on deck for fresh air, and James had to practically carry him up. His eyes seemed to be constantly pleading with James. That evening James slipped Daniel into the trunk, and the next morning he and the officer carried the trunk down to the waiting boat, which took it and the officer to freedom. As the boat disappeared toward shore, James swallowed hard and fought back the tears, knowing that it was too late to change his mind now and that a golden opportunity had slipped through his fingers.

"I can make it," he whispered to himself. "I know I can make it." He put his hands in his pocket and felt the bag of marbles that he had childishly clung to since leaving home. In sudden anger, he tossed them into the sea. He would never need them again. He felt like a tired old man as he turned back to the *Jersey* and wondered how he could make it through another day.

He did make it through, though. That day, and the next day, and the next — for three more months. Near the end of the war, he was freed in a general prisoner exchange. After the American ship, loaded with returning prisoners, docked in Philadelphia, James walked down the tiny streets of his boyhood home, wondering how the houses and streets could ever have looked huge to him. A few people glanced at him curiously, some with recognition, but James barely noticed anyone.

He was thinking of his mother and wondering if she knew he was on his way. He knew that even if she did know, she wouldn't be waiting at the door, but would be in the kitchen cooking, and would try to pretend that his walking through the door after all this time was nothing very exciting. But the smell of biscuits and gravy would soon fill the house, and her singing voice would float from the kitchen. Long before nightfall the whole neighborhood would know that Sarah Forten's boy was home.

James pushed the door open, and the aroma of cooking food filled his nostrils. She knew. When he walked into the kitchen, she didn't even look up until he whirled her around in

a bear hug. In spite of herself, she could not help crying when she saw how much James looked like his father. He was now six feet two inches tall and thin as a rail.

"You're so skinny," she said, shaking her head.

"They don't cook on the *Jersey* like you do," replied James, laughing.

"Daniel Brewton was here and told us how you slipped him off the boat," his mother said. "I'm proud of you."

She piled his plate high with rice and gravy and biscuits and pork chops and okra, just the way James had dreamed of her doing over and over again while he lay in the dark misery of the *Jersey,* counting off the passing days. It had taken two hundred ten days for the dream to come true.

James did go to work in the sail loft, as he had planned. In a short time, he was promoted to foreman. Later he became the owner of the business and invented a device that made it easier to handle the vast, heavy sails used at that time.

James Forten used his wealth and position in the community in support of the rights of women and blacks. He was active in opposing slavery, and he taught black children in his home when they were excluded from public schools. Throughout his life, he never stopped fighting for the justice that he knew all people deserved.

Author

Brenda Johnston has written books for adults as well as children. *Between the Devil and the Sea,* from which this story was taken, was chosen as a book of the year by the Child Study Association and received honorable mention from the Council on Interracial Books.

Summary Questions

Consider the difficult choices James had to make while at sea.

1. What situation became a test of James's loyalty as an American? Why was it such a difficult test?
2. Why, do you think, did James refuse Sir John's offer?
3. Why did James refuse the prisoner's offer of the chance to escape and send Daniel ashore instead?
4. James's refusal to accept either offer reveals much about his character. What words would you use to describe James? Why?

The Reading and Writing Connection

James Forten proved himself to be a brave person through the choices he made. Think of someone you know who made a courageous decision in a difficult situation. Write a paragraph telling what choice this person had to make, and why his or her decision was a sign of bravery. Try to use some of the following words in your paragraph:

> **decisively**
> **unfalteringly**
> **submissive**

From Montauk Point
by Walt Whitman

I stand as on some mighty eagle's beak.
Eastward on the sea absorbing, viewing,
   (nothing but sea and sky,)
The tossing waves, the foam, the ships in the distance
The wild unrest, the snowy, curling caps —
   that inbound urge and urge of waves,
Seeking the shores forever.

Compare and Contrast

In the last story, you read about James Forten's experiences on two British ships, the *Amphyon* and the *Jersey*. In one very important way, James's situation was the same on both ships. He was a prisoner of war. In other ways his life on the two ships was quite different. On the *Amphyon* he was treated as a friend and had considerable freedom. On the *Jersey* living conditions were terrible, and James had to struggle just to keep himself and his friend alive.

When you looked at how the two experiences were alike, you were comparing them. When you looked at the differences between the two experiences, you were contrasting them. Recognizing an author's use of comparisons and contrasts can help you understand what the author is telling you. Using comparisons and contrasts can make your own writing clearer and more interesting.

Comparing

Authors compare things in a variety of ways, such as their physical characteristics or their functions. Other ways of comparing things may vary with what is being compared.

Think about ways to compare and contrast a flower or vegetable garden in the city with one in the country. Think first of what would be the same in both places, as in the paragraph at the top of page 433.

In the paragraph, the **boldface** words and phrases signal that the author is comparing, by telling how the two things are alike.

The requirements of a garden in the city are just **like** those of a country garden. Plants have **similar** needs, no matter where they grow — good soil, enough sunshine, and enough water. In **both** city and country, one can find and develop garden plots where flowers and vegetables will thrive. In fact, many people living in the city feel that they get **just as much** pleasure from their gardens as they would from having a country garden.

The comparisons include physical characteristics (soil, sunshine, and water); functions (growing healthy plants); and ideas how city people feel about their gardens).

Contrasting

To contrast the two kinds of gardens, think how they are different, as in the following paragraph:

Unlike the country garden, the garden in the city usually must be contained within a small space. **Although** many of the same things may be grown in both, the city garden may need to be laid out **more** carefully. The city gardener may have to plant **different** kinds of vegetables — ones that take up **less** space. A city garden may provide enough vegetables for a single family. **On the other hand,** a gardener in the country may grow enough vegetables to have some to sell at the market. **However,** maintaining such a large garden requires a greater investment of time and energy.

This paragraph contrasts city gardens with country gardens. Again, the **boldface** words and phrases show differences and act as clues to the author's purpose. Reread the paragraph and find the sentences in which the author contrasts the physical characteristics and functions of the two kinds of gardens and people's ideas about them.

Using Comparing and Contrasting

When you read, look for clue words and phrases that tell you that the author is discussing how things are alike and how they are different. Think about whether the author is comparing and contrasting their physical characteristics, their functions, or other things about them.

Read the following paragraphs and be prepared to discuss the author's use of comparing and contrasting.

The bicycle and the moped are alike in that both have two wheels. Many people ride them for fun, but in some parts of the world, they serve as an important means of transportation. Because they are less expensive than cars, more people are able to own them.

The moped, unlike the bicycle, does not require human energy to run. It is powered by a small gasoline engine. Like the bicycle, the moped has pedals, but they are only used to start the engine. The power to run the bicycle comes from a person who is pedaling.

After a long trip, the moped rider would feel fairly fresh rather than be tired-out from pedaling. The moped rider would also probably arrive sooner than the bicycle rider because the moped can travel faster.

The requirements for owning and operating a moped are different from those for a bicycle. In many places the bicycle may not require a license. In contrast, most communities require a license for the moped and a license for the rider. There are usually no age limits on riding a bicycle. On the other hand, many communities have a minimum age requirement for owning a moped.

A moped usually costs more to buy than a bicycle, and is more expensive to operate. This must be taken into account when deciding which one to buy.

1. Make two columns on a sheet of paper: *Compare* and *Contrast.* List the likenesses and the differences between the moped and the bicycle. Then make a list of the words that the author used as clues to comparing and contrasting. Be prepared to discuss them with your class.
2. Write two sentences about each pair below. First compare them by telling how they are alike. Then contrast them by telling how they are different.
   A. birds and fish
   B. computers and calculators
3. Select one of the pairs in item 2. Think of other ways the two things are alike and different. Write a paragraph comparing and contrasting them. Include as many different kinds of comparisons and contrasts as you can. Underline the words and phrases that are clues to comparing and contrasting.

Skill Summary

- In comparing, the author shows how things are alike.
- In contrasting, the author shows how things are different.
- Such words as **and, alike, both,** or **same** are clues to comparing.
- Such words and phrases as **unlike, different from, on the other hand,** and **rather than** are clues to contrasting.
- Things can be compared and contrasted in terms of their physical characteristics, their functions, or ideas about them.
- Being able to compare and contrast will help you to understand what you read and will give you a technique to use in your own writing.

Science

Much of what you learn about science comes from reading science textbooks. You can get more out of your reading when you understand how the lesson is organized. Paying attention to the special characteristics of science writing and using good reading and study habits can help you understand and remember what you read.

Using SQRRR

Remember to *survey* before beginning to read. Pay special attention to each heading. This helps you to get a general idea of what the lesson is about and how the author has organized it.

Next, ask yourself *questions* about what you will read by turning each heading into a question. This will help you predict what the text will be about. Then *read,* trying to connect the new information with what you already know.

After you have read, use the *recite* and *review* steps to help you to understand and to remember what you have read. Be sure you can answer the questions within

the lesson. Often you will find further questions at the end of the chapter. Use these to review. If you have trouble with a question, go back and reread that part of the lesson.

Reading Carefully

Some topics studied in science may be somewhat new to you. For example, you probably know something about growing plants but may never have looked at plants under a microscope. An author writing about plant cell structures would try to explain the subject as clearly as possible. You must think about how this adds to what you already know.

You should read slowly and carefully. Reread when necessary to make sure you understand each part before going on to the next. Make notes of important points as you go along.

Clue words are signals to the author's purpose. Such words as *because* or *therefore* refer to cause and effect relationships. Sometimes an author describes how things are alike or different. A compare-contrast relationship may be signalled by words like *similar* and *different*.

Learning New Vocabulary

Scientific writing must describe or explain something *exactly* and without confusion. This means that the writer must use words and sentences that have precise meanings. The technical words used may be new. Some words, such as *pupil*, may have a familiar meaning in one context and a different, technical meaning in a science book. Learning the vocabulary is important in understanding what you read in science.

Often, the important words are printed in special type. You should pay careful attention to them.

As you read, make a list of the words that are new to you. Sometimes their meaning will be explained in the text or will be clear from the context. You may also get the meaning from studying the word parts. At other times you may need to stop and look up a word in order to understand what the author is saying. Many books have a glossary that gives the meaning of the technical words. After reading, study the new words

and make them part of your own science vocabulary.

Using Graphic Aids

Science books often have sketches, charts, diagrams, and other graphic aids to help you understand more about what you read. Take time to study them, paying attention to captions and labels. Often, you may find new information here. Be sure to include them in your review.

Doing Experiments

Sometimes the author will include directions for experiments to be done by yourself or with your class.

First read through all the steps. Then review the steps, asking yourself: What equipment is needed? What steps are to be carried out? What observations are to be made? What kinds of records will be kept? What special hazards need to be avoided? Try to make a mental picture. Predict what should happen. Reread until you are sure you understand what to do.

When you do the experiment, be careful to follow directions *exactly*. When you have finished the experiment, ask yourself: What should have happened? What did happen? Why did it happen? What does it help me to understand about this subject? You may be asked to prepare a written record of the experiment.

If for some reason you cannot carry out the experiment yourself, you should at least spend some time thinking carefully through all the steps. Be sure you understand what the experiment would accomplish, and why.

Summary

You will understand science better if you think about what is special about science writing. Strategies for reading science include reading slowly and carefully, rereading as needed, studying the vocabulary, paying attention to relationships among ideas, examining the graphic aids, and following the directions for experiments that are described in the book.

Preview

The next selection, "Partners in Pictures," resembles material that you might find in a science textbook. As you read it, think about *how* the author has presented the material and practice the reading and study strategies that have been described.

After you have read "Partners in Pictures," be ready to describe how the material was presented and the strategies you used in reading it.

Partners in Pictures: The Camera and the Eye

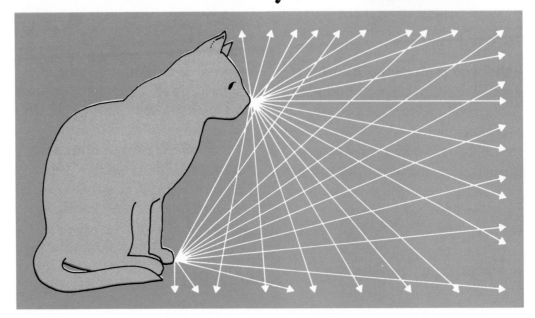

Light reflected from two points

If you want to see something, you don't close your eyes. You know that your eyes need light in order to see. Most cameras also need light in order to take pictures. Indeed, the eye and the camera use light in similar ways.

Just having light is not enough for either one to work well. They must have the right amount of light — neither too much nor too little. Both the camera and the eye can control how much light they receive.

They can also organize the light they receive. What the eye and the camera "see" is the light reflected from an object. Look at the picture of the cat. Light rays bounce off the cat in every direction. It is these rays that enter the eye or the camera. If they continue to go in all directions, they will form only a blur. In order to see or to take a picture, the rays must be focused. Both the eye and the camera have special parts which control how much light gets in and focus the incoming rays to make a clear picture. They also have a surface on which the image is projected.

439

Controlling the Light

In the camera, light enters through a small hole, called an **aperture.** It can be made larger or smaller to let in more or less light. The camera also controls how long light keeps coming in. A **shutter** covers the opening and keeps light out until the picture is taken. When the button is pushed, the shutter opens and closes. Its speed can be adjusted to let in light for a longer or shorter time.

In the eye, light enters through the **pupil,** the dark opening in the center. Around the pupil is the **iris,** the part that has color. The muscles of the iris tighten or relax to make the pupil smaller or larger, to let in more or less light as needed. (See the diagram below.)

The eye and camera are different in some ways. There is nothing inside the eye that works like a shutter. The only way to shut out light is to close your eye. The camera works only when the photographer decides to use it and sets it for the proper exposure. The eye works all the time, without conscious effort.

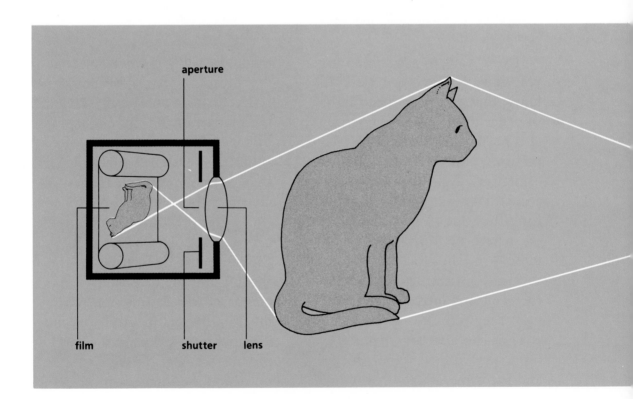

aperture

film   shutter   lens

The Screen

In both the eye and the camera, the picture is projected on a light-sensitive surface — something like projecting a movie, except that the picture is upside down and backwards. We do not notice this in the camera, since we do not see the film until the finished print is made. When we look at the print, we turn it right side up.

The eye is different. After the light enters, it falls on the **retina** at the back of the eyeball. Here are special cells, **rods** and **cones,** which react to light and color. When the light reaches the retina, the rods and cones send signals along the **optic nerve** to the brain. The brain interprets the signals and turns the picture right side up.

Focusing the Image

In both the eye and the camera, light passes through a curved **lens,** which gathers the rays and focuses them on the film or retina. How clear the picture is depends on the shape of the lens and its distance from the subject.

The camera lens is a piece of glass. To focus the camera, the lens can be moved forward or backward a bit. It cannot change its shape. The photographer may have to move nearer or farther away to get a clear picture of the subject. Special lenses can also be added for close or distant work.

The lens in the eye can change shape. It has muscles around the edge called the **ciliary body.** They can pull on the lens and stretch it thin and flat. This spreads the light rays so that distant things focus on the retina. When you look at something nearby, the muscles relax and the

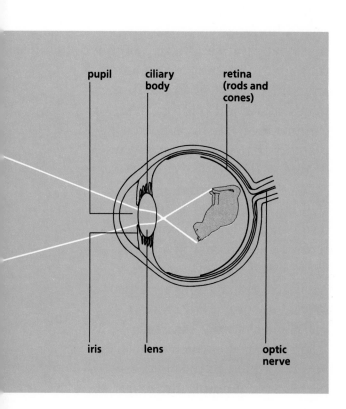

pupil · ciliary body · retina (rods and cones) · iris · lens · optic nerve

441

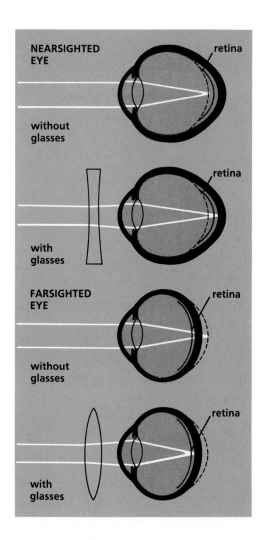

Different shapes of lenses are used to correct the focus of nearsighted and farsighted eyes. Describe the shapes of the lenses shown above.

lens thickens. Thus, the eye can correct for distance in a way the camera cannot.

However, some eyes may need help in doing this. Some people's eyes cannot focus sharply on far-away objects. Such people are said to be nearsighted. Their eyes may be longer from front to back than is usual. This causes images to focus in front of, rather than on, the retina.

Farsighted people have the opposite problem. Their eyes are often shorter from front to back. Both conditions can be corrected by lenses that are shaped to focus the image on the retina.

Picture Perfect

No matter how fine it is, the camera is still an invented object. It has been around only a little over a hundred years. In anyone's hands, it can make pictures that are a source of enjoyment, amusement, and surprise. In the hands of a good photographer, it can produce artistic and exciting pictures that show us new ways of seeing things.

The human eye has been around a lot longer than a hundred years. Our eyes constantly receive and process images at great speed without our even having to think about it. This makes our eyes even more remarkable than the camera.

Whenever you open your eyes, you see a picture that is nearly perfect. Now you know why.

Summary Questions

1. Some parts of the eye and of the camera are listed below. For each, write a sentence telling where it is and what it does.

    shutter
    ciliary body
    retina
    aperture

2. The lesson says that both the camera and the eye have a way of organizing the light they receive. Why is this important?

3. In seeing, what are the major steps that happen from the time light enters the eye through the pupil until you "see" the picture right side up?

4. On a sheet of paper, make two headings: *Alike* and *Different*. Under the headings, list the ways in which the eye and the camera are alike and different.

Pinhole Camera

A **pinhole camera** is a very simple kind of camera that can take pictures without a lens, although the pictures it takes are not very clear. Use reference sources to learn how to make and operate a pinhole camera like the one shown in the diagram below. Make one with your class and try it out.

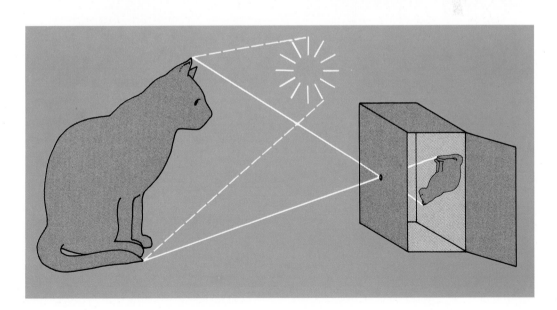

The Enchanted
Steel Mills

by Margaret Bourke-White

How could a beginning photographer capture the drama and beauty she saw in the gigantic steel mills?

For many years, Margaret Bourke-White was one of the best-known photographers in the world. She was famous for her photo essays, which told stories through pictures.

She was also a good writer. In her autobiography, Portrait of Myself, *Margaret tells about the fascinating experiment that marked the beginning of her long career.*

In the mammoth back yard of Cleveland, Ohio, lies a sprawling, cluttered area known as the Flats. Slashed across by countless railroad tracks and channeled through by the wandering Cuyahoga River, the Flats are astir with life. Locomotives slap and shove reluctant coal cars. Tugboats coax their bulging ore barges around the river bends. Overhead, traffic roars into the city on high-flung bridges. At the far edge of this clanging confusion, smokestacks on the upper rim of the Flats raise their smoking arms over the blast furnaces, where ore becomes steel.

To me in 1928, fresh from college with my camera over my shoulder, the Flats were a photographic paradise. The smokestacks ringing the horizon were the giants of an unexplored world, guarding the secrets and wonder of the steel mills. When, I wondered, would I get inside those buildings with their mysterious unpredictable flashes of light leaking out the edges?

One day while I was doing the rounds with my portfolio, I passed through the public square and saw a man standing on a soapbox. He was earnestly exhorting the air, but no one was paying the slightest attention to him. Soaring about his arms and gathered at his feet were flocks of pigeons. What a wonderful picture that was! But that day I had no camera.

Dashing to the nearest camera store, I begged to be allowed to rent or borrow a camera. The clerk eyed me curiously through his thick spectacles as I explained breathlessly about the man and the pigeons, but without delay he reached below the counter and handed me an expensive camera. I flew back to the square and found to my relief that the man was still on his soapbox.

It was only when I went back to return the camera to the clerk behind the counter that I noticed the remarkably astute and kindly expression in the blue eyes behind the thick lenses. Everything

about this clerk seemed intensified by some inner magnifying glass as strong as the spectacles he wore. When he moved, he swung strong arms from a powerful barrel-shaped chest. When he spoke, the words streamed out all in capitals, underlined, and sparked with exclamation points. Short and in his fifties, Alfred Hall Bemis was as eager to give photographic advice as I was to receive it. We went out to lunch, and I told him how I felt about steel mills.

Beme, as I came to call him, gave me badly needed technical pointers, but he never failed to recognize there was more to making pictures than technique. "Listen, child," he would say, "you can make a million technicians but not photographers, and that's the truth."

Fate was kind to me in those early Cleveland days. Various small magazines in Cleveland began publishing my garden pictures. The Cleveland Chamber of Commerce used my man with pigeons on the cover of their monthly magazine, paid me ten dollars, and ordered more covers.

Frequently, I caught in pictures the silhouette of the tantalizing steel mills over mountains of ore and coal. Sometimes I ventured as far as the guardhouse, with a request to take my camera inside. But I was always turned away at the gate.

Then, unexpectedly, Margaret Bourke-White was hired to do regular work for a big bank. She soon had earned enough money to buy a new lens for long-focus effects — "a lens worthy of any steel mill." With an introductory letter from the president of the Union Trust Bank, she went to meet Mr. Kulas, the president of the steel company.

Mr. Kulas must have been a little surprised at the intensity of this twenty-one-year-old, possessed of this strange desire to photograph a steel furnace. I, too, was a little surprised to find myself talking so fearlessly to the most powerful businessman I had ever faced.

But during my camera explorations in the Flats among the ore boats and bridges, I had done a good deal of thinking about these things. To me these industrial forms were all the more beautiful because they were never designed to be beautiful. Industry, I felt, had an unconscious beauty — often a hidden beauty that was waiting to be discovered and recorded! That was where I came in.

Mr. Kulas turned to the portfolio I had brought, looked at the pictures one by one, and stopped to study a photograph of a rock garden. "I think your pictures of flower gardens are very artistic," he said, looking up, "but how can you find anything artistic in my mill?"

"Please let me try."

And he did. He gave the word

that I was to be admitted whenever I came to the plant to take pictures. Then he did me the greatest favor of all. He went off to Europe for five months.

I did not know what a long-term task I had taken on. Without knowing it, I had picked the hardest school I could have chosen. The steel mills with their extreme contrasts of light and shade make a difficult subject even today, with all our superior techniques and equipment. But then I had no technique, almost no experience.

The mill officials grew impatient. I was doubtless in the way. They were sure I was going to break a leg or fall into a ladle of molten metal. A girl who came back night after night after night! What kind of pest was that — but the president had given his word. I had my five months.

The first night was sheer heaven. Beme talked about it when we met years later.

"You had a very joyous time watching that steel. We were standing up high someplace, and they pulled a furnace, and you were as delighted as a kid with a Fourth of July firecracker. You grabbed your camera, and you were off to a flying start.

"You weren't exactly dressed for the occasion. You had on some kind of a flimsy skirt and high-heeled slippers. And there you were dancing on the edge of the fiery crater in your velvet slippers, taking pictures like blazes and singing for joy."

My singing stopped when I saw the films. I could scarcely recognize anything on them, nothing but a half-dollar-sized disk marking the spot where the molten metal had churned up in the ladle.

I couldn't understand it. "We're underexposed," said Mr. Bemis. "Very woefully underexposed."

For weeks we struggled with floodlights, cables, and flashpans, but our illumination was simply gobbled up in the vast steel mill.

"If only I could go to someone who's been taking steel mill pictures and would be willing to advise me," I said to Beme.

"There isn't anybody," he said. "You're trying to do what nobody's done, to put the artist's touch on what others have thought a very dull mechanical problem."

I tried closer views, hoping to get more help from the light of the molten steel. The men put up a metal sheet to protect me from the heat while I set my camera in place, slipping the shield away while I made my shots. The varnish on my camera rose up in blisters, and I looked as though I had been under a tropical sun. I climbed up the hanging ladder into the overhead crane so I could shoot directly down into the molten steel during the pour. During some shots, bursts of yellow smoke at the height of the pour blotted out everything in front of the lens. During others, the crane cab started trembling during the vital moments, and all my pictures were blurred.

By this time I was living entirely for the steel mills. The jobs I was able to keep going during the daytime just about paid for the films I shot at night. Those same films filled up my wastebasket — a gluey mass of sick, limping, unprintable negatives.

Then the sales people came into my life.

The first of these was H. F. Jackson, long-armed and long-legged, with a profile like Abraham Lincoln. When he came to town, Beme called me excitedly. "I used to know Jack when we were both sixteen-year-old kids in Springfield, Massachusetts. I haven't seen him in all these years, until he turns up out of nowhere with his case full of samples. I told him how you couldn't get enough light. And he drags out these big flares with wooden handles, like Roman candles. He's on his way to Hollywood to demonstrate them for the movies. I told him if he would come with us he could see the steel mills, and he fell for it."

We had more than our usual red tape at the gate that night — a strange guard who didn't recognize our passes and phoned endlessly until he could rouse some higher-up who would admit Jack. While all this went on, a rising crescendo of rosy light glowed from the mill. We saw that we were missing a "heat" and would have to wait three hours for the next pour.

I know of no colder place than a steel mill in winter between "heats," and no hotter place than a mill during the pour. During our three hours, we roamed the windy catwalks, climbed up and down ladders with the sleet driving through, and planned our shots. I was eager to work out a side lighting that would emphasize the great hulk and roundness of the ladles and molds and still not flatten and destroy the magic of the place. To do that properly

would take two flares for each shot, Jack decided, used at each side and at varying distances from the camera.

Then in a great rush the pour began. The life of each flare was half a minute. During those thirty seconds, I steadied my camera on a railing and made exposures of eight seconds, four seconds, and two seconds. Then I dashed closer, hand holding the camera for slow shots until the flare died.

In the beginning, Beme stood at one end and Jack at the other, each holding one flare. Then as the metal rose bubbling in the ladle, with great bursts of orange smoke shrouding the mill, Jack was afraid we were not getting enough fill-in light, so we took the great gamble. He and Beme held two flares each. The last flare we saved for the last spectacular moment in the pouring of the molds — that dramatic moment when the columns of tall tubular forms are full to bursting, each crowned with sparks, and the cooling ladle in one last effort empties the final drops of its fiery load and turns away.

The next night we developed the films, and there it all was: the noble shapes of ladles, giant hooks and cranes, the dim vast sweep of the mill. When we developed the negative we had taken with the last flare, it was filled with black curving lines, as though someone had scratched it deeply with fingernails.

Beme couldn't make it out. "The film seems to be damaged in some manner."

"But the marks are so regular," I said, "like looped wire. Each one is a perfect curve."

Suddenly I knew. I had photographed the actual path of the sparks.

We reached our next roadblock after Jack had moved on to Hollywood. We were printing up our results. "Beme," I said, "these enlargements look terrible. So dull and lifeless." I couldn't understand it.

In this new crisis Mr. Bemis triumphed again. He produced another sales person. Charlie Bolwell was as plump and pink-faced as Jack had been lean. "He's taken on a job for a Belgian paper that's new in this country," Beme phoned to tell me.

My heart beat faster, and I could hear Beme's voice growing excited on the other end of the line. "I told Charlie, 'I know someone needs that paper awful bad,' and Charlie said, 'Lead me to him.' I told him, 'It's a her.' I showed him some of the prints we'd made, and he's under the impression he can do better. We're perfectly willing to let him try, aren't we, kiddo?"

Charlie Bolwell donated more than his paper samples to the cause. He taught me how to print. From Charlie I received a new conception of darkroom work, as though your hands have become an extension of the lens that took the picture, as though it were all one conscious stream of creation from the judging of the light when the picture is taken to that final sparkle in the tray when your print is what you want it to be.

By the time Charlie Bolwell had rescued my pictures, I picked the twelve best shots, put them on fresh white mounts, and the dreaded, hoped-for appointment was made.

Beme drove to the mills with me and waited outside. I got out of the car and picked up my portfolio.

Beme could see I was trembling. "Child, you've come through with an armful of pictures the like of which no one has ever seen until now. Now run along."

I walked over the long, long narrow wooden trestle that spanned the yard of the mill to the office building. I remember waiting for Mr. Kulas while he finished with some other people. Then my turn came. I remember his surprise and pleasure in the pictures. He said there had never been such steel mill pictures taken. He wanted to buy some of them. How much would they be? I assured him I would give him the pictures gladly, but if he wished to pay, the price would be quite a lot. Because of the amount of time and supplies that had gone into the work, I had decided it should be one hundred dollars a picture.

"I don't think that's a lot," said Mr. Kulas, "and in any case, I am glad to have the chance to encourage you in your pioneer work."

He picked eight photographs, commissioned me to make eight more, and laid plans for a privately printed book on *The Story of Steel,* which would contain my photographs.

Running like a madwoman, I went to tell Beme the wonderful news.

Margaret's steel pictures led to a job with Fortune, *a magazine about business and industry. She began to travel all over the United States, taking pictures of buildings and workers. In 1936, Margaret was hired as a photographer for* Life, *which became a very successful magazine. She went to Europe, China, Russia, and the Arctic. She took pictures of kings and queens and presidents. She photographed the daily lives of people everywhere.*

In 1941, when the United States went to war, Margaret Bourke-White became the first woman to work in the battle zones. For four years, she dodged bullets to get her pictures. After the war, she continued to travel all over the world on story assignments. She photographed the rich and poor of India, the miners of South Africa, and the war-torn families of Korea. Although she became ill with a disease that affected body movements, she worked until her death in 1971 at the age of sixty-seven.

Summary Questions

Think about the difficulties Margaret Bourke-White overcame to become a pioneer in her field.

1. Why did Margaret Bourke-White encounter difficulties in getting permission to photograph the steel mills? How did she overcome these difficulties?
2. What technical problems did Bourke-White face in attempting to photograph the steel mills, and how did she solve them?
3. What dangers and discomforts did Bourke-White encounter in photographing the mills?
4. Why did Bourke-White persist in her attempts to photograph the mills in spite of the frustrations and hardships she encountered?
5. Several of Margaret Bourke-White's famous photographs are shown on pages 456 and 457. Choose the one that you like the most. Explain why you chose that photograph, and tell what difficulties Bourke-White might have had in taking it.

The Reading and Writing Connection

Pretend you are Mr. Kulas and that you have received a letter from a business person in another industry who is considering commissioning Margaret Bourke-White to do some photographs. Write a letter in response that describes what you know about her skills and why you recommend her work. Try to include some of the following words in your letter:

> **commission**
> **technique**
> **intensified**
> **silhouette**

photos by
Margaret
Bourke-White

opposite: Log Rafts, 1937
left: Herero Women
bottom: Coney Island, 1952

Simile and Metaphor

To Margaret Bourke-White, the steel mills she longed to enter seemed as strange *as a fairy tale kingdom.* She described their towering smokestacks as "... *the giants of an unexplored land.*" She might have carried this comparison further by saying that from the outside the dark buildings looked *like a deserted castle taken over by a fire-breathing dragon.*

The figures of speech in the sentences above are called simile and metaphor. They describe something by comparing it to something else.

A simile uses the words *like* or *as* in the comparison. Read the following examples:

This morning I was as happy *as a* kitten with a dish of cream. Riding my bicycle to school was *like* flying on a winged horse.

A metaphor also compares two things, but does not use *like* or *as.* Metaphors may use a form of the verb *be* or another verb, as in the following sentences:

The furnace *is* a dragon. It *breathes* fire and smoke.

Similes and metaphors are used to make descriptions more interesting and colorful.

Whenever you read, notice the author's use of similes and metaphors to make the writing more vivid and interesting. Remember to use them in your own writing.

Each of the following sentences contains either a simile or a metaphor. Read each sentence and decide which kind of comparison the writer is using. Then name the two things compared.

1. The kitten's playful antics were a circus to watch.
2. Her laugh, cool as water, rippled in the air.
3. The camera clicked and whirred like an insect trapped in a net.
4. The news that we were getting an extra holiday was music to my ears.
5. From the air, the city looked like a diamond necklace draped around the shore.

Now make up your own simile or metaphor for each of the following:

a noisy old car
a still, deep pond
being hungry
running fast
waiting for your birthday

Something Extra

Put up a large sheet of paper in a convenient place in your classroom. Whenever you or your classmates come across a simile or metaphor you like, write it on the paper. If you like, make up a few of your own. Use this "word wall" to help you in your writing.

Five Under Cover

by Myrtle Nord

**Anna Strong was risking her life to spy on the British
for General Washington — but what about her
friends? Could she depend on them? Would they take
the same risk when the time came?**

Characters

Anna Strong   **Caleb Brewster**

Ben Tallmadge   **Abe Woodhull**

Robert Townsend   **Two British Soldiers**

Scene 1

Time: *Summer, 1778, during the British occupation of New York.*

Setting: *Anna Strong's home in Setauket, Long Island. A table and two chairs are center. There are a few other chairs placed around stage. At right rear is a sideboard with display dishes as well as a cup and saucer placed close to edge of counter top. A bolted door at left leads outside; a door at right leads to cellar; a door at center rear leads to rest of house.*

At Rise: Anna Strong, *who has graying hair, sits at sideboard sipping from cup. The stage is lighted only by a candle beside her. A gentle rap is heard at the front door. Startled and afraid, Anna rises as the rapping becomes louder.*

Ben: *(In hoarse whisper, offstage):* Anna. *(Louder)* Anna! *(Anna, candle in hand, moves slowly to front stage, holding light ahead of her. Ben raps again.)* It's Ben. Ben Tallmadge. Open the door!

Anna: Oh! Ben! *(Relieved, she sets candle on table and hurries to unbolt and open door. Stage lights rise.)* Come in. I'm so glad to see you!

Ben *(Furtively):* Are you alone?

Anna: Yes.

Ben: Good. (*He turns, bolting door.*)

Anna: I've been robbed twice, Ben, and when you knocked, I was afraid it was the British again.

Ben (*Grimly*): Those rascals! Now, Anna, are you sure no one could have seen me come in here?

Anna: Yes. (*Sadly*): I've been especially careful since they took Selah prisoner. He's been on a prison ship since last January. It's terrible!

Ben (*Gently leading* Anna *to chair*): Anna, I'm sorry about your husband. Come, sit down. I want to talk to you.

Anna: It's about the occupation, isn't it, Ben? The Redcoats are everywhere in Setauket, and so many of our neighbors are Loyalists now. We Patriots don't have a chance. What about you? I thought you were a lieutenant with Colonel Chester's Minutemen. (*She lowers her voice.*) You haven't gone to the other side, have you?

Ben (*Impatiently*): Of course not! But, listen — General Washington is in White Plains, while New York and all of Long Island are held by the English. He needs to know the British plans so he can block them. He needs secret information, Anna, and I'm looking for your help.

Anna: Ben! You're talking about spying!

Ben (*Calmly*): Yes, Anna — spying. Our side must have information about what the enemy is going to do. You can be sure the British have spies too. (*A step is heard offstage, then a rap at door.*)

Anna: They mustn't find you here, Ben! Quick — go to the cellar. (*The loud rapping is heard again.*) I'm coming! I'm coming! (*Then, softly to* Ben, *as she pushes him out through door at right*): If there's danger, you can escape by the outside stairs. If I drop my cup against the floor, that will be your signal to run for your life. (*More loud rapping is heard.*) Coming! (*She closes cellar door, grabs candle, goes left and opens door to Robert, who is dressed in Quaker garb.*)

Robert *(Entering):* Good evening, Mrs. Strong. I hope I didn't startle thee.

Anna *(With sigh of relief):* Oh, it's you, Robert. Come in. I've been so afraid, and so alone. . . .

Robert: That is my purpose in coming. To visit thee awhile.

Anna *(Returning candle to table):* Well, come sit down, then.

Robert *(Pulling small newspaper from pocket):* I brought the *Gazette.* I'm writing for Mr. Rivington as a regular reporter now. *(Holds out paper.)* See, here are my most recent news items.

Anna *(Taking paper and reading):* All about the parties in New York! *(She scans paper and then looks up.)* Well, I must say, Robert, you write well.

Robert: I thank thee, Ma'am.

Anna *(Again reading paper):* What's this? Benjamin Franklin ejected from the French palace? Breaking his leg? And Washington on the verge of surrender?

Robert *(Laughing):* Those are all falsehoods. Mr. Rivington's a Tory — he invents those stories. He has a remarkable imagination, and it makes his papers more salable.

Anna *(Shocked):* And you are working for him?

Robert: Yes, but I don't invent stories! *(Indignantly):* I couldn't. Even though I had to swear the oath of allegiance to England's king, I am still a Quaker! Thou knowest that, Anna Strong!

Anna: Of course I do, Robert.

Robert: Working for the *Gazette* enables me to gather news about the British. British soldiers will converse with a *Gazette* reporter.

Anna: You do a fine job, Robert.

Robert: Well, Mrs. Strong, I must be departing.

Anna: Come again, Robert. *(She accompanies him to the door.)*

Robert: Yes, whenever I return from New York. Good night to thee. *(She closes and bolts door.)*

Anna *(Going to cellar door and calling):* Ben, you can come up. *(Ben enters.)* That was Robert Townsend. Now, you were saying you need help for General Washington.

Ben: Yes, Anna. I want to talk to Abe Woodhull and Caleb Brewster tonight. They're both Patriots.

Anna: Yes, I know them.

Ben: Caleb is in Fairfield, Connecticut, serving under Colonel Smith and still working on his whaling boats.

Anna: Making successful raids, too, I hear. But Abe's resigned from the Army. After that terrible beating the Tories gave him, he's been recovering and running his father's farm.

Ben: Yes, I've heard that. That's why I thought that Abe would be willing to go to New York occasionally, make observations, and report them back to me.

Anna *(Musing):* His sister, Mary, lives there. He could visit her, as an excuse.

Ben: Exactly. But we all need to talk about it. Would you let us meet here later tonight?

Anna (*Hesitating briefly, then speaking firmly*): Of course.

Ben: Good. (*He turns to go, his hand on door bolt.*) I'll go find them.

Anna (*Stopping him, her hand on his arm*): Ben, wait a minute. Robert Townsend is writing social news for Jammy Rivington's *Gazette,* and I've been thinking. . . . He might be persuaded to help in your cause.

Ben: A Quaker? (*Shakes his head.*) I don't think so.

Anna: You might ask him. You know his father, old Samuel? Well, the Loyalists picked him up, and before they freed him they made him swear the oath of allegiance to the King. They even made Robert swear it. It went against all their beliefs.

Ben: Those Loyalists!

Anna: If you remember, it was Robert who hid Nathan Hale and got him across the British lines. Robert has connections in New York, and he's in touch with the British all the time.

Ben: I don't think he'd be of any help, but we can ask him. We'll be back this evening, Anna.

Anna: Yes, Ben. I'll be waiting. (*Ben* exits. Anna *closes door, bolts it, takes candle, and exits through rear door. Curtain*)

Scene 2

Time: *That evening.*

Setting: *The same.*

At Rise: Anna, Robert, Ben, Caleb Brewster, *and* Abe Woodhull *are sitting on stage.*

Ben: Robert, you'll not be telling tales of what you learn here tonight all over town and in New York, will you?

Robert *(Seriously):* On my word, Ben. I'll never breathe a word of it to anyone.

Ben: We all have to know what needs to be done, so I'll tell you right out. It's spying — that's what General Washington wants here in Setauket and in New York City.

Caleb *(Chuckling):* Spying, eh? Nothing I'd rather do than spy on old King George's scallawags. *(Rubs hands in satisfaction.)*

Ben: Your job, Caleb, will be running messages across the Sound from here to Fairfield. Then you'll have to deliver them to me so I can send them on to General Washington.

Caleb: Is that all?

Ben: It's no small matter, Caleb. The trick will be to cross that Sound and not get caught with secret messages.

Caleb: I'm ready to start.

Ben: Abe, we'll need you to go to New York once in a while to listen around for embattlement positions and troop movements and then to write down what you learn.

Abe *(Nervously):* I'm . . . I'm not so sure. A farmer in Manhattan? It doesn't make sense. They'd be suspicious.

Ben: But your sister Mary runs a boarding house there, so there would be no questions asked if you were visiting her.

Abe *(Uncomfortably):* I don't know. The lobsterbacks know our every move.

Ben: Look, we even have invisible ink for you to use.

Robert: Invisible ink?

Ben: Yes. No one can read it without the secret formula that brings it to light. To the British, it would only be a blank piece of paper.

Abe: I'd like to help, but why can't Robert write the messages? He's already in New York, and it sounds as if he knows what's going on.

Ben: Abe, we all know the difficult time you had with the Tories. But we need you.

Abe *(Uncertainly):* I guess I could pick up the messages at Mary's. And I could probably get them to Caleb. *(Turns to Robert):* But what about you, Robert?

Robert *(Adamantly):* I will convey to you what I see and hear about the British intentions, but I decline to write the messages.

Ben: Well, Abe?

Abe: I don't think I can do it. It's too dangerous.

Ben *(Sighing):* I'll tell you what. We'll give you a false name. How about . . . Samuel Culper? Robert will give you the news from New York. You write it down under the name of Samuel Culper and pass it along to Caleb.

Caleb *(Laughing):* And Robert can be Samuel Culper, Junior!

Abe *(Doubtfully):* I still don't know. Wouldn't the British be suspicious about why I travel to New York all the time?

Anna: You and Robert could take turns. You could go to New York once in a while to get information and Robert could bring it here sometimes. *(To Robert):* You come home to see your father quite often, don't you?

Robert: Yes. Yes, I do. *(To Ben):* This plan is agreeable to me.

Ben: Wonderful! You could meet at Mary's in New York, and in Setauket you can meet here at Anna's house.

Anna: Will you do it, Abe?

Abe *(Frantically):* But how will Caleb pick up the messages? How will he know where to meet me? I can't deliver them to the same place every time.

Ben: You won't have to. You just need a way to let Caleb know what to do. Let's figure it out now. Say Caleb comes across the Sound every week. Sometimes there will be a message, and sometimes there won't. If there's no message, he just goes back home. If there *is* a message — hmmm.

Anna: I have an idea. I can hang some things on my clothesline as a signal. How about a black petticoat? That would mean a message is ready.

Ben: Then something white. . .

Anna: Yes! Handkerchiefs! To tell the meeting place on the Sound.

Ben *(Excitedly):* Great idea! One would mean Strong's Neck Point by the oak where the lightning struck. . . .

Anna: Two would mean Setauket Harbor.

Ben: And three would mean Crane's Neck Bend!

Caleb: Four would mean Drowned Meadow, and five could be Old Man's Bay!

Ben: Anna, will you do that?

Anna: Of course I will!

Caleb: Well, Abe. Will you do it?

Abe *(After a long pause, weakly):* I'll . . . I'll try.

Ben *(Standing, pleased):* You're a good man, Abe. *(To the others):* We'll call ourselves the Samuel Culper Ring, but no one must ever know! *(Lights dim. Quick curtain)*

Scene 3

Time: *Several weeks later.*

Setting: *The same.*

At Rise: Anna *enters and hurries to front door. She unbolts lock, opens door to* Robert.

Anna *(Furtively):* Come in, Robert. Abe is already here.

Robert: Good. *(Soberly):* The news is unfavorable, Mrs. Strong. *(Bolts door.)* We must hurry.

Anna: I'll call Abe up from the cellar. *(Goes to cellar door.)* Did you have any trouble getting through today?

Robert: No. I was detained and searched, but I had no difficulties. I've used the same procedure for several weeks.

Anna *(Opening cellar door and calling):* Abe! Robert's here. *(Then, to* Robert*):* Bringing supplies for your father's store is a good method.

Robert: Yes, Ma'am. The Redcoats inspect my wagon minutely, but there's nothing there. Cabbages, flour, buttons, hatchets — there's always some different item. My father needs the supplies, in these times.

Abe (*Entering nervously, carrying ink bottle of clear liquid, pen, and white paper*): Are you sure no one saw you come, Robert?

Robert: I'm positive, Abe. I was particularly careful. (*Abe puts writing supplies on table, then pulls up chair and sits.*)

Anna: I'll hang the black petticoat on the line. (*Exits at rear.*)

Abe: Let's not delay. What's the message?

Robert: The news is discouraging. The 54th Regiment and Lord Rawdon's Corps are southward bound, and the *Greyhound* arrived last week with Cornwallis and two thousand men, destined for Carolina. (*Abe writes quickly.*) More troops have been stationed in Jamaica and Brooklyn, and the Hessians are guarding the ferries now.

Abe (*Looking up*): Is there any word that General Clinton will leave Manhattan open, giving Washington a chance to regain it?

Robert: No. They're strengthening their defense everywhere. Fortifying Governor's Island and the Narrows, and repairing the works at Paulus Hook. (*Abe continues to write.*)

Anna (*Entering*): How many handkerchiefs should I hang on the line, Abe? I need to signal Caleb while it's still daylight.

Abe: The cattle are grazing down on the bay. It will be natural for me to go there. Hang out three, Anna. That means Crane's Neck Bend. (*Anna exits rear.*) Let's continue, Robert.

Robert: Two British regiments of Colonel Fanning's Corps and a troop of Loyalists are now at White Stone. They came yesterday from Rhode Island, and their intent is to invade Connecticut — to plunder the entire colony.

Abe *(Jumping up):* Not Connecticut! Ben will need to know that right away! I'll tell Caleb about it when I see him. I'd better hurry. *(Grabs ink, paper, and quill, and hurries out through cellar door.)*

Anna *(Entering):* Has Abe gone?

Robert: Yes. He departed before we had finished. There's a British regiment headed for Connecticut, and Abe rushed off when he heard that. He was anxious that Ben be informed as soon as possible.

Anna: Connecticut? *(Sinks into chair.)* So many Patriots have gone to Connecticut for safety. *(Loud pounding on door is heard.)* Who can that be? *(Nervously):* Robert, go to the cellar. Wait there and listen. *(She gestures toward cup on sideboard.)* If there's danger, I'll drop the cup. *(Robert exits through cellar door. Anna goes to front door and unbolts it. Two British soldiers burst in and push her aside.)*

1st Soldier *(Loudly):* Search the house to see who's here. (2nd Soldier *looks through rear door.* Anna *hurries to sideboard and picks up cup.)*

Anna *(Loudly):* No need to search my house. Nobody's here but me. You've taken my husband. I'm all alone.

2nd Soldier: There's nobody else here. *(Opens cellar door, looks through doorway quickly, then closes door.)* No one down there.

1st Soldier: Now, then, missus. We just want to know a few things. (Anna *returns cup to sideboard.)*

Anna *(Feigning deafness):* Eh? I can't hear you.

1st Soldier: I say, we want to ask you some questions.

Anna *(Shouting):* Questions?

1st Soldier: Yes.

Anna *(Shouting):* You'll have to speak louder. I'm going deaf.

1st Soldier *(Shouting):* We need to know what's going on here.

Anna *(Drawing back, afraid):* I don't know anything.

2nd Soldier: We think you do. We think you're a spy.

Anna: Eh?

1st Soldier: Just tell us about those clothes hanging on your clothesline.

Anna: Clothes? What clothes?

1st Soldier: The handkerchiefs. What does three handkerchiefs on your clothesline mean?

Anna: Say that again? I can't hear you.

2nd Soldier *(Loudly):* Are those three handkerchiefs on your clothesline a signal?

Anna *(Moving toward sideboard, shouting):* Signal? *(Frowning):* Handkerchiefs? Oh! Yes, they're a signal. I need some potatoes and eggs. *(Louder):* And some milk!

1st Soldier: Potatoes? Eggs and milk? What do you mean?

Anna *(Loudly):* Now, look here! I'm an old woman, and I can't get to the store — Sam Townsend's store. So when I know Robert Townsend will be coming with supplies for his pa, I hang out some handkerchiefs.

2nd Soldier *(Suspiciously)*: Then what?

Anna *(Counting off on her fingers)*: Well, one handkerchief means potatoes. Two means eggs. And three means a can of milk. *(She shouts)*: When the black petticoat is hanging there, it means I need all three. *(She moves away from sideboard.)*

1st Soldier: Who brings it?

Anna: Robert Townsend brings me what I need. He's a good man.

2nd Soldier: Do you think he's seen your signal today?

Anna: I don't know.

1st Soldier *(Pacing closer to sideboard)*: You'd better be telling us the truth, or we'll . . . *(Swings around to point finger at Anna, and as he does so, hits cup and saucer, which crash to the floor.)*

Anna: What was that?

1st Soldier: It was a cup and saucer. And that's not all that will be broken if your Mr. Townsend doesn't show up pretty soon. Do you hear?

Anna *(Nervously)*: Yes. Yes, I hear you.

1st Soldier: Then we'll just wait here, if you don't mind. *(Soldiers sit and fold their arms. Anna peers at broken cup on floor, and in terror picks up pieces and carries them to the table.)*

Anna *(Softly)*: I wonder if I can put it back together again. Oh, dear, I wonder when Robert will come.

2nd Soldier *(Unpleasantly)*: Madam, please stop your mumbling.

1st Soldier *(To 2nd Soldier)*: Leave her alone. Once Townsend arrives, it's all over for them anyway.

2nd Soldier: *If* he comes. I'm ready to leave now. I'd like to get back to New York.

1st Soldier: So would I. But if our friend here is a spy, don't forget that we'll be commended for having found her out.

2nd Soldier: True, true. I'd like to get back to the fighting, all the same.

Robert *(Loud rapping on front door, followed by shouting from offstage)*: Anna! Anna Strong! Come and open the door. I am burdened with your foodstuffs.

Anna *(Hand to her ear, listening)*: Eh?

Robert: Anna! It's Robert!

Anna *(Softly)*: Oh, it's Robert. *(She shuffles across to door, opens it.)*

Robert *(Entering carrying gunny sack of potatoes, a bucket of eggs, and one of milk; shouting)*: Here are the foods for thee, Anna Strong. Your potatoes, eggs, and milk.

Anna: Oh, thank you, Robert.

1st Soldier (*Speaking softly as he confronts* Robert): What does four handkerchiefs mean, Robert Townsend?

Robert (*In normal tone*): Four handkerchiefs?

1st Soldier: Yes. On the clothesline.

Robert: Oh, four signifies that Mrs. Strong wants me to bring a cabbage, or carrots — some vegetable, that's all.

2nd Soldier: And what about five on the line?

Robert: Five means flour. She uses a remarkable quantity of flour.

1st Soldier: You're pretty clever, young Quaker. Now we'll test you!

2nd Soldier: If you're wrong, you'll both be locked in prison. (*He laughs*).

1st Soldier (*Turning to* Anna *and shouting*): All right, now, old woman, you've got your potatoes, eggs, and milk. What does four handkerchiefs mean?

Anna: Eh?

1st Soldier (*Yelling*): Four handkerchiefs! What does that mean out there on your clothesline?

Anna: Oh, that means I want some cabbage or some turnips or carrots or whatever Mr. Townsend has on hand.

2nd Soldier: And what does five mean?

Anna: Five? That means I need some flour for bread.

1st Soldier (*Reluctantly*): All right. We'll be going now.

Anna (*As soldiers exit*): You come back sometime and taste my bread. (Soldiers *exit and close front door.* Anna *and* Robert *sigh in relief.* Anna *shouts again.*) You're a good boy, Robert!

Robert (*Shouting*): Shall I take the handkerchiefs down for thee?

Anna (*Shouting*): Yes. Take the handkerchiefs down. (Robert *exits rear.* Anna *sinks into chair. He returns with three handkerchiefs and puts them on table. In natural voices, they continue.*)

Robert: Anna, what a narrow escape! It was so dark in the cellar I could scarcely find the potatoes or the eggs and milk. Then I feared the outside door would squeak.

Anna: I keep it well oiled. Robert, thank you for telling the story about the handkerchiefs. You did it for me.

Robert: I did not make it up, Anna Strong. I merely repeated what I heard from thee.

Anna: But you made up the story about the cabbages and the flour.

Robert: Yes, I invented that part. The imagination is a gift to be utilized for a good purpose.

Anna (*Smiling*): Well, I just hope Caleb saw the signal and Abe found him at the Bend.

Robert: What will we do now concerning our signals? We'll need to alter them after today.

Anna: We'll change them, Robert, but we'll still get our information through. And we'll never give up our fight for independence. (*Picks up bits of china on table*) I'm glad the cup is broken. It was from England. We must do the same thing with the ties they hold on America.

Robert: Dost thou think that we can sever those ties?

Anna: Yes, Robert. We must break them. (*She stands and smiles confidently.*) And somehow, Robert, break them we shall! (*Curtain*)

The End

Author

Myrtle Nord has written a number of plays for adults and young people. Her plays have been performed in many parts of the country, and two have won awards.

Summary Questions

Consider the risks and dangers involved in a spy operation.

1. What risks were Anna and her friends taking by spying for the Patriots?
2. Could Anna be sure that she could depend upon her friends to take the same risks she took when the situation became dangerous? Why or why not?
3. Why do you think Anna and her friends were willing to take such risks?
4. Anna and Robert were almost caught. How did they manage to keep the British soldiers from discovering their signaling system?
5. After the soldiers' visit, Robert told Anna that the signals must be changed. What kinds of new signals might they use?

The Reading and Writing Connection

Pretend you are a theater critic who has just attended the opening night performance of this play. Write a review of the play for the local newspaper. The review should briefly comment on the actors' performances, as well as summarize the plot. When tracing the story line, remember it is important that you do not reveal the ending. Try to use some of the following words you have learned in this selection: *feigning*, *adamantly*, *scallawags*, *utilized*.

Evaluating Information

You have learned about several propaganda techniques. When you recognize propaganda, you can make up your own mind instead of letting others tell you how to think and feel.

There are other ways you can evaluate the information an author gives you. Knowing how to evaluate what you read will help you to make decisions based on the best information.

Recognizing and Evaluating Facts

Most of what you read will present many statements given as facts. You can check a statement presented as fact to see whether or not it is true. Sometimes you will already know something that will prove a statement given as a fact to be true. Most of the time, however, you will have to use a reference book to check it.

To help you judge facts, notice the copyright date of the books you read. A book on computers written last year is more likely to have up-to-date information than a book written ten years ago. Also, the author's qualifications are helpful in judging. A book about airplanes written by someone who has studied them for many years is more likely to have correct information than a book written by someone with no background in the subject.

Recognizing and Evaluating Opinion

Sometimes writers state their opinions. An opinion is what the writer believes about something and knows that it is open to question. A statement of opinion cannot be checked to see if it is true or false. Some opinions are recognized easily. They contain words such as *I think,* or *it seems to me,* or *may.* Suppose an author wrote, "Thomas Jefferson may have been the greatest President we have had." The word *may* shows that the author knows other people may believe otherwise.

Opinions, however, are sometimes presented as facts. Suppose another author wrote, "Montana is the most beautiful state in the United States." The author is stating a personal opinion and not a proven fact about Montana.

Statements about future events are also opinions. "It will rain tomorrow" and "All automobiles will run on electricity in fifty years" are opinions. They may turn out to be true, but since no one can predict the future, these statements are opinions at the time they are given.

A statement given as a fact and a statement of opinion may be given in the same sentence. The statement "Since we've already won the state championship this year, we'll win it next year too" is an example. The first part of the sentence can be checked to see if it is true or false. It is a statement given as fact. The second part of the sentence is a prediction of the future. It is an opinion.

When you recognize a statement of opinion, you should evaluate it. One way is to look at the writer's qualifications. You would be more likely to respect the opinion of someone who has special knowledge about a subject than the opinion of someone who does not. Another way is to look for supporting evidence. You would also be more likely to respect an opinion that has evidence to support it than one without any evidence.

Recognizing and Evaluating Assumptions

An assumption is a statement given as a fact. However, the person making it does so without having any evidence that it is true. Unlike someone offering an opinion, a person making an assumption accepts it as a true statement of fact. The writer does not believe that it is open to question.

Assumptions may be misleading when they are used as evidence to persuade others. Look at the following example: "The cost of educating students in the United States is higher than in any other country. If you vote to cut taxes, our schools will remain as good as they are now."

The second sentence in the example is an opinion. It is a prediction of the future. However, the first sentence is given as a statement of fact. Figures could be checked to see whether it is true or false. Did the writer check to see if the statement is true or is it an assumption? You cannot be sure. However, there are two clues that should make you suspect that the statement is an assumption. First, the writer gives no evidence to support the statement. Second, the writer uses that statement, without evidence, to try to persuade you to do or believe something. Not all assumptions are false, but statements presented without evidence should not be accepted without careful study.

Although you cannot always be sure if a statement given as a fact is an assumption, reading with a questioning mind will help you recognize assumptions. When you read carefully, you are less likely to be misled by information that is incorrect.

Recognizing Author Viewpoint and Bias

A viewpoint is a set of ideas that lead people to think about things in a certain way. For example, if it rained on a hot summer day, the viewpoint of a farmer who needed the rain and that of someone going on a picnic would probably be quite different.

Authors, like everyone else, can be expected to have viewpoints. An American author in 1800 would probably have had a different viewpoint about the American Revolution from that of an English author. Their writings would have mirrored these different viewpoints.

Sometimes an author uses bias in his or her writings. Bias is a strong leaning for or against something or someone. A biased author finds it difficult to write fairly and objectively about a subject.

Authors who have a bias about their subject often show it in one of two ways. First, they are likely to use words that carry strong feelings. The following sentence might have been written by a movie critic; be sure to notice the emotional words. "The superb acting and the gripping story make this one of the most memorable movies you will ever see." Words such as *superb, gripping,* and *memorable* are meant to stir up strong feeling. When you notice these words, you are also aware of the author's bias.

The second way authors may show bias is by presenting evidence for only one viewpoint. Read this example:

The old office building should be torn down. The cost of heating it is too high. It no longer provides enough space. The style of the building is old-fashioned and clashes with that of its neighbors.

All the evidence given is in favor of tearing down the building. It is likely that there may be some evidence against tearing it down, but the author has shown bias by not presenting it.

When you are aware of an author's viewpoint and recognize bias in writing, you can make better decisions for yourself.

Recognizing Persuasive Techniques

Read the following selection written as a newspaper editorial. Then answer the questions about the lettered sentences.

(A) This paper strongly backs the re-election of George Simms to the House of Representatives. (B) He has been one of the finest representatives our state has ever had, and if re-elected, he will keep up his excellent work. (C) Last year George Simms was present for 97 percent of the votes in the House. (D) No other representative has a voting record like this. (E) He sponsored seven bills that passed, and each will bring money into our great state. (F) You will never regret casting your vote for George Simms.

---

1. Is Sentence A a statement given as a fact or an opinion?
2. Is Sentence B a statement given as a fact or an opinion?

3. Which sentence contains a statement given as a fact and an opinion?
4. What clue could lead you to believe that Sentence D is an assumption?
5. What is the author's viewpoint?
6. What emotional words show the author's bias?

Skill Summary

- A statement given as fact may be checked for truth through your own knowledge and experience or through reference books.
- An opinion is what someone thinks or believes to be true. Some statements of opinions have words such as *I think, may,* or *it seems to me.*
- Assumptions are ideas that are accepted as true, though they may not be.
- Bias is an author's leaning for or against a subject and biased writing often has emotional words or one-sided evidence.

The Perfect Shot

by Keith Robertson

Link was used to the noise and bustle of New York City, and it seemed there was nothing to do here at Aunt Harriet's cabin in the woods. How would he manage for a whole summer?

When Link Keller's mother decided to take a summer computer course in another state, his own summer plans had to change. Before he knew it, Link had committed himself to a summer in Michigan with his Aunt Harriet, whom he barely knew. Reluctantly, he agreed to take with him his Uncle Albert's expensive camera in order to get a picture of a rare bird, the sandhill crane.

On his second morning in Michigan, Link drove with his Aunt Harriet to her log cabin in the wilderness, where he had promised to spend at least two weeks. Its isolation and the lack of any modern conveniences were a shock to city-bred Link, and suddenly the summer began to look unbearably boring.

The cabin had only three rooms. Most of the space was taken up by one large room that served as the kitchen, dining, and living area. An old-fashioned kitchen range stood near one corner, and a big stone fireplace occupied the middle of the opposite wall. There was a cedar plank table, four straight chairs, several easy chairs that looked worn but comfortable, some built-in cupboards, and a worktable near the stove. Two doors led to the two smaller rooms. Each contained a bed, with what appeared to be a new mattress, a straight chair, an old bureau, and a small closet.

The floors were of worn planks, and the inside of the log walls had been paneled with boards. Inside, the cabin was much cozier and more inviting than Link had expected. It was clean and had none of the musty smell that houses usually have after being closed for a long time.

"Charley and his wife did a good job cleaning the place," Harriet said approvingly. "He has looked after the cabin for years — kept the roof tight, repaired the windows, things like that. When I wrote him that I was coming up this summer, he said that the squirrels and mice had got in and had ruined the mattresses, so I sent up two new ones. He's put new screens on the windows, and I noticed before we came in that he'd set out some tomato plants for us. He's a wonderful man. You'll like him."

"What is Charley's last name?" Link asked.

"Horse."

"You're not serious?"

"His real name is Running Horse," Harriet said. "He's a Chippewa Indian. He used to work in the lumber camps as a young man, and someone called him Charley and he's kept the name ever since. He knows more about the woods than anyone I've ever known. He's an expert guide."

Link unloaded the station wagon while his aunt put things away. Then he went to the pile of wood that Charley Horse had left near the edge of the clearing and brought in wood for the kitchen stove.

"We used to have an outdoor fireplace," Harriet said. "It was built of stones stacked together. If we can find the metal grill, we can rebuild it. Then we can cook out of doors part of the time. In the middle of the summer it's too hot to build a fire in the stove. We usually didn't unless it rained."

"What about a refrigerator?" Link asked, looking at the boxes of food he had carried in from the car.

"I've talked about getting one of those gas refrigerators for years," Harriet said, "but I just haven't bothered. There's a spring not very far away. We used to use it for our drinking water when your father and I were children. Later we drilled a well, but I still use the spring to keep things cold, like butter. We put whatever we want in one of those metal pails and put the pail in the water. As for bottles of milk, you just tie a string around the necks and lower them into the water. You'll be surprised how cold they'll get."

They had lamb chops, canned peas, and baking powder biscuits for dinner. Then Harriet got her cane, and with Link carrying the large metal pail full of perishables, they walked

through the gathering gloom down an overgrown path to the spring. It was not far. The trail sloped downward for a short distance and then wound around a small hillock. Water gushed out of a low ledge of rock and trickled down into a pool about ten feet in diameter. A tiny stream led the overflow away into the darkness of the woods.

"I think the water is perfectly safe to drink," Harriet said. "The real reason Dad had the well put in was that he and your father liked to come down here to take baths. Mother objected to that. She said she wasn't going to drink bath water even if it was running."

Link leaned over and put his hand in the water. "It's ice cold," he said.

"Much too cold to bathe in, I always thought," she agreed. "Mother and I carried water and took a bath with warm water in a tub."

Link found a flat rock ledge in the pool, placed the pail on it, and then weighted it down with another rock.

"That will do fine unless some bear gets too inquisitive," Harriet said. "One year I had real trouble. Charley put a rope up over that limb, and I suspended the pail out in the middle of the pool. I had to use a long stick with a hook on the end to reach out and get it."

"Are there many bears around here?" Lincoln asked, looking back into the thick depths of the woods.

"Lots of them. But if you leave them alone, they'll usually leave you alone."

It was dark by the time they returned to the cabin. Harriet lighted a kerosene lamp and showed Link how it worked. "I imagine you're tired," she said. "Up here you'll find you just naturally get up with the light and go to bed with the dark."

Link went outside and brushed his teeth at the pump and then went to bed. When he blew out the lamp, complete darkness descended. There were no distant streetlights outside his window and no occasional flash of headlights. The room was so totally dark that it bothered him. He glanced at the luminous dial of his watch just to be certain that nothing had happened to his eyes. After about ten minutes he was able to make out the square of his window, a slightly grayer shade of black in the black wall.

Suddenly he heard something rustling around outside. It sounded enormous. Charley Horse had put new screens on the windows, but would a screen discourage a bear? He tried to convince himself that if iron bars had been needed, they would have been put on. The rustling was suddenly replaced by a gnawing sound as though a rat the size of a bear were gnawing down a big tree. There were lots of trees, he decided; one more or less would make no difference as long as it didn't fall on him. He had just become resigned to the gnawing when suddenly the night was pierced with a blood-chilling screech:

"*Oouuoooouuuoo, oh oh oh!*" This brought him bolt upright in bed. Then he lay back down again. He'd read of screech owls. The screech was repeated, and then in the distance he heard a high-pitched barking, like a dog but still not a dog. "The peace and quiet of the deep woods!" he thought disgustedly. What he needed was a few trucks or cement mixers driving down the street so he could get to sleep. He covered his ears with his pillow and closed his eyes.

He drifted off to sleep in spite of the strange noises, and the next thing he knew it was light and he was awake. He got dressed, went out to the pump, and sloshed cold water over his face. On his way back he noticed the broom that had been left beside the door. It had fallen to the ground, and something had gnawed the handle through. He carried it inside and held it up for Harriet to see.

"Porcupine," she said with a laugh. "I think it's the salt in the perspiration from your hands that they're after. They'll sometimes gnaw a hoe handle in two in a night. Did you hear that owl screeching last night?"

"I heard lots of animals, and I see signs of them, but I don't see them," Link objected.

"Once in a while you will just stumble onto an animal, but usually they are very wary and cautious. So you have to be even more wary and quiet. If you stand quietly any place long enough, you'll be surprised at what you'll see."

While they ate breakfast, Harriet drew a rough map of the surrounding area, pointing out what she thought might interest him.

"It's always a good idea to carry a compass if you go very far into the woods," she cautioned. "It's not so much that a compass will keep you from getting lost, but if you do get lost, you can then keep going in one direction. Eventually, even up here, you will come to a road."

She produced a small compass, which Link stuck in his

pocket before he went exploring. He found the swamp that Harriet had indicated and the sizable stream of dark brown water that led away from it through the trees to the Manistique[1] River. He located the old beaver dam and a pond above it. And he visited the remains of what Harriet had said was an old stagecoach station. They were interesting, he admitted, but you couldn't stand around for hours and look at a beaver dam or a tumble-down log cabin. By the middle of the afternoon, he had seen practically everything on Harriet's crude map. He was on his way back to the cabin when he passed by the spring. Walking through the woods was much warmer work than he had expected, and the water looked inviting. He stripped off his clothes and stepped into the edge of the pool.

---

[1]**Manistique** (măn′ə stēk′)

The water was icy. It was so cold that his feet felt numb in a matter of seconds. He looked out at the center of the pool. The water was at least four feet deep. His father used to take a bath here, he told himself. He could at least take a quick dip. Holding his breath, he made a shallow dive toward the center. The water was deeper than he had expected; when he stood up, it came to his chin. He had never been so cold in his life. With his teeth chattering, he waded as quickly as possible to the edge and climbed out.

He found a spot of sunshine and stood shivering in it for several minutes while he tried to brush off some of the water from his body. He was covered with goose pimples. He put on his clothes and then sat down by the pool for a while. He felt wonderful. That quick dip had been the most fun of anything since his arrival in Michigan — but that was only a minute. What was he going to do with an entire summer?

The next day he went into town with his aunt to buy some milk and a few other staples. They visited the Seney National Wildlife Refuge headquarters and looked at the exhibits, and Link watched some Canada geese on the pond just outside the main building. When they returned to the cabin, he wrote several letters and took several short, aimless walks into the woods. The following morning he weeded the area around the tomato plants and then thumbed aimlessly through one of his aunt's bird books.

"You're bored, aren't you?" Harriet asked in the middle of lunch.

The sudden question caught Link unprepared. "Well, I don't know what you find to do all summer up here," he admitted finally. "What did my dad do when he was a boy?"

"He was like me. He could lie hidden in the underbrush and watch a beaver or a heron all day long. You have to love the creatures of the wild to like it here, I guess. I find New York City terribly dull." She reached out a hand and touched him on the arm. "I suppose in a way the whole idea of coming up here was selfish. Now that I am partially disabled by arthritis, I don't feel up to staying here alone the way I once did. So I told myself that you would enjoy it, so that I could come. I love it here. I can go outside and just sit watching and have a wonderful time. And of course there *was* the chance that you might like it too. Would you like to leave?"

"Well, I haven't really given it a trial yet," Link said, reluctant to hurt her by saying that he would.

"You've run out of things to do," Harriet observed. "I suppose you ought to try to get that picture your uncle wanted before you leave."

"Yes, I'd forgotten that," Link agreed. "Where would I go to find sandhill cranes?"

"Lakes, marshes, wet areas," Harriet said. "There are a number of these around within a few miles. Why don't we leave it that you will stay long enough to get your pictures? Then we'll pack up and leave."

"That's fair enough," Link said, feeling much better.

"I want to go pay Charley Horse for his work here and see several other people," Harriet said, getting up from the table. "You don't mind being left here alone?"

"Not at all," Link said.

He went to his room, got out his Uncle Albert's camera, and picked a 105 mm lens. There were only four exposures left on the roll of film, so he went outside and used them up taking pictures of the cabin. Then he reloaded the camera, tucked his aunt's bird guide in his pocket, and started off through the woods. There might be a sandhill crane at the old beaver pond. "Wet areas," Harriet had said. He might be lucky and get his pictures right away. If he did, he wouldn't say anything but wait until he got the developed slides back. He could put up with another week or so buried in the woods. Then Harriet wouldn't feel she had completely wasted her money having the cabin repaired.

He spent the next hour crouched beside the pond, trying to sit quietly, but it was almost impossible. Tiny insects buzzed around his face, crawled down his collar, and generally made him miserable. At first he tried to swat them but decided this was a waste of time. Finally he crawled underneath a low shrub and, with the leaves almost brushing his face, managed to find a little peace.

He waited as patiently as he knew how, but he saw nothing that resembled either a crane or a crane's nest. According to his bird book they didn't build much of a nest — just a shallow cluster of sedge grass and twigs on the ground. The trouble was that the edges of the pond were thick with sedges, reeds, and cattails, and it would have been difficult to see a standing crane, much less a nest. He was about to give up and move on, when suddenly, almost in front of him in the middle of the pond, there was a floating bird. It looked slightly like a small duck with a long, slender neck. Its back was gray-brown, and it had a white bill. Link raised his camera to his eyes and looked through the telescopic lens. There was a black band around the whitish bill. He snapped pictures and then put his camera down gently. He began thumbing through the book, trying to find a picture of the floating bird. He made a slight sound as he turned the pages, and when he looked up, the bird was slowly sinking into the water. It sank lower and lower until finally just its eyes were above the water. He watched, fascinated, as it disappeared entirely. He waited and waited until he decided that something must have pulled it under and eaten it. Then suddenly it popped to the surface about twenty feet farther away. Link watched as the bird dived several times. It could disappear in a flash or sink slowly and then reappear fifteen or twenty feet away. He wished that he could swim like

that underwater. Finally it disappeared for a much longer period of time. His eyes searched the surface of the pond looking for it. Then, entirely by chance, he saw its head slowly emerging in the reeds, not very far from where he sat. It came up slowly, its neck turning cautiously like a submarine periscope. Suddenly it hopped onto what seemed to be a floating pile of reeds. It scratched away some covering reeds and sat down on a nest.

Slowly and cautiously, Link raised his camera and took several pictures. He had been sitting within a few yards of the nest for some time without seeing it. He understood now what Harriet had meant when she said if he sat still long enough, he would see things.

After ten minutes of thumbing through his book, he decided that the strange bird that could impersonate a submarine was a pied-billed grebe. He sat quietly for another hour.

He saw blue jays and several songbirds that he could not identify, and then — for a few hopeful minutes — he thought he saw a sandhill crane. An enormous bird flew high overhead on slow, flapping wings. Link looked at it through his camera lens. It was blue-gray, but it had no red crown on its head. His Uncle Albert had warned him not to confuse the great blue heron with the sandhill crane.

"A crane flies with its neck stretched out straight, and a heron curves its neck in an *S* curve," Albert had said.

He was growing stiff and restless, and buzzing insects continued to plague him, so he decided to call it a day, go back, and have a quick dip in the spring. He took a slightly different route and passed through a small natural clearing that he had not visited before. He was partway across when he realized that several birds, including a particularly noisy blue jay, were screaming excitedly about something. He stopped and looked around carefully, searching for the cause of all the fuss. He looked first at the ground and then at the lower branches of the trees. Suddenly he saw an animal about eighteen inches long up in a maple tree at the edge of the clearing. Whether it was the cause of the birds' alarm or not he had no idea, but it was so grotesque looking that he forgot about the birds. He raised his camera to use the lens as his binoculars. The animal had sort of yellowish-tinged hair and a back and tail covered with white spikes. It was a porcupine! It seemed to be staring straight at him.

He moved slowly toward the tree. The porcupine made no move to run away or even to hide behind the tree trunk.

That would make quite a picture, he thought, as he watched the animal with its ratlike face and eyes. The trouble was that a branch partially blocked his view. He circled, trying to get a clear shot. Either maple leaves or the feathery branches of a nearby spruce kept him from getting a good picture. The porcupine still showed no sign of being afraid.

He looked at a low branch thoughtfully. If he climbed up about level with the animal, he could get a beautiful shot. There would be nothing in the way, and he could take the picture from the correct angle as far as the light was concerned. What a story that would make when he got back home! "I was in the same tree as the porcupine when I took this shot," he would say casually.

He slung the camera over his shoulder so that it hung against his back. Then he reached up, grabbed the lowest limb, and began climbing. It was not difficult, but he went slowly and cautiously, keeping a wary eye on the porcupine. He got up about ten feet, just slightly below the porcupine, propped himself in a reasonably secure position, and got his camera. He took several shots and then moved a trifle closer. The porcupine began to show signs of nervousness. It retreated along its branch, moving about three feet farther out.

The porcupine's fear of him gave Link courage. He climbed one branch higher and leaned over to get at just the right angle. He snapped one picture and then leaned farther to the left. He was too intent on getting the picture, and his right foot slipped. He began to topple. He grabbed frantically for the nearest branch — which was the one on which the porcupine was perched. He caught it. The sudden weight on the small branch shook the porcupine off. Link was too busy to notice or care what happened to the porcupine. His right foot slipped off the branch completely, throwing most of his weight on his left foot. The branch on which it was resting was small, and it snapped. That left him with only his right hand grasping one branch. His left hand still held the precious camera. The branch was too big around to hold properly, and it was doubtful if he could have held himself by one hand anyway. He did manage to hold on long enough to allow his feet to swing over so that he was dangling upright. Then he let go and dropped.

It was not a long drop, and he landed on his feet on soft ground. Slightly off balance, he stumbled backward and sat down heavily. There was an instant, searing pain. He let out a yelp of agony and dropped the camera. It fell only a few inches to the ground, which was carpeted with leaves and pine needles. Link was not much interested in whether the camera was safe or not. He was in too much agony. He felt as though he were sitting on a red-hot stove. He rolled over until he was on his hands and knees. Then he reached back and felt the seat of his pants with his hand, half expecting to feel blood. Instead he felt what seemed to be stiff needles. He looked around suddenly for the porcupine. It was gone, but it had left plenty to remember it by. The entire seat of his pants was filled with quills! He had landed either on or beside the porcupine when he sat down.

Slowly and gingerly he got to his feet. Each movement was painful. He reached around and carefully took hold of the nearest quill he could see. He gave a yank. Nothing happened except he felt a sharp pain.

He picked up the camera and slowly started toward the cabin. Each step was torture. He paused every few feet, but he couldn't sit down. There was nothing to do but plod onward, trying to move with the least amount of pain. About two-thirds of the way, he leaned against a tree and examined the camera. It seemed unharmed. He blew away a few specks of dirt on the lens and got the lens cap from his pocket and put it on. At least he had got some good shots before he fell — and what a story he would have to tell now when he showed the family those slides!

He reached the cabin, went to his room, and lay face down on his bed. Once more he tried pulling a quill. He had no more success than before. Those things were in there to stay! He could see himself being wheeled into a hospital, face down on the stretcher. The doctor would operate while the nurses and everyone stood around laughing.

He was wondering how he would ever get to the hospital when he heard his aunt drive in. He waited until she had entered the cabin.

"Would you come in here, Aunt Harriet?" he called. "I had an accident!"

Harriet came into the room. Link turned to look at her. She glanced at him without changing her expression and said, "Yes, you certainly did, and I'll bet it's painful! What did you do, sit on the porcupine?"

"I guess," he said. "I climbed a tree to take its picture, and we both fell."

"Hurt yourself otherwise?" she asked.

"Nope. It was rough walking home, though."

"I'll bet it was," she said. "Well, we have to get those quills out. Each quill is covered with dozens of little barbs. That makes them hard to pull out. But if you don't pull them out, they work deeper. You can't possibly take off your pants. I'll have to pull the quills out through the cloth. The best way is to take a pair of pliers and give a quick yank. I've got some antiseptic that has sort of a chilling effect, and I'll try to spray you thoroughly with that. Maybe it will soak through your trousers and deaden the pain a little. But I warn you, it will hurt."

"Go ahead," Link said, relieved that he wouldn't have to go to the hospital.

Harriet left and returned a few minutes later with a pair of pliers from the car and a can of antiseptic spray. She sprayed Link and then asked, "Ready?"

"I guess as ready as I'll ever be," Link said. He pressed his lips together.

There was a sudden stab of pain, and Harriet said, "That's one! There's quite a few to go!"

"Don't count them," Link said. "I don't want to know how many until it's all over."

"The Indians dyed porcupine quills and used them to decorate deerskin shirts and pouches and moccasins," she said some time later as she yanked out the fifteenth quill.

"I'm going to save these and use them to decorate a poster that says 'Beware of Porcupines,'" Link said. He clenched his teeth as she gave another yank.

She pulled out twenty-two quills altogether. Link was sore, and he knew he would be unable to sit comfortably for several days, but at least he could walk without pain.

"You'd better take off your clothes and examine yourself closely to be certain we haven't missed any. Then spray yourself with disinfectant again."

Link followed her suggestion and then dressed. "I'm going down to the spring," he announced as he walked into the main room of the cabin. "The other day when I waded in, my feet were numb by the time I'd gone three feet. Maybe if I sit down for fifteen minutes, I can get the same results."

Harriet gave a slight chuckle. "I don't blame you." He had reached the door when she said, "Link."

He turned.

"I want you to know that I realize how painful that was," she said almost shyly. "Nobody could have complained less."

She was much more sympathetic than he had thought, he decided as he went on toward the spring, but she didn't know how to express it. He was beginning to understand her a little, and the more he understood her the better he liked her. She was really quite a good egg.

After Link recovered from his painful adventure, Harriet persuaded him to camp alone on an island in order to get closer to the elusive sandhill cranes. Link did, and his search for the cranes drew him into some unexpected and exciting adventures and led him to an interesting discovery about his aunt. You can share Link's eventful summer by reading In Search of a Sandhill Crane, *the book from which this story was taken.*

Author

Keith Robertson says of his boyhood in the Midwest, "I was always very fond of the out-of-doors and spent a great deal of time hiking, fishing, and camping." The book from which this story was taken, *In Search of a Sandhill Crane,* was named an Outstanding Science Trade Book for Children. Mr. Robertson also wrote the Henry Reed books.

Summary Questions

Consider what caused Link to see the Michigan wilderness in a new light.

1. What was Link's attitude toward life in the woods during the first few days of his vacation?

2. What caused Link to develop a more favorable attitude toward both his vacation and his aunt?

3. How did the camera help change Link's attitude toward the woods?

4. Do you think Link will continue to enjoy photography when he returns to New York City? Why or why not? Explain how he would need to adapt his picture-taking technique to the city.

The Reading and Writing Connection

This selection talked about nature photography while the selection on Margaret Bourke-White dealt with industrial photography. Choose the one that interests you more. Then make a list of specific industries or things in nature you would like to photograph. Pick one item from your list and write a paragraph telling what your "perfect shot" would be and how you would take it. As you write, try to use some of the following words from the selection:

grotesque	**impersonate**	**inquisitive**

The Sandhill Crane

by Mary Austin

Whenever the days are cool and clear
The sandhill crane goes walking
Across the field by the flashing weir
Slowly, solemnly stalking.
The little frogs in the tules hear
And jump for their lives when he comes near,
The minnows scuttle away in fear,
When the sandhill crane goes walking.

The field folk know if he comes that way,
Slowly, solemnly stalking,
There is danger and death in the least delay
When the sandhill crane goes walking.
The chipmunks stop in the midst of their play,
The gophers hide in their hole away
And hush, oh, hush! the field mice say,
When the sandhill crane goes walking.

505

Lifeboat
in Space

by Gurney Williams

**They were 205,000 miles away from Earth, and
something had gone wrong with their spaceship.
How could they possibly get home?**

The spaceship carrying three men to the moon shuddered as if it had bumped into something. The shudder made no sense. There was nothing to bump into, 205,000 miles away from Earth in black space. Astronaut Fred W. Haise was floating between two cabins in the ship when he felt the bump. He pulled himself quickly into the main cabin, which was called the command module, as the ship continued to shake up and down. Quickly he pulled himself to his seat next to Captain James Lovell and John L. Swigert, who slammed the door shut, sealing off the cabin.

Now all three astronauts were sitting in a small compartment, about as big as a three-person tent. It was a little after 9:00 A.M. on Monday, April 13, 1970, somewhere between Earth and the moon.

Sealed into their cramped quarters, the men tried to figure out what had happened by reading dials in front of them. A few of the dials were behaving wildly. Some showed that the ship was losing electrical power. The whole ship was wobbling now, somewhat like a car with a flat tire.

Lovell tried to stop the wobbling by firing small rockets outside the ship. It didn't work. Then suddenly he hit on the problem. One of the instruments was like a fuel gauge on a car and showed how much oxygen fuel was left in one of the large tanks. The fuel provided electrical power to run the ship and was a vital source of oxygen for the men to breathe. Without fuel, the ship — and the men running it — would die.

Lovell radioed Earth about what he had found. "Our oxygen number two tank is reading zero," he said.

Then Lovell got out of his seat and glided to a window so he could see the outside of Apollo 13. He turned to the section of the ship called the service module, which was connected to one end of the command module. The service module, a large cylinder, contained the fuel tanks and the main rocket engine. In the black night of space, Lovell saw a ghostly cloud coming out of the side of the service module.

Lovell got back on the radio, flashing the news to the mission control room in Texas. "It looks to me that we are venting something," he said.

The ship, Apollo 13, had soared into the sky two days before. Now, like an old boat, it

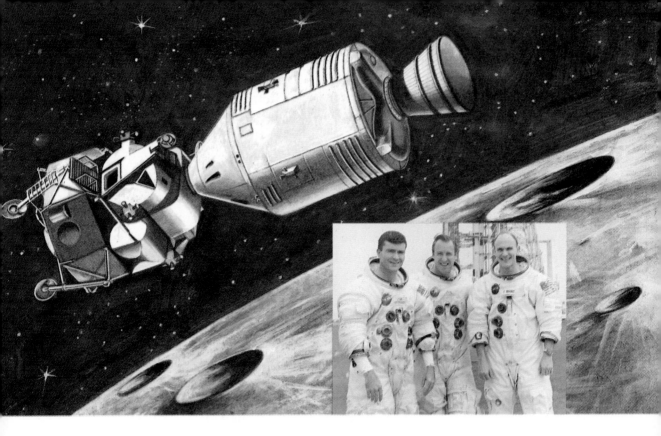

was leaking, or "venting." One of its round, silvery fuel tanks had exploded, blasting a hole right through the side of the service module. Fuel was disappearing into space, as every two seconds the ship moved a mile closer to the moon.

Dozens of people on the ground tried to figure out what to do. What they needed was a lifeboat, another rocket ship with its own supply of oxygen, its own rocket engine, to bring the men home.

In a way, Apollo 13 had such a lifeboat in Aquarius, the small but complete rocket ship at-

Apollo 13 and (left to right) Astronauts Haise, Lovell, and Mattingly

tached to the command module. It had been designed to break away and carry two men to the surface of the moon and then back up to the command module. It had its own air supply. It had its own rocket engine.

What it didn't have was space — it was only about as big as a small closet. Aquarius also lacked strength. It was built to land on the moon — not on Earth. If the astronauts tried to ride all the way home into Earth's air, it would burn to cinders. The command module was the only part of Apollo 13 designed to survive the fiery plunge back to Earth.

The people on the ground argued and sweated over what to do. Finally, they agreed on a plan and radioed it into space: Turn off everything in the command module to save what fuel is left. Climb into Aquarius. Use the Aquarius air supply and the Aquarius rocket to get home. Then when you get close to Earth, climb back into the command module to protect yourselves during landing.

Haise was the first to enter Aquarius. There were no lights except his flashlight as he floated into the dark little cabin, and there were no seats. Haise turned on some switches, and soon the cramped lifeboat was filling with its own supply of oxygen.

Lovell joined Haise, but Swigert stayed in the command module for a few minutes, turning everything off to save the little fuel left for the Earth landing. Then he, too, entered Aquarius. There was no chance now that Aquarius would land on the moon. It had a new mission: to keep three men alive.

Apollo 13, its crew huddled in one end, hurtled on through space. The ship curved around the back side of the moon, out of sight of Earth. The gray lunar surface, pocked with craters, unrolled beneath the ship at about ten times the speed of a fast jet plane on Earth. Then Earth, a blue-green ball, appeared again. It was time to see whether the small rocket on Aquarius could blast the whole ship into a good course back home to Earth. If the course adjustment failed, Apollo could miss Earth completely. The crew wouldn't survive long, and the ship would carry their bodies on an endless trip through space.

"Mark!" said a man in Texas, telling Lovell he had forty seconds to go before firing. Lovell put his hand on the firing button. "Five . . . four . . . three . . . two . . . one." At exactly the right time, the rocket began to fire, pushing the whole ship into line. It fired on, a four-minute explosion. Then a computer took over to turn the rocket off at precisely the right instant.

The astronauts in space and the mission control on the ground anxiously checked the course. The rocket had done its job. The ship was aimed for a landing in the Pacific Ocean, a quarter of a million miles away.

At least the ship was headed in the right direction. Whether it would splash down safely, no one knew.

Other problems crowded in on the men in the crippled ship.

Since fuel was low, there was not enough energy to keep Aquarius warm. The temperature was dropping, and there were no winter clothes on Apollo 13.

Fuel had been used to provide water, so now water supplies were low too. Like desert explorers, the men had carried some of the water, in plastic juice bags, from the main supply in the command module to Aquarius, but the supply was still low.

The air was bad. Back in the command module, a machine cleaned the air of dangerous gases. Aquarius had no such machine. Scientists on the ground suggested that the astronauts try to build an air cleaner out of scraps aboard the ship — plastic bags, a hose, some cards, and tape. No one knew whether the contraption would work.

By now, millions of people on Earth were worried about the voyagers from the moon. Concern had spread around the world. Thirteen countries offered to help in recovering the ship if it made it back to Earth. People gathered on the streets to watch TV reports and in churches and synagogues to pray.

In space it was cold and quiet. By early Wednesday morning, the temperature in Aquarius had dropped to fifty-five degrees. No one aboard could sleep. The men stayed awake, thirsty, tired, cold, moving around restlessly like animals in a small cage.

The air got worse. Before noon on Wednesday, a yellow light in Aquarius warned suddenly that it wasn't safe to breathe. Lovell turned on the taped-up contraption. It began to suck air through the filter.

Clean air flooded the cabin. The yellow light went off. They would be okay as long as the makeshift air cleaner worked.

The double impact of thirst and cold was making it difficult to think. At one point, Lovell was looking out the window. "The moon passed by," he said, watching a ball move slowly in front of the window. Then he corrected himself. "No, that's Earth." For an instant, the astronaut hadn't been able to tell them apart.

A sharp mind was now critical as the men began moving back into the command module to prepare to land. Landing was complicated because most of Apollo 13 had to be thrown away in space before it was safe to come down. The command module had a solid round shield on its bottom to help it survive the heat when it plunged into Earth's air. The service module and Aquarius had no such protection, and one of the astronauts' jobs was to separate the command module from Aquarius and the service module.

The service module was the first to go. Explosive charges pushed it away, and the module was spinning away into space, when Lovell spotted the damage caused by the fuel tank explosion. "There's one whole side of that spacecraft missing," he said. Haise saw it too. "It's really a mess," he reported.

As the service module disappeared in the distance, the crew aboard Apollo began to worry about a new danger. The fuel tank explosion had damaged the service module just a few feet from the heat shield that would protect the men during the last

The diagram below shows the sequence of events from the time the explosion occurred until the astronauts returned to the command module for re-entry.

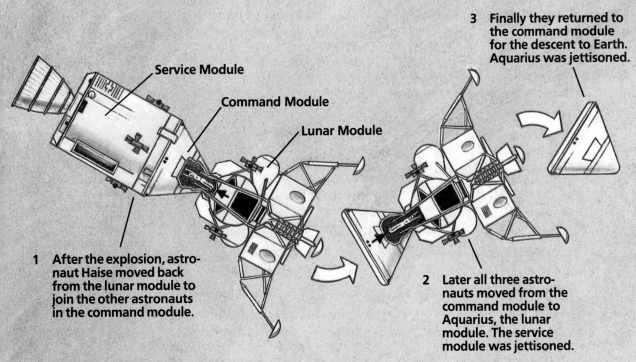

Service Module

Command Module

Lunar Module

3 Finally they returned to the command module for the descent to Earth. Aquarius was jettisoned.

1 After the explosion, astronaut Haise moved back from the lunar module to join the other astronauts in the command module.

2 Later all three astronauts moved from the command module to Aquarius, the lunar module. The service module was jettisoned.

few minutes of the flight. Suppose the explosion had also damaged the heat shield — would the command module stand the shock of re-entering Earth's atmosphere? No one talked about the possibility as Earth grew into a big, blue ball out the spaceship's window.

Lovell was the last to leave Aquarius. By the time he had eased his way back through a tunnel into the command module, the smaller rocket was filled with debris from the flight. The men switched over to the remaining oxygen in the command module, sealed off the compartment in Aquarius, and then blasted away from their lifeboat.

They were falling now, in the command module cone, at about 15,000 miles an hour. In less than an hour, they would either land or burn up.

No one was talking much. The command module was picking up speed — 17,000 miles an hour . . . 18,000 miles an hour. That meant the end of radio contact was near. The ship-to-ground radios couldn't work through the fire that would soon surround the command module.

About 400,000 feet above the Earth, the capsule began heating up. Soon flames whipped around

it, and the radio went dead. Ground scientists expected radio contact to be broken for about three and a half minutes.

At the end of three and a half minutes, there was still no word. Another half-minute ticked by. Apollo 13 remained silent. Then another half-minute. Some people began to lose hope.

"Okay, Joe." The voice was Swigert's. He was on the air again. Within minutes, white and orange parachutes rose like giant party balloons over the little command module. It splashed into the sea, and the men were picked up from their bobbing ship, which was still so cold inside that they could see their breath. They had survived.

And what of Aquarius? The lifeboat had continued to send radio signals long after it had been separated from the men it had saved. "Where did it go?" one of the astronauts had asked just before radio contact was broken.

"Oh, I don't know," replied one of the ground crew. "It's up there somewhere." A radio aboard the deserted lifeboat sputtered out one dying signal. Then lifeboat Aquarius plunged into Earth's atmosphere and burned to ashes.

Author

Like his father, Gurney Williams III has been an editor and reporter for newspapers and magazines. He has also written books for adults and for children. The selection that you have just read is from his *True Escape and Survival Stories*.

Selection Wrap-up

Summary Questions

Think about how harrowing the astronauts' experiences in space must have been.

1. What problems did the astronauts face once they moved into Aquarius? Which ones did they solve? How did they solve them?
2. What new hazard did re-entry into Earth's atmosphere create?
3. What personal characteristics did the astronauts have that helped them during their ordeal?

4. Would you describe the mission as successful? Why or why not?

The Reading and Writing Connection

Making a Table
Using reference sources, complete the mileage table at the bottom of the page.

Distance from Sun		
Planet	**Greatest Distance**	**Least Distance**

Jargon

People who work in a job or field often use special words to describe certain activities, tools, or equipment relating to their jobs. Such language is sometimes called *jargon.* Only people who know the special meaning of the word can understand jargon. However, sometimes a certain job or field is so well known that its jargon becomes known to most people. This is true of many words and phrases used by people in the space program. Read the following space words with their definitions.

astronaut   A person trained to fly in a spacecraft.

blasted   Moved into flight at great speed, propelled by rockets.

capsule   A place on a spacecraft for the crew; can be separated from the rest of the ship.

command module   The main cabin of a spacecraft.

heat shield   Special covering on the command module that protects it and its cargo from the heat of re-entry.

mission   Purpose; the job to be performed.

mission control   Space center on Earth where scientists monitor space flights and communicate with astronauts.

re-entry   The return of a spacecraft to Earth's atmosphere.

service module   A cylinder connected to the command module, containing fuel tanks and the main rocket engine.

splash down   Sea landing of a space capsule returning to Earth.

Read the beginning of the following story. Then copy it on paper, filling in each blank with one of the preceding space words or phrases. Write an ending for the story.

Hercules 7 _____ into space. Its _____ was routine: to explore an unmapped area of Earth's solar system. Joe Banks, the most experienced _____ aboard, spotted a spinning asteroid. Joe wanted to take a closer look.

"That could be Asteroid X92," Joe reported to Captain Dinah Redding. "People have been

looking for it ever since it disappeared over fifty years ago!"

"Radio _____," said Dinah,
"and tell them we're going in for
a closer look."

Now finish the story. Try to use
all of the space words listed.

Something Extra

Ask an adult friend or relative for
a list of special words used in his or
her job, giving the meaning of
each word. With your classmates,
make a dictionary of job jargon,
with a separate page for each job.

**An arrangement of photographs taken by the United States spacecraft Voyager 1.
Saturn and its rings are shown in the lower left, surrounded by six of Saturn's
moons.**

Edward Lear's

NONSENSE
BOTANY

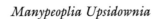

Manypeoplia Upsidownia

Pollybirdia Singularis

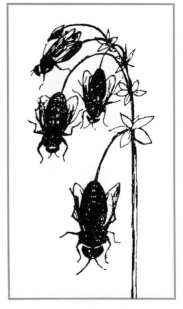

Bluebottle Buzztilentia

Guittara Pensilis

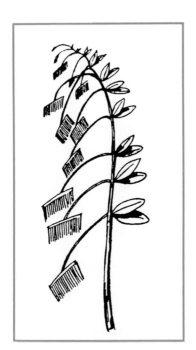

Smalltoothcombia Domestica

Bottlephorkia Spoonifolia

517

Magazine Wrap-up

Literary Skill: Character

Think about the following people you read about in this magazine. How are they alike?

- James Forten
- Margaret Bourke-White
- Anna Strong
- Captain James Lovell

Each of these people faced a difficult and dangerous situation with courage and daring. For each person, there was a goal that was worth the risk. Understanding characters' reasons, or *motivations,* for their actions is important in understanding why the events in a story happen the way they do.

On a piece of paper, write the name of each character listed and a sentence describing the dangers each faced. Then write a sentence that tells the goal that motivated the person to undertake the venture and see it through.

Vocabulary: Prefixes

Study the following prefixes with their meanings:

ante-   Before; prior to
pre-   Before; prior to
post-   After; subsequent to

Read each of the following sentences, paying attention to the boldface words. On a piece of paper, write in your own words what each boldface word means. Then rewrite the sentence, keeping the meaning the same but substituting other words for the boldface word.

1. Transportation for the field trip has been **prearranged.**
2. The nurse asked us to wait in the **anteroom.**
3. I added a **postscript** to the letter.
4. My sister went to a day camp for **preschool** children.
5. My first birthday **antedated** my last one.
6. Each of the boldface words in this lesson has a **prefix.**

Writing: Research

Use reference sources to identify different types of sailing vessels. Select one type and prepare a brief report on it. Try to include sketches or illustrations in your report. With your classmates, make a scrapbook of sailing vessels.

Books to Enjoy

Willie Bea and the Time the Martians Landed
by Virginia Hamilton

This story of love and family relationships takes place on the night of Orson Welles's radio play that frightened the country in 1938.

The Trouble with Adventurers
by Christie Harris

Six stories show the spirit of life and adventure among Pacific Northwest Indians.

Vanishing Wildlife of Latin America
by Robert M. McClung

This book discusses the plight of many unusual birds and animals in Latin America, including the West Indies and the Galapagos Islands.

Apple Is My Sign
by Mary Riskind

Harry, who is deaf and speaks in sign language, adjusts to a new school and convinces his deaf parents he can make friends.

"**Six Against the Sea**"

an excerpt from
Kon-Tiki

written by
Thor Heyerdahl

translated by **F. H. Lyon**

illustrated by
Graham Humphreys

Thor Heyerdahl set out to re-create a journey he believed had once been made by the vanished Inca people of Peru. To prove it could be done, Heyerdahl and five companions built a balsa raft like the ones the Incas had used and sailed the vast Pacific Ocean, from the coast of South America to an island halfway around the world. *Kon-Tiki* tells the story of their memorable journey and is one of the most exciting true adventure stories ever written.

KON-TIKI

by Thor Heyerdahl
illustrated by Graham Humphreys

SIX AGAINST
THE SEA

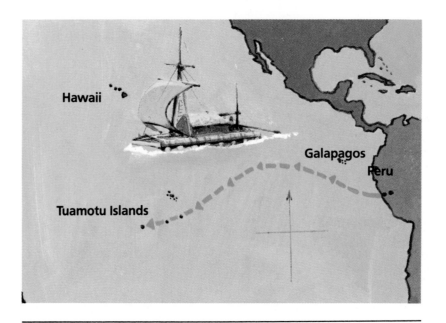

It all started with a mystery: the great stone statues, called *Tikis*, that stood on Easter Island. Where had they come from? Who had brought them there?

Explorer Thor Heyerdahl believed that they had come from Peru — that the ancient Incas had crossed the Pacific to settle the Pacific Islands, bringing with them their sun-king, Kon-Tiki.

Impossible, people said. How could the Incas have crossed thousands of miles of open sea? Heyerdahl was convinced that it was possible, that the Humboldt Current would have carried the Incas' balsa-wood rafts to the Islands.

To prove it could be done, Heyerdahl set out to cross the Pacific on a wooden raft. His companions were Bengt Danielsson, Knut Haugland, Erik Hesselberg, Torstein Raaby, and Herman Watzinger — and one green parrot.

On April 28, 1947, they set sail on the raft Kon-Tiki. *They would travel halfway around the world. The journey would take 101 days.*

By the late afternoon the trade wind was already blowing at full strength. It quickly stirred up the ocean into roaring seas, which swept against us from astern. For the first time we fully realized that here was the sea itself come to meet us; it was bitter earnest now — our communications were cut. Whether things went well now would depend entirely on the balsa raft's good qualities in the open sea. We knew that, from now onward, we should never get another onshore wind, and every day would carry us farther and farther out to sea. The only thing to do was to go ahead under full sail. If we tried to turn homeward, we should only drift farther out to sea, stern first. There was only one possible course: to sail before the wind with our bow toward the sunset.

As the troughs of the sea gradually grew deeper, it became clear that we moved into the swiftest part of the Humboldt Current. The water was green and cold and everywhere about us; the jagged mountains of Peru had vanished into the dense cloud banks astern. When darkness crept over the waters, our first duel with the elements began. We were still not sure of the sea; we were still uncertain whether it would show itself a friend or an enemy. When a white crest came groping toward us on a level with the cabin roof, we held on tight and waited uneasily to feel the masses of water smash down over us and the raft.

Every time there was the same surprise and relief. The *Kon-Tiki* calmly swung up its stern and rose skyward, while the masses of water rolled along its sides. Then we sank down again into the trough of the waves and waited for the next big sea.

About midnight a ship's light passed in a northerly direction. At three another passed on the same course. We waved our little paraffin lamp and hailed them with flashes from an electric torch, but they did not see us, and the lights passed slowly northward into the darkness and disappeared. Little did those on board realize that a real Inca raft lay close to them, tumbling among the waves. Just as little did we on board the raft realize that this was our last ship and the last trace of humans we should see till we had reached the other side of the ocean.

The next night was still worse. The seas grew higher instead of going down. So the first sixty hours passed in one continuous struggle against a chaos of waves that rushed upon us, one after another, without cessation. High waves and low waves, pointed waves and round waves, slanting waves and waves on top of other waves.

On the third night the sea went down a bit, although it was still blowing hard. About four o'clock an unexpected deluge came foaming through the darkness and knocked the raft right round before the steersmen realized what was happening. The sail thrashed against the bamboo cabin and threatened to tear both the cabin and itself to pieces. All hands had to go on deck to secure the cargo and haul on sheets and stays in the hope of getting the raft on its right course again, so that the sail might fill and curve forward peacefully. The raft would not right itself. It would go stern foremost, and that was all. The only result of all our hauling and pushing and rowing was that two men nearly went overboard in a sea when the sail caught them in the dark.

The sea had clearly become calmer. Stiff and sore, with skinned palms and sleepy eyes, we were not worth a row of beans. Better to save our strength in case the weather should call us out to a worse passage of arms. One could never know. So we furled the sail and rolled it round the bamboo yard. The *Kon-Tiki* lay sideways on to the seas and took them like a cork. Everything on board was lashed fast, and all six of us crawled into the little bamboo cabin, huddled together, and slept like mummies in a sardine tin.

We did not wake till well on in the day, when the parrot began to whistle and halloo and dance to and fro on its perch. Outside the sea was still running high, but in long, even ridges and not so wild and confused as the day before. The first thing we saw was that the sun was beating down on the yellow bamboo deck and giving the sea all round us a bright and friendly aspect. What did it matter if the seas foamed and rose high so long as they only left us in peace on the raft? What did it matter if they rose straight up in front of our noses when we knew that in a second the raft would go over the top and flatten out the foaming ridge like a steam roller, while the heavy threatening mountain of water only lifted us up in the air and rolled groaning and gurgling under the floor? A cork steam roller — that was what the balsa raft amounted to.

The sea contains many surprises for those who have their floor on a level with the surface and drift along slowly and noiselessly. People who break their way through the woods may come back and say that no wildlife is to be seen. Others may sit down on a stump and wait, and often rustlings and cracklings will begin and curious eyes peer out. So it is on the sea, too. We usually plow across it with roaring engines and piston strokes, with the water foaming round our bow. Then we come back and say that there is nothing to see far out on the ocean.

The very first day we were left alone on the sea, we had noticed fish round the raft, but we were too much occupied with the steering to think of fishing. The second day we went right into a thick shoal of sardines. Soon afterward an eight-foot blue shark came along and rolled over with its white belly uppermost as it rubbed against the raft's stern where Herman and Bengt stood steering.

Next day we were visited by tunnies, bonitos, and dorados. When a big flying fish thudded on board, we used it as bait and at once pulled in two large dorados weighing from twenty to thirty-five pounds each. This was food for several days. On steering watch we could see many fish we did not even know, and one day we came into a school of porpoises that seemed quite endless. The nearer we came to the Equator, and the farther from the coast, the commoner flying fish became. When at last we came out into the blue water where the sea rolled by majestically, sunlit and serene, ruffled by gusts of wind, we could see them glittering like a rain of projectiles that shot from the water and flew in a straight line till their power of flight was exhausted and they vanished beneath the surface.

If we set the little paraffin lamp out at night, flying fish were attracted by the light and, large and small, shot over the raft. They often struck the bamboo cabin or the sail and tumbled helpless on the deck. Unable to get a take-off by swimming through the water, they just remained lying

527

and kicking helplessly. They always came at a good pace
and snout first. If they struck us full in the face it burned
and tingled, but the attack was quickly forgiven by the
injured party — for with all its drawbacks, we were in a
land of enchantment where delicious fish dishes came
hurling through the air. We used to fry them for breakfast, and whether it was the fish, the cook, or our
appetites, they reminded us of fried troutlings once we
had scraped the scales off.

Knut was much upset one morning because, when he
was standing operating with the frying pan, a flying fish
struck him on the hand instead of landing right in the
cooking fat.

It was a few nights later. It was overcast and pitch dark, and Torstein had placed the paraffin lamp close by his head so that the night watches could see where they were treading when they crept in and out over his head. About four o'clock Torstein was awakened by the lamp tumbling over and something cold and wet flapping about his ears. "Flying fish," he thought and felt for it in the darkness to throw it away. He caught hold of something long and wet, which wriggled like a snake, and let go as if he had burned himself. The unseen visitor twisted itself away and over to Herman, while Torstein tried to get the lamp lighted again. Herman started up, too, and this made me wake, thinking of the octopus which came up at night in these waters.

When we got the lamp lighted, Herman was sitting in triumph with his hand gripping the neck of a long thin fish, which wriggled in his hands like an eel. The fish was over three feet long, as slender as a snake, with dull eyes and a long snout with a greedy jaw full of long sharp teeth. The teeth were as sharp as knives and could be folded back into the roof of the mouth to make way for what was swallowed.

Bengt, too, was awakened at last by all the noise, and we held the lamp and the long fish under his nose. He sat up drowsily in his sleeping bag and said solemnly, "No, fish like that don't exist," with which he turned over quietly and fell asleep again.

Bengt was not far wrong. It appeared later that we six sitting round the lamp in the bamboo cabin were the first to have seen this fish alive. Only the skeleton of a fish like this one had been found a few times on the coast of South America and the Galapagos Islands; ichthyologists called it *Gempylus,* or snake mackerel, and thought it lived at the bottom of the sea at a great depth because no one had ever seen it alive.

On May 24, we were lying drifting on a leisurely swell in exactly 95° west by 7° south. It was about noon, and we had thrown overboard the guts of two big dorados we had caught earlier in the morning. I was up on the edge of the raft looking at a fish as it passed quietly, when I heard a wild war whoop from Knut, who was sitting aft behind the bamboo cabin. He bellowed, "Shark!" till his voice cracked. As we had sharks swimming alongside almost daily without creating such excitement, we all realized that this must be something extra-special and flocked to Knut's assistance.

Knut had been squatting there, washing his pants in the swell, and when he looked up for a moment he was staring straight into the biggest and ugliest face any of us had ever seen in the whole of our lives. The head was broad and flat like a frog's, with two small eyes right at the sides, and a toadlike jaw that was four or five feet wide and had long fringes drooping from the corners of the mouth. Behind the head was an enormous body ending in a long thin tail with a pointed tail fin that stood straight up and showed that this sea monster was not any kind of whale. The body looked brownish under the water, but both head and body were thickly covered with small white spots.

The monster came quietly, lazily swimming after us. It grinned like a bulldog and lashed gently with its tail. The large round dorsal fin projected clear of the water, and sometimes the tail fin as well, and the water flowed about the broad back as though washing around a submerged reef. In front of the broad jaws swam a whole crowd of pilot fish in fan formation, and large remora fish and other parasites sat firmly attached to the huge body and traveled with it through the water, so that the whole thing looked like a curious zoological collection crowded round something that resembled a floating deep-water reef.

When the giant came close up to the raft, it rubbed its back against the heavy steering oar, which was just lifted up out of the water. Now we had ample opportunity of studying the monster at the closest quarters — at such close quarters that I thought we had all gone mad, for we roared stupidly with laughter and shouted overexcitedly at the completely fantastic sight we saw. Walt Disney himself, with all his powers of imagination, could not have created a more hair-raising sea monster than the one that suddenly lay with its terrific jaws along the raft's side.

The monster was a whale shark, the largest shark and the largest fish known in the world today. It is exceedingly rare, but scattered specimens are observed here and there in the tropical oceans. The whale shark has an average length of fifty feet and weighs fifteen tons. It is said that large specimens can attain a length of sixty feet.

One harpooned baby had a liver weighing six hundred pounds and three thousand teeth in each of its broad jaws.

Our monster was so large that when it began to swim in circles round us and under the raft, its head was visible on one side while the whole of its tail stuck out on the other. Again and again it described narrower and narrower circles just under the raft, while all we could do was to wait and see what might happen. When it appeared on the other side, it glided amiably under the steering oar and lifted it up in the air, while the oar blade slid along the creature's back.

In reality the whale shark went on encircling us for barely an hour, but to us the visit seemed to last a whole day.

We were visited by whales many times. Sometimes they passed like ships on the horizon, now and again sending a cascade of water into the air, but sometimes they steered straight for us. We were prepared for a dangerous collision the first time a big whale altered course and came straight toward the raft in a purposeful manner. As it gradually grew nearer, we could hear its blowing and puffing, heavy and long drawn, each time it rolled its head out of the water. It came straight toward our port side, where we stood gathered on the edge of the raft, while one man shouted that he could see seven or eight more making their way toward us.

The big, shining, black forehead of the first whale was not more than two yards from us when it sank beneath the surface of the water, and then we saw the enormous blue-black bulk glide quietly under the raft right beneath our feet. It lay there for a time, dark and motionless, and we held our breath as we looked down on the gigantic curved back of a mammal a good deal longer than the whole raft. Then it sank slowly through the bluish water and disappeared from sight. Meanwhile the whole school were close upon us, but they paid no attention to us. The whole morning we had them puffing and blowing round us in the most unexpected places without their even pushing against the raft or the steering oar. They quite enjoyed themselves, gamboling freely among the waves in the sunshine. About noon the whole school dived as if on a given signal and disappeared for good.

The marine creature against which the experts had begged us to be most on our guard was the octopus, for it could get on board the raft. The National Geographic Society in Washington, D.C., had shown us reports and photographs from an area in the Humboldt Current where monstrous octopuses had their favorite resort and came up onto the surface at night. They had arms that could do away with a big shark and set ugly marks on great whales, and a beak like an eagle's hidden among their tentacles. We were reminded that they lay floating in the darkness and that their arms were long enough to feel about in every small corner of the raft, if they did not care to come right on board. We did not at all like the prospect of feeling cold arms round our necks, dragging us out of

534

our sleeping bags at night, and we provided ourselves with machete knives, one for each of us.

For a long time we saw no sign of octopuses, either on board or in the sea. Then one morning we had the first warning that they must be in those waters. When the sun rose, we found an octopus on board, in the form of a little baby the size of a cat. It had come up on deck unaided in the course of the night and now lay dead with its arms twined round the bamboo outside the cabin door.

Young octopuses continued to come aboard. One sunny morning we all saw a glittering shoal of something that shot up out of the water and flew through the air like large raindrops, while the sea boiled with pursuing dolphins. At first we took it for a shoal of flying fish, for we had already had three different kinds of these on board. When they came near, and some of them sailed over the raft at a height of four or five feet, one ran straight into Bengt's chest and fell slap on the deck. It was a small octopus. Our astonishment was great. When we put it into a sailcloth bucket, it kept on taking off and shooting up to the surface, but it did not develop speed enough in the small bucket to get more than half out of the water.

It is a known fact that the octopus ordinarily swims on the principle of the rocket-propelled airplane. It pumps sea water with great force through a closed tube alongside its body and can thus shoot backward in jerks at a high speed. Our experience showed that young octopuses, which are a favorite food of many large fish, can escape their pursuers by taking to the air in the same way as flying fish. They pump sea water through themselves till they get up speed, and then they steer up at an angle from the surface by unfolding pieces of skin like wings. Like the flying fish, they make a glider flight over the waves for as far as their speed can carry them. After that, when we had to begin to pay attention, we often saw them sailing along for fifty to sixty yards, singly and in twos and threes. The fact that they can "glide" has been a novelty to all the zoologists we have met.

The closer we came into contact with the sea and what had its home there, the less strange it became and the more at home we ourselves felt. We learned to respect the old primitive peoples who lived in close converse with the Pacific and therefore knew it from a quite different standpoint from our own. True, we have now estimated its salt content and given tunnies and dolphins Latin names. They had not done that. Nevertheless, I am afraid that the picture the primitive peoples had of the sea was a truer one than ours.

We no longer had the same respect for waves and sea. We knew them and their relationship to us on the raft. Even the shark had become a part of the everyday picture; we knew it and its usual reactions. We did not even move away from the side of the raft if a shark came up alongside. On the contrary, we were more likely to try and grasp its back fin as it glided along the logs. This finally developed into a quite new form of sport — tug of war with shark without a line.

We began quite modestly. We caught all too easily more dorados than we could eat. To keep a popular form of amusement going without wasting food, we hit on comic fishing without a hook for the mutual entertainment of the dorados and ourselves. We fastened unused flying fish to a string and drew them over the surface of the water. The dorados shot up to the surface and seized the fish. Then we tugged, each in our own direction, and had a fine circus performance, for if one dorado let go another came in its place. We had fun, and the dorados got the fish in the end.

Then we started the same game with the sharks. We had either a bit of fish on the end of a rope or often a bag with scraps from dinner, which we let out on a line. Instead of turning on its back, the shark pushed its snout above the water and swam forward with jaws wide to swallow the morsel. We could not help pulling on the rope just as the shark was going to close its jaws again, and the cheated animal swam on with an unspeakably foolish, patient expression and opened its jaws again for the offal, which jumped out of its mouth every time it tried to swallow it. It ended by the shark's coming right up to the logs and jumping up like a begging dog for the food, which hung dangling in a bag above its nose. It was just like feeding a gaping hippopotamus in a zoological gardens.

But our respect for the five or six rows of razor-sharp teeth that lay in ambush in the huge jaws never altogether disappeared.

The last stage in our encounter with sharks was that we began to pull their tails. Pulling animals' tails is held to be an inferior form of sport, but that may be because no one has tried it on a shark. For it was, in truth, a lively form of sport.

To get hold of a shark by the tail we first had to give it a real tidbit. It was ready to stick its head high out of the water to get it. Usually it had its food served dangling in a bag. For, if one has fed a shark directly by hand once, it is no longer amusing. If one feeds dogs or tame bears by hand, they set their teeth into the meat and tear and worry it till they get a bit off or until they get the whole piece for themselves. If one holds out a large dorado at a safe distance from the shark's head, the shark comes up and smacks its jaws together, and without one's having felt the slightest tug, half the dorado is suddenly gone, and one is left sitting with a tail in one's hand. We had found it a hard job to cut the dorado in two with knives, but in a fraction of a second the shark, moving its triangular saw teeth quickly sideways, had chopped off the backbone and everything else like a sausage machine.

When the shark turned quietly to go under again, its tail flickered up above the surface and was easy to grasp. The shark's skin was just like sandpaper to hold on to, and inside the upper point of its tail there was an indentation that might have been made solely to allow a good grip. If we once got a firm grasp there, there was no chance of our grip's not holding. Then we had to give a jerk, before the shark could collect itself, and get as much as possible of the tail pulled in tight over the logs. For a second or two the shark realized nothing, but then it began to wriggle and struggle with the fore part of its body. Without the help of its tail a shark cannot get up any speed. The other fins are only for balancing and steering. After a few desperate jerks, during which we had to keep a tight hold of the tail, the surprised shark became quite crestfallen and apathetic. As the loose stomach began to sink down toward the head, the shark at last became completely paralyzed.

When the shark had become quiet and, as it were, hung stiff awaiting developments, it was time for us to haul in with all our might. We seldom got more than half the heavy fish up out of the water; then the shark, too, woke up and did the rest itself. With violent jerks it swung its head round and up onto the logs, and then we had to tug with all our might and jump well out of the way, and that pretty quickly, if we wanted to save our legs. For now the shark was in no kindly mood. Jerking itself round in great leaps, it thrashed at the bamboo wall, using its tail as a sledge hammer. Now it no longer spared its iron muscles. The huge jaws were opened wide, and the rows of teeth bit and snapped in the air for anything they could reach.

The parrot was quite thrilled when we had a shark on deck. It came scurrying out of the cabin and climbed up the wall at frantic speed till it found itself a good, safe lookout post on the roof. There it sat shaking its head or

fluttering to and fro along the ridge, shrieking with excitement. It had at an early date become an excellent sailor and was always bubbling over with humor and laughter. We reckoned ourselves as seven on board — six of us and the green parrot. At night the parrot crept into its cage under the roof of the cabin. In the daytime it strutted about the deck or hung on to guy ropes and stays and did the most fascinating acrobatic exercises.

We enjoyed the parrot's humor and brilliant colors for two months, till a big sea came on board. When we discovered that the parrot had gone overboard, it was too late. We did not see it, and the *Kon-Tiki* could not be turned or stopped. If anything went overboard, we had no chance of turning back for it — numerous experiences had shown that.

The loss of the parrot had a depressing effect on our spirits the first evening; we knew that exactly the same thing would happen to ourselves if we fell overboard on a

541

solitary night watch. We tightened up on all the safety regulations, brought into use new life lines for the night watch, and frightened one another out of believing that we were safe because things had gone well in the first two months. One careless step, one thoughtless movement, could send us where the green parrot had gone, even in broad daylight.

On July 21, the wind suddenly died away. It was oppressive and absolutely still, and we knew from previous experience what this might mean. Right enough, after a few violent gusts from east and west and south, the wind freshened up to a breeze from southward, where black, threatening clouds had rushed up over the horizon. Suddenly Torstein's sleeping bag went overboard. What happened in the next few seconds took a much shorter time than it takes to tell it.

Herman tried to catch the bag as it went, took a rash step, and fell overboard. We heard a faint cry for help amid the noise of the waves and saw Herman's head and a waving arm, as well as some vague green object in the water near him. He was struggling for life to get back to the raft through the high seas that had lifted him out from the port side. Torstein, who was at the steering oar aft, and I myself, up in the bow, were the first to perceive him, and we went cold with fear. We bellowed "Man overboard!" at the top of our lungs as we rushed to the nearest lifesaving gear. The others had not heard Herman's cry because of the noise of the sea, but in a trice there was life and bustle on deck. Herman was an excellent swimmer, and though we realized at once that his life was at stake, we had a fair hope that he would manage to crawl back to the edge of the raft before it was too late.

Torstein, who was nearest, seized the bamboo drum 'round which was the line we used for the lifeboat. It was the only time on the whole voyage that this line got caught up. Herman was now on a level with the stern of the raft but a few yards away. His last hope was to crawl to the blade of the steering oar and hang on to it. As he missed the end of the logs, he reached out for the oar blade, but it slipped away from him. There he lay, just where experience had shown we could get nothing back. While Bengt and I launched the dinghy, Knut and Erik threw out the life belt. Carrying a long line, it hung ready for use on the corner of the cabin roof, but today the wind was so strong that when it was thrown it was simply blown back to the raft. After a few unsuccessful throws, Herman was already far astern of the steering oar, swimming desperately to keep up with the raft, while the distance increased with each gust of wind. He realized that the gap would simply go on increasing, but he set a faint hope on the dinghy, which we had now got into the water. Without the line, which acted as a brake, it would perhaps be possible to drive the rubber raft to meet the swimming man. Whether the rubber raft would ever get back to the *Kon-Tiki* was another matter. Nevertheless, three men in a rubber dinghy had some chance; one man in the sea had none.

543

Then we suddenly saw Knut take off and plunge headfirst into the sea. He had the life belt in one hand and was heaving himself along. Every time Herman's head appeared on a wave back Knut was gone, and every time Knut came up, Herman was not there. Then we saw both heads at once; they had swum to meet each other and both were hanging on to the life belt. Knut waved his arm, and as the rubber raft had meanwhile been hauled on board, all four of us took hold of the line of the life belt and hauled for dear life, with our eyes fixed on the great dark object that was visible just behind the two men. This same mysterious beast in the water was pushing a big greenish-black triangle up above the wave crests; it almost gave Knut a shock when he was on his way over to Herman. Only Herman knew then that the triangle did not belong to a shark or any other sea monster. It was a corner of Torstein's watertight sleeping bag. The sleeping bag did not remain floating for long after we had hauled the two men safe and sound on board. Whatever dragged the sleeping bag down into the depths had just missed a better prey.

"Glad I wasn't in it," said Torstein and took hold of the steering oar again.

Otherwise there were not many wisecracks that evening. We all felt a chill running through nerve and bone for a long time afterward, but the cold shivers were mingled with a warm thankfulness that there were still six of us on board.

We had a lot of nice things to say to Knut that day — Herman and the rest of us too.

There was not much time to think about what had already happened, for as the sky grew black over our heads the gusts of wind increased in strength, and before night a new storm was upon us.

For five whole days the weather varied between full storm and light gale. Then on the fifth day, the heavens split to show a glimpse of blue, and the malignant, black cloud cover gave place to the ever victorious blue sky as the storm passed on. We had come through the gale with the steering oar smashed and the sail rent. The centerboards hung loose and banged about like crowbars among the logs, because all the ropes that had tightened them up under water were worn through — but we ourselves and the cargo were completely undamaged.

As early as July 3, when we were still one thousand sea miles from Polynesia, Nature was able to tell us, as it was able to tell the primitive raftsmen from Peru in their time, that there really was land ahead somewhere out in the sea. When we were a good thousand sea miles out from the coast of Peru we had noted small flocks of man-o'-war birds. They disappeared at about 100° west, and after that we saw only small petrels, which have their home on the sea. On July 3 the man-o'-war birds reappeared, at 125° west, and from now onward small flocks of them were often to be seen. As these birds did not come from America astern of us, they must have their homes in another country ahead.

On the night before July 30, there was a new and strange atmosphere about the *Kon-Tiki*. Perhaps it was the deafening clamor from all the sea birds over us that showed that something fresh was brewing. The screaming of birds with many voices sounded hectic and earthly after the dead creaking of lifeless ropes, which was all we had heard above the noise of the sea in the three months we had behind us. The moon seemed larger and rounder than ever as it sailed over the lookout at the masthead. In our fancy it reflected palm tops; it did not shine with such a yellow light over the cold fishes out at sea.

At six o'clock Bengt came down from the masthead, woke Herman, and turned in. When Herman clambered up the creaking, swaying mast, the day had begun to break. Ten minutes later he was down the rope ladder again and was shaking me by the leg.

"Come out and have a look at your island!"

His face was radiant, and I jumped up, followed by Bengt, who had not quite gone to sleep yet. Hard on one another's heels, we huddled together as high as we could climb, at the point where the masts crossed. There were many birds around us, and a faint violet-blue veil over the sky was reflected in the sea as a last relic of the departing night. Over the whole horizon away to the east, a ruddy glow had begun to spread, and far down to the southeast it gradually formed a blood-red background for a faint shadow, like a blue pencil line, drawn for a short way along the edge of the sea.

Land! An island! We devoured it greedily with our eyes and woke the others, who tumbled out drowsily and stared in all directions, as if they thought our bow was about to run on to a beach. Screaming sea birds formed a bridge across the sky in the direction of the distant island, which stood out sharper against the horizon as the red background widened and turned gold with the approach of the sun and the full daylight.

The long journey did not end with the first sight of land. For several days, the winds and currents carried the Kon-Tiki *past one island after another. Finally, on the 101st day at sea, the* Kon-Tiki *ran aground on a coral reef near a small, uninhabited island. The voyagers waded ashore to radio news of their arrival and to await the ship that would take them home again.*

547

Summary Questions

1. Why were Thor Heyerdahl and his companions willing to undertake a venture that people thought impossible?
2. How would you describe Thor Heyerdahl as a leader?
3. How would their experience of the sea have been different if the explorers had traveled in a power boat?
4. If you were making a short film about this story, which parts would you think it most important to include? Why?

The Kon-Tiki in its final home in the Kon-Tiki Museum in Oslo, Norway

Author

Thor Heyerdahl, the noted Norwegian explorer, adventurer, and author, shared all the excitement of his voyage to Polynesia in the book *Kon-Tiki*. His account of this adventure became a best-seller and was acclaimed throughout the world. It has been translated into sixty-four languages and was made into a documentary film, which received an Academy Award.

Thor Heyerdahl was awarded a doctorate by the University of Oslo, in Norway. Other scientific trips, and books about them, all brought him further fame. He now lives in Italy, where he has restored a little medieval village on a hilltop by the sea.

Illustrator

Graham Humphreys was born and educated near Birmingham, in England. He studied graphic design at Leicester College of Art. Before becoming a full-time professional illustrator, he taught in a London grammar school. He now teaches in the Department of Visual Communications at Birmingham Polytechnic. He has illustrated children's books, textbooks, and book jackets.

Glossary

Some of the words in this book may have pronunciations or meanings you do not know. This glossary can help you by telling you how to pronounce those words and by telling you their meanings.

You can find out the correct pronunciation of any glossary word by using the special spell-ing after the word and the pro-nunciation key at the bottom of each left-hand page.

The full pronunciation key below shows how to pronounce each consonant and vowel in a special spelling. The pronuncia-tion key at the bottom of each left-hand page is a shortened form of the full key.

Full Pronunciation Key

Consonant Sounds

b	bib		p	pop
ch	church		r	roar
d	deed		s	miss, sauce, see
f	fast, fife, off, phase, rough		sh	dish, ship
			t	tight
g	gag		th	path, thin
h	hat		*th*	bathe, this
hw	which		v	cave, valve, vine
j	judge		w	with
k	cat, kick, pique		y	yes
l	lid, needle		z	rose, size, xylophone, zebra
m	am, man, mum			
n	no, sudden		zh	garage, pleasure, vision
ng	thing			

Vowel Sounds

ă	pat		ô	alter, caught, for, paw
ā	aid, they, pay		oi	boy, noise, oil
â	air, care, wear		o͝o	book
ä	father		o͞o	boot, fruit
ĕ	pet, pleasure		ou	cow, out
ē	be, bee, easy, seize		ŭ	cut, rough
ĭ	pit		û	firm, heard, term, turn, word
ī	by, guy, pie		yo͞o	abuse, use
î	dear, deer, fierce, mere		ə	about, silent, pencil, lemon, circus
ŏ	pot, horrible		ər	butter
ō	go, row, toe			

Stress Marks

Primary Stress ′
bi·ol′o·gy   (bī ŏl′ə jē)

Secondary Stress ′
bi′o·log′i·cal   (bī′ə lŏj′ĭ kəl)

ab·stract (ăb′străkt′)*or*(ăb străkt′) *adj.* **1.** Difficult to understand. **2.** In art, concerned with designs or shapes that do not represent any recognizable person or thing.

a·cre·age (ā′kər ĭj) *n.* Land area measured in units, each equal to 4,840 square yards, called acres.

ad·a·mant (ăd′ə mənt) *or* (-mănt′) *adj.* Firm and unyielding. —**ad·a·mant·ly** *adv.*

ad·van·tage (əd văn′tĭj) *n.* A benefit or favorable position: *My early start gave me an advantage.*

a·gue (ā′gyoo) *n.* **1.** A fever, like that of malaria, in which there are periods of chills, fever, and sweating. **2.** A chill.

aisle (īl) *n.* **1.** A passageway between rows of seats, as in a theater. **2.** Any passageway, as between counters in a department store.

aisle

al·lot·ment (ə lŏt′mənt) *n.* Something given out or distributed: *Each sailor received an allotment of meat and beans before the voyage.*

am·a·teur (ăm′ə choor′) *or* (-chər) *or* (-tyoor′) *n.* A person who engages in an art, science, or sport for enjoyment rather than for money.

a·mi·a·bly (ā′mē ə blē) *adv.* To do or say something in a friendly, good-natured manner.

a·nal·y·sis (ə năl′ĭ sĭs) *n., pl.* **a·nal·y·ses** (ə năl′ĭ sēz). **1.** The process of separating a subject into its parts and studying them so as to determine its nature. **2.** A report of information made from the careful study of a subject.

an·tic (ăn′tĭk) *n.* An action that is odd or funny and makes no sense; prank.

an·tiq·ui·ty (ăn tĭk′wĭ tē) *n., pl.* **an·tiq·ui·ties.** **1.** Ancient times. **2.** Considerable age.

an·ti·sep·tic (ăn′tĭ sĕp′tĭk) *adj.* Thoroughly clean. *n.* A substance capable of destroying germs.

an·vil (ăn′vĭl) *n.* A heavy block, usually of iron or steel, with a smooth, flat top on which objects are shaped by hammering.

ap·a·thet·ic (ăp′ə thĕt′ĭk) *adj.* Lacking or not showing strong feeling: uninterested; indifferent.

ap·er·ture (ăp′ər chər) *n.* The opening in a camera lens that allows the amount of light passing through it to be controlled.

ap·pre·hen·sive (ăp′rĭ hĕn′sĭv)*adj.* Anxious or fearful; uneasy.

ar·chae·ol·o·gist (är′kē ŏl′ə jĭst) *n.* A person who studies the remains of past human activities, such as buildings, tools, and pottery.

ă pat / ā pay / â care / ä father / ĕ pet / ē be / ĭ pit / ī pie / î fierce / ŏ pot / ō go / ô paw, for / oi oil / oŏ book / oō boot / ou out / ŭ cut / û fur / *th* the / th thin / hw which / zh vision / ə ago, item, pencil, atom, circus

ar·id (ăr′ĭd) *adj.* Having little or no rainfall; dry: *The settlers irrigated the arid land.*

ar·ter·y (är′tə rē) *n., pl.* **ar·ter·ies.** Any of the blood vessels that carry blood from the heart to other parts of the body.

ar·ti·fact (är′tə făkt′) *n.* Usually an object of unsophisticated art.

as·sail (ə sāl′) *v.* To attack physically or with words.

a·stern (ə stûrn′) *adj.* Behind a ship or toward the rear of one.

as·tute (ə stoot′) *or* (ə styoot′) *adj.* Keen in judgment; shrewd: *an astute decision.*

au·to·graph (ô′tə grăf′) *n.* A person's signature in his or her own writing. — *v.* To write one's signature in or on: *I asked the author to autograph my book.*

az·ure (ăzh′ər) *n.* A light to medium blue, like that of the sky on a clear day.

bar·bar·i·an (bär bâr′ē ən) *adj.* Rough and uncivilized; savage.

bar·ren (băr′ən) *adj.* Lacking or unable to produce growing plants or crops: *barren soil.*

bel·lig·er·ent (bə lĭj′ər ənt) *adj.* Inclined to fight; hostile.

bel·lows (bĕl′ōz) *or* (-əz) *n.* *(used with a singular or plural verb)* A device for pumping air, consisting of a chamber with openings controlled by valves so that air can enter only at one and leave only at another as the chamber is forced to expand and contract.

bin·oc·u·lar (bə nŏk′yə lər) *or* (bī) *adj.* Of or involving both eyes at once: *binocular vision.* — *n.* Often **binoculars.** Any optical device, such as a microscope or a pair of field glasses, used by both eyes at once.

bi·ol·o·gy (bī ŏl′ə jē) *n.* The scientific study of living things and life processes, including growth, structure, and reproduction.

biv·ou·ac (bĭv′oo ăk) *or* (bĭv′wak) *n.* A temporary camp made by soldiers in the field.

blur (blûr) *n.* Something unclear, hard to see: *The distant crowd seemed just a blur of faces.* — *v.* **blurred, blur·ring.** To make or become unclear.

bole (bōl) *n.* The trunk of a tree.

bole

boon (boon) *n.* A help or benefit, often unexpected.

borscht (bôrsht) *n.* A Russian beet soup served hot or cold, often with sour cream.

brack·en (brăk′ən) *n.* **1.** A large fern with branching leaves. **2.** A place overgrown with such ferns.

brack·et (**brăk′**ĭt) *n.* **1.** A support or fixture fastened to a surface and sticking out to hold something, such as a shelf, candle, etc. **2.** A shelf supported by brackets.

brusque (brŭsk) *adj.* Rudely abrupt in manner or speech.

bulk (bŭlk) *n.* Great size, mass, or volume: *We couldn't move the couch because of its bulk.*

bu·reau (**byoŏr′**ō) *n., pl.* **bu·reaus** (**byoŏr′**ōz). A chest of drawers.

bureau

cap·tiv·i·ty (kăp **tĭv′**ĭ tē) *n., pl.* **cap·tiv·i·ties.** A period or the condition of being held prisoner.

car·a·pace (**kăr′**ə pās′) *n.* A hard outer covering, such as the upper shell of a turtle or the armorlike covering of a lobster.

car·cass (**kär′**kəs) *n.* The dead body of an animal.

cas·ing (**kā′**sĭng) *n.* A metal pipe or tubing used as a lining in wells.

cat·a·logue (**kăt′**ə lôg′) *v.* **cat·a·logued, cat·a·logu·ing.** To make a list of items, usually in alphabetical order, with a description of each.

cau·tion (**kô′**shən) *n.* **1.** Care so as to avoid possible danger or trouble: *He climbed the icy steps with caution.* **2.** A warning: *a word of caution.* — *v.* To warn against possible trouble or danger: *She cautioned them not to go near that dog.*

ce·les·tial (sə **lĕs′**chəl) *adj.* **1.** Of or related to the sky: *Stars and planets are celestial bodies.* **2.** Of heaven; divine: *Angels are celestial beings.*

ces·sa·tion (sĕ **sā′**shən) *n.* The act of stopping; a halt: *a cessation of activity.*

cha·os (**kā′**ŏs′) *n.* Great disorder or confusion.

chis·el (**chĭz′**əl) *n.* A metal tool with a sharp, beveled edge, used in cutting and shaping stone, wood, or metal.

cho·re·o·graph (**kôr′**ē ə grăf′) *or* (-grăf′) *or* (**kōr′**-) *v.* To create the arrangement of a ballet or other stage work.

coax (kōks) *v.* **1.** To persuade or try to persuade by gentle urging: *He coaxed the monkey into the cage.* **2.** To obtain by such persuasion: *coax a smile from the baby.*

com·mis·sion (kə **mĭsh′**ən) *v.* To place an order for: *commissioned a portrait.*

com·mit·ment (kə **mĭt′**mənt) *n.* A pledge or obligation, as to follow a certain course of action: *a commitment to work for peace.*

ă pat / ā pay / â care / ä father / ĕ pet / ē be / ĭ pit / ī pie / î fierce / ŏ pot / ō go / ô paw, for / oi oil / oŏ book /
oō boot / ou out / ŭ cut / û fur / *th* the / th thin / hw which / zh vision / ə ago, item, pencil, atom, circus

com·pet·i·tive (kəm **pĕt′**ĭ tĭv) *adj.* Of, in, or decided by striving against others to win something.

com·pile (kəm **pīl′**) *v.* **com·piled, com·pil·ing.** To put together into a single list or collection.

com·rade·ship (**kŏm′**răd shĭp′) *n.* Companionship; a sharing of one's activities.

con·cept (**kŏn′**sĕpt′) *n.* A general idea or understanding, especially one based on known facts or observation: *the concept that all matter is made up of elements.*

con·front (kən **frŭnt′**) *v.* To come face to face with.

con·scious (**kŏn′**shəs) *adj.* **1.** Done with awareness: *Make a conscious effort to speak clearly.* **2.** Able to see, feel, hear, and understand what is happening: *The patient is ill but still conscious.*

con·sec·u·tive (kən **sĕk′**yə tĭv) *adj.* Following in order, without a break or interruption; successive: *It rained for five consecutive days.*

con·ster·na·tion (kŏn′stər **nā′** shən) *n.* Great alarm, shock, or amazement; dismay.

con·tem·plate (**kŏn′**təm plāt′) *v.* **con·tem·plat·ed, con·tem·plat·ing.** To think about doing (something).

con·trail (**kŏn′**trāl) *n.* A visible trail of water droplets or ice crystals sometimes forming in the wake of an aircraft.

con·trap·tion (kən **trăp′**shən) *n.* A mechanical device; gadget.

con·verse[1] (kən **vûrs′**) *v.* **con·versed, con·vers·ing.** To talk informally with others: *converse about family matters.* **con·verse** *n.* Association.

con·verse[2] (**kŏn′**vûrs′) *n.* The opposite or reverse of something: *Dark is the converse of light.*

con·vul·sive (kən **vŭl′**sĭv) *adj.* Of or like a seizure or fit.

cop·pice (**kŏp′**ĭs) *n.* A thicket or grove of small trees.

copse (kŏps) *n.* A group of small trees or bushes.

copse

cor·rode (kə **rōd′**) *v.* **cor·rod·ed, cor·rod·ing.** **1.** To dissolve or wear away (a material, structure, etc.), especially by chemical action. **2.** To be dissolved or worn away.

cor·ru·gat·ed (**kôr′**ə gāt′ĭd) *or* (**kŏr′**-) *adj.* Shaped or folded into alternating and parallel ridges and grooves.

coun·ter·part (**koun′**tər pärt′) *n.* A person or thing exactly or very much like another, as in function, relation, etc.: *The modern counterpart of a horse and buggy is a car.*

cra·dle (**krād′**l) *v.* **cra·dled, cra·dling.** To hold closely; support.

cres·cen·do (krə **shĕn′**dō) *or* (-**sĕn′**-) *n., pl.* **cres·cen·dos.** A gradual increase.

crest·fall·en (**krĕst′**fô lən) *adj.* Dejected; sad.

crit·i·cal (**krĭt′**ĭ kəl) *adj.* **1.** Inclined to judge severely; likely to find fault. **2.** Exercising careful evaluation and judgment: *critical reading.* **3.** Necessary; essential.

cru·cial (**krōo′**shəl) *adj.* Of the utmost importance; decisive: *a crucial decision.*

crus·ta·cean (krŭ **stā′**shən) *n.* Any of a group of animals, such as a lobster, crab, or shrimp, that live mostly in water and have a body with a hard outer covering.

cue (kyōo) *n.* A word or signal given to remind a performer to begin a speech or movement.

cul·vert (**kŭl′**vərt) *n.* A drain or sewer crossing under a road or embankment.

culvert

cun·ning (**kŭn′**ĭng) *n.* Slyness; craftiness: *The fox is an animal of great cunning.*

cyl·in·der (**sĭl′**ən dər) *n.* A hollow or solid object shaped like a tube or pipe.

de·bris, also **dé·bris** (də **brē′**) *or* (**dā′**brē) *n.* The scattered remains of something broken or destroyed.

de·but *or* **dé·but** (dā **byōo′**) *or* (**dā′**byōo′) *n.* A first public appearance, as of a performer.

de·ci·sive (dĕ **sī′**sĭv) *adj.* Firm. — **de·ci·sive·ly** *adv.*

ded·i·ca·tion (dĕd′ĭ **kā′**shən) *n.* The act of giving or committing oneself fully to something.

deign (dān) *v.* To be kind or gracious enough to: *The speaker deigned to answer the protestors' questions.*

del·uge (**dĕl′**yōoj) *n.* A great flood; heavy downpour.

des·ig·nat·ed (**dĕz′**ĭg nāt′ĭd) *adj.* Selected for a particular duty, office, or purpose; appointed.

des·o·late (**dĕs′**ə lĭt) *adj.* **1.** Having little or no vegetation; barren. **2.** Having few or no inhabitants; deserted: *a desolate wilderness.*

de·tain dĭ **tān′**) *v.* To delay.

de·tour (**dē′**tōor′) *or* (dĭ **tōor′**) *n.* **1.** A road used temporarily instead of a main route. **2.** A change from a direct route or course. — *v.* To take or cause someone to take a detour.

dev·as·tate (**dĕv′**ə stāt′) *v.* **dev·as·tat·ed, dev·as·tat·ing.** To lay waste; ravage; spoil.

de·vour (dĭ **vour′**) *v.* **1.** To eat up greedily. **2.** To take in eagerly.

ă pat / ā **pay** / â care / ä father / ĕ pet / ē be / ĭ pit / ī pie / î fierce / ŏ pot / ō go / ô paw, for / oi oil / ōo book / ōo boot / ou out / ŭ cut / û fur / *th* **the** / th thin / hw **which** / zh vision / ə **ago,** item, pencil, atom, circus

dis·cour·age (dĭ skûr′ĭj) *v.* **dis·cour·aged, dis·cour·ag·ing. 1.** To make less hopeful or enthusiastic. **2.** To try to prevent or hinder; deter: *They lit a fire to discourage mosquitoes.*

dis·may (dĭs mā′) *n.* A sudden loss of courage or confidence that can prevent a person from acting effectively.

dog·ged (dô′gĭd) *or* (dŏg′ĭd) *adj.* Not giving up easily; stubborn. **—dog′ged·ly** *adv.*

dol·ly (dŏl′ē) *n.* A low platform that moves on small wheels or rollers, used for moving heavy loads.

down·y (dou′nē) *adj.* **down·i·er, down·i·est.** Of or like soft, fluffy, feathers.

dron·ing (drōn′ing) *adj.* Making a continuous low, dull humming sound.

drought (drout) *n.* A period of little or no rain.

drowse (drouz) *v.* **drowsed, drows·ing.** To be half asleep; doze: *A dog drowsed in the sun.*

duct (dŭkt) *n.* A tube or pipe through which liquid or gas flows.

dug·out (dŭg′out′) *n.* A long, low shelter at the side of a baseball field in which team members stay when they are not playing.

dugout

dy·nam·ic (dī năm′ĭk) *or* **dy·nam·i·cal** (dī năm′ĭ kəl) *adj.* Energetic; vigorous.

ed·dy (ĕd′ē) *n., pl.* **ed·dies.** A current, as of a liquid or gas, that moves against the direction of a main current, especially in a circular motion.

e·ject (ĭ jĕkt′) *v.* To throw out forcefully; expel.

e·late (ĭ lāt′) *v.* **e·lat·ed, e·lat·ing.** To raise the spirits of; make very happy or joyful: *elated by victory.*

e·lu·sive (ĭ loo′sĭv) *adj.* **1.** Tending to avoid or escape. **2.** Difficult to describe.

e·ma·ci·at·ed (ĭ mā′shē āt′ĭd) *adj.* Thin, as from starvation or illness.

em·bat·tle·ment (ĕm băt′l mənt) *or* (ĭm-) *n.* A low protective wall containing positions that soldiers have prepared to defend.

en·dur·ance (ĕn door′əns) *or* (ĕn dyoor′əns) *n.* The ability to withstand strain, pain, hardship, or use.

e·nor·mi·ty (ĭ nôr′mĭ tē) *n., pl.* **e·nor·mi·ties. 1.** Great wickedness. **2.** Hugeness; a thing of great size.

en·ter·prise (ĕn′tər prīz′) *n.* **1.** An undertaking or venture: *a new business enterprise.* **2.** Economic activity: *free enterprise.* **3.** Initiative in undertaking new projects; adventurous spirit.

en·vi·ous (ĕn′vē əs) *adj.* Wanting something that someone else has.

etch (ĕch) *v.* **1.** To make (a shape or pattern) on a metal plate by dissolving parts of it with acid. **2.** To show clearly as in a print.

ewe (yo͞o) *n.* A female sheep.

ex·as·per·a·tion (ĭg zăs′pə rā′shən) *n.* The condition of extreme irritation.

ex·ca·va·tion (ĕks′kə vā′shən) *n.* The act of uncovering by digging and exposing to view: *They found many tools during the excavation.*

ex·hort (ĭg zôrt′) *v.* To urge by strong argument, appeal, etc.

ex·pel (ĭk spĕl′) *v.* **ex·pelled, ex·pel·ling.** To force or drive out; to eject forcefully; *expel air from the lungs.*

ex·po·sure (ĭk spō′zhər) *n.* The act of allowing light to reach and act on a photographic film, or the length of time that the film is exposed to light.

fal·low (făl′ō) *adj.* Plowed and tilled but left unseeded during a growing season: *a fallow field.*

fal·ter (fôl′tər) *v.* To act or speak in an unsteady way.

fea·si·ble (fē′zə bəl) *adj.* **1.** Capable of being accomplished or carried out; possible: *a feasible project.* **2.** Likely; logical: *His answer seems feasible enough.* **—fea′si·bil′i·ty** *n.* **—fea′si·bly** *adv.*

feign (fān) *v.* To give a false appearance of; pretend: *feign illness.*

flail (flāl) *v.* To beat, flap, or thrash with the arms or with some long object: *Flailing the water with his arms, he tried to stay afloat.*

flint (flĭnt) *n.* A very hard stone that makes sparks when struck with steel and that can be used to start fires.

fo·cus (fō′kəs) *v.* **1.** To adjust in order to produce a clear image: *We focused the camera so we could take a picture.* **2.** To concentrate.

fod·der (fŏd′ər) *n.* Food, such as chopped cornstalks or hay, for horses, cattle, etc.

for·age (fôr′ĭj) *or* (fŏr′-) *v.* **for·aged, for·ag·ing.** To search for food or provisions.

for·lorn (fər lôrn′) *or* (fôr-) *adj.* **1.** Deserted; abandoned. **2.** Wretched or pitiful in appearance or condition.

frag·ment (frăg′mənt) *n.* **1.** A piece or part broken off or detached from a whole: *a fragment of a china plate.* **2.** Something incomplete or unfinished: *a sentence fragment.*

fren·zy (frĕn′zē) *n., pl.* **fren·zies.** Wild excitement or a display of emotion suggesting madness, often accompanied by violent activity.

ă pat / ā pay / â care / ä father / ĕ pet / ē be / ĭ pit / ī pie / î fierce / ŏ pot / ō go / ô paw, for / oi oil / oͦo book / oͦo boot / ou out / ŭ cut / û fur / *th* the / th thin / hw which / zh vision / ə ago, item, pencil, atom, circus

froth·y (frô'thē) or (frŏth'ē) adj.
froth·i·er, froth·i·est. 1. Of,
like, or covered with foam: *a wave's
frothy spray.* **2.** Light, frivolous,
and playful: *a frothy comedy.*

frus·tra·tion (frŭs trā'shən) n.
The condition of being prevented
from accomplishing a goal; a feeling of discouragement.

fun·nel (fŭn'əl) n. **1.** A utensil
with a narrow open tube at one
end, used in pouring something
into a container with a small
opening. **2.** Something shaped
like a funnel, as a tornado.

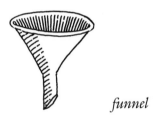

funnel

fur·tive·ly (fûr'tĭv lē) adv.
Stealthily; shiftily.

fu·tile (fyōōt'l) or (fyōō'tīl') adj.
Having no useful result; useless;
vain: *futile efforts.*

gal·va·nized steel (găl'və nīzd'
stēl) n. Steel that is coated with
zinc to protect it from rust.

gam·bol (găm'bəl) v. **gam·boled**
or **gam·bolled, gam·bol·ing** or
gam·bol·ling. To play or frolic
about.

gaunt·ness (gônt'nĭss) n. The
condition of being thin and bony.

gey·ser (gī'zər) n. A natural hot
spring that throws out a spray of
steam and water from time to time.

gin·ger·ly (jĭn'jər lē) adv. In a
very cautious or careful way: *He
gingerly patted the large dog.*

gloom (glōōm) n. **1.** Partial or
total darkness: *He peered into the
gloom.* **2.** Lowness of spirit; sadness; depression: *the gloom that
defeat always brings.*

gloom·y (glōō'mē) adj. **gloom·i·
er, gloom·i·est 1.** Partly or
completely dark. **2.** Sad: *gloomy
about his future.*

gorge (gôrj) n. A deep, narrow
passage with steep, rocky sides, as
between mountains.

gour·met (gōōr'mā') or (gōōr mā')
n. A person who likes and knows fine
food and drink.

grim·ace (grĭm'ĭs) or (grĭ-mās')
n. A tightening and twisting of
the face to express pain, contempt,
or disgust.

gro·tesque (grō-tĕsk') adj. **1.**
Distorted and odd: *a grotesque
monster.* **2.** Outlandish; very
strange.

ham·let (hăm'lĭt) n. A small
village.

hand·i·cap (hăn'dē kăp') n. Any
defect in the structure or function-
ing of the body or mind that
prevents someone from living normally; a disability.

har·poon (här **poon′**) *n.* A spear with a rope attached, used for catching sea animals.

harpoon

hawk (hôk) *v.* To offer for sale by shouting.

haz·ard (**hăz′**ərd) *n.* Something that can harm or cause injury; danger.

hence (hĕns) *adv.* **1.** For this reason; therefore. **2.** From this time: *thirty years hence.*

herb (ûrb) *or* (hûrb) *n.* A plant with leaves, roots, or other parts used to flavor food or as medicine.

her·i·tage (**hĕr′**ĭ tĭj) *n.* **1.** Property that is or can be inherited. **2.** Something other than property passed down from preceding generations; legacy; tradition: *Every country has its heritage of folk music.*

hill·ock (**hĭl′**ək) *n.* A small hill.

hob·ble (**hŏb′**əl) *v.* **hob·bled, hob·bling.** To walk with a limp or a slow, awkward motion: *The horse hobbled along on its injured leg.*

horde (hôrd) *or* (hōrd) *n.* A large group or crowd; swarm.

hos·til·i·ty (hŏ **stĭl′**ĭ tē) *n., pl.* **hos·til·i·ties. 1.** The condition of feeling ill will; hatred. **2. hostilities.** Open warfare.

hy·dro·phob·ic (hī′drə **fō′**bĭk) *adj.* **1.** Having a fear of water. **2.** Having rabies, a serious disease that attacks the central nervous system.

hy·po·der·mic (hī′pə **dûr′**mĭk) *n.* A hollow needle that pierces the skin and through which a dose of medicine can be injected.

i·dol (**īd′**l) *n.* **1.** An image that is worshiped as a god. **2.** A person or thing adored or greatly admired.

il·lu·mi·na·tion (ĭl loo′mə **nā′** shən) *n.* The act of providing or brightening with light.

il·lu·sion (ĭ **loo′**zhən) *n.* **1.** An appearance or impression that has no real basis. **2.** A mistaken notion or belief.

im·per·son·ate (ĭm **pûr′**sə nāt′) *v.* To act the character or part of; to pretend to be.

im·pulse (**ĭm′**pŭls′) *n.* **1.** A short, sudden burst of energy: *an electrical impulse.* **2.** A sudden urge; whim.

in·ces·sant (ĭn **sĕs′**ənt) *adj.* Continuing without interruption; constant; unceasing.

in·ex·pli·ca·bly (ĭn **ĕk′**splĭ kə blē) *or* (ĭn′ĭk **splĭk′**ə blē) *adv.* In an unexplainable manner.

in·fal·li·ble (ĭn **făl′**ə bəl) *adj.* Not capable of making a mistake.

ă **pat** / ā **pay** / â **care** / ä **father** / ĕ **pet** / ē **be** / ĭ **pit** / ī **pie** / î **fierce** / ŏ **pot** / ō **go** / ô **paw, for** / oi **oil** / oo **book** / oo **boot** / ou **out** / ŭ **cut** / û **fur** / *th* **the** / th **thin** / hw **which** / zh **vision** / ə **ago, item, pencil, atom, circus**

in·jec·tion (ĭn **jĕk′**shən) *n.* The process of forcing a liquid medicine into the body by the use of a hypodermic needle.

in·quis·i·tive (ĭn **kwĭz′**ĭ tĭv) *adj.* **1.** Eager to learn: *an inquisitive mind.* **2.** Unduly curious; prying.

in·stinct (**ĭn′**stĭngkt′) *n.* **1.** An inner feeling or way of behaving that is automatic rather than learned. **2.** A natural talent or ability.

in·su·late (**ĭn′**sə lāt′) *or* (**ĭns′**yə-lāt′) *v.* **in·su·lat·ed, in·su·lat·ing.** To cover, surround, or line something with material that slows or stops the passage of heat, sound, or electricity.

in·ten·si·fy (ĭn **tĕn′**sə fī′) *v.* **in·ten·si·fied, in·ten·si·fy·ing.** To make or become forceful, strong, or concentrated.

in·ter·pret (ĭn **tûr′**prĭt) *v.* **1.** To see or understand in a certain way. **2.** To explain the meaning of.

in·un·date (**ĭn′**ŭn dāt′) *v.* **in·un·dat·ed, in·un·dat·ing.** To overwhelm, as with a flood: *The courts are inundated with cases.*

in·va·lid (**ĭn′**və lĭd) *n.* A sick, weak, injured, or disabled person, especially someone in poor health for a long time.

in·var·i·a·bly (ĭn **vâr′**ē ə blē) *adv.* In a manner that is constant or unchanging.

i·so·la·tion (ī′sə **lā′**shən) *n.* The condition of being kept apart from others: *living in isolation from the world.*

jade (jād) *n.* Either of two minerals that are used as gemstones and as materials from which objects are carved.

lark[1] (lärk) *n.* Any of several mostly European songbirds that often sing as they fly high in the air.

lark[2] (lärk) *n.* A merry adventure, prank, or romp.

lit·er·al·ly (**lĭt′**ər ə lē) *adv.* **1.** Word for word. **2.** Really or actually.

loath·ing (**lō′**thĭng) *n.* Extreme dislike or hatred.

lon·gev·i·ty (lŏn **jĕv′**ĭ tē) *n.* Long life.

loom (lōōm) *v.* **1.** To come into view, often with a threatening appearance: *Storm clouds loomed on the horizon.* **2.** To seem close at hand.

lo·tus (**lō′**təs) *n., pl.* **lo·tus·es.** Any of several plants related to the water lily, having large white, pink, or yellow flowers.

lotus

lu·mi·nous (**lōō′**mə nəs) *adj.* Giving off light: *a luminous sign.*

lunge (lŭnj) *v.* **lunged, lung·ing.** To make a sudden, forceful movement forward, toward, or for something: *The player lunged at the ball.*

ma·chet·e (mə **shĕt′**ē) *or* (**-chĕt′**ē) *n.* A large, heavy knife with a broad blade, used for cutting vegetation and as a weapon.

mag·a·zine (măg′ə **zēn′**) *or* (**măg′** ə zēn′) *n.* **1.** A periodical containing written matter, such as articles or stories, and usually also illustrations and advertising. **2.** A place where ammunition is stored.

ma·lig·nant (mə **lĭg′**nənt) *adj.* **1.** Having or showing ill will; malicious: *malignant thoughts.* **2.** Threatening to life or health.

mal·lard (**măl′**ərd) *n.* A wild duck of which the male has a glossy green head and neck.

mallard

mam·moth (**măm′**əth) *adj.* Huge; gigantic.

man·da·rin (**măn′**də rĭn) *n.* In imperial China, a high public official.

ma·neu·ver (mə **noo′**vər) *or* (mə-**nyoo′**) *v.* To make or cause to make one or more changes in a course or position.

ma·raud·ing (mə **rôd′**ing) *adj.* Roving in search of or raiding to seize booty.

mat·i·nee *or* **mat·i·née** (măt′n **ā′**) *n.* A theatrical performance given in the afternoon.

mauve (mōv) *n.* A light reddish or grayish purple.

me·an·der (mē **ăn′**dər) *v.* **1.** To follow a winding and turning course: *The river meanders through the town.* **2.** To wander aimlessly and idly. —**me·an′der·ing** *adj.*

men·ace (**měn′**əs) *v.* **men·aced, men·ac·ing.** To threaten with harm; endanger: *an oil slick menacing the shoreline of California.* —**men′ac·ing** *adj.: a menacing look.*

me·te·or·ol·o·gist (mē′tē ə **rŏl′**ə- jĭst) *n.* A scientist who studies weather and weather conditions.

miffed (mĭft) *adj.* Offended or annoyed.

min·i·a·tur·ize (**mĭn′**ē ə chə rīz′) *or* (**mĭn′**ə-) *v.* **min·i·a·tur·ized, min·i·a·tur·iz·ing.** To plan or make on a greatly reduced scale.

mi·nute (mī **noot′**) *or* (**-nyoot′**) *or* (mĭ-) *adj.* Exceptionally small; tiny.

mod·est·ly (**mŏd′**ĭst lē) *adv.* **1.** Playing down one's own talents, abilities, or accomplishments. **2.** In a reserved manner.

ă pat / ā pay / â care / ä father / ĕ pet / ē be / ĭ pit / ī pie / î fierce / ŏ pot / ō go / ô paw, for / oi oil / oo book / oo boot / ou out / ŭ cut / û fur / *th* the / th thin / hw which / zh vision / ə ago, item, pencil, atom, circus

mod·ule (mŏj′o͞ol) *or* (mŏd′yo͞ol) *n.* Any of the self-contained parts of a spacecraft, each of which is used for a particular job.

mol·ten (mōl′tən) *adj.* Made liquid by heat; melted.

mon·i·tor (mŏn′ĭ tər) *n.* A device used to record or control a process or activity. —*v.* To keep watch over, record, or control.

moon·stone (mo͞on′stōn′) *n.* A pearly stone that lets light pass through, valued as a gem.

mor·sel (môr′səl) *n.* A small piece, especially of food; a bit.

mot·tled (mŏt′ld) *adj.* With spots or streaks.

mu·ral (myo͝or′əl) *n.* A large picture or decoration applied directly to a wall or ceiling.

muse (myo͞oz) *v.* **mused, mus·ing.** To consider at length; ponder; meditate.

ob·sta·cle (ŏb′stə kəl) *n.* Something that stands in the way of reaching a goal.

of·fal (ô′fəl) *or* (ŏf′əl) *n.* Waste parts, especially of a butchered animal.

ok·ra (ō′krə) *n.* **1.** A tall tropical or semitropical plant. **2.** The edible pods of the okra plant, used in soups or as a vegetable.

o·men (ō′mən) *n.* A thing or event regarded as a sign of future good or bad luck.

o·paque (ō pāk′) *adj.* **1.** Not capable of letting light pass through: *Metals and some minerals are opaque.* **2.** Not reflecting light; not shiny; dull.

op·pres·sive (ə prĕs′ĭv) *adj.* **1.** Difficult to bear; tyrannical. **2.** Causing physical or mental distress: *an oppressive silence.*

op·ti·mis·tic (ŏp′tə mĭs′tĭk) *adj.* Taking a hopeful view of a situation, expecting the best possible outcome.

o·va·tion (ō vā′shən) *n.* A loud and enthusiastic display of approval, usually in the form of shouting or hearty applause.

pains·tak·ing (pānz′tā′kĭng) *adj.* Involving or showing great care, thoroughness, etc.; careful. —**pains′tak′ing·ly** *adv.*

par·ka (pär′kə) *n.* A warm fur or cloth jacket with a hood.

parka

par·ti·tion (pär tĭsh′ən) *n.* Something, as a partial wall, that divides a room or space.

pa·thet·ic (pə thĕt′ĭk) *adj.* Arousing pity, sympathy, or sorrow; sad; pitiful.

pa·tron (**pā′**trən) *n.* A person who supports a certain activity or institution: *a patron of the arts.*

pen·dant (**pĕn′**dənt) *n.* A hanging ornament, as one worn dangling from a necklace or from the ear.

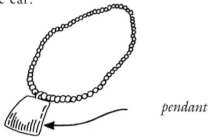

pendant

pen·du·lum (**pĕn′**jə ləm) *or* (-dyə-) *n.* An object suspended from a fixed support so that it swings freely.

per·ish (**pĕr′**ĭsh) *v.* **1.** To die, especially in a violent manner: *Ten people perished in the accident.* **2.** To pass from existence; disappear gradually: *The dinosaur perished from the earth.*

per·ish·a·bles (**pĕr′**ĭ shə bəlz) *pl. n.* Things, such as food, that spoil or decay easily.

per·plexed (pər **plĕks′**d) *adj.* Confused or puzzled; bewildered.

per·sist·ent (pər **sĭs′**tənt) *adj.* Refusing to give up or let go.

pla·guy (**plā′**gē), also **pla·guey.** *adj. Informal.* Irritating; bothersome; annoying.

plain·tive (**plān′**tĭv) *adj.* Sad; mournful: *a plaintive song.*

pli·a·ble (**plī′**ə bəl) *adj.* **1.** Easily bent or shaped without breaking; flexible: *pliable strips of wood.* **2.** Tending to be easily influenced or dominated: *a pliable mind.*

plun·der (**plŭn′**dər) *v.* To take booty or valuables from; rob: *Pirates plundered the coastal city.*

poise (poiz) *v.* **poised, pois·ing. 1.** To balance or be balanced: *He poised the flashlight on the edge of the table.* **2.** To remain in one spot as if suspended: *A hummingbird poises over a flower.*

port·age (**pôr′**tĭj) *or* (**pōr′**-) *v.* **port·aged, port·ag·ing.** To carry boats or supplies overland between waterways.

port·fo·li·o (pôrt **fō′**lē ō) *or* (pōrt-) *n., pl.* **port·fo·li·os.** A portable case for holding loose papers, documents, etc.

pro·ceeds (**prō′**sēdz′) *n.* All the money that comes from a business or fund-raising activity.

pro·ject (prə **jĕkt′**) *v.* To cause a beam of light to put an image of a picture or shadow onto a surface: *The slides were projected onto the wall.*

pro·jec·tile (prə **jĕk′**təl) *or* (-tīl′) *n.* An object, such as a bullet or an arrow, that is fired, thrown, or otherwise launched through space.

prom·is·ing (**prŏm′**ĭ sĭng) *adj.* Giving hope of future success: *The scientist made a promising discovery.*

prop (prŏp) *v.* **propped, prop·**

ă pat / ā pay / â care / ä father / ĕ pet / ē be / ĭ pit / ī pie / î fierce / ŏ pot / ō go / ô paw, for / oi oil / ōō book /
ōō boot / ou out / ŭ cut / û fur / *th* the / th thin / hw which / zh vision / ə ago, item, pencil, atom, circus

ping. **1.** To keep from falling; support. **2.** To place in a leaning or resting position: *propped her chin in her hands and listened.* — *n.* A vertical support used to keep something from falling.

pros·pect (**prŏs′**pĕkt′) *n.* **1.** Something expected or foreseen; an expectation. **2.** A possible candidate, as for a team or position.

pro·spec·tive (prə **spĕk′**tĭv) *adj.* Likely to happen; expected.

Pull·man (**poŏl′**mən) *n.* Often **Pullman car.** A railroad car having private sleeping compartments.

pun·gent (**pŭn′**jənt) *adj.* Sharp to the taste or smell: *a pungent sauce.*

rap·ture (**rāp′**chər) *n.* Overwhelming delight; great joy.

rasp (răsp) *or* (räsp) *v.* To make a harsh, grating sound.

ra·vine (rə **vēn′**) *n.* A deep, narrow cut, similar to a canyon or gorge, in the earth's surface.

re·as·sure (rē′ə **shoŏr′**) *v.* **re·as·sured, re·as·sur·ing.** To make less fearful or worried; to restore confidence to.

re·con·struct (re′kən **strŭkt′**) *v.* **1.** To build again; restore. **2.** To determine or trace from information or clues: *reconstruct the events that preceded the accident.*

re·en·act (rē ĕn **ăkt′**) *v.* To act something out again: *re-enact the events leading up to the accident.*

re·luc·tant (rĭ **lŭk′**tənt) *adj.* Unwilling. — *adv.* **re·luc·tant·ly.**

rem·i·nisce (rĕm′ə **nĭs′**) *v.* **rem·i·nisced, rem·i·nisc·ing.** To remember and tell of past experiences or events.

re·mote (rĭ **mōt′**) *adj.* **re·mot·er, re·mot·est.** Far away; not near.

ren·dez·vous (**rän′**dā voō) *or* (-də-) *n., pl.* **ren·dez·vous** (**rän′**dā voōz′) *or* (-də-) A prearranged meeting: *a rendezvous of the explorers in the wilderness.*

re·signed (rĭ **zīnd′**) *adj.* Accepting what is happening without complaining.

re·source·ful (rĭ **sôrs′**fəl) *adj.* Clever and imaginative, especially in finding ways to deal with a difficult situation.

re·ver·ber·ate (rĭ **vûr′**bə rāt′) *v.* **re·ver·ber·at·ed, re·ver·ber·at·ing.** To echo back; resound.

rho·do·den·dron (rō′də **dĕn′**drən) *n.* A shrub with evergreen leaves and clusters of white, pinkish, or purplish flowers.

rhododendron

rig (rĭg) *n.* Any special equipment or gear.

rub·ble (**rŭb′**əl) *n.* **1.** Irregular, broken pieces of rock. **2.** Fragments of stone or other material left after the destruction or decay of a building.

ruth·less (rōōth′lĭs) *adj.* Showing no pity; cruel.

sal·a·ble (sāl′ə bəl) *adj.* Fit and suitable to sell or capable of attracting buyers.

sal·vage (săl′vĭj) *v.* **sal·vaged, sal·vag·ing. 1.** To save from loss or destruction. **2.** To save or rescue (anything of use or value) that would otherwise be lost, discarded, damaged, or destroyed.

scal·a·wag (skăl′ə wăg) also **scal·ly·wag** (skăl′ē-) *n.* A dishonest, unprincipled person.

scraw·ny (skrô′nē) *adj.* **scraw·ni·er, scraw·ni·est.** Thin and bony; skinny.

scur·ry (skûr′ē) *v.* **scur·ried, scur·ry·ing, scur·ries. 1.** To move with or as if with light, rapid steps; scamper. **2.** To race about in a hurried or confused manner; rush.

self-suf·fi·cient (sĕlf′sə fĭsh′ənt) *adj.* Able to provide for oneself without help; independent.

sen·try (sĕn′trē) *n., pl.* **sen·tries.** A person, especially a soldier, posted at some spot to warn of approaching attackers or to check persons seeking admittance; a guard. — *adj.* Relating to a sentry: *He took sentry duty.*

se·rene (sə rēn′) *adj.* **1.** Peaceful and calm. **2.** Perfectly clear and bright.

shaft (shăft) *n.* **1.** A spear or arrow or the long, slender stem of a spear or arrow. **2.** A long, narrow passage or opening, such as one leading into a mine.

sham·ble (shăm′bəl) *v.* **sham·bled, sham·bling.** To walk in an awkward or lazy way, dragging the feet; shuffle.

sheep·ish (shē′pĭsh) *adj.* **1.** Embarrassed and apologetic. **2.** Meek; timid.

shud·der (shŭd′ər) *v.* To tremble or shiver suddenly, especially from fear or cold.

si·dle (sīd′l) *v.* **si·dled, si·dling.** To move sideways or edge along.

sil·hou·ette (sĭl′ōō ĕt′) *n.* An outline of something that appears dark against a light background.

smug (smŭg) *adj.* **smug·ger, smug·gest.** Too pleased or satisfied with oneself. — **smug′ly** *adv.*

sol·i·tar·y (sŏl′ĭ tĕr′ē) *adj.* Being or living alone: *I saw a solitary runner at the side of the road.*

som·ber·ly (sŏm′bər lē) *adv.* In a gloomy manner.

spas·mod·ic (spăz mŏd′ĭk) *adj.* Happening occasionally; in sudden bursts.

spec·i·men (spĕs′ə mən) *n.* A sample of something that one studies.

ă pat / ā pay / â care / ä father / ĕ pet / ē be / ĭ pit / ī pie / î fierce / ŏ pot / ō go / ô paw, for / oi oil / ōō book /
ōō boot / ou out / ŭ cut / û fur / *th* the / th thin / hw which / zh vision / ə ago, item, pencil, atom, circus

spec·tac·u·lar (spĕk tăk′yə lər) *adj.* Sensational, marvelous: *a spectacular view.*

spi·ral (spī′rəl) *v.* Circling around to form a series of constantly changing planes, like a coil spring.

spiral

splay·foot·ed (splā′foŏt′ĭd) *adj.* Walking with feet turned outward.

sta·ple[1] (stā′pəl) *n.* **1.** A major product grown or produced in a region: *Rice and rubber are the staples of Southeast Asia.* **2.** A basic food always produced and sold in large amounts because of steady demand: *Bread and potatoes are staples of their diet.*

sta·ple[2] (stā′pəl) *n.* A thin piece of wire, put through sheets of paper to hold them together.

stark (stärk) *adj.* **stark·er, stark·est. 1.** Plain and blunt; unmistakable: *stark evidence.* **2.** Unadorned; barren; grim: *the stark lunar landscape.*

stat·ure (stăch′ər) *n.* Reputation gained by achievement.

stench (stĕnch) *n.* A strong, unpleasant smell; a stink.

ster·e·o·phon·ic (stĕr′ē ə fŏn′ĭk) *or* (stîr′-) *adj.* Of, indicating, or used in a sound-reproduction system that uses two separate channels to give a more natural effect of the distribution of the sound sources.

stol·id (stŏl′ĭd) *adj.* Having or showing little emotion. — **stol′id·ly** *adv.*

stra·ta (strā′tə) *or* (străt′ə) *pl. n.* Layers of rock usually made of the same substance.

stray (strā) *n.* An animal or person that has roamed or wandered from a group or proper place.

stub·ble (stŭb′əl) *n.* **1.** Short, stiff stalks, as of grain, left after a crop has been harvested. **2.** Something resembling this, such as a short, stiff growth of beard.

sub·mis·sive (səb mĭs′ĭv) *adj.* Yielding; obedient.

sub·mit (səb mĭt′) *v.* **sub·mit·ted, sub·mit·ting.** To yield or surrender (oneself) to the will or authority of another.

sul·len (sŭl′ən) *adj.* Showing ill humor or resentment; sulky.

su·per·vi·sor (soō′pər vī′zər) *n.* A person who watches over, directs, and inspects action, work, or performance.

sym·bol·ize (sĭm′bə līz′) *v.* **sym·bol·ized, sym·bol·iz·ing.** To serve as something that stands for something else: *The poet used rain to symbolize sadness.*

sym·pa·thet·ic (sĭm′pə thĕt′ĭk) *adj.* **1.** Of, feeling, expressing, or resulting from understanding or affection between persons. **2.** In agreement.

syn·chro·nize (sĭng′krə nīz′) *or* (sĭn′-) *v.* **syn·chro·nized, syn·chro·niz·ing. 1.** To operate at the same rate and together in time. **2.** To cause (two or more things) to operate in this way.

syn·di·cate (sĭn′dĭ kĭt) *n.* An organization of people formed for a specific purpose.

tak·en a·back (tā′kən ə **băk′**) *adv.* Surprised: *I was taken aback by your decision to leave your job.*

tan·ta·liz·ing (tăn′tə-līz′ĭng) *adj.* Teasing as if by allowing to see something desired but keeping it out of reach.

tech·ni·cal·i·ty (tĕk′nĭ **kăl′**ĭ tē) *n.* **1.** A detail. **2.** Something only a specialist would be interested in.

tech·nique (tĕk **nēk′**) *n.* A procedure or method by which a task, especially a difficult or complicated one, is accomplished.

tee·ter (tē′tər) *v.* **1.** To walk or move unsteadily or unsurely, before or as if before falling; totter. **2.** To waver; show signs of failure about to happen.

tel·e·scop·ic (tĕl′ə **skŏp′**ĭk) *adj.* Seen by means of an instrument that makes distant objects appear closer and larger.

tell (tĕl) *n.* An ancient mound consisting of the accumulated remains of several cities.

ten·ta·tive (tĕn′tə tĭv) *adj.* Not certain or permanent; experimental. **—ten·ta·tive·ly** *adv.* In an uncertain manner; indefinite: *tentatively scheduled.*

tern (tûrn) *n.* Any of several sea birds related to and resembling the gulls but generally smaller and with a forked tail.

tern

ter·rain (tə **rān′**) *or* (tĕ-) *n.* A tract of land: *hilly terrain.*

Tex·as lea·guer (tĕk′səs lē′gər) *n. Baseball.* A fly ball that drops between the infielder and the outfielder for a hit.

the·o·ry (thē′ə rē) *or* (thîr′ē) *n., pl.* **theories. 1.** An idea or set of ideas made up to explain why something happened or continues to happen. **2.** An assumption or guess based on limited information or knowledge.

ther·a·pist (thĕr′ə pĭst) *n.* Someone who specializes in treating a physical or mental illness.

this·tle (thĭs′əl) *n.* Any of several prickly plants with usually purplish flowers and seeds tufted with silky fluff.

ă pat / ā **pay** / â care / ä father / ĕ **pet** / ē be / ĭ **pit** / ī **pie** / î **fierce** / ŏ **pot** / ō go / ô **paw, for** / oi **oil** / ŏŏ **book** / ŏŏ **boot** / ou **out** / ŭ **cut** / û **fur** / *th* **the** / th **thin** / hw **which** / zh vision / ə **ago, item, pencil, atom, circus**

thong (thông) *or* (thŏng) *n.* A narrow strip of leather used to fasten something.

trans·con·ti·nen·tal (trăns′kŏn tə-nĕnt′tl) *adj.* Crossing one of the main masses of the earth: Africa, Antarctica, Asia, Australia, Europe, North America or South America.

tread (trĕd) *v.* **trod** (trŏd), **tread·ing.** To walk on, over, or along.

tres·tle (trĕs′əl) *n.* A framework made up of vertical, horizontal, and slanting supports, used to hold up a bridge.

trestle

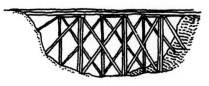

tri·um·phant (trī ŭm′fənt) *adj.* —**tri·um·phant·ly** *adv.* Victorious, successful.

trough (trôf) *n.* **1.** A long, narrow hollow, as between ocean waves. **2.** A long, narrow container for holding food or water for animals.

tun·dra (tŭn′drə) *n.* An area of arctic regions with no trees and few other plants.

tur·bu·lent (tûr′byə lənt) *adj.* Violently moving or disturbed; stormy: *turbulent waters.*

turf (tûrf) *n.* **1.** An upper layer of earth containing much grass and roots; sod. **2.** A piece cut from this.

un·a·bashed (ŭn′ ə băsht′) *adj.* Not embarrassed or ashamed.

un·ceas·ing·ly (ŭn sē′sĭng lē) *adv.* In a continuous manner.

un·der·es·ti·mate (ŭn′dər ĕs′tə-māt′) *v.* **-es·ti·mat·ed, -es·ti·mat·ing.** To judge or guess too low the value, amount, quality, or capacity of.

un·fal·ter·ing·ly (ŭn fôlt′ər ing lē) *adv.* Without wavering or hesitating.

un·in·hab·it·ed (ŭn′ĭn hăb′ĭ tĭd) *adj.* Without people; not lived in.

un·sea·son·a·bly (ŭn sē′zə nəb lē) *adv.* In a manner that is not suitable for the season.

ush·er (ŭsh′ər) *n.* A person who shows people to their seats, as in a theater.

u·til·ize (yōōt′l īz′) *v.* **u·til·ized, u·til·iz·ing.** To put to use for a certain purpose: *utilizing the stream's water to run the mill.*

vague (vāg) *adj.* **vagu·er, vagu·est.** **1.** Not clearly expressed; lacking clarity: *a vague statement; a vague promise.* **2.** Lacking definite shape, form, or character.

van·tage point (văn′tĭj point) *n.* A position from which a person has a commanding view or outlook.

var·nish (**vär′**nĭsh) *n.* An oil-based paint that dries to leave a surface coated with a thin, hard, glossy film that is relatively transparent and almost colorless.

vast (văst) *adj.* Very great in area, size, or amount: *The ship sailed the vast ocean.*

ver·vain (**vûr′**vān′) *n.* Any of several varieties of plants having slender spikes of small blue, purplish, or white flowers.

vi·cious (**vĭsh′**əs) *adj.* **1.** Cruel; mean: *vicious lies.* **2.** Savage and dangerous: *a vicious shark.* **3.** Violent; intense: *found shelter from the vicious wind.*

vin·dic·tive (vĭn **dĭk′**tĭv) *adj.* Having or showing a desire for revenge; vengeful.

vi·tal (**vīt′**l) *adj.* **1.** Necessary to life: *The heart and lungs are vital organs.* **2.** Very important: *A good education is vital to a satisfying and successful career.*

wan (wŏn) *adj.* **wan·ner, wan·nest.** **1.** Unnaturally pale, as from illness: *a wan face.* **2.** Weak or faint: *a wan smile.*

war·y (**wâr′**ē) *adj.* **war·i·er, war·i·est.** **1.** Alert to danger; watchful: *The possibility of discovery kept him wary.* **2.** Distrustful: *wary of the weather.*

wick (wĭk) *n.* A cord or strand of soft fibers, as in a candle or oil lamp, that draws up fuel, such as melted wax or oil, to be burned.

wick

wor·ry (**wûr′**ē) *or* (**wŭr′**ē) *v.* **wor·ried, wor·ry·ing.** **1.** To feel or cause to feel uneasy or anxious: *worried about his health.* **2.** To grasp and tug at repeatedly: *a kitten worrying a ball of yarn.*

wretch·ed (**rĕch′**ĭd) *adj.* **1.** Full of or attended by misery or woe. **2.** Shabby. **3.** Inferior in quality: *a wretched performance.*

zo·o·log·i·cal (zō′ə **lŏj′**ĭ kəl) *or* **zo·o·log·ic** (zō ə **lŏj′**ĭk) *adj.* Of animals or the scientific study of animals: *a zoological collection.* **—zo′o·log′i·cal·ly** *adv.*

zwie·back (**zwī′**băk′) *or* (-băk′) *or* (**zwē′**-) *or* (**swī′**-) *n.* A type of biscuit first baked in the form of a slightly sweetened loaf of bread and then sliced and oven-toasted.

ă pat / ā pay / â care / ä father / ĕ pet / ē be / ĭ pit / ī pie / î fierce / ŏ pot / ō go / ô paw, for / oi oil / oͦo book /
oͦo boot / ou out / ŭ cut / û fur / *th* the / th thin / hw which / zh vision / ə ago, item, pencil, atom, circus

Read
Write
Listen
Speak

Read

Use these aids to help you read words you have not seen before.

❶ Use the letter sounds and the context, the sense of nearby words, phrases, and sentences.

- Sometimes the general sense of the passage may be the best context clue.

  The quarrel with his brother had left John feeling **fractious.** (*fractious:* "irritable")

- Sometimes a passage will include a direct explanation of the word.

  The Queen wore a **tricorn,** a three-cornered hat. (*tricorn:* "three-cornered hat")

- A synonym, a word with nearly the same meaning, can be a context clue.

  The **skittish** deer was so nervous it jumped when a frog splashed. (*skittish:* "nervous")

- A contrast word such as *but* or *although* will sometimes let you know that a word of opposite meaning is given.

  This morning the book display was neat and orderly, but now it is a **haphazard** jumble. (*haphazard:* "not neat or orderly")

❷ Look for a base word with a prefix, a suffix, or both. Use the context and the meanings of the word parts to figure out the meaning of the word.

I made no **prejudgment** but waited to see the evidence.

Prefix	Base Word	Suffix	Meaning
pre-	judge	-ment	"action of judging"

3 If you cannot figure out the meaning, use a glossary or a dictionary.

abstract / archaeologist

ab·stract (ăb′străkt′)*or*(ăb străkt′) *adj.* **1.** Difficult to understand. **2.** In art, concerned with designs or shapes that do not represent any recognizable person or thing.

a·cre·age (ā′kər ĭj) *n.* Land area measured in units, each equal to 4,840 square yards, called acres.

ad·a·mant (ăd′ə mənt) *or* (-mănt′) *adj.* Firm and unyielding. **—ad·a·mant·ly** *adv.*

ad·van·tage (əd văn′tĭj) *n.* A benefit or favorable position: *My early start gave me an advantage.*

a·gue (ā′gyōō) *n.* **1.** A fever, like that of malaria, in which there are periods of chills, fever, and sweating. **2.** A chill.

aisle (īl) *n.* **1.** A passageway between rows of seats, as in a theater. **2.** Any passageway, as between counters in a department store.

aisle

al·lot·ment (ə lŏt′mənt) *n.* Something given out or distributed: *Each sailor received an allotment of meat and beans before the voyage.*

am·a·teur (ăm′ə chŏŏr′) *or* (-chər) *or* (-tyŏŏr′) *n.* A person who engages in an art, science, or sport for

enjoyment rather than for money.

a·mi·a·bly (ā′mē ə blē) *adv.* To do or say something in a friendly, good-natured manner.

a·nal·y·sis (ə năl′ĭ sĭs) *n., pl.* **a·nal·y·ses** (ə năl′ĭ sēz). **1.** The process of separating a subject into its parts and studying them so as to determine its nature. **2.** A report of information made from the careful study of a subject.

an·tic (ăn′tĭk) *n.* An action that is odd or funny and makes no sense; prank.

an·tiq·ui·ty (ăn tĭk′wĭ tē) *n., pl.* **an·tiq·ui·ties. 1.** Ancient times. **2.** Considerable age.

an·ti·sep·tic (ăn′tĭ sĕp′tĭk) *adj.* Thoroughly clean. *n.* A substance capable of destroying germs.

an·vil (ăn′vĭl) *n.* A heavy block, usually of iron or steel, with a smooth, flat top on which objects are shaped by hammering.

ap·a·thet·ic (ăp′ə thĕt′ĭk) *adj.* Lacking or not showing strong feeling; uninterested; indifferent.

ap·er·ture (ăp′ər chər) *n.* The opening in a camera lens that allows the amount of light passing through it to be controlled.

ap·pre·hen·sive (ăp′rĭ hĕn′sĭv)*adj.* Anxious or fearful; uneasy.

ar·chae·ol·o·gist (är′kē ŏl′ə jĭst) *n.* A person who studies the remains of past human activities, such as buildings, tools, and pottery.

ă pat / ā pay / â care / ä father / ĕ pet / ē be / ĭ pit / ī pie / î fierce / ŏ pot / ō go / ô paw, for / oi oil / ŏŏ book / ōō boot / ou out / ŭ cut / û fur / th the / th thin / hw which / zh vision / ə ago, item, pencil, atom, circus

552

arid / bracken

ar·id (ăr′ĭd) *adj.* Having little or no rainfall; dry: *The settlers irrigated the arid land.*

ar·ter·y (är′tə rē) *n., pl.* **ar·ter·ies.** Any of the blood vessels that carry blood from the heart to other parts of the body.

ar·ti·fact (är′tə făkt′) *n.* Usually an object of unsophisticated art.

as·sail (ə sāl′) *v.* To attack physically or with words.

a·stern (ə stûrn′) *adj.* Behind a ship or toward the rear of one.

as·tute (ə stōōt′) *or* (ə styōōt′) *n.*

trolled by valves so that air can enter only at one and leave only at another as the chamber is forced to expand and contract.

bin·oc·u·lar (bə nŏk′yə lər) *or* (bī) *adj.* Of or involving both eyes at once: *binocular vision.* — *n.* Often **binoculars.** Any optical device, such as a microscope or a pair of field glasses, used by both eyes at once.

bi·ol·o·gy (bī ŏl′ə jē) *n.* The scientific study of living things and life processes, including growth

Houghton Mifflin

Dictionary

Student

An American Heritage Dictionary

Reading Stories

When you read stories, you read for enjoyment. You read to find out about characters and events. Follow these suggestions to understand and remember the stories you read.

Before You Read

1 **Read the title, and look at the pictures. If the story has an introduction, read it.**
- What will the story be about?
- What do you already know about the topic?

2 **Read the author's name.**
- Have you read other stories by this author? What were those stories about?
- Is any information given about the author? What does it tell you?

3 **Think about what you want to look for when you read a story.**
- Who are the main characters?
- What is the setting?
- How does the story begin?
- What happens in the story?
- How does the story end?

While You Read

1 **Remember the important characters and events in the story.**

2 **Make predictions about what will happen next.**

3 **Check your predictions.**
- Were your predictions right or wrong?

- Did you predict something that didn't happen? Why didn't it happen?

④ Try to picture the characters and the scenes.

⑤ Ask questions about what you are reading.

- Does the story make sense to you?
- Are any parts hard to understand? Which parts?

⑥ If any parts are unclear, read them again.

- Decide if you need to use a glossary or a dictionary.

After You Read

① Think about the characters and events.

- If you were going to tell someone about the story, what would you say?

② Decide how you feel about the story.

- Did you enjoy the story? Why or why not?
- Are there any parts you especially liked? Why?
- Would you like to read another story by the author? Why or why not?

③ Compare the events in the story with your own life.

- What problems have you faced that are like the ones the main characters had?
- What have you done that is similar to what any of the characters did?
- How are you like the characters? How are you different?

④ Think about how the author told the story.

- What did the author want you to think about?
- How did the author want you to feel? What words and descriptions give you that feeling?

⑤ Think about other stories you have read.

- How was this story like others you have read? How was it different?

When you read articles, textbook chapters, and nonfiction books, you are reading to learn. Follow these suggestions to understand and remember the information you read.

Before You Read

1 Survey the material.
- Read the title and headings.
- Read any introductory and summary statements.
- Look at the pictures. Read any captions.

2 Think about the topic.
- What do you already know about the topic?
- What do you think you will find out about the topic?

While You Read

1 Read the material under each heading.
- Read as carefully as you need to. Take time to understand.
- Think about paragraph topics. Think about a sentence that states the main idea of each paragraph. Look for details that support each main idea.
- Make sure you understand the meanings of any special terms.
- Pay attention to words such as *first* and *next*. They help you understand *when* things happened.
- Pay attention to words such as *because* and *so*. They help you understand *why* things happened.
- Notice if the author compares one thing to another. Look for the ways the two things are alike or different.

② **Ask yourself questions about what you are learning.**

③ **Check your understanding.**

- Is the meaning clear?
- Do you need to reread any sections?

After You Read

① **Think about the information.**

- What was the topic?
- What facts did you learn about the topic?
- What special terms did you learn?
- What do you know about the topic now that you didn't know at the start?

② **Answer any questions you asked as you were reading.**

③ **Decide how you would learn more about the topic.**

A Study Plan

You can also follow the five steps of the SQRRR method to learn and remember information. Each letter of SQRRR stands for a different step.

Step One: Survey. Look over the headings. Look at the pictures, and read the captions.

Step Two: Question. Turn each heading into a question to set the purpose for reading each section.

Step Three: Read. Read each section to answer the question you made from the heading.

Step Four: Recite. Answer your question in your own words.

Step Five: Review. Look again at each heading, and recite once again the answers to your questions.

Write

The Writing Process

1 Prewriting

Before you begin to write, decide what you want to write about. Here is one way to choose a topic.

- Make a list of several ideas.
- Think about each idea on your list.

    Do you know enough about this idea to write about it, or can you find information about it?

    Is there too much to tell?

    Would the idea be interesting to write about?

    Would your readers be interested in it?

- Decide which idea is best to write about.
- Circle that idea. It will be your topic.

Lynn's class has finished their study of ancient Roman life. The teacher has assigned them to write an article that compares and contrasts something in an ancient Roman city with something in the modern world. Lynn listed several pairs of things that she could compare and contrast. She thought about each idea and circled the best one.

> *Roman baths and modern swimming pools*
>
> *(Roman apartment houses and modern apartment buildings)*
>
> *Roman roads and modern superhighways*

After you decide on a topic, make a plan showing the important details you will include.

Here is one way to plan an article of comparison and contrast.

- List the ways the things are alike.
- List the differences.

Lynn's plan for her article looked like this.

Apartment Buildings in Ancient Rome and Modern Cities	
Alike	*Different*
5 or 6 stories high	*no plumbing or cooking facilities in Rome*
built of concrete, brick, or wood	*stoves provided heat in Rome*
balconies around buildings	*no glass on windows in Rome*

❷ Write a First Draft

After you have a plan, write a first draft. A first draft is a first try at getting your ideas down on paper. Write on every other line so that there will be room to make changes. Do not worry about mistakes. You can correct them later.

Here are some things to think about as you write an article of comparison and contrast.
- Look at the similarities and differences in your plan.
- Decide whether you will begin with a paragraph that compares or a paragraph that contrasts.
- Introduce each paragraph with a sentence that states the main idea.
- Try to use words such as *same* and *unlike,* which point out similarities and differences.

Here is part of Lynn's first draft of her article.

A modern apartment building is like an ancient Roman apartment house in many ways. Buildings in ancient Rome often reached a height of five or six stories and ~~they~~ were made of wood, brick, and concrete. ~~They had~~ There were balconies around the buildings. Today balconies are still common in many European and American cities.

There are important diferences between roman and modern buildings. Unlike modern apartments, the windows had no glass. ~~People could not~~ heating, plumbing

❸ Revise

When you revise, look at your writing to make changes. The kinds of changes you make may depend on the kind of writing you are doing. Here are some ways to revise an article of comparison and contrast.

- Read the article to yourself.

  Does each paragraph clearly show comparisons or contrasts?
  Are your details interesting?
  Have you included compare/contrast clue words?
  Is any important information missing?

- Change words and sentences to make the writing clearer.
- Read your story to a listener. Think about what your listener asks or suggests.
- Revise your writing so that it will interest your readers.

Lynn read her article to her friend Carl. Carl listened carefully.

Carl: It seems clear, and you stuck to the topic.

Lynn: Is there anything I should explain better?

Carl: There was no glass in the windows. Did they have any way to cover them?

Lynn: That's a good question. I'll try to find out.

Carl: Also, try to tell more about the differences in heating.

Lynn read over her draft again. She made some changes. She did research to find the details that Carl had asked about. Here is part of Lynn's revised article.

~~They had~~ There were balconies around the
buildings. Today *buildings with* balconies are still common
in many European and American cities.

There are important diferences between
roman and modern buildings. Unlike
modern apartments, the windows *windows* *in these ancient buildings were* had no
covered with wood shutters, not Roman
glass. ~~People could not~~ heating, plumbing
and cooking facilities were poor and they *Romans*
had no way of puping water to the upper
levles. Modern apartments have central
heating systems, but *wood-burning* stoves were the only
sorce of heat. *in the Roman apartments.*
Luckily, the weather in Rome is very mild, so
the ancient Romans probably were not too cold.

❹ Proofread

Slowly reread what you have written, word by word. Check for mistakes, and correct them.

● Use the proofreading checklist and marks to fix your draft.

Proofreading Checklist

Did I

☑ 1. indent each paragraph?

☑ 2. use complete sentences?

☑ 3. use capital letters and end marks correctly?

☑ 4. use other punctuation marks correctly?

☑ 5. spell every word correctly?

☑ 6. use the proper format?

Proofreading Marks

ꟼ Indent a paragraph.

∧ Add something.

ℓ Take out something.

⋀ Add a comma.

ꚃꚃ Add quotation marks.

⊙ Add a period.

≡ Capitalize.

/ Make a small letter.

∿ Reverse the order.

— Fix spelling.

Here is part of Lynn's revised article after she proofread it.

There are important *differences* ~~diferences~~ between roman and modern buildings. Unlike modern apartments, the windows *windows in these ancient buildings were* had no *covered with wood shutters, not Roman* glass. ~~People could not~~ heating, plumbing and cooking facilities were poor, *Romans* and they had no way of *pumping* ~~puping~~ water to the upper *levels* ~~levles~~. Modern apartments have central heating systems, but *wood-burning* stoves were the only *source* ~~sorce~~ of heat in the Roman apartments. *Luckily, the weather in Rome is very mild, so the ancient Romans probably were not too cold.*

583

⑤ Publish

When you are ready to share what you have written, make a final copy.

- Copy your revised and proofread draft in your best handwriting.
- Proofread once again. Correct any mistakes.
- Think of a special way to share your work.

Lynn and her classmates decided to put their articles together in a book called *Ancient Rome and Modern Times — Comparisons and Contrasts*. Lynn used a computer to type her article. Then she illustrated it and added the article and drawing to the book. The book was displayed in the school library.

Listen and Speak

Listening

When you listen, think about your purpose for listening.

1 Listening to a story for enjoyment
- Listen for important events.
- Think about how each event leads to another.
- Try to picture the people and places.

2 Listening to a lesson or report for information
- Think about the topic.
- Listen for details about the topic.
- Listen for important terms.
- Listen for any opinions stated by the speaker and for the facts that support them.
- Think of questions to ask.

3 Listening for directions
- Listen for each step. Think about the order of steps.
- Try to picture each step.
- Listen for words that describe actions.
- Ask questions if you do not understand each step.

Speaking

When you give a talk or read aloud, you want your listeners to pay attention to your words. You want to inform and entertain them.

1 Giving a talk
- Choose a topic that will interest your listeners.

- Gather information on that topic. Decide which ideas you will tell about and the order in which you will present them.
- Write key words and phrases on cards or slips of paper.
- Practice your talk until you can give it just by glancing at your notes as you speak.
- Speak clearly and with expression.
- Look at different people in your audience.
- Try to relax.

2 Reading aloud
- Read silently anything you plan to read aloud. Then practice reading aloud to yourself until you are reading smoothly.
- Read loudly enough for all to hear, and pronounce the words clearly.
- Hold the book so that your audience can see your face. Hold your head up so that your voice is not blocked by the book.
- Read in natural phrases by grouping words instead of reading word by word.
- Look at your audience as often as you can without losing your place.
- Adjust your voice and reading rate to the mood of the story.
- Read lines of conversation as you think the story characters would say them. Read the other parts of the story as if the author were speaking.
- Read informational material slowly and clearly, the way you think the author might speak if telling the information to an audience.

Discussing Writing

When you are getting ready to revise something you have written, read it aloud to a friend. You and your listener can discuss the writing to make it better.

1 A writer may ask these questions.
- Was my beginning interesting?
- Was anything not clear?
- Are there any details I should add?

2 A listener should follow these guides.
- Listen carefully as the writer reads.
- Tell something you liked about the writing.
- Ask questions about anything you did not understand.
- Make suggestions if the writer asks for help.
- Be polite.

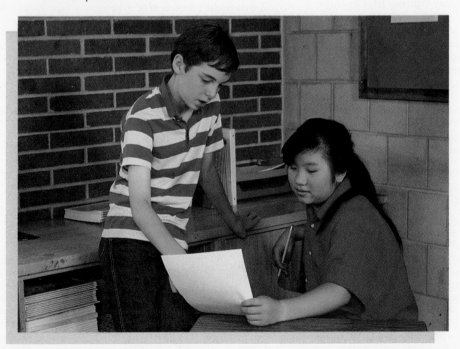

Bibliographical Note
The study method described in the "Student Handbook" is based on the widely used SQ3R system developed by Francis P. Robinson in *Effective Study,* 4th ed. (New York: Harper & Row, Publishers, Inc., 1961, 1970).

Credits

Cover and title page illustrated by D. J. Simison
Magazine openers illustrated by Higgins Bond

Illustrators: **8–9** Higgins Bond **12–26** Paul
Van Munching **29** Catherine Bleck
30 Bill Ogden **47–48** (top) Omnigraphics
48 (bottom), **55** Susanah Brown
59 Omnigraphics **60–71** Chris Calle
73 Roger Tory Peterson **74–75** Sheryl
Regester **80–92** Tony Smith **95** Paul
Goodnight **97–102** George M. Ulrich
104–108 Judy Sue Goodwin-Sturges **109** Meg
Kelleher **110–127** (illustrations) Cherie Wyman
(borders) © Mitchell & Malik **130** Bill Ogden
134–135 Higgins Bond **138–151** Floyd
Cooper **162–172** Anthony Accardo
178–186 Eric Velasquez **190–200** Francien
van Westering **212–213** Susanah Brown
220–228 Julie Downing **233–262** Jan
Pyk **266–267** Higgins Bond **270–285**
James Watling **316–317** Omnigraphics
330 Susanah Brown **359** Cecilia von
Rabenau **360–368** Mou-sien Tseng
375–376 Omnigraphics **378–405**
(illustrations) Ben F. Stahl (borders)
© Mitchell & Malik **410–411** Higgins
Bond **414–427** Tony Smith **439–443**
Omnigraphics **460–474** Charles Shaw
481 Bill Ogden **484–501** Robert Giuliani
504–505 Laura Cornell **508–510**
Peter Gregory **521–544** Graham Humphreys
550–570 George M. Ulrich **571–587** Linda
Phinney **578–580, 582, 583** Marsha Goldberg

Photographers: **32, 37** courtesy of Maria Tall-
chief Paschen **42** © Martha Swope
52–55 © Howard B. Bluestein/University
of Oklahoma **56** © Dan McCoy/Rainbow
96 © Aaron M. Levin/Taurus Photos **97**
© Mark Godfrey/Archive **98** (top) British
Museum **98** (bottom) © Dr. E. R.
Degginger/Bruce Coleman Inc. **99** Aerofilms
100 © Frank Siteman/Stock Boston **101**
© Peter Menzel **102** Pat Lanza Field/
Bruce Coleman Inc. **154–155** © Focus on
Sports **176** © Jim Pickerell/Black Star
203 RESTING IN THE WOODS by John
George Brown/Collection of JoAnn & Julian
Ganz, Jr. **207** © Michal Heron
215–216 Nebraska Historical Society
217 The Bettmann Archive **218**
Nebraska Historical Society **290–291**
© James A. Sugar/Black Star **292–305**
Steve Rubicam/Reese-Gibson **308** Michal
Heron **309** © Michael Phillip Manheim/
After Image **310** © Lynn Johnson/Black
Star **311** © David Moore/Black Star
314 © Peter Argentine **315** Jeffrey Mark
Dunn **319** © Rosemary Chastney/Ocean
Images Inc. **320** Jeffrey Mark Dunn
322 WGBH Boston **324–325** Jeffrey
Mark Dunn **328–329** THE CHASM OF
COLORADO by Thomas Moran/US Department
of the Interior **331–342** © Scribner's
Monthly **345** © David Lissy/Focus on
Sports **346–357** © Randall Davis
430–431 SUNLIGHT ON THE COAST
by Winslow Homer/Toledo Museum of Art
444–446 © Margaret Bourke-White/Life
Magazine © (Time Inc.) **450–453**
© Margaret Bourke-White/George Arents
Research Library (Syracuse University)
456–458 © Margaret Bourke-White/
Life Magazine © (Time Inc.) **506–
508** (inset), **515** NASA **516–517**
Historical Pictures Service, Chicago **520–521**
© Hans Wendler/The Image Bank
548 A. Husmo/Mittet Foto **571** © Richard
Hutchings **578, 581, 584, 587** Michal Heron